Scalable and Distributed Cloud Continuum Orchestration for Next-Generation IoT Applications: Latest Advances and Prospects

Scalable and Distributed Cloud Continuum Orchestration for Next-Generation IoT Applications: Latest Advances and Prospects

Guest Editors

Dimitrios Dechouniotis
Ioannis Dimolitsas

MDPI

Basel • Beijing • Wuhan • Barcelona • Belgrade • Novi Sad • Cluj • Manchester

Guest Editors
Dimitrios Dechouniotis
Department of Electrical and Computer Engineering
National Technical University of Athens
Athens
Greece

Ioannis Dimolitsas
School of Electrical and Computer Engineering
National Technical University of Athens
Athens
Greece

Editorial Office
MDPI AG
Grosspeteranlage 5
4052 Basel, Switzerland

This is a reprint of the Special Issue, published open access by the journal *Future Internet* (ISSN 1999-5903), freely accessible at: https://www.mdpi.com/journal/futureinternet/special_issues/2706CA5DI1.

For citation purposes, cite each article independently as indicated on the article page online and as indicated below:

Lastname, A.A.; Lastname, B.B. Article Title. *Journal Name* **Year**, *Volume Number*, Page Range.

ISBN 978-3-7258-8377-6 (Hbk)
ISBN 978-3-7258-8378-3 (PDF)
https://doi.org/10.3390/books978-3-7258-8378-3

Contents

About the Editors

Dimitrios Dechouniotis

Dimitrios Dechouniotis is an assistant professor in the Electrical and Computer Engineering Department of the University of Peloponnese, Greece. He has participated in more than 10 national and European research projects on modern 5G communications, cyber–physical systems and Industry 4.0. His research interests include control theory, cloud computing, cyber-physical systems, industrial modeling and process optimization.

Ioannis Dimolitsas

Ioannis Dimolitsas received his Diploma (2018) and Ph.D. (2023) degrees from the School of Electrical and Computer Engineering, National Technical University of Athens (NTUA). Currently, he is a postdoctoral researcher in the Network Management and Optimal Design (NETMODE) Laboratory at NTUA. He has participated in several national and European projects in the fields of next-generation networks, edge and cloud computing, and cyber–physical systems. His research interests include multi-criteria optimization, dynamic resource allocation, edge and cloud computing modeling, network optimization, and digital twins.

future internet

Editorial

Scalable and Distributed Cloud Continuum Orchestration for Next-Generation IoT Applications: Latest Advances and Prospects

Dimitrios Dechouniotis * and Ioannis Dimolitsas

Department of Electrical and Computer Engineering, National Technical University of Athens, 15780 Athens, Greece; jdimol@netmode.ntua.gr
* Correspondence: ddechou@netmode.ntua.gr

1. Introduction

With the advent of the Internet of Things (IoT), the centralized cloud computing service delivery paradigm has been gradually transformed into a cloud continuum that includes edge and fog computing and heterogeneous IoT devices with varying computing and power capabilities. At the same time, the dawn of the 5G era requires advanced orchestration solutions that guarantee that the requirements of time-/mission-critical IoT-enabled applications are met. Under this setting, the cloud continuum is defined as the infrastructure that includes remote cloud datacenters, edge clusters, and IoT/end-devices with heterogeneous computing capabilities.

However, several challenges still need to be addressed regarding these capabilities. The orchestration of such complex applications requires, for example, heterogeneous resources spread across the cloud continuum. The core advantage of edge computing is the placement of computational resources at the network edge to alleviate the computation burden of IoT devices, which are also augmented with enhanced computational capabilities. In this context, the orchestration of such applications requires solutions for distributed service embedding, task offloading, resource autoscaling, and service migration in real time and in a scalable fashion. With the evolution of the IoT and the advent of 5G/6G and massive machine-type communications, extremely dense networks are expected to be created, placing even more strain on the available infrastructure across the cloud continuum.

2. Contributions

In this Special Issue, a range of articles tackle interesting challenges and propose novel solutions for various research problems involving the cloud continuum.

Hazrati et al. [1] focus on Information-Centric Networks (ICNs) and the caching problem. They denote data freshness and build a router-based mechanism to compute the cache hit rate and freshness score of the content stored in caches. Furthermore, they introduce an AI-based prediction mechanism to enhance caching efficiency. This proactive approach reduces unnecessary data replacements and ensures that the cache retains the most relevant and current data.

The authors of the second article [2] present a benchmarking framework for assessing deep learning (DL) models, which have been deployed and utilized across the cloud continuum for the delivery of intelligent IoT services. They focus on evaluating DL model scaling across three key performance axes during model inference: classification accuracy, computational overhead, and latency. Working in this direction, they employ several

 https://doi.org/10.3390/fi17040141

model structures from three popular DL application domains and utilize publicly available and pre-trained model architectures (BERT, EfficientNet, and MLP) and openly available datasets (i.e., GLUE-MRPC and ImageNet).

Sturley et al. [3] share a comparative study on virtualization and containerization in the computing continuum. They focus on these major methods for application deployment at the network edge and compare them, considering several criteria, such as compatibility based on user experience and the ease of installation/deployment, scalability based on the automatic elasticity facing the workload, and energy efficiency in terms of energy and computer resources.

The authors of the fourth article [4] explore the application of collaborative virtual and augmented reality in a cloud continuum context, focusing on designing, implementing, and verifying three reference architectures for deployment in five collaborative VR/AR use cases. These architectures consider the distribution of the computational workload between cloud and edge. The first processes all requests in the cloud, while the second balances the workload between cloud and edge infrastructure. Finally, the third architecture handles the workload entirely at the network edge.

Abinayaa et al. [5] focus on detecting Denial of Service (DDoS) attacks in wireless sensor networks. Their approach utilizes the CatBoost classifier (Cb-C) and the Lyrebird Optimization Algorithm (LOA). The latter is used to optimize the hyperparameters of the Cb-C, which is used as a classification methodology for predicting various types of attacks.

The paper by Kuaban, Godlove Suila et al. investigates the adoption of IoT technologies in the Silicon Mountain technology ecosystem in Cameroon [6]. Through a survey-based approach, the authors identify key barriers such as standardization issues, financial constraints, labor shortages, educational gaps, market challenges, government policies, security concerns, and inadequate power supply. Market challenges, including high marketing costs and socio-economic crises, are particularly significant. The authors suggest strategies such as enhancing tax policies, improving infrastructure, and promoting IoT education to overcome these challenges.

Shahid, Kamal et al. conducted a comparative analysis of routing protocols, namely, EIGRP, OSPF, and BGP, in IPv6-based load-sharing and link failover systems [7]. Using tools such as Wireshark, VMWare, GNS3, and Iperf3, this study evaluated network performance metrics, including convergence time, packet loss, jitter, and delay. The findings reveal that EIGRP achieves superior failover convergence and lower packet loss, while OSPF excels in managing link failures. The study's route-mapping strategy and recommended BGP hold times provide practical guidance for network engineers in optimizing IPv6 infrastructure.

In their article, Karthick, Gayathri, and Glenford Mapp [8] introduce a Secure Service Ecosystem (SSE) to enable real-time, secure service migration in Intelligent Edge Environments for smart cities. The key mechanisms developed include a Resource Allocation Algorithm, a Resource Allocation Secure Protocol (RASP), and a Secure Service Protocol (SSP). By verifying the protocol's safety with ProVerif, this study shows the potential of the SSE in enhancing performance and security in smart city applications.

The paper by Tsikteris Sean et al. [9] introduces a novel model for optimizing resource allocation and server selection in multi-access edge computing (MEC) environments. The proposed "TRUST-ME" model leverages a trust-based framework that evaluates the reliability of MEC servers based on both direct interactions and social feedback from other IoT devices, enabling more informed decision-making. An optimistic Q-learning algorithm is employed to allow IoT devices to autonomously select the most suitable MEC server.

Satish et al. [10] addresses the challenge of bufferbloat, which affects the performance of real-time applications such as video conferencing, cloud gaming, and IoT services. The authors propose a novel solution by integrating the Low Latency, Low Loss, and Scalable Throughput (L4S) architecture into the Asynchronous Advantage Actor-Critic (A3C) reinforcement learning algorithm within the FreeBSD networking stack. This approach involves a dual-queue coupled active queue management (AQM) system to manage queues and reduce packet loss, while A3C dynamically adjusts the base drop probability in response to network conditions.

A decentralized global registry system leveraging blockchain and NFT technology to address key challenges in digital asset management, such as security, interoperability, and scalability, is presented in the final article [11]. Through detailed system design and a comparative analysis with traditional centralized registries and existing blockchain-based solutions, this paper highlights the advantages of enhanced security, transparency, and efficiency. Additionally, the legal, ethical, and social implications of NFT-based tokenization are explored, particularly in intellectual property management.

3. Conclusions

This Special Issue on "Scalable and Distributed Cloud Continuum Orchestration for Next-Generation IoT Applications: Latest Advances and Prospects" showcases the latest contributions in the orchestration of cloud continuum- and IoT-based applications. The articles published in this Special Issue span a diverse range of topics, including information-centric networks, deep learning, cyber security, MEC resource orchestration, active queue management, comparative analyses of routing protocols, and smart city applications. These studies collectively highlight how the cloud continuum enables innovative applications and address technical challenges facing 5G and the IoT.

Conflicts of Interest: The authors declare no conflict of interest.

References

1. Hazrati, N.; Pirahesh, S.; Arasteh, B.; Sefati, S.S.; Fratu, O.; Halunga, S. Cache Aging with Learning (CAL): A Freshness-Based Data Caching Method for Information-Centric Networking on the Internet of Things (IoT). *Future Internet* **2025**, *17*, 11. [CrossRef]
2. Trihinas, D.; Michael, P.; Symeonides, M. Evaluating DL Model Scaling Trade-Offs During Inference via an Empirical Benchmark Analysis. *Future Internet* **2024**, *16*, 468. [CrossRef]
3. Sturley, H.; Fournier, A.; Salcedo-Navarro, A.; Garcia-Pineda, M.; Segura-Garcia, J. Virtualization vs. Containerization, a Comparative Approach for Application Deployment in the Computing Continuum Focused on the Edge. *Future Internet* **2024**, *16*, 427. [CrossRef]
4. Di Martino, B.; Pezzullo, G.J.; Bombace, V.; Li, L.H.; Li, K.C. On Exploiting and Implementing Collaborative Virtual and Augmented Reality in a Cloud Continuum Scenario. *Future Internet* **2024**, *16*, 393. [CrossRef]
5. Abinayaa, S.S.; Arumugam, P.; Mohan, D.B.; Rajendran, A.; Lashab, A.; Wei, B.; Guerrero, J.M. Securing the edge: Catboost classifier optimized by the lyrebird algorithm to detect denial of service attacks in internet of things-based wireless sensor networks. *Future Internet* **2024**, *16*, 381. [CrossRef]
6. Kuaban, G.S.; Nkemeni, V.; Nwobodo, O.J.; Czekalski, P.; Mieyeville, F. Internet of Things Adoption in Technology Ecosystems Within the Central African Region: The Case of Silicon Mountain. *Future Internet* **2024**, *16*, 376. [CrossRef]
7. Shahid, K.; Ahmad, S.N.; Rizvi, S.T.H. Optimizing Network Performance: A Comparative Analysis of EIGRP, OSPF, and BGP in IPv6-Based Load-Sharing and Link-Failover Systems. *Future Internet* **2024**, *16*, 339. [CrossRef]
8. Karthick, G.; Mapp, G. Developing a Secure Service Ecosystem to Implement the Intelligent Edge Environment for Smart Cities. *Future Internet* **2024**, *16*, 317. [CrossRef]
9. Tsikteris, S.; Rahman, A.B.; Siraj, M.S.; Tsiropoulou, E.E. TRUST-ME: Trust-Based Resource Allocation and Server Selection in Multi-Access Edge Computing. *Future Internet* **2024**, *16*, 278. [CrossRef]

10. Satish, D.; Kua, J.; Pokhrel, S. Active Queue Management in L4S with Asynchronous Advantage Actor-Critic: A FreeBSD Networking Stack Perspective. *Future Internet* **2024**, *16*, 265. [CrossRef]
11. Kuznetsov, O.; Frontoni, E.; Kuznetsova, K.; Shevchuk, R.; Karpinski, M. NFT Technology for Enhanced Global Digital Registers: A Novel Approach to Tokenization. *Future Internet* **2024**, *16*, 252. [CrossRef]

future internet

MDPI

Article

Cache Aging with Learning (CAL): A Freshness-Based Data Caching Method for Information-Centric Networking on the Internet of Things (IoT)

Nemat Hazrati [1], Sajjad Pirahesh [1], Bahman Arasteh [2,3,4,*], Seyed Salar Sefati [2,5], Octavian Fratu [5,6] and Simona Halunga [5,6,*]

[1] Department of Computer Engineering, Tabriz Branch, Islamic Azad University, Tabriz 5157944533, Iran; nemat.hazrati@stu.iaut.ac.ir (N.H.); pirahesh@iaut.ac.ir (S.P.)
[2] Department of Software Engineering, Faculty of Engineering and Natural Science, Istinye University, Istanbul 34460, Türkiye; sefati.seyedsalar@upb.ro
[3] Department of Computer Science, Khazar University, Baku AZ1096, Azerbaijan
[4] Applied Science Research Center, Applied Science Private University, Amman 11937, Jordan
[5] Faculty of Electronics, Telecommunications and Information Technology, National University for Science and Technology POLITEHNICA Bucharest, 060042 Bucharest, Romania; octavian.fratu@upb.ro
[6] Academy of Romanian Scientists, 050044 Bucharest, Romania
* Correspondence: bahman.arasteh@istinye.edu.tr (B.A.); simona.halunga@upb.ro (S.H.)

Abstract: Information-centric networking (ICN) changes the way data are accessed by focusing on the content rather than the location of devices. In this model, each piece of data has a unique name, making it accessible directly by name. This approach suits the Internet of Things (IoT), where data generation and real-time processing are fundamental. Traditional host-based communication methods are less efficient for the IoT, making ICN a better fit. A key advantage of ICN is in-network caching, which temporarily stores data across various points in the network. This caching improves data access speed, minimizes retrieval time, and reduces overall network traffic by making frequently accessed data readily available. However, IoT systems involve constantly updating data, which requires managing data freshness while also ensuring their validity and processing accuracy. The interactions with cached data, such as updates, validations, and replacements, are crucial in optimizing system performance. This research introduces an ICN-IoT method to manage and process data freshness in ICN for the IoT. It optimizes network traffic by sharing only the most current and valid data, reducing unnecessary transfers. Routers in this model calculate data freshness, assess its validity, and perform cache updates based on these metrics. Simulation results across four models show that this method enhances cache hit ratios, reduces traffic load, and improves retrieval delays, outperforming similar methods. The proposed method uses an artificial neural network to make predictions. These predictions closely match the actual values, with a low error margin of 0.0121. This precision highlights its effectiveness in maintaining data currentness and validity while reducing network overhead.

Keywords: information-centric networking; Internet of Things; in-network caching; data freshness; cache replacement strategy

1. Introduction

The future of the internet will extend far beyond conventional computers and software applications, bringing connectivity to countless everyday items and even devices integrated into the human body [1,2]. This transformation, driven by the Internet of Things (IoT), promises a world where almost everything around us, from household appliances to wearable health monitors, is part of a vast, interconnected network [3]. Internet usage primarily focuses on content retrieval and information exchange, often overshadowing two-way host-to-host communication. In the traditional model, users specify a server to request information, restricting the network layer from sourcing data from alternative locations [4].

Information-centric networking (ICN) [5], which uses content-based naming, in-network caching, and name-based routing, provides a more versatile approach [6]. In ICN, users request data by name without specifying their source, allowing any node holding a copy of the data to respond, thus enhancing content accessibility [7]. A central feature of ICN is in-network caching, where intermediary nodes store data ready to be retrieved quickly when requested again [8]. This efficiency depends on factors like cache size, communication cost, and cache policies (including cache decision and eviction criteria) [9]. However, IoT data are often transient and require updates, making data freshness crucial [10]. A caching system must manage data by replacing outdated information with updated content as needed by the user [11]. The accuracy of cached data is crucial for making effective cache decisions [12,13]. Before, IoT systems only determined the data source and freshness of information.

A caching system must manage data by replacing outdated information with updated content that the user needs. Beyond merely retaining recently updated data, the interactions with cached data, including validation of their relevance and timely replacement, ensure that the network delivers accurate and up-to-date information. Robust mechanisms are essential to assess data currentness and validity in IoT systems, considering access frequency and timing. Ensuring data freshness, correctness, and accuracy is crucial for making real-time, critical decisions. Our proposed method goes beyond traditional freshness-based caching strategies by integrating metrics that assess data validity, prioritize updates, and ensure optimized caching actions in dynamic IoT environments. ICN is a network architecture focused on content retrieval rather than traditional end-to-end host communication [12]. It enables efficient data sharing, improved security, and better scalability.

This paper proposes an eight-step method to optimize caching and data freshness in ICN-IoT networks. The process begins with routers identifying whether an incoming message is a data request or a data response. For data request messages, the router checks its cache for availability (cache hit) or unavailability (cache miss) of the requested data. If a cache hit occurs, the router calculates the freshness score of the data to verify their validity and decides whether to deliver the data or forward the request to the next hop. For data response messages, the router checks for duplicates in the cache, replacing older entries when a match is found. If no duplicate exists, the router evaluates whether there is space in the cache for the new data; otherwise, it calculates the time validity of cached entries to remove expired data. If no expired data are found, the router eliminates the data entry with the lowest freshness score to accommodate the new data. This systematic process guarantees caching only the most relevant and current information, enhancing network efficiency. It significantly improves response times in ICN-IoT systems. The contributions of this paper are:

- Enhancing the cache hit ratio by maintaining only recently updated and relevant data in the cache. This avoids ambiguity and uses a more standard term to describe the data;
- Enabling intermediate routers to independently calculate data freshness and make caching decisions based on it, effectively optimizing traffic load;

- Structuring data request messages to include sensor identifiers and data types, which enables efficient data retrieval management based on specific time intervals;
- Improving cache performance by ensuring it contains only current data, which increases cache hits, reduces response delay, and lowers network traffic load.

The rest of the article proceeds as follows: Section 2 includes related work about the data caching method; Section 3 describes the proposed fresh-based caching method; Section 4 explains and discusses the simulation results; and Section 5 concludes the paper.

2. Related Work

The data caching method is designed to optimize data storage and retrieval by selectively caching data at strategic points within a network [14]. In this approach, nodes in the network temporarily store data based on specific criteria, such as data freshness, access frequency, and relevance, allowing for faster data access and reduced communication overhead. When a request is made, cached data can be retrieved from an intermediate node rather than the source, significantly lowering latency and network traffic [15]. This method incorporates caching policies to determine when to store, update, or remove data, focusing on maximizing cache utility and efficiency. This section discusses previous papers and the motivation for conducting this research.

Vural and Navaratnam [16] proposed a distributed probabilistic caching strategy where cache nodes adjust their caching probability based on the distance between the producer and the consumer and the data's freshness. In this approach, the closer a caching node is to the producer, the fresher the data it can provide. Data received directly from the producer are the freshest but involve higher communication costs due to more hops. Conversely, data retrieved from an intermediate router's cache have lower freshness but incur a reduced multi-hop retrieval cost. This method seeks to balance the tradeoff between "data freshness" and the cost of multi-hop data retrieval to optimize overall data access in a multi-hop network path.

Quevedo and Corujo [17] proposed a consumer-driven algorithm to confirm information freshness in content-centric networking. This paper first caches data packets with a freshness parameter defined by the data source. In the second step, a consumer requests data based on a specified freshness level. The freshness parameter at the source is important and can either boost or reduce network performance. In this paper, the authors try to reduce negative impacts by having the data producer respond based on the consumer's specified requirements. The benefit of this proposed method is that consumers can control the freshness of the data, which improves data relevance and freshness.

Hail and Amadeo [18] presented a probabilistic caching strategy for IoT (Pcasting) systems, considering data freshness, energy, and each IoT sensor's cache space. This proposed method helps decrease energy consumption and delays in data retrieval. The Pcasting method is flexible and compatible with various routing protocols. It can also be adjusted to include extra parameters when needed. The results show that this strategy significantly boosts network efficiency. It provides a flexible, energy-efficient caching solution for IoT environments.

Vural and Wang [19] suggested a model for in-network caching in the IoT that balances communication costs with data freshness. This paper first explores the benefits of caching temporary data in internet routers. It considers both the rate of data requests and the data's lifetime. Data lifetime refers to the duration for which data stay valid. In the second phase, when a router receives data, it checks freshness by looking at the data's arrival time, generation time, and expected lifetime. This evaluation helps ensure that only relevant data are stored.

Doan Van and Ai [20] proposed a caching decision algorithm called the Multi-Attribute Cache Decision Strategy (MACDS) for ICN-IoT. The MACDS algorithm considers several important factors, such as energy use, memory space, data freshness, and the hop count between nodes. These attributes allow the MACDS to make smart decisions on data caching locations. The proposed method optimizes resource efficiency while ensuring data accessibility, making it highly suitable for IoT environments with frequent resource constraints. It helps maintain up-to-date information across connected devices. The MACDS algorithm boosts energy efficiency by cutting down on unnecessary data transfers. It also improves network performance by caching frequently requested data in readily accessible locations. This leads to quicker data retrieval and extends the network's overall lifespan.

Meddeb and Dhraief [21] proposed a caching method for IoT networks that keeps updated data while lowering caching costs. Their approach includes a freshness mechanism that regularly checks cached data, replacing outdated information. This strategy's careful handling of data freshness keeps information relevant and accurate in constantly changing IoT environments. It ensures that data remain up to date despite frequent updates. The caching process selects nodes directly connected to consumers along the data path to store data. This setup shortens the time needed to retrieve data by reducing the number of hops. This approach speeds up response times and boosts network efficiency. Combining data freshness checks with smart cache placement allows this approach to tackle major IoT challenges. This makes it a useful solution for real-time, data-driven applications in networks with limited resources.

Asmat and Din [22] proposed the Enhanced Edge-Linked Caching (EELC) algorithm and Policy Optimization (PPO) to optimize caching in IoT networks. This proposed method dynamically adapts to current network conditions and prioritizes popular content to make the system more efficient. The EELC scheme stores frequently used data close to users, which reduces energy consumption, server load, and delays in accessing data. This method is an improvement over older techniques, like Edge-Linked Caching (ELC) and Leave Copy Everywhere (LCE), in both efficiency and speed. EELC places frequently accessed data closer to users, which speeds up data access and improves efficiency. This approach also reduces unnecessary data transfers, boosting overall network responsiveness. EELC requires regular updates and monitoring, which takes considerable processing power. This demand can be challenging for devices that have limited resources.

Mishra and Jain [23] presented a smart content replacement strategy designed for ICN in IoT networks, focusing on better cache management by keeping important data readily available. Traditional IoT networks running on TCP/IP face issues like limited address space, high data traffic, and reduced efficiency. ICN, however, allows in-network caching, where data are stored temporarily in intermediate nodes, supporting faster data retrieval and reducing network load. Traditional caching policies, like First In, First Out (FIFO); Least Recently Used (LRU); and Least Frequently Used (LFU), fail to account for the transient nature of IoT data, leading to frequent eviction of critical content. To address this, the authors introduced a novel replacement policy—evaluating data requests, content freshness, and upcoming request wait times (URWTs) to prioritize cache content effectively. Preemptively tracking these attributes in the Pending Interest Table (PIT) enables their method to remove less critical data while retaining high-value content efficiently.

Luo and Yan [24] proposed the Caching Algorithm based on Random Forest (CARF) for low earth orbit satellite mega-constellations, applying ICN to the IoT environment. The CARF uses the "viscosity" concept to integrate content popularity and satellite node location predictions to enhance cache placement accuracy. The Random Forest (RF) algorithm in the CARF allows for proactive caching of popular content at ideal satellite locations, effectively reducing access delays. This strategic placement enhances cache hit rates and throughput, ensuring faster data retrieval for users. As a result, the CARF demonstrates superior performance compared to traditional methods, like Leave Copy Everywhere (LCE) and Leave Copy Down (LCD). The method improves caching efficiency but demands significant computational resources and relies on precise satellite location prediction, which may limit its applicability under resource constraints or unexpected satellite path deviations. Table 1 shows the pros and cons of the proposed methods.

Table 1. Advantages and disadvantages of the proposed methods.

Author	Proposed Method	Advantage	Disadvantage
Vural and Navaratnam [16]	Distributed probabilistic caching strategy adjusting cache probability by distance and freshness.	Balances data freshness with multi-hop retrieval costs.	Retrieval from distant caches may reduce data freshness.
Quevedo and Corujo [17]	Consumer-driven caching in content-centric networking, where consumers specify freshness level.	Allows consumers to define data relevance, enhancing freshness and network efficiency.	Producer-specified freshness may negatively impact network performance if not optimally set.
Hail and Amadeo [18]	Probabilistic Caching Strategy (Pcasting) in the IoT considering data freshness, battery level, and cache occupancy.	Adaptive to various protocols, improving energy efficiency and network flexibility.	Limited by dependency on specific routing protocols for full efficiency.
Vural and Wang [19]	In-network caching for the IoT, balancing communication costs with data freshness based on data lifetime.	Effectively caches relevant, timely data by considering data lifetime and request frequency.	Increased complexity due to continuous data freshness assessments; limited to static data.
Doan Van and Ai [20]	Multi-Attribute Cache Decision Strategy (MACDS) for ICN-IoT considering energy, memory, freshness, and hops.	Enhances energy efficiency and accessibility, ideal for resource-constrained IoT environments.	Complex decision-making may increase the computational load on low-resource nodes.
Meddeb and Dhraief [21]	Freshness-focused caching for the IoT with continuous data validity monitoring and reduced retrieval delays.	Effective in dynamic environments, reducing hops and latency.	High resource demand due to continuous data freshness monitoring.
Asmat and Din [22]	Enhanced Edge-Linked Caching (EELC) scheme using PPO for optimal cache placement based on content popularity.	Minimizes data transfer, reducing energy and access times.	High processing requirements for reinforcement learning may strain low-resource devices.
Mishra and Jain [23]	Content replacement strategy for ICN in the IoT, retaining essential data based on freshness and future requests.	Prioritizes high-value content, reducing unnecessary data loss.	Dependency on accurate data request predictions limits efficacy under unpredictable conditions.
Luo and Yan [24]	Caching Algorithm based on Random Forest (CARF) for low earth orbit satellites, optimizing cache placement.	Reduces data access delay, improving cache hit rates and throughput in satellite IoT networks.	Demands significant computational resources and precise satellite location data; limited by resource constraints.

Research Motivation and Identified Gaps

This study's motivation arises from the need to address several persistent challenges in data caching within IoT networks, particularly those utilizing ICN. Existing methods, while innovative, have limitations that affect network efficiency, data freshness, cache management, and overall QoS. These gaps, highlighted in the existing literature, provided the impetus for our proposed method to tackle deficiencies in previous caching strategies.

A primary challenge identified in prior works is balancing data freshness with caching efficiency. Studies by Vural et al., Vural and Navaratnam [16], and Quevedo and Corujo [17] attempted to incorporate data freshness into their caching strategies, yet they often relied on static parameters or distance-based caching that did not fully capture real-time fluctuations in data validity. Our work addresses this gap by implementing dynamic data freshness calculations, enabling more precise caching decisions, and optimizing data relevancy across variable IoT traffic loads. Furthermore, solutions like those proposed by Hail and Amadeo [18] and Doan Van and Ai [20] introduced adaptive caching parameters, such as energy and memory. However, these approaches overlooked the cumulative impact of cache decision delays on network latency, leading to suboptimal performance in highly time-sensitive IoT environments. Our method seeks to mitigate latency without imposing excess computational load on network nodes by focusing on cache decision timeliness and utilizing a multi-criteria approach.

Another key gap in the literature involves the need for flexible mechanisms for cache eviction based on data expiration or redundancy. Traditional methods, like the LRU and probabilistic models, frequently need to accommodate the dynamic nature of IoT-generated data. Techniques like EELC by Asmat and Din [22] provided an early attempt at context-based cache decisions but struggled with scalability due to heavy computational requirements. In contrast, our proposed method utilizes a lightweight, freshness-based eviction strategy tailored to maximize cache utility while minimizing resource consumption, thus enhancing scalability for resource-constrained IoT networks.

Finally, the limitations of predictive caching and traffic load distribution models prompted us to introduce a proactive caching approach that considers historical data patterns. While models like those by Meddeb and Dhraief [21] and Mishra and Jain [23] addressed data validity, they lacked predictive insights for high-demand scenarios. Incorporating data freshness indicators with predictive cache placement enables our method to anticipate better and meet peak traffic demands. This approach optimizes cache hit ratios, reduces network delays, and lowers traffic load. This study, therefore, fills critical gaps by combining real-time freshness validation, optimized cache replacement strategies, and predictive cache management, enhancing the overall responsiveness and reliability of IoT caching systems.

3. Problem Statement

Maintaining data freshness in IoT systems within ICN architectures is crucial yet challenging due to the continuous generation of time-sensitive data by IoT devices [25]. In these networks, routers save data along the path to reduce delay and improve bandwidth use. Without a way to verify data freshness, outdated information could be sent to IoT clients [26]. This can result in poor decisions and slower system responses. This issue becomes more complex as IoT networks grow, with data demands constantly changing.

The quick aging of sensor data also raises the risk of sending outdated information. A strong system is needed to ensure that only updated and relevant data are stored and quickly accessible to users [27]. Traditional ICN [28] caching methods do not effectively manage data freshness, which can lead to poor cache use. This often results in lower cache hit rates and less efficient network performance. These methods usually do not account for real-time factors to check if data are still valid, like comparing when data were created to when they were requested. They also overlook how often the data are requested, which affects their relevance. Without precise freshness management, outdated data can remain in caches, taking up valuable space. Since IoT applications need reliable, up-to-date data for tasks like monitoring and control, a better caching method is urgently needed [29,30]. This approach must accurately assess data freshness and prioritize which data to replace in the cache based on their usefulness and validity. This ensures the cache performs well and keeps reliable data available across IoT networks.

3.1. QoS Formula

The cache hit rate metric shows how well a caching system performs by calculating the percentage of requests fulfilled directly from the cache rather than fetching data from slower storage [22,31]. A higher cache hit rate usually means quicker data access, less delay, and better Quality of Service (QoS) by reducing the strain on backend resources [32]. A high cache hit rate in network systems can also lower bandwidth usage because data are retrieved locally from the cache instead of repeatedly pulling from the main source. Optimizing cache hit rates is crucial for applications requiring rapid data access, such as content delivery networks (CDNs) and real-time data processing in IoT systems [33]. Effective caching algorithms, like the proposed method in your simulations, aim to maximize cache hits over time, outperforming traditional methods like LRU under various operational conditions. Equation (1) is used to calculate the cache hit rate:

$$Cache\ Hit\ Rate = \frac{Number\ of\ Cache\ Hits}{Total\ Number\ of\ Requests} \tag{1}$$

Number of cache hits refers to the successful instances where the requested data were found in the cache. The total number of requests is the overall number of requests made during the simulation period.

Network delay (D) represents the time taken for data to travel from the source to the destination across a network, affecting the overall response time in networked systems [31]. High network delays can result from long transmission paths, heavy network traffic, or processing delays at intermediate nodes. Reducing network delay is essential for applications requiring low-latency communication, including real-time video streaming, IoT systems, and online gaming. Effective caching mechanisms, such as the proposed method in your simulations, help lower network delay by reducing the need for frequent data retrievals from the source. Caching frequently accessed and up-to-date data enables the network to achieve faster response times and improve QoS, outperforming traditional caching approaches, such as LRU. Equation (2) was used to evaluate the delay [34]:

$$D = T_{rtt} + T_{proc} + T_{queue} + T_{trans} \tag{2}$$

T_{rtt}, measured in milliseconds (ms), represents the round-trip time delay for data to travel to and from the source. T_{proc}, in milliseconds (ms), denotes the processing time at each network node or router. T_{queue} is the queuing delay for packets waiting to be processed or transmitted and T_{trans} is the transmission time for data across the network.

Traffic load (TL) measures the volume of data or requests that pass through a network over a certain period, reflecting network demand and potential congestion. High traffic load can strain network resources, resulting in slower response times and increased packet loss, which negatively impacts QoS [35]. Caching frequently requested data closer to users reduces traffic load as fewer requests need to reach the original data source, alleviating network burden. In the simulations, the proposed caching method reduced traffic load more effectively than the LRU algorithm by serving additional requests from intermediate caches. This decrease in traffic improves network efficiency, saves bandwidth, and lowers latency, which is beneficial for applications needing quick data access and minimal delay. Traffic load was calculated by Equation (3):

$$TL = \frac{Total\ Number\ of\ Requests \times Data\ Size\ per\ Request}{Simulation\ Time} \tag{3}$$

Root mean square error (RMSE) is a standard metric for measuring the accuracy of predictive models by showing the average difference between predicted and actual values [36]. It is calculated by finding the square root of the average of squared differences between observed and predicted values, keeping the result in the same units as the original data. A lower RMSE indicates more accurate predictions. This metric is especially valuable in regression and time series forecasting, where accurate predictions are critical, as it reveals the average error size in predictions [37]. This metric helps pinpoint areas where improvements could enhance overall model performance. Equation (4) was used to calculate the value of RMSE:

$$RMSE = \sqrt{\frac{1}{n}\sum_{i=1}^{n}\left(F_{rate_{pred,i}} - F_{rate_{obs,i}}\right)^2} \quad (4)$$

In Equation (4), n is the total number of observations, $F_{rate_{pred,i}}$ represents the predicted or estimated value for the i-th observation, and $F_{rate_{obs,i}}$ represents the actual or measured value for the i-th observation. When $i = 2$, the term $\left(F_{rate_{pred,i}} - F_{rate_{obs,i}}\right)^2$ represents the squared difference between the predicted and observed values for the second observation. This contributes to the overall sum of squared errors. The formula applies to all $i = 1, 2, \ldots, n$, ensuring the RMSE is calculated as a single, unique value representing the average error over all observations.

3.2. Calculating Data Freshness

The proposed method utilizes data freshness calculations within the Named Data Network (NDN)-based ICN-IoT architecture to efficiently manage cached data in response to consumer requests. This approach uses freshness as a primary criterion for determining whether data should be retrieved from cache, forwarded, or replaced, optimizing response times and cache utilization. Each step of the method is described below.

Step 1: Start and Check for Message Type

The process begins when the router receives an incoming message, either a data request message or a data response message from a consumer. A data request message specifies a request for specific information while a data response message carries the requested data. The type of message determines the router's subsequent actions. To classify the message, let M denote the incoming message. The router determines whether M belongs to the set of data request messages (τ) or the set of data response messages (D) based on its contents. This classification can be represented by Equation (5):

$$M = \begin{cases} Data\ request\ message\ \ if\ M \in \tau \\ Data\ Message\ if\ M \in D \end{cases} \quad (5)$$

Here, τ represents the set of data request messages, which contain information such as the requested data type, sensor ID, and request time, while D represents the set of data response messages, which include the actual sensor data. The router determines the set membership $(M \in \tau\ or\ M \in D)$ by analyzing specific fields in the message, such as headers or metadata. If $M \in \tau$, the router checks its cache for the requested data. If $M \in D$, the router evaluates caching decisions based on the recency and validity of the data.

Step 2: Check Cache for Requested Data

In the proposed method of this study, the data request message is sent by the client and received by a router along the transmission path. Each request message specifies the sensor number and the data item type (R_{type}). For example, the client may request the average temperature of a room over the last 15 min. Here, the "average temperature over the last 15 min" corresponds to the data item type (R_{type}) while the specific temperature request for a particular room refers to a sensor with a unique identifier.

Upon receiving a data request message, the router searches its cache or Content Store (CS) for the requested data. This process determines whether a cache hit (data are found) or a cache miss (data are not found) occurs. The cache status is represented by Equation (6), where $Cache_{Status} = 1$ indicates a cache hit and $Cache_{Status} = 0$ signifies a cache miss:

$$Cache_{Status} = \begin{cases} 1 & if\ (Sensor\ number,\ data\ type) \in CS \\ 0 & if\ Otherwise \end{cases} \tag{6}$$

Step 3: Calculate Data Freshness

If the data are found in the cache, the router calculates the data freshness to verify their validity. Freshness V is determined by Equation (7):

$$V = 1 - \frac{RT - CDTS}{R_{type}} \tag{7}$$

RT (Request Time) represents the time when a consumer requests data while CDTS (Cached Data Time Stamp) indicates the time when the data are stored in the cache. R_{type} (Requested Data Type) is a numerical value representing the refresh rate of the requested data type. V is the freshness score, with values closer to 1 indicating fresher data. If $V > 0$, the data are considered valid and ready to be sent to the consumer.

Step 4: Cache Hit or Cache Miss Decision

Depending on the result of the freshness calculation, the router decides whether to deliver the data or forward the request. If $V > 0$, indicating a cache hit with valid data, the router sends the data to the consumer. If $V \leq 0$, or if the cache does not contain the requested data, a cache miss occurs, and the data request message is forwarded to the next step. The decision to forward is calculated by Equation (8). Forward = 1 means the data request message is forwarded while Forward = 0 indicates the data are sent directly to the consumer:

$$Forward = \begin{cases} 1 & if\ Cache_{status} = 0\ or\ V \leq 0 \\ 0 & Otherwise \end{cases} \tag{8}$$

Step 5: Check for Data with a Matching Sensor Number and Type in the Cache

When a data message is received, the router first checks whether the cache already contains data with the same sensor number and data type. This is expressed by Equation (9). If $Duplicate_{Check} = 1$, the old data are removed and the new data are cached; otherwise, the router proceeds to the next step.

$$Duplicate_{Check} = \begin{cases} 1 & if\ (Sensor\ number,\ data\ type) \in CS \\ 0 & Otherwise \end{cases} \tag{9}$$

Step 6: Check for Empty Space in the Cache

If no duplicate data are found, the router checks if there is space in the cache for the new data. Cache space is represented by Equation (10). If $Cache_{Space} = 1$, the new data are cached; if $Cache_{Space} = 0$, the router moves to the next step:

$$Cache_{Space} = \begin{cases} 1 & if\ available\ space > 0 \\ 0 & Otherwise \end{cases} \tag{10}$$

Step 7: Check for Expired Data in the Cache

If the cache is full, the router checks for expired data by calculating the time validity of cached entries. Time validity is calculated by Equation (11):

$$Time_{validation} = 1 - \frac{NDTS - CDTS}{NDtype} \tag{11}$$

$NDTS$ ($New\ Data\ Time\ Stamp$) represents the time when new data become available for caching, $CDTS$ ($Cached\ Data\ Time\ Stamp$) indicates the time when the data were originally stored in the cache, and $NDtype$ ($New\ Data\ Type$) reflects the refresh rate of the new data type. If $Time_{validation} \leq 0$, the cached data are deemed expired and removed to accommodate the new data.

Step 8: Remove Data with the Lowest Freshness Score if No Expired Data are Found

If no expired data exist, the router calculates the freshness score $V(i,j)$ of all cache entries and removes the data with the lowest score to cache the new data. The overall validity score is calculated by Equation (12):

$$\mathrm{V(i,j)} = (\alpha \times F_{Rate}) + ((1-\alpha) \times Time_{validation}) \tag{12}$$

$V(i,j)$ represents the combined freshness and validity score, where α is a weighting coefficient that balances the importance of freshness and validity in the calculation. Additionally, α is considered a network-specific constant because its value is chosen based on the specific characteristics and requirements of the network environment, such as the frequency of data updates, the priority of real-time data, or the caching strategy employed. For example, in networks where data freshness is critical, α may be set closer to 1 to provide further weight to freshness. Conversely, in scenarios where data validity or historical relevance is more important, α may be set closer to 0 to emphasize validity. The freshness rate F_{Rate} is calculated by Equation (13):

$$F_{Rate} = \frac{SRN}{TR} \tag{13}$$

Here, the same request number (SRN) represents the count of requests made specifically for a particular data type while total requests (TR) denotes the overall number of requests during the observation period. A *higher F* value indicates that the data type is more frequently requested, making it more likely to be prioritized for caching.

This systematic process ensures that only the most relevant and up-to-date data are retained in the cache, optimizing resource utilization and enhancing response times for consumers in the ICN-IoT network. Algorithm 1 shows the proposed method pseudocode.

Algorithm 1: Pseudocode of the proposed method.

```
START

//Step 1: Check for Message Type

1. RECEIVE M //Incoming message
2. IF M ∈ τ THEN //If M is a data request message
3.         MESSAGE_TYPE ← "REQUEST"
4. ELSE IF M ∈ D THEN //If M is a data response message
5.         MESSAGE_TYPE ← "RESPONSE"
6. ELSE
7.         RETURN "Invalid Message"
```

Algorithm 1: *Cont.*

```
//Step 2: Check Cache for Requested Data
IF MESSAGE_TYPE = "REQUEST" THEN
    CHECK_CACHE(M.sensor_number, M.data_type)
    IF (M.sensor_number, M.data_type) ∈ CS THEN
        Cache_Status ← 1 //Cache hit
    ELSE
        Cache_Status ← 0 //Cache miss
    END IF

//Step 3: Calculate Data Freshness
    IF Cache_Status = 1 THEN
        V ← 1 - (RT - CDTS)/R_type
        IF V > 0 THEN
            SEND_DATA_TO_CONSUMER( )
        ELSE
            FORWARD_REQUEST()
        END IF
    ELSE
        FORWARD_REQUEST()
    END IF

//Step 4: Cache Hit or Cache Miss Decision
ELSE IF MESSAGE_TYPE = "RESPONSE" THEN

//Step 5: Check for Matching Data in Cache
    IF (M.sensor_number, M.data_type) ∈ CS THEN
        REMOVE_OLD_DATA(M.sensor_number, M.data_type)
        CACHE_NEW_DATA(M)
    ELSE

//Step 6: Check for Empty Space in Cache
        IF AVAILABLE_CACHE_SPACE > 0 THEN
            CACHE_NEW_DATA(M)
        ELSE

//Step 7: Check for Expired Data in Cache
            FOR EACH DATA_ENTRY IN CS DO
                Time_validation ← 1 - (NDTS - CDTS)/NDtype
                IF Time_validation ≤ 0 THEN
                    REMOVE_EXPIRED_DATA(DATA_ENTRY)
                    CACHE_NEW_DATA(M)
                    BREAK
                END IF
            END FOR
```

Algorithm 1: *Cont.*

```
//Step 8: Remove Data with Lowest Freshness Score
            IF NO_EXPIRED_DATA_FOUND THEN
                CALCULATE_FRESHNESS_AND_VALIDITY()
                REMOVE_LOWEST_SCORE_DATA()
                CACHE_NEW_DATA(M)
            END IF
        END IF
    END IF
END IF

END
```

3.3. *Predicting Data Freshness*

The CAL method incorporates a prediction mechanism using the Nonlinear Autoregressive (NAR) neural network to enhance caching efficiency. In the fourth step of the caching process, routers predict the data's freshness rate and calculate the validity of cached data based on the predicted freshness. This proactive approach reduces unnecessary data replacements and ensures that the cache retains the most relevant and current data. The NAR model forecasts future data freshness by analyzing past traffic patterns. Specifically:

- **Input Layer:** Processes historical request data, such as the sensor request number (SRN) and total requests (TRs) for specific data types;
- **Hidden Layer:** Configured with an optimized number of neurons to balance learning complexity and computational efficiency;
- **Output Layer:** Produces the predicted freshness rate ($F_{rate_{pred}}$) for the specified data;

For requests specific to a sensor ID or data type, the corresponding historical request counts are used as inputs to forecast the future request rate.

These predictions are utilized in the CAL method to calculate data validity, guiding decisions about which data to retain or replace in the cache. The combination of historical traffic data and neural network predictions enables CAL to maintain high accuracy in its caching strategy while reducing computational overhead and network traffic. Predicted freshness values are computed as follows:

- The network uses past request data to predict PSRN (predicted SRN) and PTR (predicted total requests);
- Equation (14) calculates the predicted freshness rate (F_{rate}):

$$F_{rate_{pred}} = \frac{SRN + PSRN}{TR + PTR} \tag{14}$$

- Equation (15) evaluates the predicted validity (V_{pred}):

$$V_{pred}(i,j) = \left(\alpha * F_{rate_{pred}}\right) + ((1-\alpha) * \text{Time\_validation}) \tag{15}$$

The predicted freshness values guide the CAL method's caching decisions, allowing routers to prioritize more relevant data. This integration minimizes unnecessary cache replacements and enhances the overall efficiency of IoT data dissemination.

4. Evaluation

This section thoroughly analyzes the simulated scenario, including the selection and justification of the parameters used to accurately represent real-world conditions within the network environment. The scenario aims to reflect typical usage patterns and operational constraints encountered in a NDN-based ICN-IoT architecture, ensuring the results.

4.1. Simulation Scenario

As shown in Figure 1, the simulation scenario is a network consisting of six consumer nodes (servers), fifteen router nodes, and six data producer nodes. Each consumer node is connected to the producer nodes through different routes via multiple routers. The communication paths between each server and the producers are statically determined. Each producer node is connected to three sensors, which collect data and send it to the requesting consumer. The sensors are Wi-Fi stations connected to a wireless access point (producer node) in infrastructure mode. All communications in this topology are wireless and the routers are Mikrotik Netmetal 5 devices with MIPS architecture.

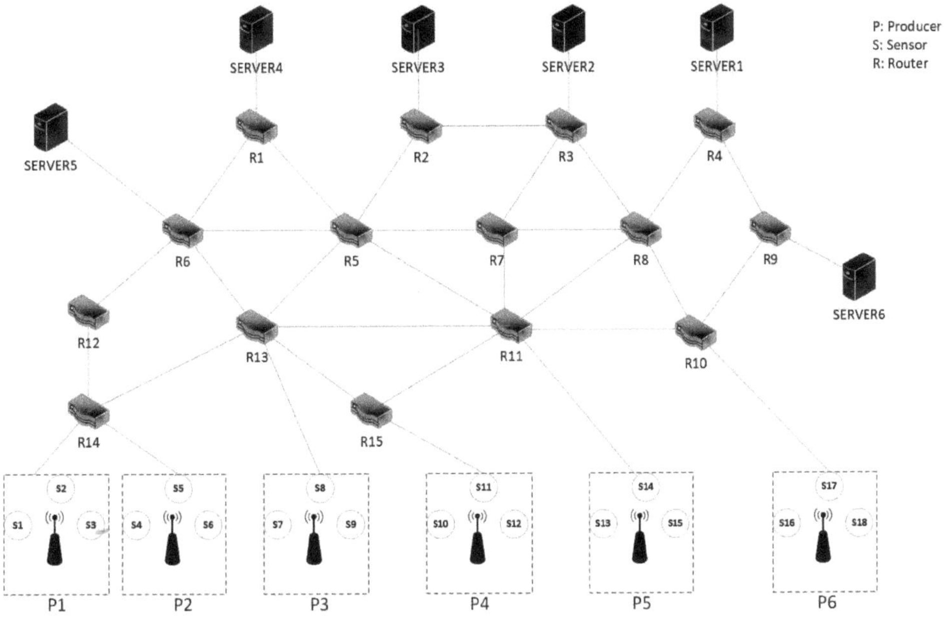

Figure 1. Topology of the simulated scenarios.

4.2. Simulation Parameters

Table 2 summarizes the parameters used to simulate the proposed approach scenario.

In the simulations, messages are randomly generated using MATLAB. Each data request message includes the request number, applicant number, request time, requested sensor number, and data item type. Once generated, the data request message is sent according to their request times. According to the topology in Figure 2, each requesting node sends its message along a specific path to the data producer identified in the request. Each path consists of multiple hops and the data request message passes through several intermediate routers. If the cache cannot fulfill the request, it is forwarded to the producer. In this simulation scenario, network delays are modeled by considering each data exchange's propagation and transmission delays and the processing time and data handling at each router. The size of the exchanged data packets determines the traffic load for each period. The scenario is simulated using the LRU method and the proposed approach, each tested separately in eight modes based on simulation time, period length, and the number of requests. MATLAB version R2022 was used for all simulations.

Table 2. Simulation parameters.

Parameter Description	Parameter Value
Router cache size	10 records
Data item type	The average of the last 5 min, 10 min, 15 min, 20 min, and 30 min
The distance of the consumer to the connected router	95 m
Distance between routers	7 km
The distance of the producer to the connected router	10 km
Wireless propagation speed	$3 \times (10^8)$ m per s
Propagation delay	$\frac{\text{Distance}}{\text{Wireless speed}}$
Transmission delay	$\frac{\text{Load\_size}}{\text{Wireless BW}}$
Wireless bandwidth	200 Mbps
Packet size	1472 bytes
Constant (α)	0.8

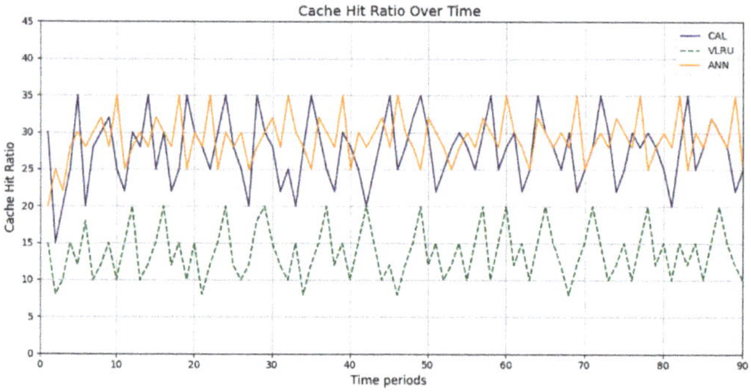

Figure 2. Cache hit ratio of the caching methods in Model 1.

Simulation metrics included:

- **Cache Success Rate**: The percentage of data requests the cache satisfies;
- **Network Traffic Load**: Total network bandwidth utilized for data retrieval;
- **Response Time**: Time taken to retrieve requested data.

4.3. Discussion

The proposed method integrates time series analysis to handle the temporal nature of data freshness in IoT environments. Each data packet is tagged with time stamps, including the Cached Data Time Stamp (CDTS) and Request Time (RT), to calculate a freshness score dynamically. This approach ensures that cache decisions are based on the temporal relevance of the data, prioritizing recently updated or frequently requested information. Additionally, the time-dependent patterns observed in request frequencies are considered in predictive models, such as the Artificial Neural Network (ANN), to optimize caching decisions proactively. These time-dependent variables enable the method to effectively handle the ever-changing nature of data generated in IoT environments.

The ANN employed in this study was designed to predict key performance metrics, such as cache hit ratios and network delays, under various simulation scenarios. The ANN architecture consisted of three hidden layers, each comprising sixty-four neurons.

The ReLU activation function introduced non-linearity, ensuring the model could capture complex relationships between input features. The input features for the ANN included request frequency, data freshness, and historical cache hit ratios, which were generated and extracted from simulation scenarios using MATLAB. The network leveraged these features to identify patterns and trends in the data, facilitating more accurate predictions of system behavior. Training the ANN involved splitting the data into a training set (70% of the total data) and a validation set (30%), ensuring the model could generalize effectively to unseen data. Backpropagation with a mean squared error (MSE) loss function was used during training to iteratively minimize prediction errors, enhancing model accuracy over successive iterations. The RMSE metric was used to assess the ANN's performance, providing a quantitative measure of prediction accuracy. Lower RMSE values indicated the ANN's reliability in forecasting key outcomes, such as the likelihood of cache hits and delays. The ANN's role extended beyond predictions—it served as a baseline for comparison with the proposed caching method, especially in scenarios where predictive models could enhance decision making. Analyzing patterns in historical data, the ANN showcased the benefits of integrating machine learning techniques into caching systems. This highlights their capacity to anticipate system demands and enhance performance.

The simulation results were assessed across three key performance metrics: cache hit ratio, network delay, and traffic load. Our proposed cache aging with learning (CAL) method was compared with two established techniques, the ANN and Variable Least Recently Used (VLRU) algorithms. Results indicate that under extended simulation durations and frequent, high-volume data requests, CAL outperformed the alternatives by effectively caching data while preserving their freshness. This contributed to reduced network delays and optimized traffic load. The findings underscore efficient cache management's importance in handling high-demand scenarios in networked environments, enhancing data availability and system responsiveness. However, if fewer requests are sent over longer intervals, the method's benefits are less noticeable. Therefore, we focused on scenarios with longer simulation times, higher request volumes, and shorter intervals, as shown in Table 3, where the results demonstrate the method's effectiveness in achieving our study's goals.

Table 3. Simulation modes.

Simulation Mode	Simulation Time	Period Length	Number of Requests
Mode 1	3 h	180 s	3000
Mode 2	10 h	120 s	1000
Mode 3	3 h	120 s	3000
Mode 4	10 h	120 s	3000

However, the results also reveal that CAL's effectiveness compared to the ANN was insignificant in certain scenarios. Specifically, CAL showed marginal improvements in cases with lower request frequencies or longer intervals between requests. This is because CAL primarily focuses on real-time data freshness, which limits its adaptability to fluctuating traffic patterns. In contrast, the ANN's predictive modeling capabilities enable it to anticipate system demands and optimize cache decisions accordingly, giving it a distinct advantage in such scenarios.

This performance gap can also be attributed to the static nature of CAL's cache aging mechanism. While CAL effectively prioritizes recently updated data, it lacks the flexibility to dynamically adjust its parameters based on observed trends or historical request patterns. Conversely, the ANN utilizes a dynamic learning process that continuously adapts its caching strategies as new patterns emerge. This allows the ANN to maintain a higher cache hit ratio in environments with variable or unpredictable request frequencies as it can allocate resources more efficiently.

Another contributing factor is the reliance of CAL on pre-defined thresholds for determining data freshness. These thresholds, while effective in scenarios with consistent data traffic, may lead to suboptimal performance in situations where traffic intensity varies significantly. The ANN mitigates this issue using real-time input features, such as request frequency and historical data, to make more informed caching decisions. As a result, the ANN exhibits better overall responsiveness to the inherent variability in IoT environments, particularly in cases with less frequent or irregular request patterns.

Figures 2–5 present the simulation results in four different modes, as outlined in Table 3. Figure 2 illustrates the cache hit rate of the proposed method in the first simulation model, which includes 3000 requests over 180 s. As shown in Figure 2, the cache hit ratio of the proposed method is higher than that of the VLRU method. Figure 3 depicts the cache hit ratio of the caching methods in the second simulation model, where the proposed method again achieves a considerably higher cache hit ratio than the VLRU algorithm. The proposed caching method outperforms the VLRU method in terms of the cache hit ratio across different simulation models. The simulation results indicate a significant difference in cache hit rate between the proposed method and the VLRU method; the proposed method substantially improves cache hit rate performance.

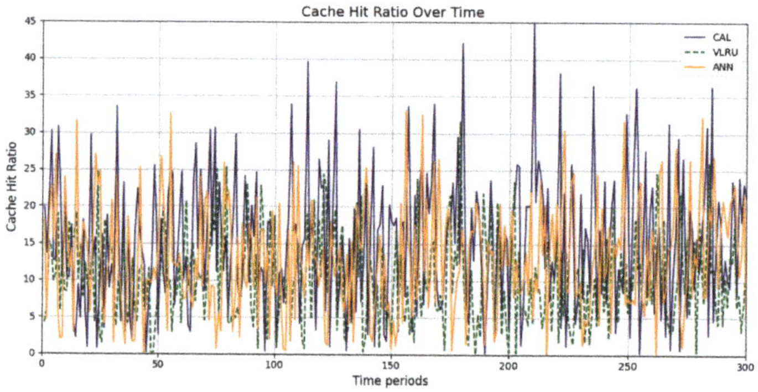

Figure 3. Cache hit ratio of the caching methods in Model 2.

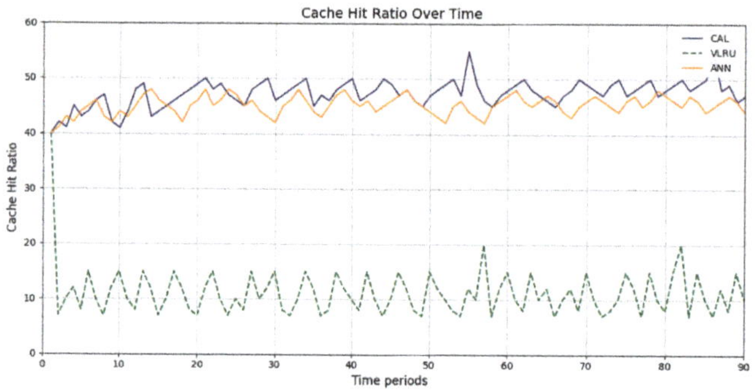

Figure 4. Cache hit ratio of the caching methods in Model 3.

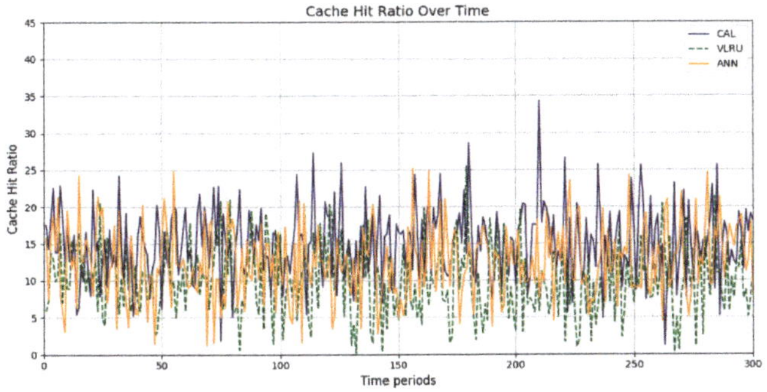

Figure 5. Cache hit ratio of the caching methods in Model 4.

Figures 4 and 5 show the simulation results for Models 3 and 4. The third model's simulations include 3000 requests over 120 s. As shown in Figure 4, the cache hit rate of the proposed method is significantly higher than that of the VLRU method and is approximately equal to the values estimated by the ANN. Figure 5 depicts the cache hit ratio of the caching methods in the fourth simulation model, where the cache hit ratio of the proposed method is again a bit higher than that of the VLRU algorithm. The simulation results across all four models confirm the superiority of the proposed method in terms of cache hit rate, demonstrating a significant improvement in cache hit rate performance.

Making cache decisions based on data freshness allows routers to cache data that are more likely to be re-requested by other consumers. Due to the high cache hit ratio and the lack of frequent reference to the data source, network delay has been reduced compared to the VLRU method. It should be noted that a large part of the network delay for the proposed method in the diagrams is related to the execution time of the router processes for cache decisions. Due to the implementation of this method in the simulation environment, the computational time for the simulated processing of routers is longer than in the natural environment. If implemented in the real environment, the network latency is significantly less than in the simulation results. The caching methods impose performance overhead on the system. The imposed performance overhead by the caching techniques should be evaluated as the other criteria. Network delay and traffic load are the leading performance overhead assessed in this study.

Figures 6 and 7 show the network delay of the caching methods in the first simulation model with and without estimated values by the ANN. Similar experiments have been performed for the second model. Figures 8 and 9 show the results of the simulations in the second model. Figures 10 and 11 show the network delay imposed by the caching methods in the third simulation model with and without estimated results. The results of the simulations indicate that the proposed method has a lower network delay than the VLRU method. The results of the fourth model simulations have been shown in Figures 12 and 13. The results of the fourth model simulation are similar to those of the second simulation model. The imposed performance overhead in Simulation Model 2 is like the VLRU method (shown in Figures 8 and 9). Overall, the network delay imposed by the proposed method is lower than that of the VLRU method. The proposed method provides a higher cache hit ratio with lower network delay.

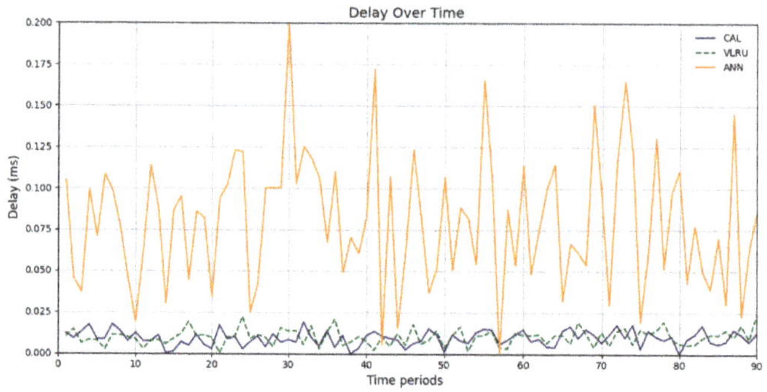

Figure 6. Network delay of the caching methods in Model 1.

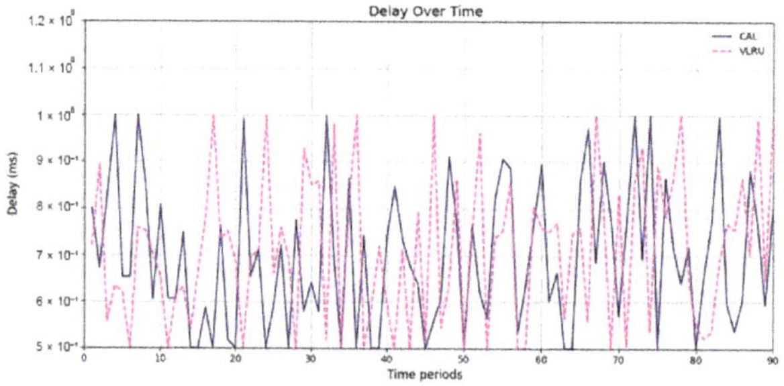

Figure 7. Network delay of the caching methods in Model 1 without estimation.

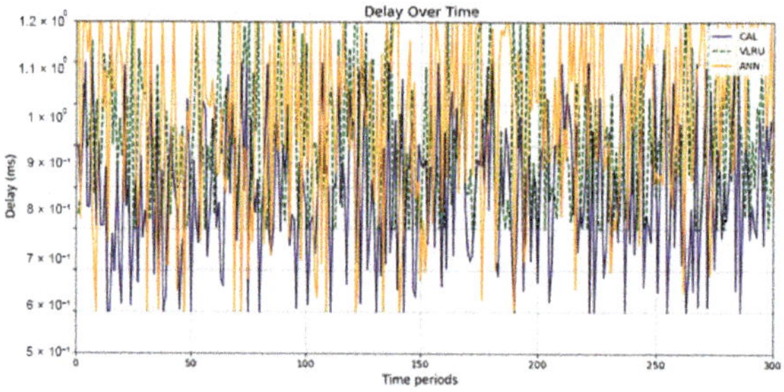

Figure 8. Network delay of the caching methods in Model 2.

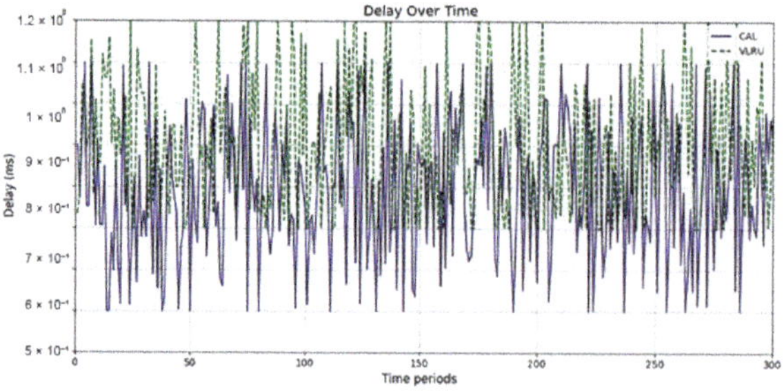

Figure 9. Network delay of the caching methods in Model 2 without prediction.

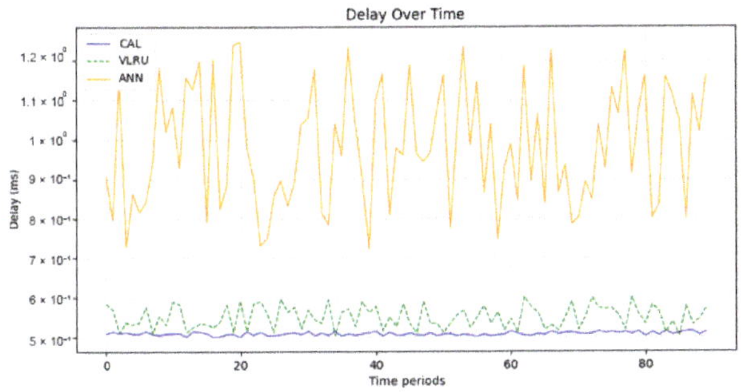

Figure 10. Network delay of the caching methods in Model 3.

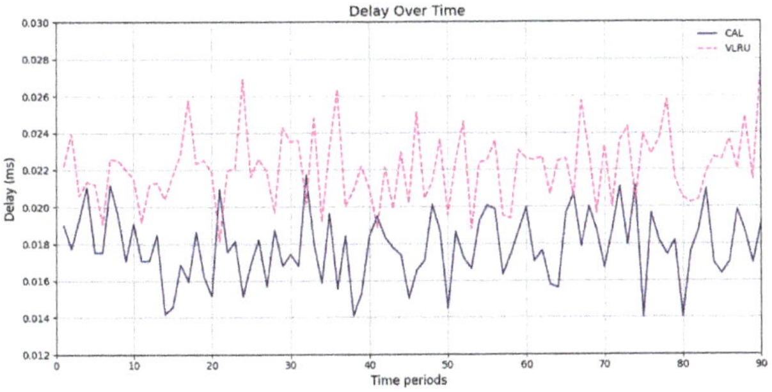

Figure 11. Network delay of the caching methods in Model 3 without estimation.

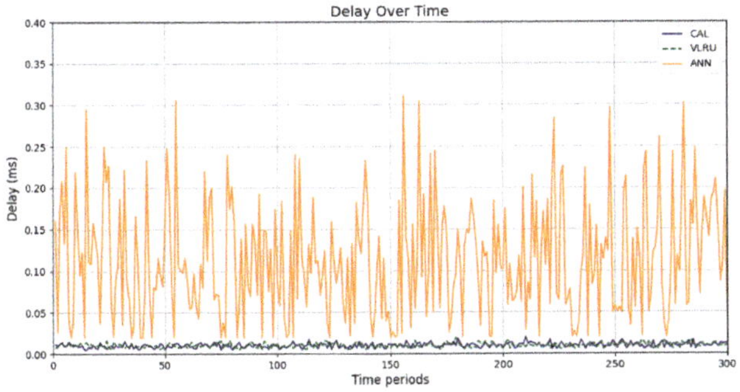

Figure 12. Network delay of the caching methods in Model 4.

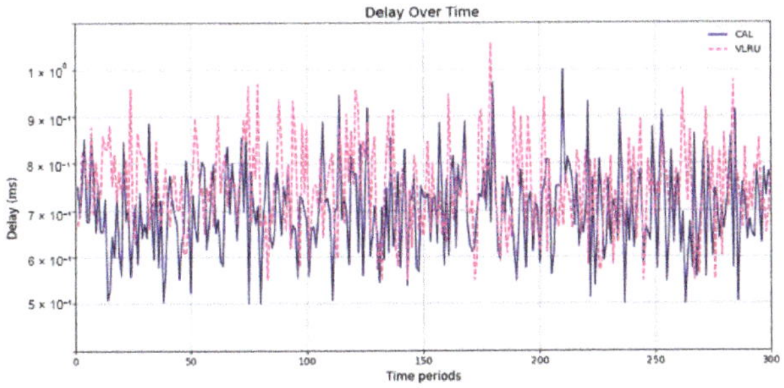

Figure 13. Network delay of the caching methods in Model 4 without estimation.

The results confirm that the proposed method considerably improves the cache hit ratio without imposing network delay; this is its main merit. Traffic load is the other criterion for the caching methods that should be considered. Figures 14 and 15 show the traffic load of the proposed method and VLRU in the conducted simulations in four models. The average value of the imposed traffic load by the proposed method is lower than the VLRU method in Simulation Models 1 and 2. Figure 5 shows the traffic load of the chachi methods in Simulation Models 3 and 4. The traffic load of the proposed method is lower than that of the other method. The lower traffic load is the other merit of the proposed method over the previous methods. In all simulation models, in the worst case, the traffic load is equal to the traffic load of the VLRU method. The proposed method optimizes the traffic load since intermediate routers answer most requests. To evaluate the accuracy of the results, the results obtained by the proposed method were compared with the predicted results by the ANN. The RMSE was used according to Equation (4) to compare the predicted and the measured values. The RSME obtained for Simulation Model 1 is 0.0139 and for Model 4 is 0.0121. Figure 16 shows the F_{rate} values in the simulations.

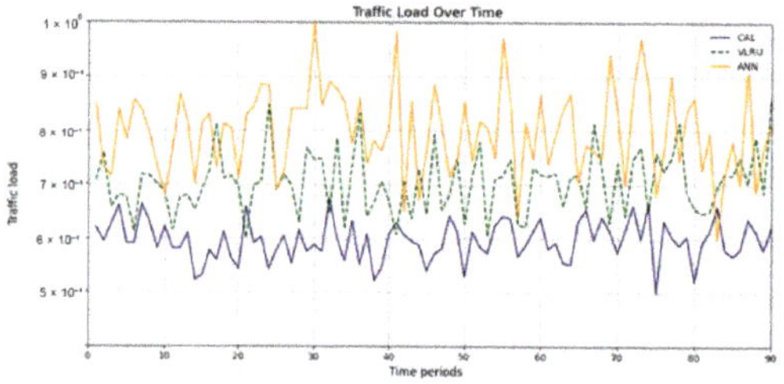

(**a**) Simulation Model 1

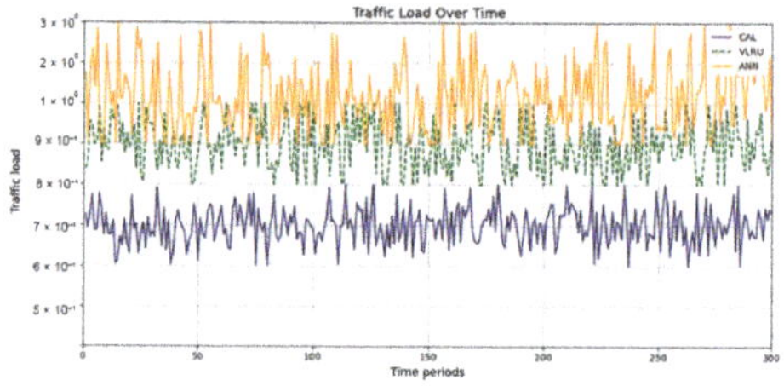

(**b**) Simulation Model 2

Figure 14. Traffic load of the caching methods in Models 1 and 2.

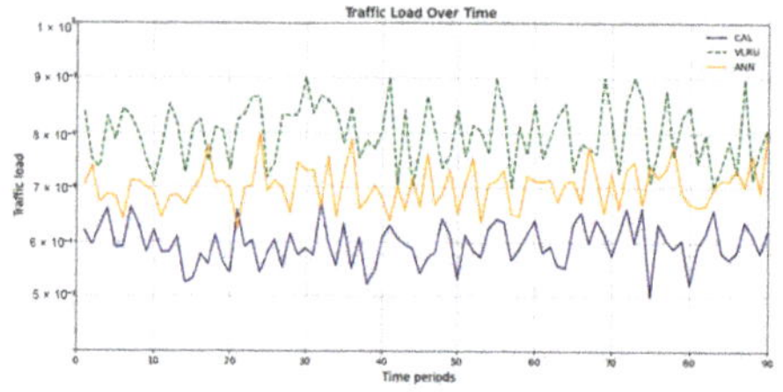

(**a**) Simulation Model 3

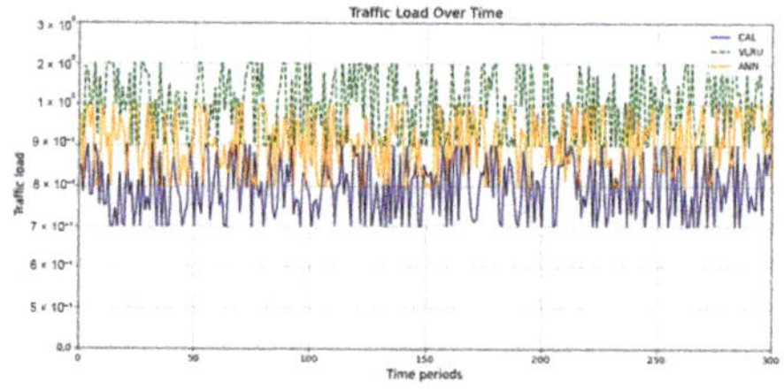

(**b**) Simulation Model 4

Figure 15. Traffic load of the caching methods in Models 3 and 4.

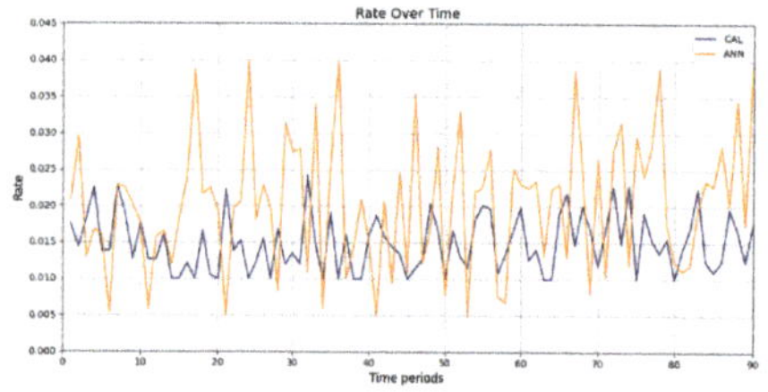

(**a**) Model 1

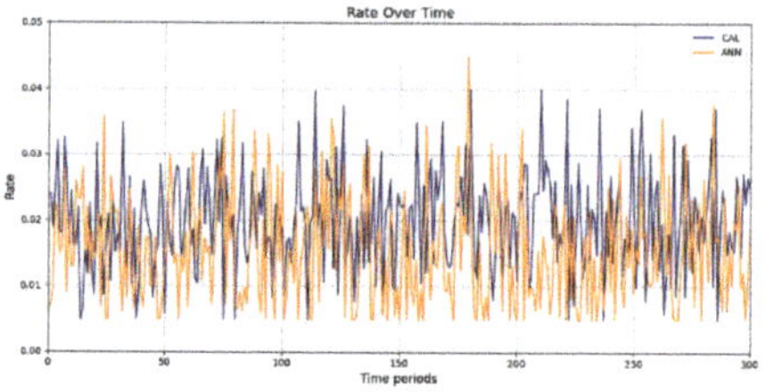

(**b**) Model 2

Figure 16. F_{rate} values in simulation Models 1 and 4.

5. Conclusions and Future Works

Due to the instability and transience of data on the IoT and the need for a mechanism for data freshness to control the validity of cached data, in this regard, we proposed an approach for in-network caching in ICN. Calculating the data freshness in the ICN-IoT is an approach that is proposed to increase the cache hit ratio, reduce traffic load, and decrease network delay in data retrieval. In this approach, the freshness of cache data is calculated by routers and the cache decision is made based on the results. The simulation and evaluation of results represent the achievement of the expected targets of this study. The proposed approach in this research has significantly increased the cache hit ratio compared to the VLRU method by enhancing data freshness in the cache of the routers. Reducing network delays and optimizing traffic load are the other two objectives of this research. The suggested method facilitates the data exchange in communication paths between the consumer and the data producer.

Predicting requests and data freshness based on traffic information for datasets and using the expected information for cache decisions by routers is another idea that can be considered for future work. In the proposed approach of this research, the routers process and calculate the data freshness and cache decision. Due to the limited resources in the IoT, using the capabilities of Software-Defined Networking can be another idea for future works. The most common advantages of SDN are separation of the control plane from the data plane, centralized network management and traffic load, scalability, improved network control and responsiveness, reliability, and reduced network latency. If the proposed approach in this paper is combined with a software-based network, control processes will be removed from the routers and performed by the central unit and the routers will be managed centrally. Centralized network management and central control can reduce network latency by reducing the computational load of routers and speeding up the necessary processing. Utilizing different hybrid machine learning algorithms [38] instead of the ANN can improve the performance of the suggested method.

Author Contributions: Conceptualization, N.H., B.A., O.F. and S.H.; Methodology, S.P.; Software, S.P.; Validation, B.A. and S.S.S.; Formal analysis, S.S.S.; Investigation, O.F. and S.H.; Data curation, B.A.; Writing—original draft, N.H. and S.P.; Writing—review & editing, N.H., B.A., S.S.S. and S.H.; Visualization, S.P. and S.S.S.; Supervision, B.A. and S.H.; Project administration, O.F. and S.H.; Funding acquisition, O.F. and S.H. All authors have read and agreed to the published version of the manuscript.

Funding: This work was supported by the project "Mobility and Training for beyond 5G ecosystems (MOTOR5G)", funded by the European Union's Horizon 2020 Program under the Marie Skłodowska Curie Actions (MSCA) Innovative Training Network (ITN) under Grant 861219. The present work is also supported by the H2020-MSCA-RISE "Research Collaboration and Mobility for Beyond 5G Future Wireless Networks (RECOMBINE)" project with GA no. 872857.

Data Availability Statement: The data relating to the current study are available in google.drive and can be freely accessed by the following link: https://drive.google.com/drive/folders/1TwRWsJf65-YJxS87F8FZEvABFtDd-hfG?usp=share_link, accessed on 31 October 2024.

Conflicts of Interest: The authors declare that there are no conflicts of interest regarding the publication of this paper.

References

1. Alnaser, A.M.A.; Saloum, S.S.; Sharadqh, A.A.; Hatamleh, H. Optimizing Multi-Tier Scheduling and Secure Routing in Edge-Assisted Software-Defined Wireless Sensor Network Environment Using Moving Target Defense and AI Techniques. *Future Internet* **2024**, *16*, 386. [CrossRef]
2. Sefati, S.S.; Haq, A.U.; Craciunescu, R.; Halunga, S.; Mihovska, A.; Fratu, O. A Comprehensive Survey on Resource Management in 6G Network Based on Internet of Things. *IEEE Access* **2024**, *12*, 113741–113784. [CrossRef]
3. Yalli, J.S.; Hasan, M.H.; Badawi, A. Internet of things (iot): Origin, embedded technologies, smart applications and its growth in the last decade. *IEEE Access* **2024**, *12*, 91357–91382. [CrossRef]
4. Ekwonwune, E.N.; Chigozie, U.C.; Ekekwe, D.A.; Nwankwo, G.C. Analysis of Secured Cloud Data Storage Model for Information. *J. Softw. Eng. Appl.* **2024**, *17*, 297–320. [CrossRef]

5. Arshad, S.; Azam, M.A.; Rehmani, M.H.; Loo, J. Recent advances in information-centric networking-based Internet of Things (ICN-IoT). *IEEE Internet Things J.* **2018**, *6*, 2128–2158. [CrossRef]
6. Anjum, A.; Agbaje, P.; Mitra, A.; Oseghale, E.; Nwafor, E.; Olufowobi, H. Towards named data networking technology: Emerging applications, use cases, and challenges for secure data communication. *Future Gener. Comput. Syst.* **2024**, *151*, 12–31. [CrossRef]
7. Glazkov, R.; Moltchanov, D.; Srikanteswara, S.; Samuylov, A.; Arrobo, G.; Zhang, Y.; Feng, H.; Himayat, N.; Spoczynski, M.; Koucheryavy, Y. Provisioning of Fog Computing over Named-Data Networking in Dynamic Wireless Mesh Systems. *Sensors* **2024**, *24*, 1120. [CrossRef]
8. Xing, M.; Deng, H.; Han, R. A Method for 5G–ICN Seamless Mobility Support Based on Router Buffered Data. *Future Internet* **2024**, *16*, 96. [CrossRef]
9. Ioannou, A.; Weber, S. A survey of caching policies and forwarding mechanisms in information-centric networking. *IEEE Commun. Surv. Tutor.* **2016**, *18*, 2847–2886. [CrossRef]
10. Henze, M.; Matzutt, R.; Hiller, J.; Mühmer, E.; Ziegeldorf, J.H.; van der Giet, J.; Wehrle, K. Complying with data handling requirements in cloud storage systems. *IEEE Trans. Cloud Comput.* **2020**, *10*, 1661–1674. [CrossRef]
11. Din, I.U.; Hassan, S.; Khan, M.K.; Guizani, M.; Ghazali, O.; Habbal, A. Caching in information-centric networking: Strategies, challenges, and future research directions. *IEEE Commun. Surv. Tutor.* **2017**, *20*, 1443–1474. [CrossRef]
12. Feng, Y.; Zhang, W.; Feng, Z.; Zhong, X.; Liu, F. An MTD-driven Hybrid Defense Method Against DDoS Based on Markov Game in Multi-controller SDN-enabled IoT Networks. In Proceedings of the 2024 IEEE/ACM 32nd International Symposium on Quality of Service (IWQoS), Guangzhou, China, 19–21 June 2024; pp. 1–6.
13. Sefati, S.S.; Halunga, S. Ultra-reliability and low-latency communications on the internet of things based on 5G network: Literature review, classification, and future research view. *Trans. Emerg. Telecommun. Technol.* **2023**, *34*, e4770. [CrossRef]
14. Zhang, P.; Xu, W.; Liu, Y.; Qin, X.; Niu, K.; Cui, S.; Shi, G.; Qin, Z.; Xu, X.; Wang, F. Intellicise wireless networks from semantic communications: A survey, research issues, and challenges. *IEEE Commun. Surv. Tutor.* **2024**, 1. [CrossRef]
15. Chen, C.; Wang, C.; Qiu, T.; Atiquzzaman, M.; Wu, D.O. Caching in vehicular named data networking: Architecture, schemes and future directions. *IEEE Commun. Surv. Tutor.* **2020**, *22*, 2378–2407. [CrossRef]
16. Vural, S.; Navaratnam, P.; Wang, N.; Wang, C.; Dong, L.; Tafazolli, R. In-network caching of Internet-of-Things data. In Proceedings of the 2014 IEEE International Conference on Communications (ICC), Sydney, Australia, 10–14 June 2014; pp. 3185–3190.
17. Quevedo, J.; Corujo, D.; Aguiar, R. Consumer driven information freshness approach for content centric networking. In Proceedings of the 2014 IEEE Conference on Computer Communications Workshops (INFOCOM WKSHPS), Toronto, ON, Canada, 27 April–2 May 2014; pp. 482–487.
18. Hail, M.A.; Amadeo, M.; Molinaro, A.; Fischer, S. Caching in named data networking for the wireless internet of things. In Proceedings of the 2015 International Conference on Recent Advances in Internet of Things (RIoT), Singapore, 7–9 April 2015; pp. 1–6.
19. Vural, S.; Wang, N.; Navaratnam, P.; Tafazolli, R. Caching transient data in internet content routers. *IEEE/ACM Trans. Netw.* **2016**, *25*, 1048–1061. [CrossRef]
20. Doan Van, D.; Ai, Q. An efficient in-network caching decision algorithm for I nternet of things. *Int. J. Commun. Syst.* **2018**, *31*, e3521. [CrossRef]
21. Meddeb, M.; Dhraief, A.; Belghith, A.; Monteil, T.; Drira, K.; AlAhmadi, S. Cache freshness in named data networking for the internet of things. *Comput. J.* **2018**, *61*, 1496–1511. [CrossRef]
22. Asmat, H.; Din, I.U.; Almogren, A.; Altameem, A.; Khan, M.Y. Enhancing Edge-Linked Caching in Information-Centric Networking for Internet of Things with Deep Reinforcement Learning. *IEEE Access* **2024**, *12*, 154918–154932. [CrossRef]
23. Mishra, S.; Jain, V.K.; Gyoda, K.; Jain, S. Distance-based dynamic caching and replacement strategy in NDN-IoT networks. *Internet Things* **2024**, *27*, 101264. [CrossRef]
24. Luo, H.; Yan, T.; Hu, S. Caching Policy in Low Earth Orbit Satellite Mega-Constellation Information-Centric Networking for Internet of Things. *Sensors* **2024**, *24*, 3412. [CrossRef]
25. Rafique, W.; Hafid, A.S.; Cherkaoui, S. Complementing IoT services using software-defined information centric networks: A comprehensive survey. *IEEE Internet Things J.* **2022**, *9*, 23545–23569. [CrossRef]
26. Tyagi, V.; Saraswat, A.; Kumar, A.; Gambhir, S. Securing IoT Devices Against MITM and DoS Attacks: An Analysis. *Reshaping Intell. Bus. Ind. Converg. AI IoT Cut. Edge* **2024**, *237–249*. [CrossRef]
27. HS, S.; Boregowda, U. Quality-of-service-linked privileged content-caching mechanism for named data networks. *Future Internet* **2022**, *14*, 157. [CrossRef]
28. Djama, A.; Djamaa, B.; Senouci, M.R. TCP/IP and ICN networking technologies for the Internet of Things: A comparative study. In Proceedings of the 2019 International Conference on Networking and Advanced Systems (ICNAS), Annaba, Algeria, 26–27 June 2019; pp. 1–6.

29. Ahanger, A.S.; Masoodi, F.S.; Khanam, A.; Ashraf, W. Managing and Securing Information Storage in the Internet of Things. In *Internet of Things Vulnerabilities and Recovery Strategies*; Auerbach Publications: Boca Raton, FL, USA, 2024; pp. 102–151.
30. Sefati, S.S.; Craciunescu, R.; Arasteh, B.; Halunga, S.; Fratu, O.; Tal, I. Cybersecurity in a Scalable Smart City Framework Using Blockchain and Federated Learning for Internet of Things (IoT). *Smart Cities* **2024**, *7*, 2802–2841. [CrossRef]
31. Din, I.U.; Hassan, S.; Almogren, A.; Ayub, F.; Guizani, M. PUC: Packet update caching for energy efficient IoT-based information-centric networking. *Future Gener. Comput. Syst.* **2020**, *111*, 634–643. [CrossRef]
32. Khan, Y.; Mustafa, S.; Ahmad, R.W.; Maqsood, T.; Rehman, F.; Ali, J.; Rodrigues, J.J. Content caching in mobile edge computing: A survey. *Clust. Comput.* **2024**, *27*, 8817–8864. [CrossRef]
33. Bamhdi, A.M. CDCA: Transparent Cache Architecture to Improve Content Delivery by Internet Service Providers. *Int. J. Adv. Comput. Sci. Appl.* **2023**, *14*, 847–867. [CrossRef]
34. Sefati, S.S.; Fartu, O.; Nor, A.M.; Halunga, S. Enhancing Internet of Things Security and Efficiency: Anomaly Detection via Proof of Stake Blockchain Techniques. In Proceedings of the 2024 International Conference on Artificial Intelligence in Information and Communication (ICAIIC), Osaka, Japan, 19–22 February 2024; pp. 591–595.
35. Sefati, S.S.; Arasteh, B.; Halunga, S.; Fratu, O.; Bouyer, A. Meet User's Service Requirements in Smart Cities Using Recurrent Neural Networks and Optimization Algorithm. *IEEE Internet Things J.* **2023**, *10*, 22256–22269. [CrossRef]
36. Li, K.-Q.; Yin, Z.-Y.; Liu, Y. A hybrid SVR-BO model for predicting the soil thermal conductivity with uncertainty. *Can. Geotech. J.* **2023**, *61*, 258–274. [CrossRef]
37. Chicco, D.; Warrens, M.J.; Jurman, G. The coefficient of determination R-squared is more informative than SMAPE, MAE, MAPE, MSE and RMSE in regression analysis evaluation. *PeerJ Comput. Sci.* **2021**, *7*, e623. [CrossRef]
38. Arasteh, B. A new Hybrid Model using Case-Based Reasoning and Decision Tree Methods for improving Speedup and Accuracy. In Proceedings of the Iadis International Conference, Salamanca, Spain, 18–20 February 2007.

future internet MDPI

Article

Evaluating DL Model Scaling Trade-Offs During Inference via an Empirical Benchmark Analysis

Demetris Trihinas [1,*], Panagiotis Michael [1] and Moysis Symeonides [2]

[1] Department of Computer Science, School of Sciences and Engineering, University of Nicosia, Nicosia CY-2417, Cyprus; michael.p15@live.unic.ac.cy
[2] Department of Computer Science, University of Cyprus, Nicosia CY-2109, Cyprus; symeonidis.moysis@ucy.ac.cy
* Corresponding: trihinas.d@unic.ac.cy

Abstract: With generative Artificial Intelligence (AI) capturing public attention, the appetite of the technology sector for larger and more complex Deep Learning (DL) models is continuously growing. Traditionally, the focus in DL model development has been on scaling the neural network's foundational structure to increase computational complexity and enhance the representational expressiveness of the model. However, with recent advancements in edge computing and 5G networks, DL models are now aggressively being deployed and utilized across the cloud–edge–IoT continuum for the realization of in situ intelligent IoT services. This paradigm shift introduces a growing need for AI practitioners, as a focus on inference costs, including latency, computational overhead, and energy efficiency, is long overdue. This work presents a benchmarking framework designed to assess DL model scaling across three key performance axes during model inference: classification accuracy, computational overhead, and latency. The framework's utility is demonstrated through an empirical study involving various model structures and variants, as well as publicly available datasets for three popular DL use cases covering natural language understanding, object detection, and regression analysis.

Keywords: deep learning; artificial intelligence; cloud computing; benchmarking

1. Introduction

Deep learning (DL) has emerged as an influential tool that drives innovation efforts for the advancement of mission-critical applications such as the prediction of environmental phenomena [1], object detection and classification [2], natural language understanding and generation [3], and autonomous navigation and steering [4]. DL is inspired by how the human brain is structured and functions, with the foundation and premise attributed to Deep Neural Networks (DNNs). In DNNs, multiple layers of interconnected artificial neurons form a network of hierarchies aimed at enhancing the network's ability to automatically derive low-dimensional representations from unstructured and high-dimensional data, such as human-written text and images [5].

With the last decade featuring several breakthroughs in the area of generative AI, such as Generative Adversarial Networks (GANs) [6], transformers [7], and Large Language Models (LLMs) [8,9], model scaling is gaining significant interest. Model scaling refers to the expansion of the underlying structure of the DNN [10]. Early research attempted to advocate for the addition of more neurons in DNNs, leading to increased network depth [11]. By scaling the DNN, users can select among several model variants to enhance utility for different application aspects and deployment sites (i.e., data centers or edge computing) [12]. More recent examples have suggested increasing multiple dimensions of the DNN structure together, such as the popular EfficientNet model architecture for object detection that features eight model variants with different network depths, widths, and input resolutions [13]. However, as the underlying DNN structure expands, so does the computational complexity of the network to increase the representational power of the DNN and improve accuracy while also generalizing better over newly introduced tasks [14]. A recent study by OpenAI revealed that since 2012, the amount of computational effort required by DL models has increased exponentially and doubled every 4 months [15]. Nonetheless, while IoT and edge computing hardware are vastly improving, they are not doing so at a rate capable of catering to the advancements in deep learning [16,17]. Hence, although the AI community was, in the past, focused solely on improving model accuracy metrics, a paradigm shift is now being observed where runtime performance during inference and energy efficiency are gaining industry interest [18,19].

This brings us to the focal point and motivation that support our work. With so many different scaling strategies for DNNs, it becomes extremely difficult for users to select a model variant that will meet different QoS requirements. Models can scale in terms of depth, width, and clarity of input data, and different parameters can be set (e.g., batch size and training epochs). All these configurations can significantly impact the performance of a DL application. The majority of existing works that empirically evaluate model scaling focus on either a single model structure [13,20] and/or introduce findings that are tailored to solely evaluating accuracy and overhead during the model training stage [21,22]. We deviate from the norm and focus on the impacts of different model scaling strategies during runtime inference. Specifically, we focus on three key performance axes: classification accuracy, computational overhead, and latency. By offering a detailed examination of trade-offs during model inference, our work aims to guide AI practitioners in selecting and tuning DL models for efficient and effective deployment of intelligent IoT services in resource-constrained environments.

The main contributions of our work are summarized as follows:

- We introduce a high-level description of a benchmarking framework for the assessment of the various trade-offs that occur when scaling the underlying network of a DL model across different dimensions (i.e., depth and width). This modular and extensive framework provides performance insights on the impact of DL model scaling during runtime inference in light of classification accuracy and model loss, computational overhead, and the model's latency footprint.
- We demonstrate the utility of our framework by introducing an empirical study evaluating DL model scaling strategies and their impacts on the QoS of runtime inference. We employ several model structures from three popular DL application domains. For our work, we utilize publicly available and pre-trained model architectures (BERT, EfficientNet, and MLP), and for inference workloads, we employ openly available datasets (i.e., GLUE-MRPC and ImageNet).

The rest of this article is structured as follows: Section 2 presents a brief overview of model scaling for DNNs as the premise of our work. Section 3 elaborates on the benchmark methodology employed for the evaluation and empirical study. Section 4 introduces three different DL use cases and the datasets used during validation. Section 5 documents the performance metrics used during the empirical study, while Section 5 presents a comprehensive overview of the results. Section 6 provides an overview of recent related works, while Section 7 concludes the article and outlines future work.

2. Background

The following subsections introduce an overview of the architecture pattern encompassing deep neural networks (DNNs) and the premise of model scaling for DNNs.

2.1. *Deep Neural Networks*

Deep learning is synonymous with many-layered artificial neural networks that are well-recognized and referred to as deep neural networks (DNNs). It is in these networks that data are hierarchically represented, achieving excellent results in high-level abstraction and intricate pattern recognition when working with tasks connected to unstructured data such as images, audio, and text [23].

An exemplary image of a DNN is depicted in Figure 1. The key constituents of deep learning are neurons, layers, weights, biases, and activation functions. Neurons are the basic units that process input and produce output through an activation function. Layers are collections of neurons and can be classified into three types: input layers, hidden layers, and output layers. The input type layer first accepts initial data, like pixel values in image data or word embeddings in text. These layers' neurons represent traits of the data. Hidden layers process the flow of data by identifying complex patterns. Neural networks with one hidden layer are called shallow neural networks (SNNs), and networks with typically more than one layer are called deep neural networks (DNNs) [24]. The neurons within layers receive inputs, process them, and transmit information to successive layers. The output layer delivers the results, such as class labels in a classification task or numerical values in regression, with the number of neurons representing the number of categories or outputs. Weights and biases are parameters integrated into the model to learn during training and make the model accurate in making predictions. Activation functions introduce non-linearity into the network for the learning of complex patterns.

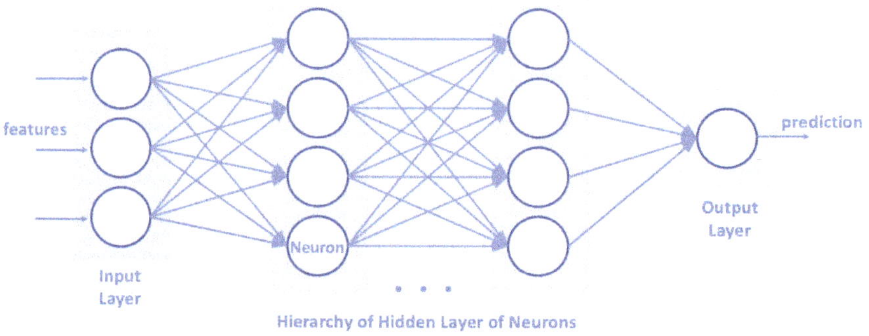

Figure 1. High-level overview of a deep neural network.

2.2. Model Scaling for Deep Neural Networks

Model scaling is the method where the capacity of the DNN is enlarged by expanding the underlying architectural structure to meet the varying requirements of different workloads [20,25].

Structure-wise, the baseline of a neural network can be expanded as follows:

- In terms of *depth* by adding more layers to capture a richer set of features and generalize when introduced to new tasks;
- In terms of *width* by embedding more neurons per layer to capture more fine-grained features and intricate relationships within the data;
- In terms of *data clarity* (i.e., resolution for images) to potentially capture more fine-grained patterns in the given input.

An example of a neural network model structure that can be scaled depth-wise to introduce new variants are the popular Residual Networks (ResNets) [11]. The naming convention of a ResNet (i.e., ResNet-50 or ResNet-152) includes a number denoting the number of layers in the network.

While scaling towards one dimension can increase model accuracy, as a network deepens (or widens), training speed is impacted due to the vanishing gradient problem where convergence is slowed down as the network parameters become very small while propagated back through the layers [26]. To compensate, *compound scaling* is considered the norm today, where multiple dimensions are scaled together. An example of a family of neural networks adopting compound scaling is EfficientNet models for object detection, where depth, width, and input resolution are uniformly scaled based on a compound coefficient. By doing so, EfficientNet models can achieve accuracy similar to that of other DNNs (i.e., ResNets) while utilizing fewer computational resources during model training and extracting meaningful cost savings [13].

3. DNN Model Scaling Benchmark Framework

To perform the benchmarking of a diverse set of DNN use cases, we created an automated process where a user needs to specify a dataset, the selected DNN use case, and the user's preferences about the model scaling parameters.

Figure 2 depicts a high-level overview of our pipeline. The framework provides a lightweight Python library through which users can submit their preferences by either filling in the library's programming interfaces or by passing their parameters written in a configuration file (in YAML format).

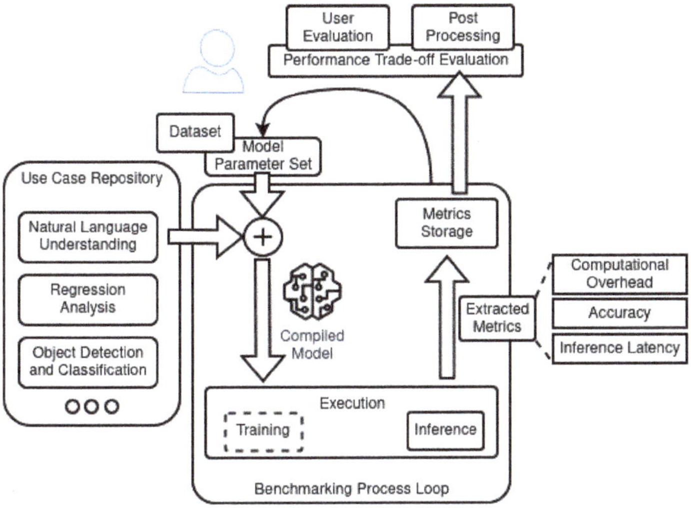

Figure 2. Pipeline of performance evaluation trade-offs.

An example of the configuration file is depicted in Listing 1. In this example, the user selects *MLP* as the DNN use case (*use_case*). Then, the user must define the parameter space (*parameter_space*) of the respective use case, which includes the available parameters, along with the selected evaluation values. In this example, the user sets three different values for network depth (*network_depth: [4, 5, 7]*), two values for network width and batch size parameters (*network_width: [32, 64]; batch_size: [32, 128]*), and three values for epochs (*epochs: [1, 3, 5]*). The system generates all possible permutations of these parameters, resulting in a search space of 36 unique runs for this use case.

Next, the monitoring metrics that for the system to expose are selected. The available metrics include *computational_overhead*, *accuracy*, and *latency*. We then examine a set of execution-related parameters, including the boolean parameter *training*, which specifies whether the system retrains the model; *dataset*, which indicates the dataset location; and *times*, which defines the number of experimental executions. It is worth noting that how the dataset is loaded depends on the specific use-case implementation, so the *dataset* parameter could refer to either a file or a folder where the dataset resides (e.g., a folder of images for object detection and classification use cases).

After that, the framework generates a set of model scaling parameters based on user preferences and combines them with a specified ML use case. If users wish to create their own use cases, they should extend the DNN Model Scaling Benchmark programming interface and add them to the *use-case repository*. By default, our system includes a *use-case repository* with three predefined DL use cases—*natural language understanding*, *regression analysis*, and *object detection and classification*—each with its respective scaling parameters (see Section 4). With the parameters and chosen use case defined (via the configuration file or programmatically), the system generates a model whose structure reflects the specified *model parameter set*, resulting in a *compiled model*.

Listing 1: DNN parameters of the model scaling benchmark framework.

```
use_case: MLP
parameter_space:
   network_depth: [ 4, 5, 7 ]
   network_width: [ 32, 64 ]
   batch_size: [ 32, 128 ]
   epochs: [ 1, 3, 5 ]
metrics:
   - computational_overhead
   - accuracy
   - latency
training: True
dataset: "..."
times: 1
```

The next phase of our pipeline is *execution*. This phase has two steps, namely *training* and *inference*. Specifically, the pipeline splits the dataset into training and testing subsets. This split is configurable with default values of 80% for training and 20% for the testing set. After that, the pipeline performs the training, updating the weights of the *compiled model*. We should note that the training step is optional, since the users may introduce their own pre-trained models. Next, the trained model is utilized to perform inference on the testing subset, extracting the performance metrics, namely *inference latency*, *accuracy/error*, and *computational overhead*. Since the test subset is already annotated, we can easily extract accuracy for classification tasks or error for regression tasks. For the inference latency, the framework keeps the timestamp before the inference process starts and the timestamp when it is over, subtracts them, and divides by the number of data points. Finally, for the computational overhead, our system extracts the number of Floating-Point Operations (FLOPs) from the compiled ML model. A more detailed description of the metrics can be found in Section 5. The pipeline stores the *extracted metrics* in *metric storage*; then, the system selects another set of model parameters and repeats the process until there are no more parameter sets to be examined.

Once all *model parameter sets* (and trials) for a given ML use case have been evaluated, users can conduct a *performance trade-off evaluation*. This step enables the system to automatically facilitate various *post-processing* tasks, such as fitting trend lines, plotting performance metrics, detecting outliers, and generating the respective reports. Additional post-execution metrics are also made available, such as model complexity (γ), which reflects the model's FLOPs relative to the most complex model configuration in the use case. Thus, users can intuitively analyze the effects of different parameter configurations, observing trends across a range of ML parameters and model structures. By visualizing these trade-offs, users gain insights into the balance between computational demands, accuracy, and other performance metrics, supporting informed decision making for optimal model selection in alignment with their specific goals and constraints.

4. DL Use Cases and Validation Datasets

Our DL repository comprises of three use-cases originating from different application domains and covering three out of the seven important domains for advancing AI as identified by MLcommons [27]. All use cases employ open model structures with publicly available variants, and the datasets utilized for the inference workloads are also publicly available. Moreover, we note that although, inherently, any set of values can be used to alter the problem dimensions of a model structure, we embrace the reference value sets suggested by the model designers (e.g., Google Research) that lead to optimal fine tuning of the model accuracy for a given computational budget. These configurations enable all experimental results of the empirical analysis to be realistic, reproducible, and verifiable. Table 1 provides a summary of the DNN model architectures for the DL use cases, as well as their scaling dimensions and their parameterization, for quick reference.

Table 1. DL DNN model architectures and scaling dimensionalities for DL use cases.

DNN Model Architecture	No. of Variants	Scaling Dimensions	Experimental Value Sets
BERT	20	Network depth (D); Hidden embeddings (H)	D = {2, 4, 6, 8, 10}, H = {128, 256, 512, 768}
EfficientNet	6	Network depth (D); Network width (W); Input resolution (R); Dropout rate (O)	D = {1.0, 1.1, 1.2, 1.4, 1.8, 2.2}, W = {1.0, 1.0, 1.1, 1.2, 1.4, 1.6}, R = {224, 240, 260, 300, 380, 456}, O = {0.2, 0.2, 0.4, 0.4, 0.6, 0.6}
MLP	120	Network depth (D); Network width (W); Batch size (B); Epochs (E)	D = {1, 2, 3, 4, 5, 6, 7, 8, 9, 10}, W = {32, 64, 128}, B = {32, 64, 128, 256}, E = {1, 3, 5}

For EfficientNet, values are expressed as coefficients from the baseline B_O model and the i_{th} value of each dimension was paired together to produce the 6 variants.

4.1. *Natural Language Understanding*

This use case involves natural language understanding, where the DL application setup is responsible for processing a series of text-based inference tasks using a language model to semantically interpret the provided text. The chosen model architecture for this use case is the well-known Bidirectional Encoder Representations from Transformers (BERT) model. BERT, as a model structure, was first introduced in 2019 by Google and is considered one of the most novel model structures for NLP tasks, language reasoning, and conversational AI. In brief, BERT is structured with stacked quantized transformer encoder layers, where each layer comprises self-attention mechanisms and feed-forward neural networks [3]. BERT was intentionally designed to pre-train deep bidirectional representations, adopting a large English text corpus (i.e., Wikipedia), by jointly conditioning on both left and right contexts in all layers [28]. With this, BERT models can capture intricate patterns and dependencies in text-based datasets, making them powerful for understanding the nuances of language.

For the empirical study, we utilize 20 BERT model variants that have been introduced by Google Research (https://github.com/google-research/bert/ accessed on 7 November 2024) and referenced as suitable for edge computing. These models vary in network depth (D = {2, 4, 6, 8, 10}) and hidden embedding sizes (H = {128, 256, 512, 768}). For the workload of inference tasks, we use the widely recognized GLUE-MRPC dataset released by Microsoft Research (https://www.microsoft.com/en-us/download/details.aspx?id=52398 accessed on 7 November 2024), with the validation set containing 1125 sentence pairs automatically extracted from online news sources, along with human annotations indicating whether the sentences in each pair are semantically equivalent (paraphrase).

4.2. *Object Detection and Classification*

This use case centers on object detection, where the DL application setup is configured to handle a series of inference tasks to detect objects within a set of given images and classify the objects by assigning appropriate labels from a pre-defined label set. The chosen model architecture for this purpose is the widely used EfficientNet convolutional neural network [13]. EfficientNet was first introduced in 2020 by GoogleAI to provide object detection for mobile and IoT services run at the network edge. For EfficientNet, the baseline network (denoted as B_0) exploits a multi-objective neural architecture search that optimizes for both accuracy and FLOPS by adopting a hierarchy of mobile inverted bottleneck convolution layers and the use of squeeze-and-excitation optimization to ultimately enhance representational capacity [29]. However, the most popular feature of EfficientNet is the introduction of compound scaling, where the network structure can uniformly scale in depth, width, and resolution by taking advantage of a fixed set of scaling coefficients tailored to increase the network's computational efficiency without impacting representational accuracy.

The publicly released variants of EfficientNet are code-named as `Bx`, with `x` denoting the model complexity rank ($B_0 - B_7$) and each varying in network depth, width, resolution, and dropout rate. For this empirical study, we utilize the first six models ($B_0 - B_5$), which are all openly available in the Keras pre-trained model library (https://keras.io/api/applications/efficientnet/ accessed on 7 November 2024). Hence, we note that, as shown in Table 1, for EfficientNet, the value of each dimension is expressed as a coefficient factor of the base variant (B_0), and the six variants are formed by taking the i_{th} value from each dimension to form its dimensional value set. As an example, B_4 takes values of $D = 1.8$, $W = 1.4$, $R = 380$, and $O = 0.6$. For the inference workload, we use images extracted from the well-known and publicly available Tiny ImageNet dataset hosted on Hugging Face (https://huggingface.co/datasets/zh-plus/tiny-imagenet accessed on 7 November 2024), which includes a validation set of 10,000 color images (64 × 64 pixels) categorized into 200 label classes.

4.3. Regression Analysis for Predicting Numerical Outcome

For this use case, we tested 120 Multi-Layer Perceptron (MLP) model variants. In brief, MLPs are fully connected feed-forward artificial neural networks. As MLPs are fully connected, each neuron in layer $D - 1$ is connected to every neuron in the subsequent layer (D). For this use case, the MLP networks' goal is to ingest data points and, through a regression analysis, predict the numerical value of a target variable. A leaky Rectified Linear Unit (ReLU) is embraced for the neuron activation function. These 120 different model configurations differ by network depth (D = {1, 2, 3, 4, 5, 6, 7, 8, 9, 10}), neurons per layer (W = {32, 64, 128}), batch size (B = {32, 64, 128, 256}), and epochs (E = {1, 3, 5}).

As our inference workload, we use the open and publicly available California Housing dataset from StatLib provided via Keras (https://keras.io/api/datasets/california_housing/ accessed on 7 November 2024). Specifically, the dataset captures 20Ksamples, with each composed of eight attributes (e.g., house age and number of rooms), and the target variable for reference is the median house value per California district, expressed USD.

5. Benchmark Framework Metrics for Comparison

The benchmark framework supports the evaluation of the reference DL use cases against three performance axes, all evaluated during model inference tasks. Specifically, all use-case model variants are evaluated in terms of accuracy, computational overhead, and inference latency.

The following details how each metric is measured.

5.1. Classification Accuracy and Prediction Error During Inference

For use cases 1 and 2, accuracy is measured as the precision of the DL classification tasks per use case. In brief, classification precision is defined as the ratio of the number of correct predictions to the total number of predictions, where correct predictions include true positives and true negatives, as shown below:

$$CA = \frac{TP + TN}{TP + TN + FP + FN} \tag{1}$$

For use case 3, where regression is employed, accuracy (or less inaccuracy) is measured by computing the Mean Square Error (MSE) for the predictions output by the regression analysis of the model variant. Specifically, the MSE computes the average squared difference between the observed (y) and predicted (y) values of a sample comprising N values, as shown below:

$$MSE = \frac{1}{N}\sum_{i=1}^{N}(y_i - \hat{y}_i)^2 \quad (2)$$

For the comparison of the model variants in terms of accuracy, the outcome for each input data point of the validation dataset is recorded during runtime inference. Upon the completion of the experimental run, the accuracy metric per model variant is computed and can be used to compare against experimental runs utilizing other model variants.

5.2. Computational Overhead During Inference

The computational overhead of a DL model is attributed to the processing effort required by the model to perform the requested inference task (e.g., classification or regression) and output a result for a given data point. To measure the computational overhead imposed by a DL model variant during an experimental run, our benchmark framework counts floating-point operations, denoted as FLOPs. In brief, FLOPs measure the total number of mathematical operations involving floating-point values across the computational path of the DNN during runtime inference to output a prediction after receiving a new data point as input. FLOPs are a key metric for evaluating computational efficiency for DL models, as they provide measurable and hardware-independent results suitable for comparison among DL model variants [30]. To measure the FLOPs for each model variant, our benchmark framework utilizes the open and popular `flopth` (https://github.com/vra/flopth accessed on 7 November 2024) Python library, which supports the measurement of the FLOPs performed during DNN inference.

5.3. Inference Latency

The third performance evaluation metric of our benchmark framework is inference latency. Inference latency for DL models is defined as the total amount of time required by the DNN variant to output a prediction after receiving a new data point as input and perform the necessary (mathematical) operations imposed throughout the computational path of the layered neural network during runtime inference. A customized monitoring probe has been created to extract the inference latency from open and popular ML backends, including TensorFlow and PyTorch, as used in the two DL use-cases.

5.4. Model Complexity

To ease both the depiction of the results and to easily identify models among a large corpus of variants per use case, we introduce a new metric definition. *Model complexity*, denoted as $\gamma \in (0, 1]$, is defined as the proportional difference of a model variant relative to the most complex model (m_N) under consideration ($\gamma = 1.0$).

For instance, assuming a set of N models denoted as M, where all variants differ only by network depth (layers), then if M_N has a network depth of 10 layers, a model ($m_i \in M$) with $\gamma = 0.3$ has a depth of three layers. For the introduced use cases where multiple DNN dimensions can be scaled, a normalized γ is computed and used as a reference for each model variant. For this, first, each scaling dimension is normalized; next, all dimensions are multiplied, and finally, the intermediate product is divided by the γ of M_N.

As an example, the normalized model complexity vector for the EfficientNet variants of use case 2 is the following: $\gamma = [0.070, 0.082, 0.160, 0.235, 0.597, 1.0]$. With this vector, we can now place variants in an orderly fashion and can denote proportional differences to estimate the computational overhead and latency of inference, as we see from the experimentation. Finally, we note that in all introduced plots, we employ the model complexity as the independent variable and show how accuracy, computational overhead, and latency are affected when scaling the model's complexity.

6. Evaluation

In this section, we embrace our benchmark framework to conduct an empirical analysis to understand various trade-offs during runtime inference and assess their impacts on the introduced DL use cases.

6.1. Testbeds

For experimentation, we opted for two testbeds: a public and a private cloud infrastructure. Our aim is to enhance the replication of the empirical study so that the results from DL use-case benchmarking can be reproduced and verified by anyone interested in this study.

To this end, all experiment runs for the BERT (UC1) and MLP-Regression (UC3) use cases were executed on a testbed supported by Google Colaboratory (https://colab.google/ accessed on 7 November 2024). Specifically, this testbed provides the benchmark framework with a dedicated DL execution environment featuring 16 GB of memory for model storage and performance of the computational experimentation, as well as an Nvidia T4 GPU featuring 2560 CUDA cores and 320 Turing tensor cores that are specialized for neural network training and inference. In turn, the experimental runs for the EfficientNet use case (UC2), which requires significant memory for both the model variants and the ImageNet workload, were run on an HP Proliant DL380 G9 server with an Intel Xeon E5-2680 processor embedding 44 cores clocked at 2.50 GHz and 176 GB memory. Finally, we note that all model variants embraced for UC1 and UC2 are the pre-trained versions of these models provided by Google Research and made publicly available in the HuggingFace and Keras repositories, respectively (see Sections 4.1 and 4.2). This enables both the verification of the study findings (e.g., classification accuracy) with minimal human effort and the necessary computational overhead to reproduce the experimental settings.

6.2. Experimental Analysis

Figures 3–5 depict the results of empirical study in which several model variants per DL use case were run and evaluated during runtime inference. It should be noted that all plots are presented with the x axis (independent variable) capturing the normalized complexity of each model variant as introduced in Section 5.4.

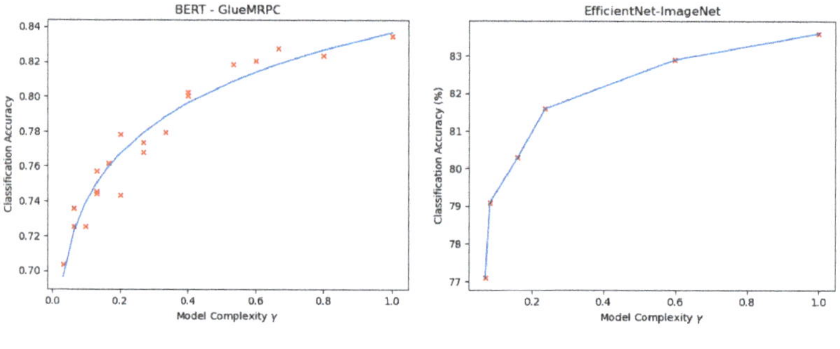

(**a**) (**b**)

Figure 3. *Cont.*

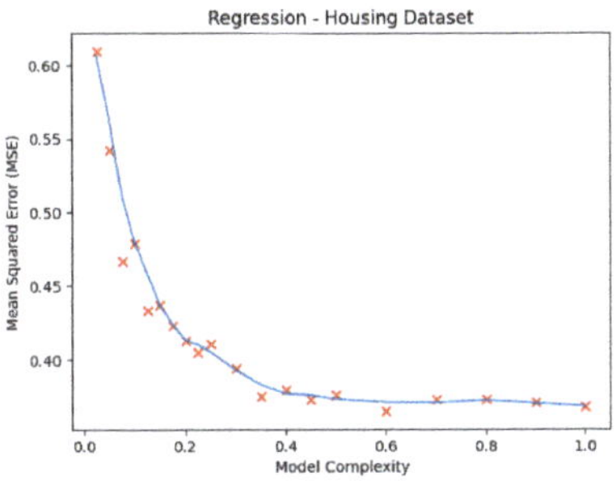

(c)

Figure 3. Inference quality (classification accuracy and MSE) with respect to model complexity. The presented plots include: (**a**) BERT model variants, (**b**) EfficientNet model variants, and (**c**) MLP-Regression model variants.

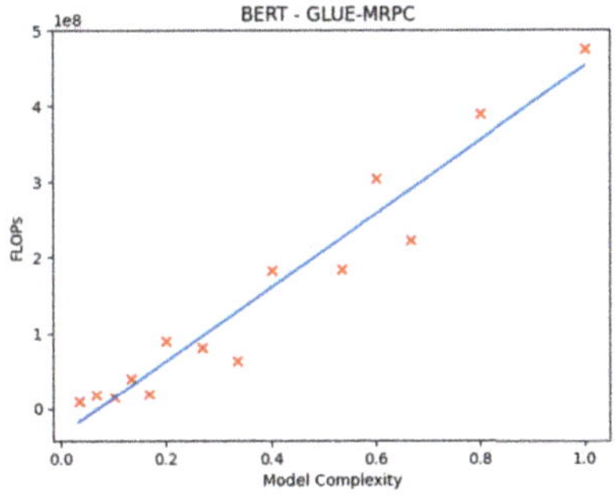

(a)

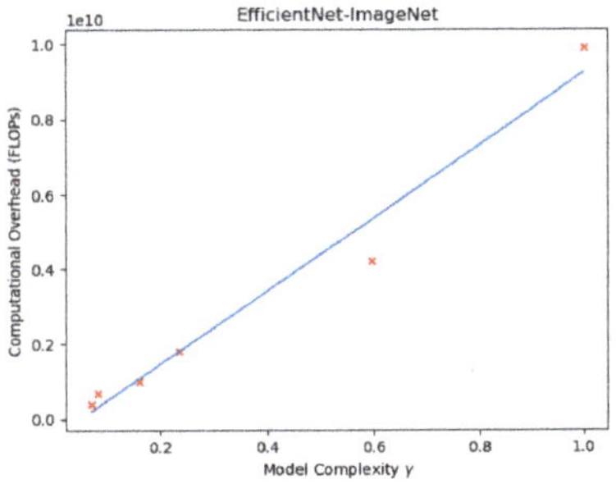

(b)

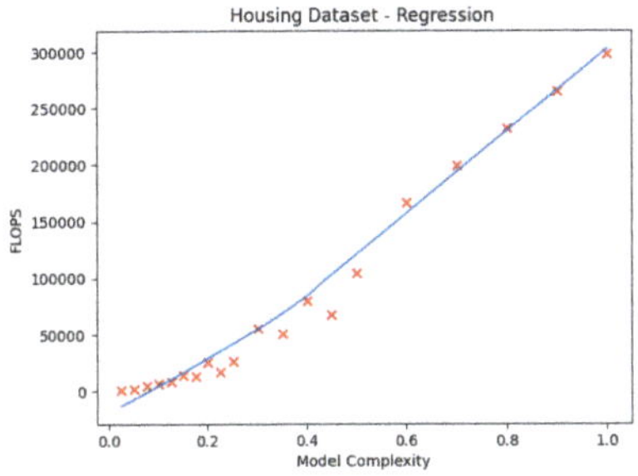

(c)

Figure 4. Computational overhead of inference with respect to model complexity. The presented plots include: (**a**) BERT model variants, (**b**) EfficientNet model variants, and (**c**) MLP-Regression model variants.

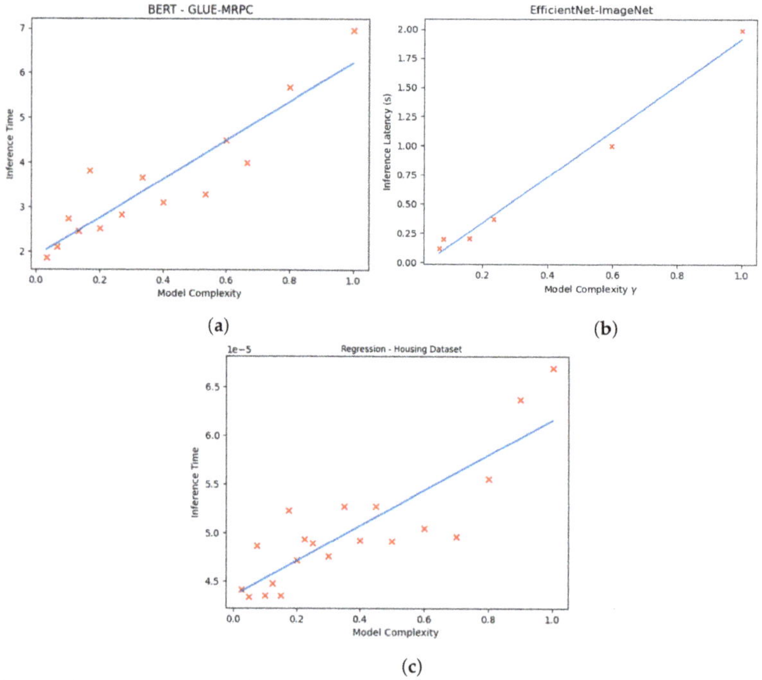

Figure 5. Inference latency with respect to model complexity. The presented plots include: (**a**) BERT model variants, (**b**) EfficientNet model variants, and (**c**) MLP-Regression model variants.

6.3. Inference Quality

Let us start the discussion of the empirical study with the plots presented in Figure 3. These plots depict the classification accuracy (UC1 and UC2) and MSE (UC3) for the introduced model variants for each use case. First, it is evident that in all use cases, given enough data during training, quality can be improved by increasing the complexity of the model. In the case of the BERT (Figure 3a) and EfficientNet (Figure 3b) models, the classification accuracy increases, while in the case of the MLP regression models (Figure 3c), the mean square error decreases. Hence, scaling the DNN structure's dimensionality (e.g., network depth and width) by creating more computationally complex variants is beneficial for improving the inference quality during runtime inference.

The second insight from the empirical study is that, for all use cases, the learning ratio of simpler models plateaus at some point. An illustrative example is provided by the plots in Figure 3a,b. Scaling the EfficientNet-B0 structure by the first compound scaling coefficient increases the model's classification accuracy by more than 2.2%, but scaling from the B4 variant to the B5 variant introduces minimal gains in accuracy that are less than 0.5%. This can also be confirmed by looking at the MLP-Regression plot (Figure 3c) where performing a further study, one can establish the non-linear nature of the error and the diminishing error reduction through a Ramsey REST test (r-test I-value = 0.000826).

Third, as is evident in the MLP-Regression plot (Figure 3c) the global minimum is achieved for $\gamma = 0.6$, and afterwards, more complex models present a slight increment in their reported MSE values. This occurs as the DNN model structure scales and becomes too complex, which results in overfitting to the randomized effects that are present only in the specific (California Housing) dataset used for training. In this regard, although the expressive power of a model is (somehow) dependent on model complexity, a mathematical expression for estimating inference quality irrespective of the DL use-case domain does not exist [31]. This is inherently due to the phenomenon introduced in the second (learning plateau) and third (overfitting) insights.

6.4. Computational Overhead of Inference

The plots in Figure 4 depict the effect of model scaling on the computational overhead imposed on the underlying model serving as infrastructure during runtime inference for each of the referenced DL use cases.

From these plots, it is immediately evident that when the model complexity increases, so does the computational overhead. Moreover, the model complexity and the computational overhead present an almost linear relationship. For example, in the BERT case (Figure 4a), the coefficient of determination (R squared) is $R^2 = 0.913$, and for the EfficientNet use case (Figure 4b), $R^2 = 0.984$. These value indicate a well-fit linear relationship. Furthermore, for the MLP-Regression case (Figure 4c), we observe two distinct phases of linearity, the second of which presents a higher linear coefficient that the first phase.

6.5. Inference Latency

The plots in Figure 5 depict the effect of model scaling on the latency observed by users submitting inference tasks to the DL model serving the application during runtime inference for each of the referenced DL use cases. In these plots, we observe that the linear relationship between model complexity and inference latency holds, especially for the BERT (Figure 5a) and EfficientNet (Figure 5b) use cases, although it is less perfect. The coefficients of determination for these two use cases are $R^2 = 0.871$ and $R^2 = 0.972$, respectively. The reduction can be attributed to the fact that although latency is highly correlated with the computational overhead (FLOPs) of the DNN required to output a result, other factors contribute to increased latency. Specifically, latency also depends on data pre-processing to shape the input data points to meet the processing requirements of the DNN and DNN optimizations that can affect memory access patterns. While these factors can (slightly) influence the overall latency, the inference delay observed in the MLP-Regression use case (Figure 5c) is highly affected by overfitting after the global minimum is achieved ($\gamma = 0.6$), distorting the depicted linear relationship between model complexity and latency ($R^2 = 0.597$).

Finally, a key observation among the three performance axes must be made. A specific model complexity (e.g., $\gamma = 0.2$) and computational budget (in FLOPs) can be achieved by utilizing different scaling policies (i.e., depth only, compound coefficient on depth/width, etc.). For example, in the case of the BERT models in which two dimensions are available for scaling (network layers (d), embedding sizes (e)) a $\gamma = 0.2$ can be achieved with (d, h) pairs that are equivalent to (2, 768) and (6, 256). In the first example, the classification accuracy is 74.2%, and latency is 2.2 s, while in the second case, accuracy is 77.8%, and the latency is 2.79 s. Therefore, model scaling can have a significantly different effect on the classification accuracy and inference latency. Hence, benchmarking various model scaling strategies to evaluate the performance outcome during DL model inference is of utmost importance when striving to achieve cost savings in geo-distributed deployments and under resource constraints.

7. Related Work

The following introduces relevant scientific works split into two subsections, the first of which briefly discusses DL model scaling and the latter of which introduces empirical evaluations in the field of DL model scaling.

7.1. DL Model Scaling

Several DL model scaling techniques have been proposed throughout the last decade according to which the underlying structure of the DNN can be expanded in terms of either depth [11] or width [26], or adopt higher data clarity for the provided input [32]. However, as the DNN structure increases towards only a single dimension (i.e., depth), the computational costs become prohibited, and model quality can be impacted as well due to parameter redundancy [33]. To overcome these challenges, Tan et al. [13] and Han et al. [34] proposed the use of compound scaling with the introduction of EfficientNet and TinyNet models, respectively. Compound scaling, as previously described, suggests that the DNN structure can expand uniformly towards multiple dimensions by embracing a suitable scaling coefficient. With this, DNNs can achieve accuracy similar to that of other (competitive) DNNs while utilizing fewer computational resources during model training and, thus, extracting meaningful cost savings.

7.2. Empirical Evaluations of DL Model Scaling

The following presents both recent and notable scientific works introducing empirical evaluations for DL model scaling.

Lin et al. [20] investigated the pitfalls of one-dimensional model scaling for convolutional neural networks (CNNs) and proposed a scaling method for CNNs that utilizes dimensional relationship and runtime proxy constraints to improve accuracy and inference latency. In turn, Hestness et al. [35] introduced a study where they empirically projected the computational requirements for future DL applications based on the representational growth achieved (and targeted) by the AI community.

Dollár et al. [14] presented an evaluation study to demonstrate how different compound scaling strategies affect the model parameters; activations; and, consequently, training time for different CNN model structures, focusing primarily on EfficientNet and RegNet models. With a focus on language models that adopt a transformers-based architecture, Kaplan et al. [21] empirically showed that performance (measured by test loss) improves and follows a power-law relationship as the model size, dataset size, and availability of computational power are scaled during model training. When only scaling one factor to achieve the referenced performance, the other two must not become bottlenecks. For optimal performance, the authors showed that all three factors must be scaled-up in tandem.

In a recent study, Bahri et al [22] capitalized on the previously mentioned work to show how scaling the model and dataset size can be explained under variance-limited and/or resolution-limited scaling regimes. In the end, the authors provided a theoretical framework that can be used to estimate upper and lower bounds for model loss depending on the aforementioned scaling regimes. Furthermore, Aach et al. [36] presented an empirical analysis of three open and popular distributed deep learning frameworks to assess their performance and scalability during model training with experiments focusing on ResNet and ImageNet models as the examined workload. Finally, Wang et al. [37] introduced an empirical study that examined a large corpus of DL model variants investigating unit test adoption and if/how metrics beyond accuracy are used to improve model robustness and reliability.

Based on the provided list of existing works empirically evaluating model scaling, it is obvious that the majority of the aforementioned studies either focus on a single model structure (e.g., ResNet, RegNet, or CNN models) and/or introduce findings that are tailored to solely evaluating accuracy and overheads during the model training stage. We deviate from the norm and focus on the impacts different model scaling strategies have during runtime inference. By offering a detailed examination of trade-offs during model inference, our work can contribute to guiding AI practitioners in selecting and tuning DL models for efficient and effective deployment of intelligent IoT services in resource-constrained environments. Moreover, we note that although a direct comparison against other empirical studies cannot be performed, as the body of related work focuses on performance and accuracy during the model training phase, several of our findings can be confirmed by the aforementioned studies. For example, Lin et al. [20] showcased that compound model scaling positively impacts classification accuracy for DNNs, while Bahri et al. [22] confirmed this but also noted (as we do) that the gains in terms of accuracy diminish and can plateau as a model attempts to scale using large compound coefficients. In turn, Dollár et al. [14] showed that although two model variants can present the same computational complexity, the output classification accuracy can (significantly) differ.

8. Conclusions and Future Work

This article presents an empirical benchmarking study focused on understanding the correlation between DL model scaling and three performance axes during runtime inference. These axes cover accuracy, computational effort, and latency. This distinguishes our work from other studies that solely studied model accuracy and training duration during the training phase for different model variants. To this end, we designed and presented a prototype of a DL model scaling benchmark framework, along with details about its execution and functionalities. Moreover, we introduced three diverse DL use cases from the domains of natural language understanding, object detection, and regression analysis. All three use cases embrace open DNN model architectures, multiple and different scaling techniques, and the use of popular datasets for workload generation.

With the three developed DL use cases, we then performed an empirical analysis with the use of our benchmark framework to discover various insights and trade-offs introduced across the three performance axes during runtime inference when examining multiple model variants per use case. Some key observations from the analysis are the following. Across all three DNN use cases, increasing model complexity generally led to improved inference quality—higher accuracy for classification tasks and lower MSE for regression tasks—but only up to a point. As model complexity continued to increase, the improvements began to plateau. Moreover, scaling the model complexity beyond a certain point that is both use-case and database-dependent, may lead to the model overfitting to the training data, capturing noise rather than meaningful patterns, which can degrade performance on new data. We also observed an almost linear relationship between model complexity and computational overhead (measured in FLOPs). In addition, the inference latency increased with model complexity, correlating with computational overhead, although the relationship was not perfectly linear due to additional factors like data pre-processing effort and memory access patterns influenced by model optimizations. Finally, our study highlights that models with the same complexity but different configurations can have significantly different impacts on accuracy and latency.

Our future work includes several key areas of development to enhance the capabilities and applicability of our benchmarking framework. Initially, we plan to introduce new use cases covering more real-world problems that will include more complex DNN models, like LLMs or generally generative AI. To that end, we plan to integrate our system with online model repositories (e.g., HuggingFace) in order to further automate our analysis. Secondly, we envision an extension of our monitoring subsystem to capture not only DNN performance metrics but also underlying utilization metrics, e.g., compute utilization (GPU/CPU), memory usage, disk I/O, etc. This will reveal hidden correlations between the structures of specific DNN models and their effects on the execution environment. Furthermore, our plans include the introduction of an intuitive user interface, along with a visualization library that will include post-experimentation advanced plotting and analysis functions. This new module will alleviate the difficulties faced by end users in extracting correlations between different parameters, find the sweet spot for their deployment, and extract useful insights. Finally, we would like to create a recommendation service that suggests (near-)optimal configurations for DNN-enabled applications without requiring every possible permutation to be tested. This service will be especially beneficial for beginners, providing a strong starting point to reduce evaluation time and help them choose the best-fit DNN model for their requirements.

Author Contributions: Conceptualization, D.T., M.S. and P.M.; methodology, D.T., P.M. and M.S.; software, P.M. and M.S.; validation, P.M.; writing—review and editing, M.S., D.T. and P.M.; project administration, D.T. All authors have read and agreed to the published version of the manuscript.

Funding: This work is part of AdaptoFlow, which is indirectly funded by the European Union's Horizon Europe research and innovation action programme via the TRIALSNET Open Call issued and executed under the TrialsNet project (Grant Agreement no. 101017141).

Data Availability Statement: The study used open and publicly available pre-trained model variants for the DL use cases, and the workloads feature open and popular ML/DL datasets. Links to the model and data repositories are provided throughout the article. The data generated by the benchmark framework are made publicly accessible in a Github repository available at the following link: https://github.com/unic-ailab/ModelScalingBench accessed on 7 November 2024.

Conflicts of Interest: The authors declare no conflicts of interest.

References

1. Elbes, M.; AlZu'bi, S.; Kanan, T. Deep Learning-Based Earthquake Prediction Technique Using Seismic Data. In Proceedings of the 2023 International Conference on Multimedia Computing, Networking and Applications (MCNA), Valencia, Spain, 19–22 June 2023; pp. 103–108. [CrossRef]
2. Simonyan, K.; Zisserman, A. Very deep convolutional networks for large-scale image recognition. *arXiv* **2014**, arXiv:1409.1556.
3. Devlin, J.; Chang, M.W.; Lee, K.; Toutanova, K. BERT: Pre-training of Deep Bidirectional Transformers for Language Understanding. *arXiv* **2019**, arXiv:cs.CL/1810.04805. http://arxiv.org/abs/1810.04805
4. Teichmann, M.; Weber, M.; Zöllner, M.; Cipolla, R.; Urtasun, R. MultiNet: Real-time Joint Semantic Reasoning for Autonomous Driving. In Proceedings of the 2018 IEEE Intelligent Vehicles Symposium (IV), Changshu, China, 26–30 June 2018; pp. 1013–1020. [CrossRef]
5. Ren, J.; Xia, F. Brain-inspired Artificial Intelligence: A Comprehensive Review. *arXiv* **2024**, arXiv:2408.14811.
6. Goodfellow, Ian and Pouget-Abadie, Jean and Mirza, Mehdi and Xu, Bing and Warde-Farley, David and Ozair, Sherjil and Courville, Aaron and Bengio, Yoshua. Generative adversarial nets. *Commun. ACM* **2020**, *63*, 139–144. [CrossRef]
7. Vaswani, A. Attention is all you need. In Proceedings of the 31st Conference on Neural Information Processing Systems (NIPS 2017), Long Beach, CA, USA, 4–9 December 2017.
8. Radford, A. Improving language understanding by generative pre-training. **2018**, *Preprint*.
9. Chowdhery, A.; Narang, S.; Devlin, J.; Bosma, M.; Mishra, G.; Roberts, A.; Barham, P.; Chung, H.W.; Sutton, C.; Gehrmann, S.; et al. Palm: Scaling language modeling with pathways. *J. Mach. Learn. Res.* **2023**, *24*, 1–113.
10. Szegedy, C.; Liu, W.; Jia, Y.; Sermanet, P.; Reed, S.; Anguelov, D.; Erhan, D.; Vanhoucke, V.; Rabinovich, A. Going deeper with convolutions. In Proceedings of the IEEE Conference on Computer Vision and Pattern Recognition, Boston, MA, USA, 7–12 June 2015; pp. 1–9.
11. He, K.; Zhang, X.; Ren, S.; Sun, J. Deep residual learning for image recognition. In Proceedings of the IEEE Conference on Computer Vision and Pattern Recognition, Las Vegas, NV, USA, 27–30 June 2016; pp. 770–778.
12. Touvron, H.; Bojanowski, P.; Caron, M.; Cord, M.; El-Nouby, A.; Grave, E.; Izacard, G.; Joulin, A.; Synnaeve, G.; Verbeek, J.; et al. ResMLP: Feedforward Networks for Image Classification With Data-Efficient Training. *IEEE Trans. Pattern Anal. Mach. Intell.* **2023**, *45*, 5314–5321. [CrossRef] [PubMed]
13. Tan, M.; Le, Q.V. EfficientNet: Rethinking Model Scaling for Convolutional Neural Networks. *arXiv* **2020**, arXiv:cs.LG/1905.11946. http://arxiv.org/abs/1905.11946
14. Dollár, P.; Singh, M.; Girshick, R. Fast and accurate model scaling. In Proceedings of the IEEE/CVF Conference on Computer Vision and Pattern Recognition, Nashville, TN, USA, 20–25 June 2021 ; pp. 924–932.
15. Amodei, D.; Hernandez, D. AI and Compute. 2018. Available online: https://openai.com/research/ai-and-compute (accessed on 7 November 2024).
16. Gujarati, A.; Elnikety, S.; He, Y.; McKinley, K.S.; Brandenburg, B.B. Swayam: Distributed autoscaling to meet SLAs of machine learning inference services with resource efficiency. In Proceedings of the 18th ACM/IFIP/USENIX Middleware Conference, New York, NY, USA, 9 December 2017; Middleware'17, pp. 109–120. [CrossRef]
17. Trihinas, D.; Symeonides, M.; Georgiou, J.; Pallis, G.; Dikaiakos, M.D. Energy-Aware Streaming Analytics Job Scheduling for Edge Computing. In Proceedings of the 2023 IEEE International Conference on Cloud Computing Technology and Science (CloudCom), Naples, Italy, 4–6 December 2023 ; pp. 161–168. [CrossRef]
18. Wu, C.J.; Raghavendra, R.; Gupta, U.; Acun, B.; Ardalani, N.; Maeng, K.; Chang, G.; Aga, F.; Huang, J.; Bai, C.; et al. Sustainable AI: Environmental Implications, Challenges and Opportunities. In Proceedings of the Machine Learning and Systems, Santa Clara, CA, USA, 29 August–1 September 2022; Marculescu, D., Chi, Y., Wu, C., Eds.; Volume 4, pp. 795–813.
19. Trihinas, D.; Michael, P.; Symeonides, M. Towards Low-Cost and Energy-Aware Inference for EdgeAI Services via Model Swapping. In Proceedings of the 2024 IEEE International Conference on Cloud Engineering (IC2E), Paphos, Cyprus, 24–27 September 2024. [CrossRef]
20. Lin, C.; Yang, P.; Wang, Q.; Qiu, Z.; Lv, W.; Wang, Z. Efficient and accurate compound scaling for convolutional neural networks. *Neural Netw.* **2023**, *167*, 787–797. [CrossRef]
21. Kaplan, J.; McCandlish, S.; Henighan, T.; Brown, T.B.; Chess, B.; Child, R.; Gray, S.; Radford, A.; Wu, J.; Amodei, D. Scaling laws for neural language models. *arXiv* **2020**, arXiv:2001.08361.
22. Bahri, Y.; Dyer, E.; Kaplan, J.; Lee, J.; Sharma, U. Explaining neural scaling laws. *Proc. Natl. Acad. Sci. USA* **2024**, *121*, e2311878121. [CrossRef] [PubMed]

23. Goodfellow, I.; Bengio, Y.; Courville, A. *Deep Learning*; MIT Press: Cambridge, MA, USA , 2016. Available online: http://www.deeplearningbook.org (accessed on 7 November 2024).
24. LeCun, Y.; Bengio, Y.; Hinton, G. Deep learning. *Nature* **2015**, *521*, 436–444. [CrossRef] [PubMed]
25. Zhai, X.; Kolesnikov, A.; Houlsby, N.; Beyer, L. Scaling vision transformers. In Proceedings of the IEEE/CVF Conference on Computer Vision and Pattern Recognition, New Orleans, LA, USA, 18–24 June 2022; pp. 12104–12113.
26. Zagoruyko, S. Wide residual networks. *arXiv* **2016**, arXiv:1605.07146.
27. MLcommons MLPerf Benchmarks. 2024. Available online: https://mlcommons.org/benchmarks/ (accessed on 7 November 2024).
28. Devlin, J.; Chang, M.W. Open Sourcing BERT: State-of-the-Art Pre-training for Natural Language Processing. *Google Res.* **2019**. Available online: https://research.google/blog/open-sourcing-bert-state-of-the-art-pre-training-for-natural-language-processing/ (accessed on 7 November 2024).
29. Tan, M.; Chen, B.; Pang, R.; Vasudevan, V.; Sandler, M.; Howard, A.; Le, Q.V. Mnasnet: Platform-aware neural architecture search for mobile. In Proceedings of the IEEE/CVF Conference on Computer Vision and Pattern Recognition, Long Beach, CA, USA, 15–20 June 2019; pp. 2820–2828.
30. Patterson, D.A.; Gonzalez, J.; Le, Q.V.; Liang, C.; Munguia, L.; Rothchild, D.; So, D.R.; Texier, M.; Dean, J. Carbon Emissions and Large Neural Network Training. *arXiv* **2021**, arXiv:2104.10350.
31. Raghu, M.; Poole, B.; Kleinberg, J.; Ganguli, S.; Sohl-Dickstein, J. On the expressive power of deep neural networks. In Proceedings of the International Conference on Machine Learning. PMLR, Sydney, Australia, 6–11 August 2017; pp. 2847–2854.
32. Howard, A.G. Mobilenets: Efficient convolutional neural networks for mobile vision applications. *arXiv* **2017**, arXiv:1704.04861.
33. Bello, I.; Fedus, W.; Du, X.; Cubuk, E.D.; Srinivas, A.; Lin, T.Y.; Shlens, J.; Zoph, B. Revisiting ResNets: Improved Training and Scaling Strategies. *Adv. Neural Inf. Process. Syst.* **2021**, *27*, 22614–22627.
34. Han, K.; Wang, Y.; Zhang, Q.; Zhang, W.; Xu, C.; Zhang, T. Model rubik's cube: Twisting resolution, depth and width for TinyNets. In Proceedings of the 34th International Conference on Neural Information Processing Systems, Red Hook, NY, USA, 6–12 December 2020; NIPS'20.
35. Hestness, J.; Ardalani, N.; Diamos, G. Beyond Human-Level Accuracy: Computational Challenges in Deep Learning. In Proceedings of the 24th Symposium on Principles and Practice of Parallel Programming, Washington, DC, USA, 16–20 February 2019.
36. Aach, M.; Inanc, E.; Sarma, R.; Riedel, M.; Lintermann, A. Large scale performance analysis of distributed deep learning frameworks for convolutional neural networks. *J. Big Data* **2023**, *10*, 96.
37. Wang, H.; Yu, S.; Chen, C.; Turhan, B.; Zhu, X. Beyond Accuracy: An Empirical Study on Unit Testing in Open-source Deep Learning Projects. *ACM Trans. Softw. Eng. Methodol.* **2024**, *33*, 1–22. [CrossRef]

future internet

MDPI

Article

Virtualization vs. Containerization, a Comparative Approach for Application Deployment in the Computing Continuum Focused on the Edge

Hamish Sturley [1,†], Augustin Fournier [2,†], Andoni Salcedo-Navarro [3,†], Miguel Garcia-Pineda [3,†] and Jaume Segura-Garcia [3,*,†]

[1] School of Computing, Engineering and Physical-Science, University of the West of Scotland, Paisley Campus, Paisley PA1 2BE, UK; b00336796@studentmail.uws.ac.uk

[2] Télécom SudParis/Orange, 91000 Evry, France; augustin.fournier2701@gmail.com

[3] Computer Science Dpt–ETSE, Universitat de València, 46100 Burjassot, Spain; andoni.salcedo@uv.es (A.S.-N.); miguel.garcia-pineda@uv.es (M.G.-P.)

* Correspondence: jaume.segura@uv.es; Tel.: +34-963-543-730

† These authors contributed equally to this work.

Abstract: With the emergence of containerization 10 years ago, we saw a compact, convenient and portable way of running apps directly concurrently with virtualization. The major difference is in the architecture. Containers share the same kernel as the guest and then do not virtualize low-layer components like the Central Processing Unit (CPU). On the one hand, they are lighter and more flexible than virtual machines (VMs). On the other hand, VMs can more precisely meet the low-layer needs and are completely autonomous systems. Nowadays, what is the best architecture to use to develop an application? In this paper, we will study the two main virtual methods of deploying this. We will compare both methods on several criteria: compatibility based on user experience and the ease of installation/deployment, scalability based on the automatic elasticity facing the workload and energy efficiency in terms of energy and computer resources. After the tests, we conclude that the containerization option is the most ecologically advantageous option in terms of energy consumption.

Keywords: containerization stack; edge computing; orchestration; performance tests; virtualization stack

1. Introduction

As digital transformation accelerates across various sectors, the adoption of advanced technologies such as e-Government, Industry 4.0, Agriculture 5.0 and Smart Cities is becoming increasingly widespread. These technologies, powered by the development of artificial intelligence (AI) and other emerging tools, offer unprecedented opportunities for institutions, governments and organizations to enhance efficiency, reduce operational costs, and achieve higher levels of automation [1]. The shift towards these technologies necessitates a critical examination of the underlying infrastructure, particularly in how software applications are deployed and managed to meet the growing demands of modern systems.

In the context of the Computing Continuum, which spans from Cloud to Edge/Fog environments, the deployment of applications requires a careful selection of the appropriate hosting environment [2]. The decision between virtualization and containerization, two prevalent technologies in this space, plays a pivotal role in determining the performance, scalability and efficiency of these deployments [3,4]. Virtualization, a well-established technology, allows multiple operating systems to run concurrently on a single physical machine by abstracting the hardware layer. In contrast, containerization offers a more lightweight approach by isolating applications within containers that share the host operating system's kernel, leading to faster deployment times and more efficient resource utilization.

As organizations increasingly shift towards Edge Computing—where data processing occurs closer to the source rather than in centralized cloud servers—the choice between virtualization and containerization becomes even more critical. Edge environments often come with constrained resources and specific Quality of Service (QoS) requirements, making it imperative to choose the right deployment strategy [5]. Virtual machines (VMs) provide robust isolation and security, which are essential in many Edge applications. However, they can also introduce significant overhead, potentially impacting performance in resource-limited settings. On the other hand, containers, while more resource-efficient, may pose challenges related to security and orchestration in diverse and distributed Edge environments [6].

The complexities involved in deploying applications across the Computing Continuum highlight the need for a comprehensive comparative analysis of virtualization and containerization technologies [2]. This paper aims to address this need by evaluating various virtualization and containerization stacks to determine the optimal environment for hosting deployments and the applications they support. The analysis will consider key factors such as performance, scalability, security and ease of management, which are crucial for meeting the unique demands of Edge Computing.

In addition to the technical evaluation, this study will also explore the broader implications of these technologies for the future of application deployment in Edge environments. As the Edge becomes an increasingly vital part of the Computing Continuum, understanding the tradeoffs between virtualization and containerization will be essential for organizations seeking to leverage these technologies effectively.

Ultimately, the findings of this research will contribute to the ongoing discourse on the best practices for deploying applications in the Computing Continuum, with a particular focus on Edge Computing. As the digital landscape continues to evolve, the ability to make informed decisions about deployment strategies will be key to unlocking the full potential of emerging technologies and ensuring their successful integration into the fabric of modern infrastructure.

Another possible research motivation in the study of the comparison between virtualization and containerization concerns the architecture of the CPU within the context of Edge Computing. Depending on the use of Intel (x86_64) or ARM architectures [7], the set of instructions used can be different. When using reduced instruction sets (RISC) in ARM and low-cost devices for Edge Computing [8], the advantages in performance, regarding the tradeoff between energy consumption and computational power, can be achieved efficiently when the proper use case is selected.

This work is presented as follows: after this introductory section, the section on related works explains some of the studies that establish the state of the art for this issue. Section 3 is focused on the materials and methodology and explains the tools, software and hardware used for the application tests with different architecture combinations. Section 4 will explain the results of the tests with different architectures, which will be discussed and concluded in Section 5.

2. State of the Art

The recent shift to Edge Computing models has placed a greater emphasis on cheaper and more power-efficient systems that are not well addressed by x86/64 architectures. Instead, many Edge Computing solutions are turning to alternative architectures, such as ARM-based processors, which are known for their lower power consumption and cost-effectiveness. These architectures are better suited for distributed, resource-constrained environments where Edge devices operate with limited power and processing capabilities. As Edge Computing continues to grow, there is an increasing demand for customized, specialized hardware that can meet these performance and energy efficiency needs, driving innovation beyond traditional x86/64 systems. This shift is helping industries deploy intelligent applications at the Edge, closer to the source of data, with reduced latency and improved scalability.

Different authors have used differing approaches to the analysis of the different options offered by virtualization and containerization for the Computing Continuum, from the Cloud to User Equipment (UE), passing through the Edge. In [9], the authors provide a systematic review of container virtualization in real-time environments in Industry 4.0, analyzing 37 papers on real-time constraints, task latency and container platforms for cyber–physical systems. Also, in [10], the authors address the need for a systematic analysis of containerization, focusing on its role as a lightweight alternative to virtual machines for deploying modern applications in diverse environments. They taxonomically classify existing research on the performance comparison between hypervisors and containers and analyze container orchestration and performance monitoring tools. In [11], the authors conduct a systematic literature review to identify the most popular container technologies and trends in their research, facilitating more informed decision-making. In [4], the authors perform a systematic mapping of research on these core technologies, revealing that most articles focus on deployment through validation and solution research, while fewer papers address orchestration, particularly in philosophical and model-related contexts. The findings highlight gaps in the literature, offering valuable insights for researchers, industries and service providers.

Regarding Cloud-centered applications for these technologies, in [12], the authors compare the performance of three Cloud architectures: Infrastructure as a Service (IaaS) , Platform as a Service (PaaS) and Software as a Service (SaaS), focusing on the differences between containerization and virtualization. The findings indicate that while containers generally perform better in SaaS and PaaS environments, the performance metrics for IaaS are nearly the same for both methods. This research aims to help users make informed decisions about their Cloud deployment strategies by providing clear, quantifiable data on these differences. Also, in [3], the authors examine the performance differences between these technologies across IaaS, PaaS and SaaS Cloud architectures. The findings indicate that containers generally offer better performance for SaaS and PaaS, while the performance for IaaS is nearly identical between the two methods, providing valuable insights for users deciding between them.

In [13], the authors focus their interest on interactive training simulations, which are used across various industries and challenge traditional computing networks due to their high-performance demands. They examine how to extend traditional high-performance computing (HPC) environments into Cloud-based services to support multiple interactive simulations while maintaining performance. Their work evaluates four HPC load-balancing techniques—virtualization, software containers and clustering—to optimize the scheduling and execution of these simulations, finding that the choice of technique should be based on cluster resources, job competition and software requirements.

Regarding Internet of Things (IoT) applications requiring high computing power and real-time processing, in [6], the authors propose to face these challenges with low-cost Small Board Computers (SBCs) by leveraging container-based technologies and fog computing to enhance device collaboration, scalability and load balancing. They compare the container orchestration platforms Docker Swarm and Kubernetes on SBC clusters, finding that Docker Swarm provides superior performance across various topologies and cluster configurations.

In [2], the authors face the problem of container and microservice management platforms like Kubernetes, which are crucial for Cloud computing but struggle with heterogeneous computing environments, where nodes have varied characteristics. They propose to replace Kubernetes' native scheduler with a customizable one that better accommodates the diverse needs of a Continuum Computing environment. Testing a batch-based scheduling approach on virtual machines demonstrates improved performance over Kubernetes' pod-by-pod method, highlighting the limitations of default scheduling in supporting complex deployment requirements.

In [14], the author exposes in a seminar a comparison between hypervisor-based and container-based virtualization, highlighting the rise in popularity of container-based virtualization due to Docker, a tool that simplifies container management. While hypervisor-based virtualization has been a dominant method for decades, container-based virtualization offers distinct advantages, leading to its increased use. The paper details the benefits and tradeoffs of both technologies, with a particular focus on container-based virtualization and Docker. It also addresses the security risks associated with containerization and provides a summary of related work in the field.

Different authors have tackled the integration of virtualization/containerization with Edge Computing. In [15], the authors investigate different works on Cloud and Edge Computing paradigms and their virtualization at the Edge. They also provide a taxonomy based on the state of the art for virtualized resources. In [16], the author analyzes the application of the concept of device virtualization in IoT/Edge Computing and carries out performance studies using single-board computers (SBCs) to efficiently deploy different low-power virtualized devices (i.e., families of Raspberry Pi and Odroid) in terms of performance when handling container-virtualized instances. Also, in [17], the authors focus their efforts in evaluating a methodology based on the study of containerization-based Edge–Cloud computing infrastructures' performance. They saw that containerization at the Edge does not introduce noticeable performance degradation in terms of communication, computing and intelligence capabilities, making it a promising technology for the Edge–Cloud computing paradigm, although they claim that there is still room for improvement, especially in time-critical industrial applications. According to them, this evaluation methodology can be used as a reference for practitioners in Edge–Cloud computing to obtain a client-perspective overview of system performance.

The massive amount of data generation today challenges current network architectures, which struggle with bandwidth, latency and privacy issues. From the Edge Computing perspective, these problems are addressed by enabling local data processing, while Network Function Virtualization (NFV) simplifies service creation by virtualizing traditional network functions. In [5], the authors compare containers and virtual machines through the implementation of a unified management and orchestration platform (MANO) for Virtualized Everything Functions (VxFs) using LXD for containers and KVM for virtual machines on a Raspberry Pi 4. The results indicate that containerization is not always suitable alone and is best used as a complementary approach to full virtualization.

3. Materials and Methods

In this section, we outline the tools and procedures used for the different experiments conducted to check the performance of the different approaches selected. First, we describe the software tools used, and later, we describe the hardware options. Finally, the tests deployed define a comparative framework between both approaches.

3.1. Stress-ng

To guarantee a consistent and dependable benchmark, it was essential to choose a tool that could apply a controlled and reproducible workload to the system. For this purpose, the `stress-ng` tool, short for Stress Next Generation, was selected. Stress-ng [18] is a powerful, Linux-based benchmarking and stress-testing tool specifically developed to evaluate the performance and stability of various hardware components under extreme conditions. It is widely used in scenarios where assessing the resilience and capability of computer systems is critical, such as in Fog (Fog Computing) and Edge Computing environments, where devices often operate under varying loads and conditions.

Stress-ng offers an extensive range of tests that can apply loads to different parts of a system, including the CPU, memory, input/output (I/O) subsystems, and more. By simulating intense workloads, Stress-ng helps to identify potential weaknesses or bottlenecks within these subsystems. This is particularly important in Fog and Edge Computing, where hardware is often deployed in remote or resource-constrained environments, requiring systems to be both robust and reliable.

The tool's metrics provide detailed insights into how a system performs under pressure. For instance, it can measure the CPU's ability to handle intensive computational tasks, the memory's capacity to manage large datasets, and the I/O subsystem's efficiency in processing data transfers. These metrics are crucial for understanding overall performance and identifying any areas that may require optimization. Additionally, Stress-ng can simulate hardware failures or resource exhaustion scenarios, allowing engineers to test a system's response to such conditions and ensure that it can recover gracefully or maintain functionality. This tool provides multiple options when configuring the input and output settings for the planned architecture.

The `--metrics` option displays the total number of "Bogo" (bogus) operations performed in the stress processes, but these are not reliable indicators of performance or throughput and are not intended for benchmarking. Instead, they provide a useful way to observe system behavior under different types of load.

Stress-ng uses an unconventional metric called "Bogo Ops", which measures the number of iterations the stressor completes during a run, indicating the overall amount of "work" done in Bogo operations (Bogo Ops). Bogo Ops provide a general idea of system performance under load conditions but are not intended to serve as precise benchmarking metrics. The other metrics used within this `--metrics` option are real time, usr time, sys time, Bogo Ops/s (real time) and Bogo Ops/s (usr + sys time). These metrics are explained in Table 1.

Table 1. Other metrics explained within stress-ng.

Metric	Explanation
real time (s)	The average wall clock duration (in seconds) of the stressor is the total wall clock time for all instances of that stressor divided by the number of stressors run.
usr time (s)	The usr time is the total user time (in seconds) consumed by running all instances of the stressor.
sys time (s)	The sys time is the total system time (in seconds) consumed by running all instances of the stressor.
Bogo Ops/s (real time)	The total Bogo operations per second based on wall clock time, which reflects the apparent runtime, increases as more processors distribute the workload, reducing wall clock time and boosting the apparent Bogo Ops rate of the system.
Bogo Ops/s (usr + sys time)	The total Bogo operations per second based on cumulative user and system time represent the real Bogo Ops rate of the system, accounting for the actual execution time across all processors, which generally decreases with more concurrent stressors due to contention on cache, memory, execution units, buses and I/O devices.

The use of the package `stress-ng` is not advised for precise and conventional measurements; it is only recommended to measure tendencies. The metrics used within this tool have no transformative operation to any other real metric, such as throughput, delay or any other. We used it as a comparative tool for the different experiments planned.

3.2. *Top System Monitor*

The `top` system monitor [19] is a powerful and widely used tool in Linux-based operating systems, providing real-time insights into system performance and resource utilization. By default, top tracks a variety of key metrics, including per-core CPU usage, memory consumption, load averages and detailed information about all running tasks and processes. The interface is dynamic, updating continuously to reflect the current state of the system, which allows users to observe how resources are being allocated and identify potential bottlenecks or issues in real time. This makes top an invaluable tool for system administrators and developers who need to monitor system health, troubleshoot performance problems or manage resources effectively.

In our planned tests, we utilized top to capture detailed performance data, which were recorded as JSON objects for later analysis. By doing so, we can systematically track how the system behaves under the stress conditions we impose, including how resources are distributed across multiple CPU cores and how memory usage fluctuates. This approach allows us to gather precise and structured data, which can be analyzed to understand the impact of different stressors on system performance. The JSON format also facilitates easy integration with other tools and workflows, enabling a more comprehensive assessment of the performance outcomes from our tests. This data-driven approach enhances the accuracy of our performance evaluations, providing a solid foundation for optimizing system configurations or identifying areas for improvement.

3.3. Power Meter Data Logger

For the performance evaluation, aside from the usual machine-based metrics, we measured the sustainability of the system in terms of power consumption. To this end, we selected a power meter logger, which was the UM24C [20] power meter data logger, due to its broad sensor suite. This logger can measure the supply voltage, supply current, supply power, cable resistance, charged capacity, temperature, USB data line voltage and USB charging mode. Table 2 shows the main operational ranges for this power meter. Logging is typically provided over the Bluetooth interface and managed through an app provided by the manufacturer; however, this was replaced with the `rdumtool` [21] command line tool, exposing sensor values as JSON objects in order to improve ease of processing.

Table 2. The main features of the um24c power monitor as stated by the manufacturer [20].

Sensor	Range	Resolution	Accuracy
Supply V	4.50–24.00 V	0.01 V	$\pm(0.2\% + 1digit)$
Supply A	0.000–3.000 A	0.001 A	$\pm(0.8\% + 3digits)$
Cable resistance	1.5–9999.9 Ω		
Temperature	−10 °C–100 °C		±3 °C

3.4. Raspberry Pi Testbed Setup

Due to the rise in ARM-based Edge Computing infrastructure, an ARM host was selected for testing to best determine results for all computing paradigms. The Raspberry Pi 4B+ was chosen as a testbed to compute resources due to the greater availability of high-accuracy low-voltage meters encouraging the selection of devices in the 5 V range. The host Raspberry Pi (rpi) was additionally subjected to tests to provide a baseline for performance, with an Operating System (OS), which was a 64-bit Rasbian 12 desktop.

The following containers and virtual machines were created in order to test the performance of each:

1. **Kubernetes and Docker:** The Kubernetes test environment was set up as a single-node Kubernetes cluster using the minikube Kubernetes stack, the Podman container runtime and a single 64-bit Debian 12 container for running the tests. The docker test environment was set up as a 64-bit `linuxserver debian 12` ssh container with stress-ng installed on the standard docker engine with Docker Compose orchestration.
2. **x86 and aarch64:** The x86 VM was run as a 64-bit QEMU virtual machine with `qemu-sysem-x86_64`, and Debian 12 was used for the tests.x86 was selected for emulation in the ARM environment to demonstrate the need for effective virtualization methods in foreign instruction sets due to the rise in ARM-based Edge Computing resources. The ARM VM was run as a 64-bit QEMU virtual machine with `qemu-system-aarch64` with the virtual machine type, the kernel virtual machine extension or KVM, allowing for the direct throughput of quest operations, which were used to best represent the capabilities of virtual machines. The arm64 version of Debian 12 was used for the tests (used as a Raspberry Pi VM).

3.5. x86 Testbed Setup

When building the test setup, it was determined that using a virtualized environment would reduce labor and complexity requirements when testing the system, ensure parity between the systems being tested and enable the sharing of computing resources. To this end, the Proxmox virtual environment was selected for use as a host for the systems evaluated.

The Proxmox virtual environment (PVE) is an enterprise-grade layer 2 hypervisor based on the Debian kernel. The main strengths of the PVE include a highly active community with excellent community and developer support, a highly capable webUI environment and support for advanced virtual storage.

Within the PVE, all evaluated systems were provided with the same hardware: 2 cores from both CPUs for a total of 4 threads, 8 Gigabytes of RAM, 100 Gigabytes of hard drive disk space and access to both the host's network and an internal virtual network, both provided through virtualized switches.

Figure 1 depicts a global scheme for the stress tests carried out in this work. These tests will also serve as a basis for the pointcloud generation use case that will be explained later.

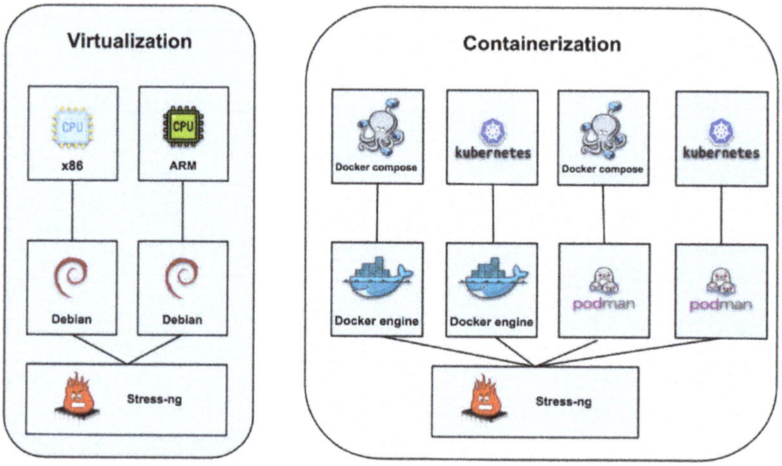

Figure 1. Global scheme of the tests.

3.6. x86 Tests

As previously mentioned, the term Bogo Ops is short for "bogus operations", and it is a metric used by stress-ng to indicate the number of operations performed by the stress test within a given time frame, which for us is 1 min and 10 min.

While Bogo Ops are not a standardized measurement like FLOPS (for floating-point operations) or IOPS (for disk), they give a rough idea of performance by showing how many iterations of a given task have been completed. The higher the Bogo Ops value, the more operations the system was able to perform during the stress test, which suggests better performance for that particular component.

When running CPU stress tests with `stress-ng`, the tool runs different types of computational workloads (like integer calculations, floating-point math, or cryptographic operations). The Bogo Ops metric in CPU tests indicates how many iterations of these workloads the CPU was able to complete.

In memory stress tests, stress-ng performs memory-intensive operations like allocating, copying, reading and writing data to and from memory. Here, the Bogo Ops metric reflects how many memory-related operations (e.g., memory reads, writes or allocations) were completed. This metric is useful for testing how well the system handles memory-intensive workloads and can reveal memory bottlenecks.

For I/O disk tests, stress-ng performs read/write operations on files to measure the disk's I/O performance. The Bogo Ops metric in I/O tests represents the number of I/O operations completed, such as file reads, writes and seeks or other disk-related operations. A large number of Bogo Ops in this context suggests that the disk subsystem can handle a larger volume of I/O operations in the given time. We performed each test three times and obtained the average value in order to have relevant values.

Kubernetes and Docker Engine are very common in companies with complicated and scalable networks. These tools enable automated scalability management, load balancing and container failure management for a complex application. The goal is to test the different cases in a simple architecture with similar solutions to quantify performance. Compared to Docker Engine, Podman does not use a centralized daemon, which allows for lighter container management, does not use root connection for security, and natively supports pod management. Podman is therefore a legitimate competitor to Docker Engine as a runtime container. For orchestrators, Kubernetes is designed to handle complex applications on a large scale and is suitable for production environments, so it has plenty of features. Docker Compose is designed for a simple application consisting of a single node. It does not have features such as scaling (too light), fault tolerance and advanced volume management, making it much easier to configure. Later on, we will describe Docker Compose as a container manager, but as having a simple command utility for the sake of simplicity.

For each container–runtime and container–manager coupling, we obtained specific metrics:

- Duration of the test: this was measured to see the influence of time on efficiency.
- Bogo Ops: This is a non-official metric used to measure the number of operations carried out by the hardware. We will use this to compare the efficiency of each method.
- User time: this is the time taken by the CPU to execute code from you or your apps.
- System time: this is the time taken by the CPU to manage and interact with other hardware components (I/O, network, memory, etc.).

3.7. Raspberry Pi Tests

In order to determine the power efficiency of the evaluated automated power meter in the different virtual environments, observations were generated via a bash script [22]. Tests were run 5 times for each virtual environment, and then Bogo Ops in a 60 s window per watt second were used to determine a value for relative power efficiency.

Due to issues with the rdumtool and maximum recording length, the measured watt hours were compared to a correspondingly adjusted Bogo Ops value.

3.8. Use Case: Dynamic Pointcloud Generation with OpenDroneMap

After testing the different architectures, we used the best option for a specific use case: pointcloud processing. Pointcloud processing and management have specific requirements for computing. Similarly to [23], we found that a good software option for processing is Open Drone Map (ODM) [24]. This is an open framework used to generate and process maps and pointclouds from Unmanned Aerial Vehicles (UAVs) [25].

In this use case, we will demonstrate how Docker and Kubernetes dynamically manage and scale pointcloud generation. Drone images are transmitted to a Raspberry Pi for preprocessing, which then requests a GPU-accelerated transformation matrix from an Edge server to align spectral bands. Kubernetes orchestrates Docker containers in the Cloud, distributing the computational load for efficient pointcloud generation. The system architecture is shown in Figure 2.

The workflow starts with the drone capturing images and transmitting them to a Raspberry Pi, which preprocesses the images for pointcloud generation. Upon receiving the first image, the Raspberry Pi requests a transformation matrix from the Edge server to align the images from different spectral bands. The Edge server, using GPU acceleration, computes the matrix, ensuring all images share the same perspective and reducing computation time.

After obtaining the transformation matrix, the Raspberry Pi extracts metadata from the images to apply vignetting corrections. It then aligns the images using the transformation matrix, ensuring consistency across all spectral bands. Once the images are preprocessed and aligned, the Raspberry Pi sends them to the Cloud environment for further processing. In the Cloud, Kubernetes orchestrates the deployment of ODM instances within Docker containers. Each instance is responsible for processing a specific spectral index, such as the NDVI, or band.

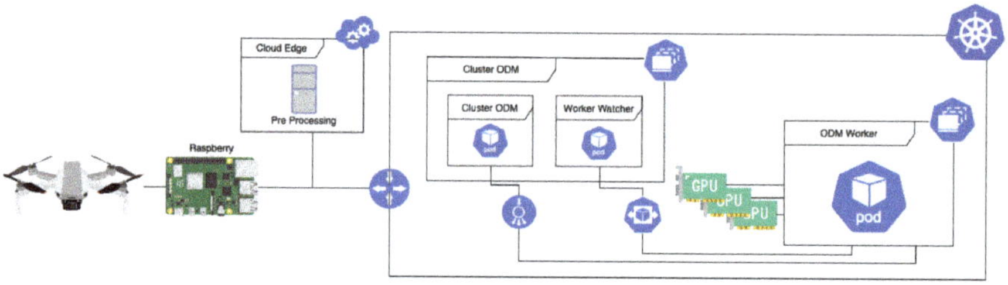

Figure 2. System architecture for pointcloud generation using distributed computing with Raspberry Pi, Edge server and Kubernetes-orchestrated Cloud environment.

The system scales dynamically by adjusting the number of ODM worker instances based on the number of spectral indices to be computed in parallel. This scalability is achieved through Kubernetes' ability to manage resources and deploy additional instances as needed. A Watcher Service operates within the Cloud environment to monitor the availability of ODM instances. It ensures that new instances are registered with ClusterODM, which functions as a load balancer, distributing tasks among the available workers.

By distributing computational tasks across multiple ODM workers, the system significantly accelerates the pointcloud generation process. The parallel processing of different spectral indices reduces the time required to obtain results. This architecture demonstrates the effectiveness of combining Kubernetes and Docker to manage complex workloads in a Cloud environment.

4. Results

4.1. Tests Results

For the tests explained in Sections 3.6 and 3.7, the average values obtained are depicted in Table 3. In this figure, we see that the payload (in terms of "Bogo Ops") for longer processes (10 min) is greater (and proportional to that of shorter processes (1 min)). The speed or apparent runtime (in terms of "Bogo Ops/s" in real time) seems to be nearly constant in both processes (the longer and shorter ones), and the runtime for the cumulative user and system time has the same behavior but on a lower scale because these do not take into account as many operations.

Table 3. Averages for tests carried out with CPU using `stress-ng` in Section 3.6.

Duration (min)	Manager	Container Runtime	Bogo Ops	Bogo Ops/s	Usr + Sys Bogo Ops/s
10	Docker Compose	Podman	311,7331.0	5195.5	1300.4
10	Docker Compose	Docker Engine	3,089,738.0	5149.6	1288.6
10	-	Docker Engine	3,093,922.3	5156.5	1290.2
10	-	Podman	3,050,764.7	5084.6	1272.4
10	Kubernetes	Podman	3,027,897.3	5046.5	1279.8
10	Kubernetes	Docker Engine	2,984,890.0	4974.8	1265.3
1	Docker Compose	Docker Engine	308,970.3	5149.4	1288.8
1	Docker Compose	Podman	309,507.7	5158.4	1293.0
1	-	Docker Engine	310,324.0	5171.9	1294.4
1	-	Podman	306,818.3	5113.5	1281.2
1	Kubernetes	Podman	299,595.3	4993.2	1267.0
1	Kubernetes	Docker Engine	296,143.0	4935.6	1254.3

For the tests described in Section 3.7, the following data are presented. Of note are the highly similar rpi, Docker and aarch64 vm measurements, demonstrating the high efficiency of containers, as well as the suitability of virtualization stacks with the appropriate extensions. On the other hand, the apparent lack of performance in Kubernetes hosted in Podman environments seems to indicate inefficiencies in the container runtime or high overheads. Finally, the extremely poor performance of the x86 virtual machine shows the difficulties in emulating legacy hardware on modern instruction set paradigms. Another interesting finding, however, is uncovered when evaluating the stress reports from the x86 host. It was discovered that completed add operations were found to be roughly equal to divide operations, as without full CPU parity, no virtual acceleration was being undertaken at all, indicating a possible area of improvement for virtualization speed when similar instructions are available.

Figures 3–7 show the percentage of additional performance based on the solution that had the lowest percentage. We consider the numbers of `usr + sys Bogo Ops/s` and `Bogo Ops/s` for the task itself to have the most reliable graph possible. The purpose of these results is to identify trends, not to consider specific measures as they are not standardized. They allow us to get an idea of performance and resource management. As expected, the Kubernetes container manager solution is less effective in our scenario because we will deploy only a few containers over a short period of time. There is a difference in CPU usage performance of 5%, which can be significant in terms of time and resources. It is difficult to come to a conclusion about runtime containers here. Although the use of Docker Compose should not affect the performance results of the containers, there is a difference in the results obtained between using Docker Compose and using the runtime container alone. This difference may be due to inaccurate measurements and other factors. The measurement and explanation of these differences may be addressed in a future study.

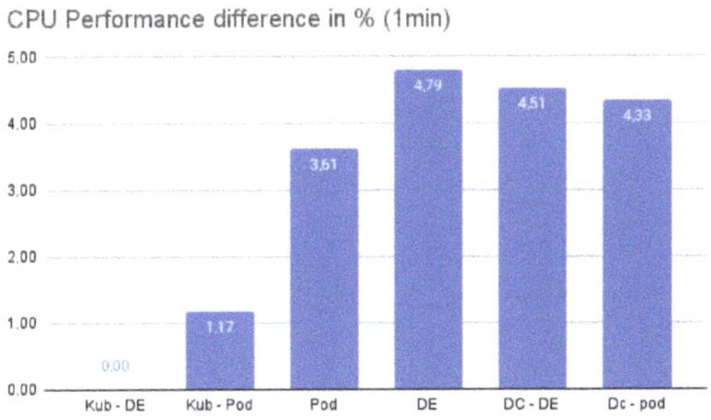

Figure 3. CPU performance difference in percent for 1 min.

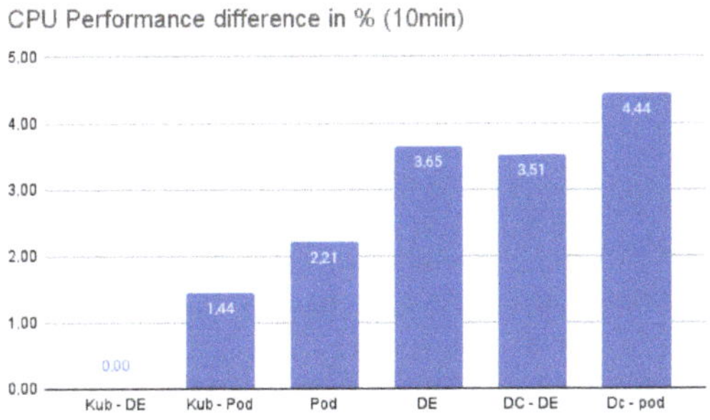

Figure 4. CPU performance difference in percent for 10 min.

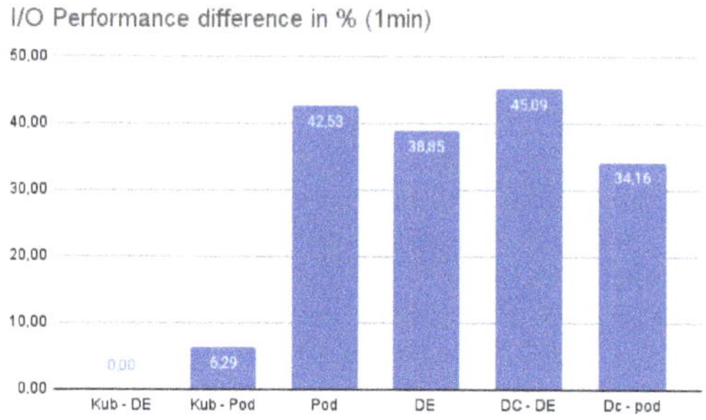

Figure 5. I/O disk performance difference in percent for 1 min.

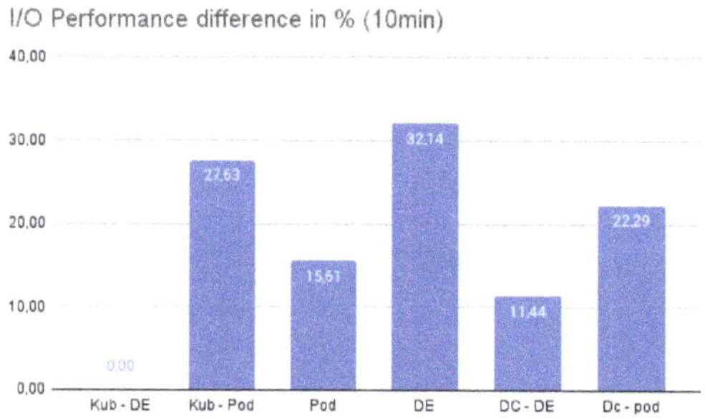

Figure 6. I/O disk performance difference in percent for 10 min.

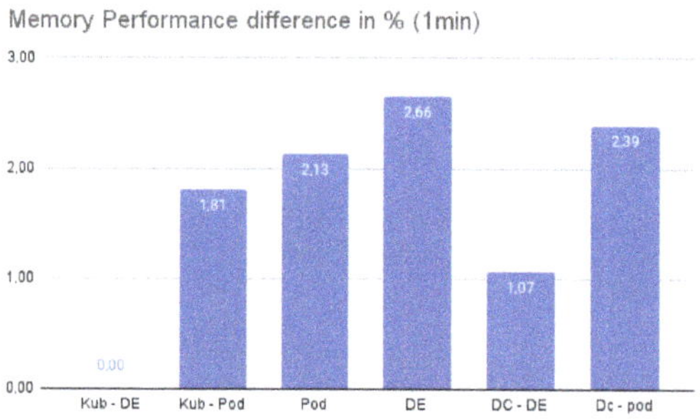

Figure 7. Memory performance difference in percent for 1 min.

For the CPU performance graph over 10 min (see Figure 4), a similar trend is obtained. It should be noted that the performance difference between Kubernetes and other solutions decreased, showing a trend that suggests that Kubernetes can perform well in the long term. With these graphs, we can see that the use of Docker Compose with Podman performs better on all levels in the context of using only a few containers over a moderate period of time. For the I/O disk performance graphs over 1 min (see Figure 5), we can see that Docker Compose acts as a better container manager in our case, being 40% more efficient on average. This can be explained because Podman does not use a daemon for managing containers. Thus, there is no overload with this and with complex network services. In addition, Kubernetes is very complex in terms of components; it needs a Kuberlet, an API server, a controller manager, etc. For this reason, Kubernetes and Docker Engine are less likely to have better results than Docker Compose and Podman.

The results for the I/O disk performance graph for ten minutes (see Figure 6) show the same trend as for CPU performance; Kubernetes' results are still worse than the others, but they significantly increased. This trend supports the hypothesis about the long-term efficiency of Kubernetes.

For the memory part (see Figure 7), the difference is less significant than CPU consumption or I/O operations. This difference can be explained by the same argument used for the I/O disk performance: the complexity of Kubernetes is more resource-consuming than the lightweight container manager Docker Compose.

We can then recommend using Docker Compose and Podman in an environment that requires resource efficiency on a one-time basis and not for a long-term service. For example, to train artificial intelligence (AI) on a model with large amounts of data, we can use Docker Compose and Podman. In the case of a complex architecture with a need for redundancy and error management or a service/application, we recommend Kubernetes, which will meet these needs adequately.

Figure 8 summarizes the whole range of tests performed in the different virtualized and containerized architectures. This figure shows that the use of Kubernetes with the Podman backend demonstrates the advantage of utilizing Kubernetes with the more popular Docker Engine; furthermore, the true extent of x86's virtualization inefficiency is revealed.

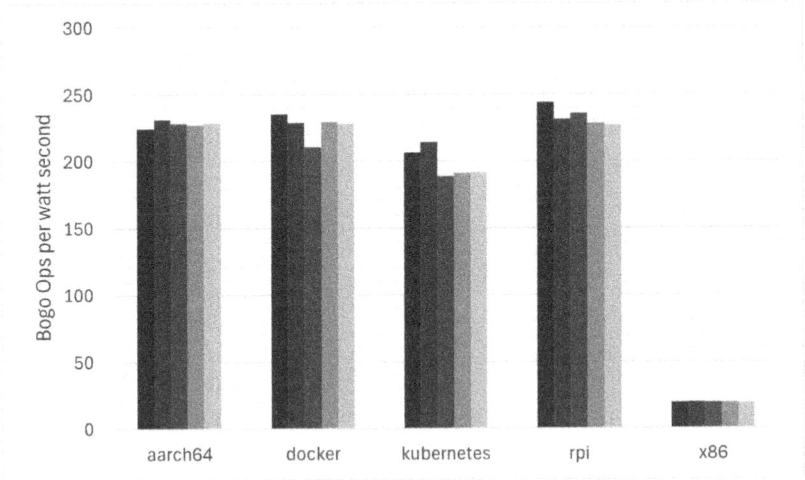

Figure 8. Comparison of all 25 tests (5 min) performed on the Raspberry Pi testbed.

Figure 9 summarizes the same set of tests as before but on a 20 min timescale instead of 5 min. This figure shows that the power efficiency of Kubernetes exceeds that of Docker when run for longer periods.

The widespread adoption of Kubernetes has fostered an extensive ecosystem of Kubernetes-compatible containers and tools, along with a supportive community of developers and users. This environment provides organizations with a powerful suite of tools, which encourages both new and existing users to engage with Kubernetes-based solutions. As a result, individuals and organizations often prefer Kubernetes-compatible solutions, even when theoretically superior alternatives may be available.

Although Kubernetes was originally designed for clustered deployments, single-node Kubernetes cluster solutions have gained substantial popularity due to their reduced resource requirements and improved performance. For instance, Canonical's MicroK8s operates as a single-node cluster by default, catering to small production environments and development needs. Similarly, Rancher Labs' K3s is optimized as a single-node solution specifically for Edge Computing and IoT applications. This trend highlights the flexibility and adaptability of the Kubernetes ecosystem in addressing modern deployment requirements.

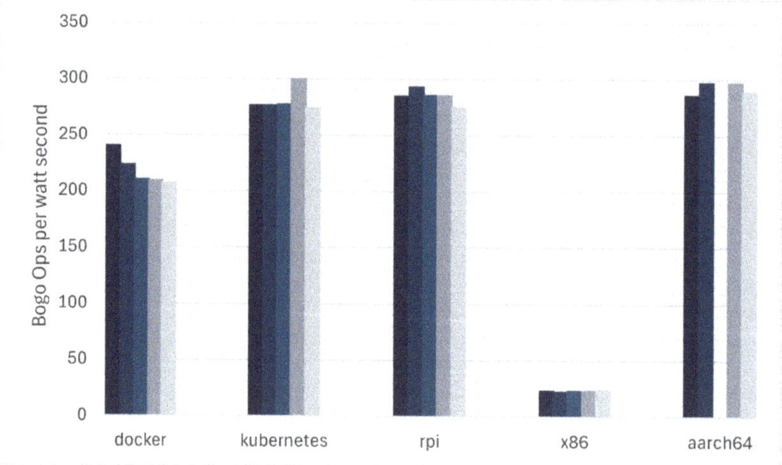

Figure 9. Comparison of all 24 tests (20 min) performed on the Raspberry Pi testbed.

The comparison between the Kubernetes experiment using the previous version and the new version (i.e., k3s) on a single node shows a difference of only 1.4%. Therefore, we consider the results of the new experiments to be compatible with those of the previous version. Also, as shown in Figure 10, the efficiency enhancement between the one-node and two-node options is around 8%.

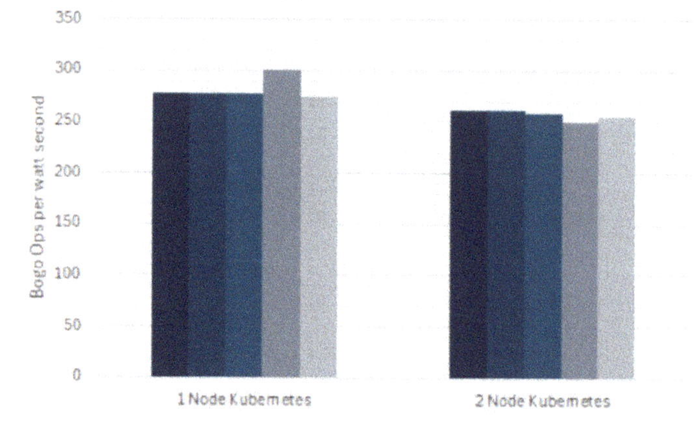

Figure 10. Tests with 2-node cluster compared to previous 1-node architecture.

4.2. Use Case Results

From the previous analysis, we found that the worst option was the use of the Kubernetes and Docker Engine stack, which in the different comparison test figures, with results given as percentages (Figures 3–7), is the reference baseline, as it underwent no improvement in performance. Our purpose here is to check this option for a use case with intensive processing.

To evaluate the performance and scalability of the use case given in Section 3.8, we conducted an experiment using a drone flight that captured 48 images. The data were processed using four ODM nodes configured in a cluster, with each node equipped with four virtual CPUs (vCPUs). The hardware specifications for the ODM nodes were based on the recommendations provided in the official documentation (https://docs.opendronemap.org/installation/ (Visited on 29 September 2024)).

The results of the experiment are summarized in Table 4. The table presents the average preprocessing time per image, the average time taken to create each transformation matrix, and the total time required to generate the pointclouds for the RGB, Red Edge (RE), Red (R) and Green (G) spectral bands.

Table 4. Performance metrics for use case given in Section 3.8.

Metric	Average Time (s)	RGB (s)	RE (s)	R (s)	G (s)
Preprocessing Time	3.67	–	–	–	–
Warp Matrix Creation	24.72	–	–	–	–
Pointcloud Time	–	912.28	868.09	875.95	858.71

The experimental results, summarized in Table 4, highlight the effectiveness of our distributed computing approach for pointcloud generation. The average preprocessing time per image was 3.67 s, and the creation of the warp matrix took an average of 24.72 s. We processed the pointclouds for the four spectral bands in parallel. The processing times were 912.28 s for RGB, 868.09 s for RE, 875.95 s for R and 858.71 s for G. This parallelization significantly accelerated the overall processing workflow, demonstrating that distributing computational tasks across multiple nodes reduces processing time and enhances efficiency in generating pointclouds from drone images.

5. Discussion and Conclusions

5.1. *Power Inefficiencies*

The data presented in Table 3 indicate a clear need to optimize both container and virtualization environments on ARM Edge devices, as the range of watt-to-operation requirements will place a greater demand on both power requirements, potentially affecting battery life, and heat output.

Moreover, this also demonstrates the similarities between containerization and virtualization environments when considering power consumption, allowing greater freedom for software deployment.

5.2. *Comparison Between Virtual Machines and Containers*

Both methods of virtualization present some advantages. On the one hand, VMs can provide a graphical user interface that is very useful for monitoring and testing without dealing with the network. Furthermore, VMs emulate low-layer components, allowing you to tune them to fit your needs. Thus, you can make VMs for use with real stuff like USB sticks, which is an impossible thing to do with containers.

On the other hand, you have containers. These involve high-layer virtualization, with only the packages you need and your code embedded. Therefore, containers are light and can be modified quickly due to the share of the host's OS. Containers can easily be made lightweight and compatible. The community has a lot of container images with software already built in. Developers can just pull the image and get rid of the prerequisites, accelerating software development and app deployment. Containers are developed in a static context. The files and apps within a container are not meant to change. Developing and testing an app or some software meant to be tested in a dynamical context in a container may cause compatibility or security issues.

So, regarding the use of virtual machines or containers, although the solution is not straightforward, we can say that it depends on the requirements, but we can conclude that a good method of virtualization is crucial for the success of a project. To separate apps on the same host without overloading the host with a virtual OS, containers are a must. Containers should be used when flexibility and resource efficiency are critical, especially in resource-constrained environments such as Edge Computing.

As much as containers share the OS of the host, some cases are not compatible with granularity in hardware devices, complete isolation, specific OS configurations and customer requirements. Thus, the use of VMs would be relevant in this case.

As a general conclusion, we can see that even in the worst case of the different stack tests (using the Kubernetes and Docker Engine stack, which is a common option for companies), the performance can be meaningful, although the computing power is quite low.

For future work, we will further study different use cases and the analysis of performance in bigger hardware architectures for Edge or Cloud. Also, different tests of these technologies on security issues in Edge environments will be performed in a later work for deploying services in distributed and resource-limited environments.

Furthermore, we will explore the performance impact arising from the differences in system requirements between virtualization and containerization when executing a greater variety of different parallel tasks at the Edge.

Author Contributions: Conceptualization, J.S.-G. and M.G.-P.; methodology, J.S.-G., H.S. and A.F.; software, H.S., A.F. and A.S.-N.; investigation, H.S., A.F. and A.S.-N.; resources, J.S.-G. and M.G.-P.; writing—original draft preparation, J.S.-G.; writing—review and editing, H.S., A.F., A.S.-N. and M.G.-P.; funding acquisition, J.S.-G. and M.G.-P. All authors have read and agreed to the published version of the manuscript.

Funding: This research was partially funded by the Spanish Ministry of Science and Innovation/Spanish Research Agency (MCIN/AEI) within the project Agriculture 6.0 with reference TED2021-131040B-C33 and the project ECO4RUPA with reference PID2021-126823OB-I00, funded by MCIN/AEI/10.13039/501100011033 and by the European Union "NextGenerationEU"/PRTR. Also, the Spanish Ministry of Universities for the grant number PRX22/000503. Also, we thank the Generalitat Valenciana for the grant CIBEST/2023/101 and the grant CIAEST/2022/91.

Data Availability Statement: Data are contained within the article.

Acknowledgments: The authors would like to thank the Spanish Ministry of Science and Innovation/Spanish Research Agency (MCIN/AEI) and the Generalitat Valenciana for the funding provided for the development of this research. Also, we thank Juan Gutierrez and Santiago Felici for their advice. Further thanks go to the academic and catering staff of the Escola Tècnica Superior d'Enginyeria for their support during the initial phases of the project.

Conflicts of Interest: The authors declare no conflicts of interest.

References

1. Javaid, M.; Haleem, A.; Singh, R.P.; Suman, R. Artificial Intelligence Applications for Industry 4.0: A Literature-Based Study. *J. Ind. Integr. Manag.* **2022**, *07*, 83–111. [CrossRef]
2. Robles-Enciso, A.; Skarmeta, A.F. Adapting Containerized Workloads for the Continuum Computing. *IEEE Access* **2024**, *12*, 104102–104114. [CrossRef]
3. M, A.; Dinkar, A.; Mouli, S.C.; B, S.; Deshpande, A.A. Comparison of Containerization and Virtualization in Cloud Architectures. In Proceedings of the 2021 IEEE International Conference on Electronics, Computing and Communication Technologies (CONECCT), Bangalore, India, 9–11 July 2021; pp. 1–5. [CrossRef]
4. Odun-Ayo, I.; Geteloma, V.; Eweoya, I.; Ahuja, R. Virtualization, Containerization, Composition, and Orchestration of Cloud Computing Services. In Proceedings of the Computational Science and Its Applications—ICCSA 2019, Saint Petersburg, Russia, 1–4 July 2019; Misra, S., Gervasi, O., Murgante, B., Stankova, E., Korkhov, V., Torre, C., Rocha, A.M.A., Taniar, D., Apduhan, B.O., Tarantino, E., Eds.; Springer: Cham, Switzerland, 2019; pp. 403–417.
5. da Cunha, H.G.V.O.; Moreira, R.; de Oliveira Silva, F. A Comparative Study Between Containerization and Full-Virtualization of Virtualized Everything Functions in Edge Computing. In *Proceedings of the Advanced Information Networking and Applications;* Barolli, L., Woungang, I., Enokido, T., Eds.; Springer: Cham, Switzerland, 2021; pp. 771–782.
6. Fayos-Jordan, R.; Felici-Castell, S.; Segura-Garcia, J.; Lopez-Ballester, J.; Cobos, M. Performance comparison of container orchestration platforms with low cost devices in the fog, assisting Internet of Things applications. *J. Netw. Comput. Appl.* **2020**, *169*, 102788. [CrossRef]
7. Ouro, P.; Lopez-Novoa, U.; Guest, M.F. On the performance of a highly-scalable Computational Fluid Dynamics code on AMD, ARM and Intel processor-based HPC systems. *Comput. Phys. Commun.* **2021**, *269*, 108105. [CrossRef]
8. Tso, F.P.; White, D.R.; Jouet, S.; Singer, J.; Pezaros, D.P. The Glasgow Raspberry Pi Cloud: A Scale Model for Cloud Computing Infrastructures. In Proceedings of the 2013 IEEE 33rd International Conference on Distributed Computing Systems Workshops, Philadelphia, PA, USA, 8–11 July 2013; pp. 108–112. [CrossRef]

9. Queiroz, R.; Cruz, T.; Mendes, J.; Sousa, P.; Simões, P. Container-based Virtualization for Real-time Industrial Systems—A Systematic Review. *ACM Comput. Surv.* **2023**, *56*, 59. [CrossRef]
10. Bhardwaj, A.; Krishna, C.R. Virtualization in Cloud Computing: Moving from Hypervisor to Containerization—A Survey. *Arab. J. Sci. Eng.* **2021**, *46*, 8585–8601. [CrossRef]
11. Silva, V.G.d.; Kirikova, M.; Alksnis, G. Containers for Virtualization: An Overview. *Appl. Comput. Syst.* **2018**, *23*, 21–27. [CrossRef]
12. Abuabdo, A.; Al-Sharif, Z.A. Virtualization vs. Containerization: Towards a Multithreaded Performance Evaluation Approach. In Proceedings of the 2019 IEEE/ACS 16th International Conference on Computer Systems and Applications (AICCSA), Abu Dhabi, United Arab Emirates, 3–7 November 2019; pp. 1–6. [CrossRef]
13. Mondesire, S.C.; Angelopoulou, A.; Sirigampola, S.; Goldiez, B. Combining virtualization and containerization to support interactive games and simulations on the cloud. *Simul. Model. Pract. Theory* **2019**, *93*, 233–244. [CrossRef]
14. Eder, M. Hypervisor- vs. Container-based Virtualization. Seminar Future Internet WS2015/16—Network Architectures and Services. July 2016. Available online: https://www.net.in.tum.de/fileadmin/TUM/NET/NET-2016-07-1/NET-2016-07-1_01.pdf (accessed on 28 August 2024).
15. Mansouri, Y.; Babar, M.A. A review of edge computing: Features and resource virtualization. *J. Parallel Distrib. Comput.* **2021**, *150*, 155–183. [CrossRef]
16. Morabito, R. Virtualization on Internet of Things Edge Devices with Container Technologies: A Performance Evaluation. *IEEE Access* **2017**, *5*, 8835–8850. [CrossRef]
17. Liu, Y.; Lan, D.; Pang, Z.; Karlsson, M.; Gong, S. Performance Evaluation of Containerization in Edge-Cloud Computing Stacks for Industrial Applications: A Client Perspective. *IEEE Open J. Ind. Electron. Soc.* **2021**, *2*, 153–168. [CrossRef]
18. King, C.I. Stress-ng. 2024. Available online: https://github.com/ColinIanKing/stress-ng (accessed on 24 August 2024).
19. Murray, C. Linux Handbook. Available online: https://linuxhandbook.com/top-command/ (accessed on 28 August 2024).
20. Ruiden, K. UM42C USB Power Meter Manual. Available online: https://fccid.io/2A5Y7-UM34C/User-Manual/User-manual-5807006.pdf (accessed on 28 August 2024).
21. Finnie, R. rdumtool—RDTech UM24C/UM25C/UM34C Bluetooth Interface Tool. Available online: https://github.com/smandon/rdumtool (accessed on 28 August 2024).
22. Undack. Containerpaper Repository. Available online: https://github.com/Undack/Containerpaper (accessed on 27 September 2024).
23. Catala-Roman, P.; Navarro, E.A.; Segura-Garcia, J.; Garcia-Pineda, M. Harnessing Digital Twins for Agriculture 5.0: A Comparative Analysis of 3D Point Cloud Tools. *Appl. Sci.* **2024**, *14*, 1709. [CrossRef]
24. OpenDroneMap. 2024. Available online: https://www.opendronemap.org/ (accessed on 20 August 2024).
25. Authors, O. ODM—A Command Line Toolkit to Generate Maps, Point Clouds, 3D Models and DEMs from Drone, Balloon or Kite Images. OpenDroneMap/ODM GitHub Page. 2020. Available online: https://github.com/OpenDroneMap/ODM (accessed on 20 August 2024).

future internet

MDPI

Article

On Exploiting and Implementing Collaborative Virtual and Augmented Reality in a Cloud Continuum Scenario

Beniamino Di Martino [1,†], Gennaro Junior Pezzullo [1,*,†], Vincenzo Bombace [1,†], Ling-Huey Li [2,†] and Kuan-Ching Li [2,*,†]

1 Department of Engineering, University of Campania "Luigi Vanvitelli", 81031 Aversa, Italy; beniamino.dimartino@unicampania.it (B.D.M.); vincenzo.bombace@studenti.unicampania.it (V.B.)
2 Department of Computer Science and Information Engineering (CSIE), Providence University, Taichung 43301, Taiwan
* Correspondence: gennaro.pezzullo@unicampus.it (G.J.P.); kuancli@pu.edu.tw (K.-C.L.)
† These authors contributed equally to this work.

Abstract: This work explores the application of collaborative virtual and augmented reality in a cloud continuum context, focusing on designing, implementing, and verifying three reference architectures for five collaborative VR/AR software deployment. The architectures designed differ in their distribution of computational load: one handles everything in the cloud, one balances the load between the cloud and the edge, and the last concentrates the load entirely on the edge. The design of the architectures was initially outlined through sequence and component diagrams and then implemented using the most appropriate technologies and frameworks. For each architecture, a specific application was developed and deployed on the various components of that architecture to test its proper functioning. Finally, the scenarios were simulated to be stressed with a significant number of users, employing tools such as Cloud Analyst to analyze performance and present well-defined and implemented reference architectures.

Keywords: cloud continuum; cloud edge; virtual reality; augmented reality; simulation

1. Introduction

In recent years, the rapid advancement of technology has led to the convergence of solutions such as cloud computing and augmented reality (AR), opening up new frontiers in human experiences. Despite these advances, there are still significant challenges regarding latency, scalability, and real-time processing, especially for applications that require highly interactive and immersive environments. A significant limitation of current systems lies in the centralized nature of cloud computing, which often needs help to meet the rigorous performance requirements for real-time applications, particularly in environments where multiple users must collaborate in a shared virtual space. This has created an urgent need for solutions to bring computational resources closer to the user, minimizing delays and improving overall performance. In this context, edge computing [1,2] has emerged as a fundamental pillar, providing a decentralized computing infrastructure that enables data processing closer to end users. This proximity reduces latency and improves the responsiveness of critical applications such as collaborative AR. The shift from traditional cloud-based models to edge computing architectures represents a paradigm shift in how data-intensive and latency-sensitive applications are designed and deployed. Collaborative AR, where multiple users can share and interact with virtual objects in real time within a common space, is an excellent example of a technology that benefits significantly from edge computing. This type of AR application requires synchronization among multiple devices, low-latency data transmission, and high computational capacity to maintain smooth interaction and collaboration among users. Failure to meet these requirements can lead to a degraded user experience, making the technology unsuitable for critical sectors such as industrial operations or healthcare, where accuracy and reliability are critical. The interplay between cloud edge computing [3] and collaborative AR can revolutionize these areas by enabling more robust and scalable systems that support real-time collaboration between geographically dispersed users. This paper will explore the connection between these two technologies through case studies, experiments, and theoretical analysis to contribute to the landscape of edge-enabled collaborative systems [4]. Specifically, the focus will be on designing, implementing, and testing different reference architectures for collaborative AR. These architectures will vary in how the computational load is distributed, gradually moving from cloud-centric models to those with more edge-based components. This work is structured as follows: In Section 2, we present a review of the state of the art, exploring current research and technological advances in edge computing and collaborative augmented reality (AR). In Section 3, we outline the specific goals of this research, which include the design, development, and testing of several reference architectures for collaborative AR. Section 4 will provide a detailed definition of the reference architectures with component realizations and sequence diagrams to outline the different modules and their interactions. These architectures will be designed with varying degrees of dependence on cloud resources. In Section 5, the technologies used to implement each architecture will be described. In addition, the several applications we implement will be described and deployed on the different architectures to validate how they work in real-world scenarios. In Section 6, we conduct performance evaluations of the implemented architectures through simulations. These tests, conducted with the Cloud Analyst simulation platform, will evaluate how the defined architectures behave as the number of users scales. Finally, in Section 7, we summarize the main research findings, discuss the broader implications of integrating edge computing with collaborative AR, and suggest directions for future work.

2. State of the Art

The numerous processes carried out in the last few decades, both in the cloud continuum and in immersive platforms in virtual, augmented [5], and hybrid reality scenarios [6], have opened the doors to numerous application scenarios for these technologies.

2.1. Cloud and Edge Computing

While cloud computing has opened the doors to unlimited resources, it suffers from intrinsic problems related to the remoteness of resources. In this context, edge computing presents itself as a solution that moves resources closer to the user. Recent studies and frameworks have highlighted the effectiveness of edge computing in improving performance in many contexts [7,8]. Among these, we include VR/AR systems due to the interaction of real-time components and the high bandwidth of the transferred data, which represents a significant challenge in this context. On the other hand, the edge has limited resources [9], which leads to poor scalability, which translates to a rapid drop in performance in terms of computation when the number of simultaneously connected users increases. For this reason, hybrid cloud edge architectures combining the strengths of cloud and edge computing allow the distribution of computational tasks between cloud servers and edge devices based on their computational needs and latency requirements. The development of hybrid architectures is supported by the continuous increase in IoT devices and the advances in network technologies such as 5G.

2.2. Collaborative Virtual and Augmented Reality

Collaborative VR/AR involves multiple users interacting with virtual objects or shared environments [10]. One of the earliest works in the context of collaborative augmented reality was Rekimoto's Transvision system, which made it possible for multiple people to simultaneously access graphical elements of a table [11]. From then on, a lot of work has been conducted in this field in the different sectors: from an entertainment context [12] to an industrial context [13,14]. This continued interest has also led to the definition of frameworks, especially in a mobile device context [15]. Current systems use a combination of cloud and edge computing to manage the synchronization of virtual environments between different users. Studies have demonstrated various approaches to manage the synchronization of user actions and the sharing of virtual assets [16], ensuring that all participants have a consistent experience; however, our study differs from others because different architectures specific to AR will be defined in which the components are gradually moved from the cloud to the edge to verify, in other contexts, which among them is the most appropriate solution for different use cases.

3. Objectives and Methodology

This paper contributes to the state of the art by offering new insights into the design of cloud edge architectures for collaborative AR systems, validating different architectural models through detailed case studies, and presenting empirical data based on simulations. The proposed solutions are tested in various real-world scenarios, showcasing their applicability and benefits in practical settings. So, the main objective of this work is to define different and valid reference architectures for deploying VR and AR applications on cloud continuum infrastructures. These architectures will be structured in such a way as to carry the computation load from the core to the edge. This work was carried out as follows to achieve the previously described objectives. First, in Section 4, we defined three different architectures using UML diagrams [17]; in particular, we used component diagrams to define the single components and sequence diagrams to show their interoperability. The next step was to determine the technologies that would implement the individual components of all architectures. After defining and implementing the different architectures to validate them, as mentioned in the introduction, ad hoc applications were developed for each architecture, which we will see in detail in the Section 5. This was carried out to validate the operation of the aforementioned architectures. Finally, the last phase involved simulation, using Cloud Analyst, to validate these architectures as users scaled up. In detail, we simulated, for the same computational capacity of edge and server components, how response times vary as users vary up to a maximum of 1000 users.

4. Architecture

In this section, different reference architectures will be shown. They are presented in the following order: we start from a cloud center architecture in which almost all operations are performed in the cloud and then gradually move the computational load to the edge. For each architecture, the scenarios and mechanisms of use will be presented.

4.1. Centralized IoT System with Prevalent Processing in the Cloud

The first architecture deals with scanning real objects and their real-time reconstruction in virtual environments through sensors. The various components are presented in the component diagram in Figure 1.

The architecture is divided into two main macro areas. The **Edge** part, in this case, consists only of the various **Client** components that represent a new *"user"* and is responsible for connecting to the cloud server to access the scene shared with other users. It also sends and receives data relating to the object previously recognized by the sensors. The goal is to have one-to-one movement between what the sensor detects and what the cloud reconstructs. The **Cloud** part, on the other hand, is divided into four main components, which are as follows:

- **Cloud Server**: The cloud server acts as a central point for managing multiplayer connections and processing the tracking data of the object to be recognized. It receives data from clients and routes them for scene processing and synchronization. It uses scalable and reliable cloud resources to ensure a stable connection and rapid data processing.
- **Object Collider**: This is the component responsible for detecting the movements of the user's object using the sensor. It captures the data relating to the position and orientation, and then transmits them to the client for 3D processing and sending to

the central server. This saving of the individual positions also allows events to be triggered when there is a collision between reconstructed objects and between a single reconstructed object and a single scene object.

- **Object Creation**: The processing component receives the object tracking data from the server and processes them by creating the associated 3D model the clients need, subsequently routing them via the server to the client.
- **Reconstruction of Data**: to create the object, it is necessary first to reconstruct the object starting from the data that construct the sensors. A rule-based approach or machine and deep learning algorithms [18] can achieve this in many ways.

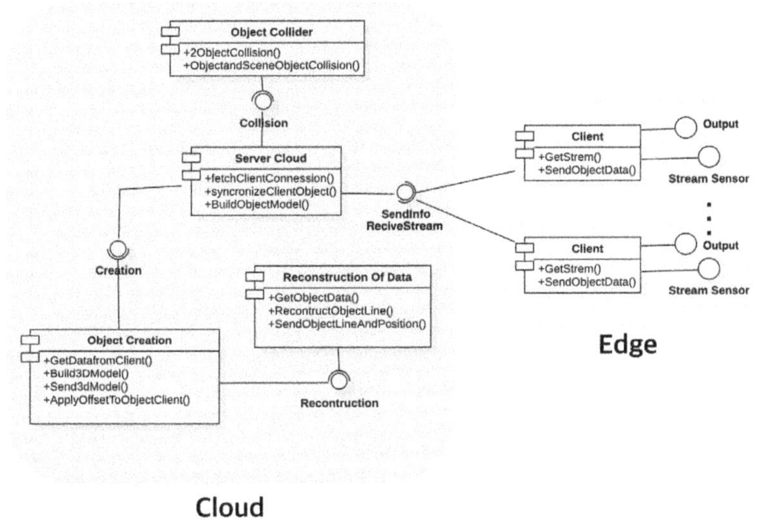

Figure 1. This figure shows a component diagram of the first reference architecture in which the entire computation is shifted to the cloud.

The sequence diagram in Figure 2 describes the interaction between these components and their workflow. The client component uses a sensor to capture external data sent to the cloud in real time. The server uses the *Object Creation* and *Reconstruction of Data* components to reconstruct the 3D object. In more detail, the Reconstruction of Data component reconstructs the object of interest from the data, and the Object Creation component maps it in 3D. For example, assuming you want to recognize a person's movements, the first component will identify the object in the data stream and map its movements, and the other will reconstruct the avatar based on the real person's movements. Furthermore, particular attention must be paid to the *ApplyOffsetToObjectClient* method (Figure 3).

Depending on the number of clients connecting, this method allows a starting offset to be assigned to the individual client reconstruction in the virtual world. The process is dynamic and recalculated each time a new user connects. This algorithm aims to ensure that the generation of 3D objects in VR is associated with a different client and never overlaps. So, the first defined architecture provides a robust and scalable infrastructure through centralized data management. In addition, maintenance and upgrades are facilitated. However, depending entirely on the cloud can cause bandwidth limitations and slow performance when managing large data sets or numerous connected devices.

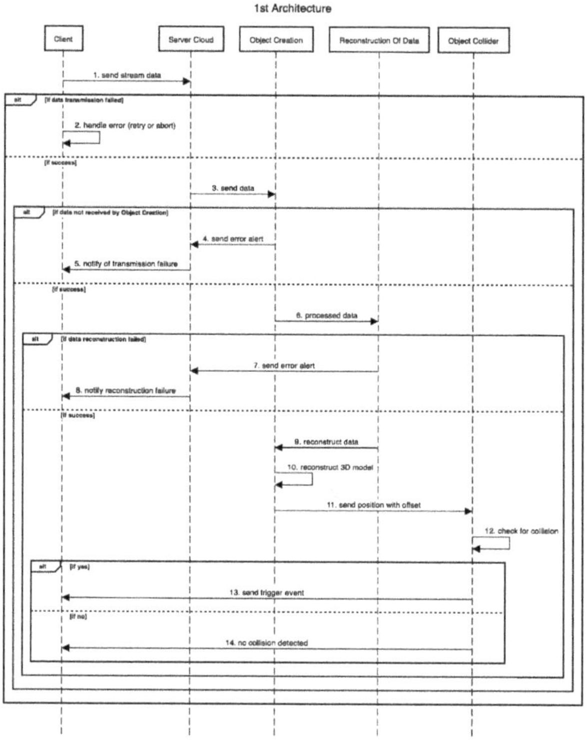

Figure 2. This diagram shows the flow and the error-handling mechanisms of the first reference architecture to send data, reconstruct a 3D model, check collisions and trigger events, involving the client, object creation, data reconstruction, and the cloud server.

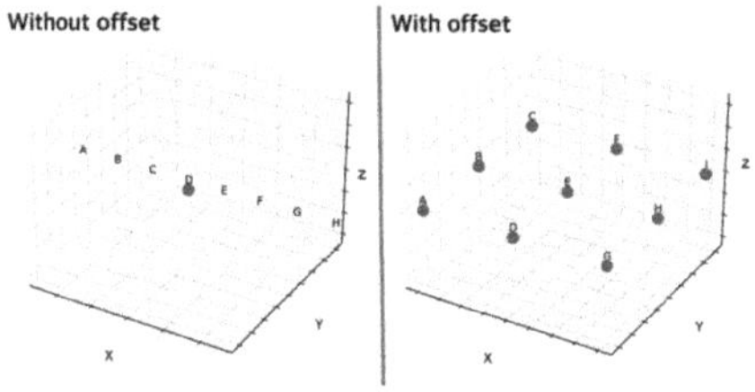

Figure 3. This figure allows you to visually understand what happens if an offset is not properly scheduled depending on the number of participants. In the first case, all the spawns are overlapped. In the second case, however, the spawns are perfectly ordered depending on the number of participants (in this specific case, nine).

4.2. Hybrid IoT Infrastructure with Balanced Processing Between Cloud and Edge

In this second architecture, there is the addition of some components that have been repositioned in an environment architecturally closer to IoT devices (Figure 4).

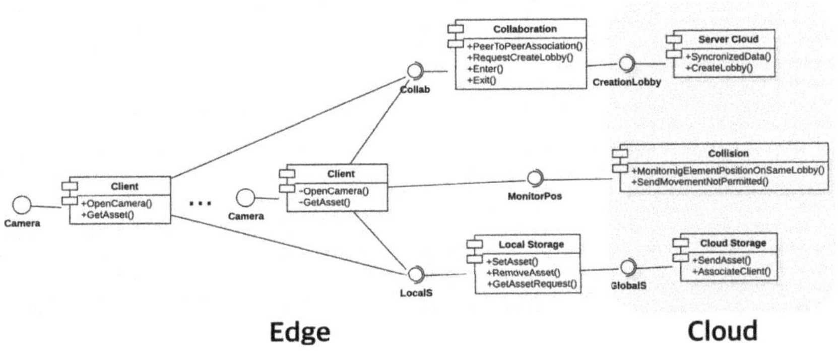

Figure 4. This figure depicts a component diagram of the second reference architecture, in which the computation is balanced between the cloud and the edge.

Even the devices themselves have been imagined to be computationally more efficient and capable of performing more complex operations than just sending and receiving data. The "Collision" component placed in the cloud functions as a monitor that can view all user locations thanks to the "Client" component at any instant and trigger events based on these locations. An example could be limiting movements to an area or triggering an event if multiple users are in the same location. "Cloud Storage" and "Local Storage" components were introduced, both dedicated to data management and storage. The choice to separate the storage function from the server compared to the previous architecture was made to allow collaboration between the "Cloud Storage" and the "Local Storage". In particular, through a specific algorithm, the saving of objects intended to be used in the scenario, both in AR and VR, is managed. This algorithm aims to optimize the loading and unloading of data from the server, keeping the most frequently used objects local. In detail, if the object has reached a usage threshold and space is available, it is saved. If there is no space, the least used item is removed and replaced with the new one. Figure 5.

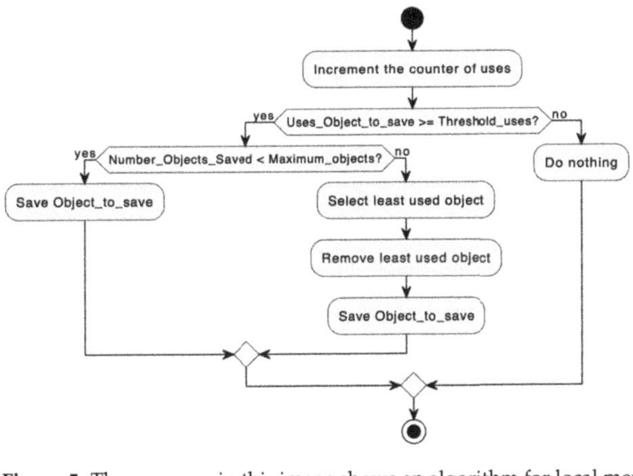

Figure 5. The sequence in this image shows an algorithm for local memory management in which an object is saved or replaced based on the number of uses and maximum memory capacity.

Finally, synchronization between multiple users has been divided into two components, one managed in the cloud and the other on the edge. The "Collaboration" component creates and manages the different lobbies. Specifically, it is responsible for processing requests based on the number of users and managing peer-to-peer connections. It instructs the "Server Cloud" to create new lobbies to optimize participant collaboration when necessary. Concerning the workflow of the various components, this is described in the component diagram in Figure 6, except the "Collision" component, since it has the same function as "Object Collider" in the previous architecture. For this reason, it was preferred to hide it so as not to make it hard to read.

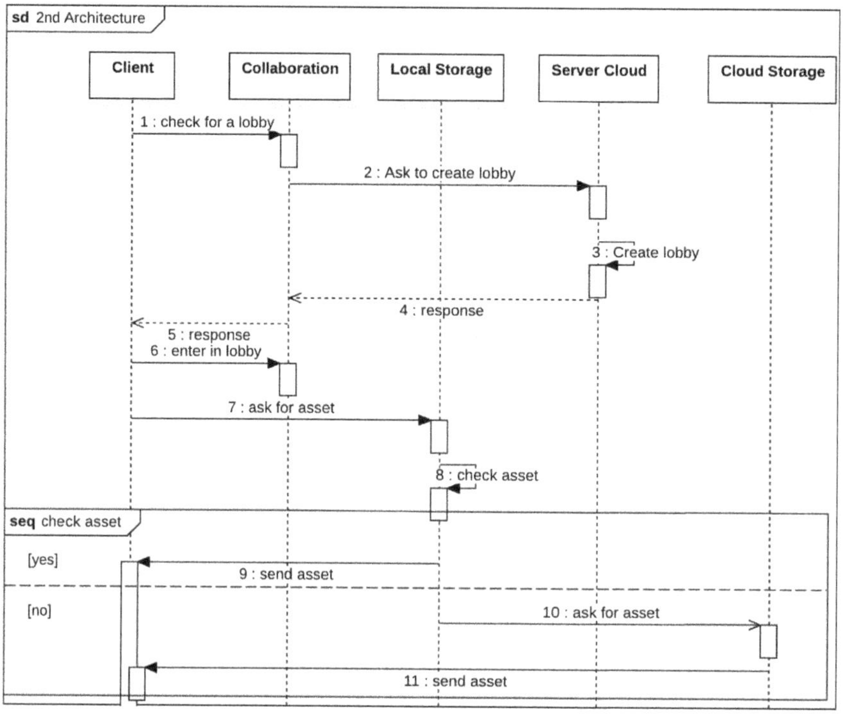

Figure 6. This sequence diagram shows the main operations of the second architecture, including lobby creation, asset management, and the interaction between local client storage, the cloud server, and cloud storage.

As you can see from Figure 6, the operation is as follows: starting from the client, it first requests to enter the lobby. If no lobby is active, the *Server Cloud* component is asked to create one. After carrying out this request, different objects can be inserted into the AR and/or VR scene through a request made via the client, first to the local storage, and in the cases where it does not possess the requested asset, to the cloud storage. During the entire session, the positions of the assets are continuously updated and monitored by the *Collision* component in the cloud, which takes care of unleashing triggers based on the type of collision. Thus, the second architecture represents a balanced compromise between cloud and edge processing. Some operations are handled locally in this context, easing network traffic and optimizing bandwidth usage. However, it requires more powerful devices and may suffer from synchronization problems when connections are unstable.

4.3. Decentralized IoT Solution with Prevalent Processing at the Edge

In our presented architecture, the computational load has been wholly repositioned towards the edge, leaving only storage and synchronization functions to the cloud (Figure 7).

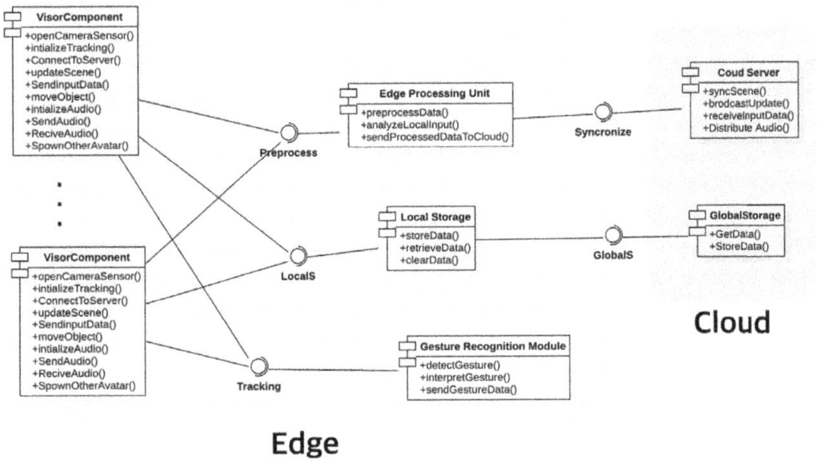

Figure 7. This figure shows a component diagram of the third reference architecture, in which most of the operations are shifted to the edge.

In fact, only two components have been placed within the cloud, which are the cloud server and Global Storage. The former is the heart of the synchronization logic and management of collaborative sessions, supporting crucial operations such as the following:

- **SyncScene**: Ensures all devices display an updated and synchronized scene version.
- **BroadcastUpdate**: Broadcasts changes made to the scene to all participants, ensuring consistency in the shared experience.
- **ReceiveInputData**: Processes input received from users to update the state of the scene accordingly.
- **DistributeAudio**: Handles the distribution of audio signals among participants, allowing voice interactions within the virtual environment.

As for cloud storage, this operates in exactly the same way as defined in the previous architecture and shown in Figure 5. For these reasons, we will not describe it a second time. As for the edge side, this is composed of the main component, the **Visor Component**, which constitutes the interface through which users interact with the augmented reality environment, offering a range of essential features:

- **OpenCameraSensor**: Activates the camera sensors to integrate virtual elements into the real scene visible to the user.
- **InitializeTracking**: Initializes the tracking of the user's movements and position, allowing intuitive interactions with the virtual scene.
- **ConnectToServer**: Establishes a connection with the cloud server to access the shared scene and synchronize the experience with other users.
- **UpdateScene**: Updates the virtual scene display based on user inputs and updates from the cloud server.
- **SendInputData**: Transmits input data to the cloud server, such as movements and selections.
- **MoveObject**: Allows users to change the position of objects within the virtual scene.
- **InitializeAudio**: Prepares the audio system for user voice communication.
- **SendAudio/ReceiveAudio**: Manages the sending and receiving of audio streams, facilitating real-time communication.
- **SpawnOtherAvatar**: Generates virtual representations of other users, enriching the shared scene with their virtual presence.

The other supporting components are in **Local Storage**, which works similarly to Global Storage (Figure 5). A component called the **Gesture Recognition Module** will be responsible for interpreting the gestures and associating them with a movement. Finally, the Edge Processing Unit has the task of preprocessing the data to send to the cloud Server. Let us now analyze the interactions between these components by analyzing a communication prototype using a sequence diagram Figure 8.

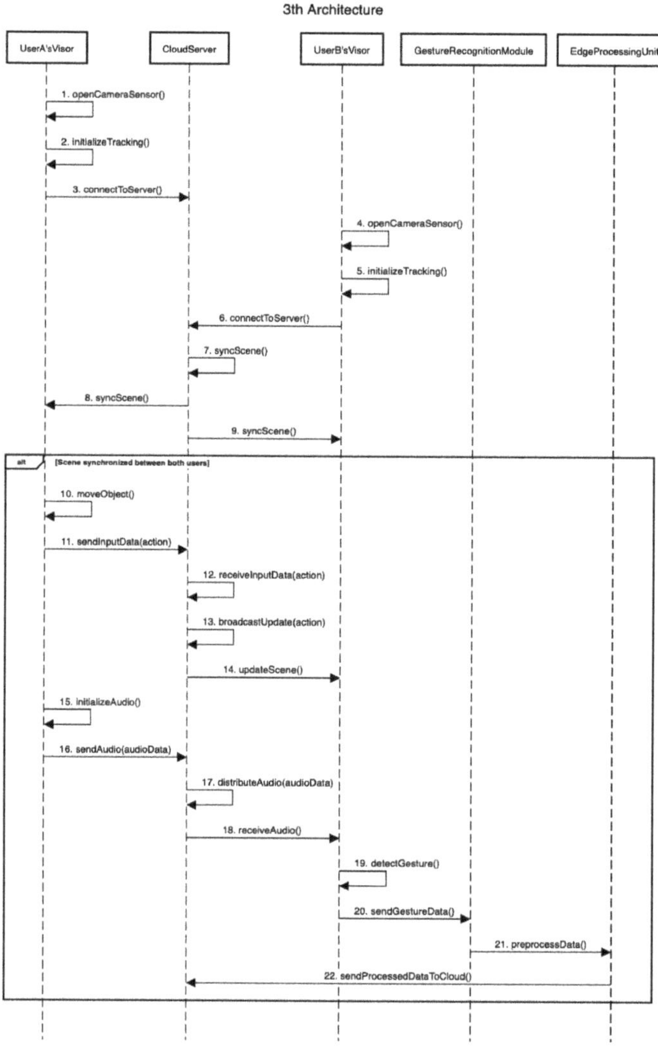

Figure 8. This sequence diagram shows the main operations for synchronizing a scene and sharing audio data between two users (User A and User B), using viewers, cloud servers, gesture recognition modules, and processing units at the edge. The flow includes opening camera sensors, synchronizing the scene, updating objects, and sharing real-time audio and gesture data.

This sequence reflects a typical workflow that allows users to share and interact within the same virtual scene superimposed on the real world, highlighting the collaborative capabilities of the application. At the start of the session, User A and User B activate their respective headsets, which begin tracking their movements and position through the *initializeTracking()* method that calls the **Gesture Recognition Module** component. This is essential to allow the system to interpret and respond to the movements and interactions of the users within the physical environment. Subsequently, the headsets connect with the cloud server via *connectToServer()*, a crucial step that allows users to access the same virtual scene and collaborate in real-time. Once the connection is established, the server proceeds with the initial synchronization of the scene for both users, sending the current state of the virtual environment via *syncScene()*, ensuring that User A and User B see a consistent and up-to-date representation of the shared scene. User A interacts with a virtual object during the session by moving it within the scene. Their headset captures this action via *sendInputData(action)*, then communicates the update to the cloud server. The server processes the input received and, through *broadcastUpdates(action)*, propagates the changes to all connected users, including User B, who receives the update and sees the modified scene thanks to updateScene(). At the same time, an audio communication dimension develops between the users. User A sends audio data (such as words or sounds) that, passing through the server via *sendAudio(audioData)* and *distributeAudio(audioData)*, reach User B, allowing them to listen to User A in real time. When User B moves within the environment, their actions are transmitted to the server, which, in turn, updates User A on the new position of User B in the virtual scene, ensuring that the changes are visible to all participants. It is worth noting that at the same time as the user's movement tracking initialization process, a series of routines are started that involve all the sensors, including the camera, which is essential for the success of an augmented reality application. Finally, it is worth noting that a routine that is constantly called is *UpdateScene()*, which calls the camera update for each frame. The last architecture moves processing almost entirely to the network edge, dramatically reducing latency and making the system more independent of cloud disruptions. The decentralized model is also well suited for use in areas with limited connectivity.

5. Implementation

After logically defining three reference architectures, this section will show the technologies used to implement them, mapping them for each component. Only then, before proceeding with simulations, will different applications be developed to demonstrate the correct design for each of the three architectures. Each application will be a concrete example of use, showing how each architecture behaves in real-life usage contexts.

5.1. Technologies Used

The main technologies used are shown in the Figure 9. They are described in detail below, specifying the technologies used and the relevant version implemented:

- **Python, v3.6**: the language used to implement the motion capture system.
- **Unity 2022.3.19f1 and C#**: Unity was used as the main framework for the design of the three different architectures. Furthermore, specific scripts were created in C# for the more complex tasks.
- **OpenCV v3.2**: a fundamental Python library for implementing the first architecture, as it allows the use of pre-trained machine learning models [19].
- **Flusk v1.1**: a framework that allows the easy implementation of multiplayer software, particularly optimized for Unity.
- **Docker v4.30**: mainly used to create volumes capable of storing pre-loaded 3D assets [20].
- **Android Studio and Xcode**: used to convert applications created in Unity for the iOS and Android operating systems, respectively [21].
- **Firebase**: mainly used as online storage through the Firestore and Storage services [22].
- **Normcore**: a cloud service mainly used to share real-time data. After implementing the different architectures, each was validated through different case studies to verify their functioning and performance [23].

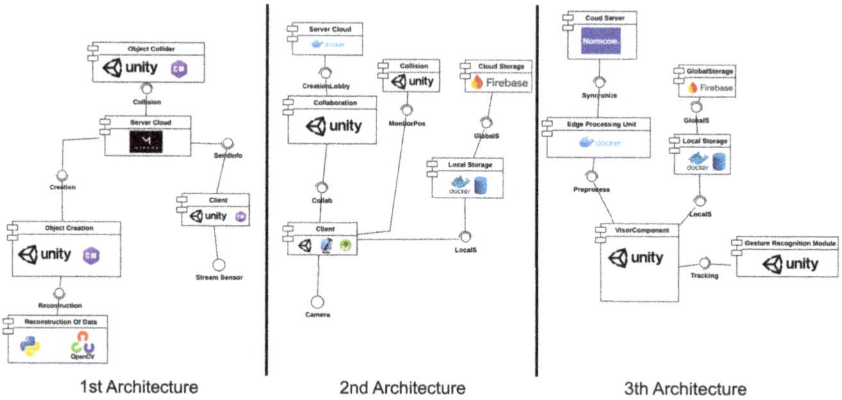

Figure 9. This figure shows the three reference architectures mapped with the most appropriate technologies to implement.

The following subsections present several case studies we implemented to evaluate the effectiveness and performance of the reference architectures described in Section 4. These case studies focus on different interaction paradigms, using both virtual reality (VR) and augmented reality (AR) technologies to create collaborative environments.

5.2. Case Study for First Architecture: Collaborative Virtual Reality with Hand Recognition

For the first reference architecture mentioned in the previous section, an application was implemented to verify its proper functioning. It is a virtual space where different users can interact with each other or virtual objects. The user's hand represents the connection point between the real and virtual worlds. The operation is as follows: the user places his or her hand, left or right, in front of the camera. This captures the video stream and sends it in real time to the cloud. Here, the Object Creation component deals with virtual hand reconstruction using a rule-based approach, leveraging the Reconstruction of Data component, which identifies 21 different hand landmarks through a specific model called the Hand Landmarks Detection Model [24–26] (Figure 10).

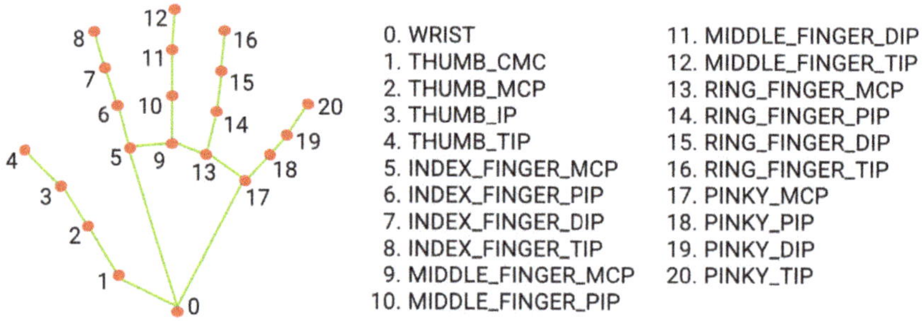

Figure 10. This figure conceptually illustrates the division of the hand into 21 points, allowing real-time tracking of the independent movements of each finger or the entire hand.

Depending on the number of connected users, the arrangement of individual hands within the virtual space changes, as described in the architecture. Collaboration was implemented through two different approaches: the possibility for each user to interact with virtual objects, which, in this scenario, are simple geometric figures embedded in the environment, and the possibility of interaction between multiple users (Figure 11).

Figure 11. Screenshot of the application in operation, deployed on the first architecture, with three different users connected. Through its hand reconstruction, one of them interacts with the shared objects within the scene, specifically the cubes.

5.3. Case Studies for Second Architecture: Collaborative Augmented Reality with the Use of a Smartphone

For the second architecture, two different case studies based on smartphones were deployed, involving using three-dimensional objects collaboratively within a real environment. The creation of this applications is also based on the use of Unity [27,28]; unlike the previous case, the edge part manages the spawning of objects and interactions with them. For collaboration, the devices will use the local network to create a "room", thanks to which each client will communicate to all room members, through P2P [29] messages, the positions or movements of an object.

Once the user selects an object, the activated edge component is in local storage. At this stage, an initial request is sent to the local storage, which searches its Docker volume [30].The local storage contains previously downloaded objects from the cloud and sends them directly to the client for use if the object is already present. If, on the other hand, the object is not available locally, a new request is generated for cloud storage based on Firebase. The cloud storage system is structured through key-value logic, optimized to speed up the search for and retrieval of needed items.

Several users tested the applications by downloading an APK file to their Android devices, allowing them to experience them on their own. For iOS devices, on the other hand, users had to go to dedicated booths, where the application was built directly from a PC to enable its installation and use. This approach ensured a smooth and customized experience for both operating systems. Two separate applications were developed. The first, created for the "We Make Future" fair in Bologna, Italy, at the MiC (Ministry of Culture) booth and illustrated in Figure 12, allowed multiple users to interact with shared virtual objects. The second application, presented as a prototype at an exhibition at the Central State Archives in Rome, was later deployed to enable use in a collaborative scenario, where participants could browse several digitized historical volumes collaboratively.

Figure 12. The two frames show the two different collaborative applications related to the two case studies described and developed. In the first frame, the action represents the translation of an object, visible in real-time to all participants, who can observe the interaction simultaneously. The second frame, on the other hand, is a collaborative experience in which a book is browsed and shown, with all participants viewing the process in real-time. Both applications highlight the possibilities for shared interaction within augmented virtual environments.

5.4. *Case Studies for Third Architecture: Collaborative Hybrid Virtual and Augmented Reality with Use of Headset*

Finally, for the third architecture, two separate applications were developed and deployed, both characterized by the fact that most of the processing is shifted to the edge, using visors that handle real-time tracking of users' head and hand movements. In the first case, the main goal was to create an augmented reality (AR) experience by overlaying virtual elements on top of the real-world video stream users perceive. For this project, the library *MixedRealityToolkit* [31] provides an integrated framework for handling advanced inputs such as gestures and spatial interactions. This framework enables the development of immersive experiences without programming basic functionality from scratch. The scenario implemented (depicted in Figure 13) involves each user viewing, via his or her viewer, a combination of the real environment and an overlaid virtual layer when the application is started. The latter contains various interactive objects that can be shared and manipulated collaboratively among multiple users. In addition, each participant can move freely within their physical space, and their position and movements are represented to other participants in the room through virtual avatars. This system promotes interaction and collaboration in an enriched environment where physical and virtual reality merge. In the second case, an AR application was built and deployed that allows users to interact with both NPC (non-player character) avatars and other connected users (clients). In this context, real users can freely communicate with each other, while NPCs follow a predefined behavior: they can answer questions or ask questions based on a programmed script. This second scenario differs from the first in that the interaction is shifted from collaboration on virtual objects to social interaction between participants and NPCs, adding a narrative dimension to the experience.

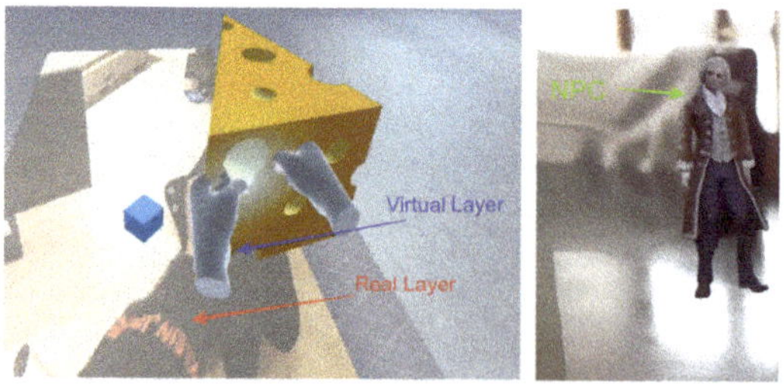

Figure 13. Two different frames were captured. While using the application, the former shows how the real flow (the user's arm) is superimposed on a virtual flow (reconstructed hands and a shared usable object). The latter shows the interaction with an NPC in the real-world.

6. Testing and Validation

This section shows the simulations performed, and the results obtained are discussed (see Table 1). CloudAnalyst [32] was used for all simulations. It is a simulation tool based on CloudSim [33,34], specifically designed to model and analyze the impact of the geographic distribution of cloud computing resources on performance.

It provides an interface to characterize the nodes regarding computational capacity, storage space, geographic location, network characteristics, and the number of concurrent users. After preparing the environment, it is possible to launch the simulation and obtain performance measures through the use of this tool, which we will analyze in this section. The Cloud Analyst tool was configured to simulate the three different architectures defined in Section 4 with the nodes represented in Figure 14. In detail, the characterizing nodes are as follows: UB_1, UB_2, UB_3, UB_4, and UB_5 represent the various pulls of users that can vary from a value n to a value n′. In our specific case, four different simulations were carried out for each of the three architectures. The number of UB_S was set to 5, the peak user hours for each UB were set from 3:00 P.M. to 9:00 P.M., and the number of users varied in the following way. NUB_{min} is denominated as the minimum number of users for each UB, NUB_{max} is the number of connected users for each UB, N_{max} is the maximum number of total connected users, and N_{min} is the minimum number of connected users. The configurations considered are as follows:

1. $NUB_{\text{min}} = 0$ and $NUB_{\text{max}} = 1 \Rightarrow N_{\text{min}} = 0$ and $N_{\text{max}} = 5$.
2. $NUB_{\text{min}} = 1$ and $NUB_{\text{max}} = 10 \Rightarrow N_{\text{min}} = 5$ and $N_{\text{max}} = 50$.
3. $NUB_{\text{min}} = 10$ and $NUB_{\text{max}} = 100 \Rightarrow N_{\text{min}} = 50$ and $N_{\text{max}} = 500$.
4. $NUB_{\text{min}} = 100$ and $NUB_{\text{max}} = 1000 \Rightarrow N_{\text{min}} = 500$ and $N_{\text{max}} = 5000$.

As for the components in red, these represent the cloud and edge resources on which we deployed the components described in the section dedicated to architectures (e.g., Server Cloud is SC). In the simulations carried out, the virtual machines created for the server were equipped with 10 TB of storage, 150 GB of RAM and Intel Xeon processors. The edge virtual machines, on the other hand, had 500 GB of storage, 10 GB of RAM, and a 4-core ARM CPU. Since most of the services used came from America, we simulated the resources as if they were allocated by consistently setting the data transmission time with this design choice. As for the edge components, these were simulated by setting the latency time appropriately low to simulate a resource allocated close to the IoT devices and a reduced computational capacity based on the preliminary tests performed in the implementation.

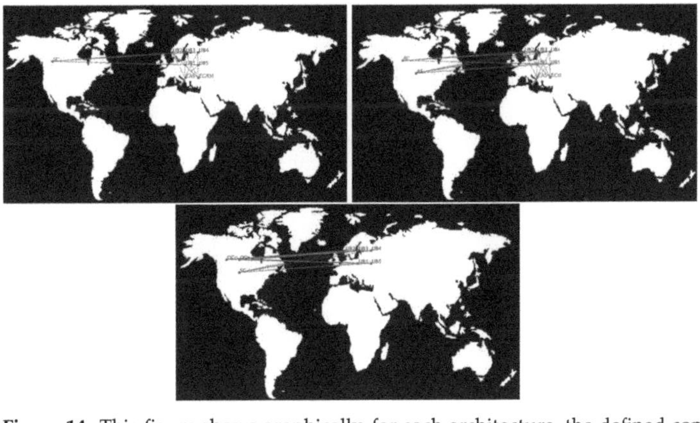

Figure 14. This figure shows graphically, for each architecture, the defined components and user groups, highlighting the interactions between the users and the various components.

Table 1. Simulation results: average, minimum, and maximum response times of the three architectures in the different designated scenarios. The critical values for experiment replication are highlighted in bold.

Simulation	Average Response Time (ms)	Min (ms)	Max (ms)
1Arch0_1	297.66	44.12	621.06
1Arch1_10	329.92	43.76	673.30
1Arch10_100	800.68	73.04	1819.52
1Arch100_1000	**5222.49**	**218.75**	17,223.80
2Arch0_1	**48.00**	**36.72**	**62.64**
2Arch1_10	76.27	36.70	269.22
2Arch10_100	409.71	34.53	2131.46
2Arch100_1000	4051.75	**39.34**	**27,742.37**
3Arch0_1	47.61	**35.30**	64.73
3Arch1_10	74.46	**33.75**	269.02
3Arch10_100	353.02	37.72	1886.20
3Arch100_1000	**3423.89**	37.59	23,583.14

Figure 15 shows that the resource distribution and optimized configuration of architectures two and three make them more scalable and efficient. Moreover, among all architectures, the minimum response times are relatively stable and low, especially for architectures two and three, indicating that systems can handle isolated requests more efficiently, especially with a low user load. Going into more detail, several critical values essential for interpreting the results emerge from the table. The generic simulation is described by the code NArchi_i_j, where N represents the simulated architectures in the order they are described in Section 4, i represents the minimum number of users for each connected userbase, and j represents the maximum number of connected users. The highest response times under a high load (1000 users) are observed in the first architecture, with an average of 5222.49 ms and a minimum of 218.75 ms. These values demonstrate the limitations of the first architecture as user numbers increase. In contrast, architectures two and three, which exploit edge devices, show significantly lower average response times. For example, architecture two manages a minimum response time of 39.34 ms even under a load of 1000 users. Furthermore, in the one-user scenario, architecture two achieves the lowest average response time of 48.00 ms, and the extreme values remain very low, with a minimum of 36.72 ms and a maximum of 62.64 ms. So, the data show that architectures two and three consistently outperform architecture one in terms of stability, as evidenced by the lower range between the minimum and maximum response times under varying loads. The highlighted values serve as benchmarks for evaluating the scalability and efficiency of the architectures.

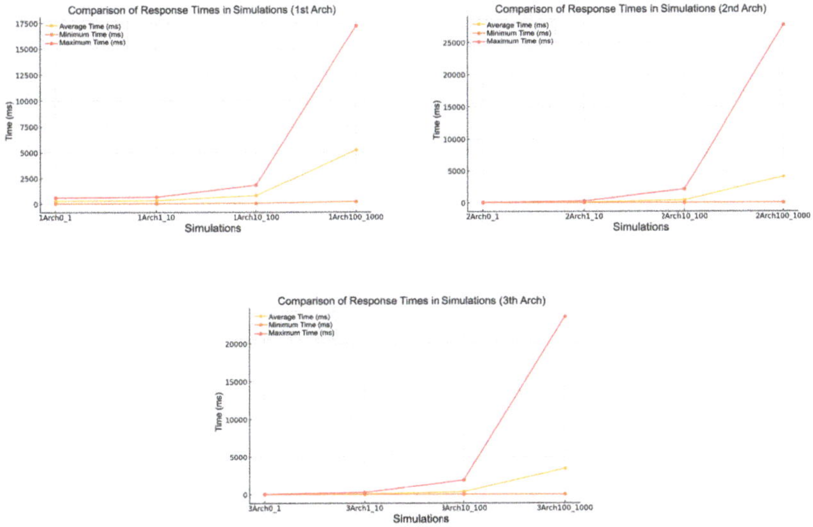

Figure 15. Graphical representation of performance as the number of users changes for three different architectures, with the figures sorted according to the order of the architectures presented. For each architecture, the orange line indicates the minimum time, the red line the maximum time, and the yellow line the average time.

7. Concluding Remarks and Future Work

This work explored the deployment and performance of collaborative virtual and augmented reality systems in a cloud continuum context, focusing on integrating and comparing cloud-centric and edge-centric hybrid architectures. Strengths and weaknesses emerged for each architecture defined and are summarized in Table 2.

Table 2. Comparison of strengths and limitations of different IoT architectures.

Architecture	Strengths	Limitations
Centralized IoT (Cloud)	High computing power, easy updates, centralized management.	High latency, cloud dependency, bandwidth limitations in multi-device scenarios.
Hybrid IoT (Cloud–Edge)	Reduced latency, efficient bandwidth usage, better for real-time interactions.	Requires powerful edge devices, potential synchronization issues in unstable networks.
Decentralized IoT (Edge)	Minimal latency, independent from cloud interruptions, suitable for critical applications.	Higher hardware costs, higher power consumption for edge devices.

Several key insights and conclusions emerged through the definition and implementation of these architectures and their subsequent validation through simulations. As shown in Section 6 with the increase in the number of users, the cloud-centric architecture showed substantial degradation in performance, highlighting the limits of an utterly centralized approach. Instead, hybrid architectures have balanced performance and scalability by distributing computational loads between cloud and edge resources. However, all simulations were conducted by fixing the computational capabilities of both the cloud and the edge. It would be interesting to investigate whether the results obtained remain valid even when these parameters vary, since a different distribution of computational resources could affect the performance of the architectures. Exploring this aspect could lead to the definition of a reference architecture that optimizes the load distribution between the cloud and edge and identifies the best specifications each machine should possess to ensure optimal performance. Among the future developments, of considerable importance is to consider the privacy and security aspects by exploring methods of secure data transmission and storage adapted to these distributed architectures. Different scheduling algorithms could also be applied to evaluate the various approaches to determine which maximizes the number of concurrent users. Furthermore, using other case studies to include more application scenarios, such as the healthcare, military, and educational fields, could provide further insights into the versatility and limitations of the proposed architectures. All of these advances could lead to the definition of a unified reference architecture for the AR/VR scenario, capable of adapting to all possible application contexts and being deployed modularly, depending on available resources and the specific needs of the case study.

Author Contributions: Conceptualization, G.J.P., V.B. and B.D.M.; methodology, G.J.P. and V.B.; software, G.J.P., V.B. and L.-H.L.; validation, G.J.P. and V.B.; investigation, G.J.P., V.B. and B.D.M.; data curation, V.B.; writing—original draft preparation, G.J.P., V.B. and B.D.M.; writing—review and editing, K.-C.L. and L.-H.L.; visualization, L.-H.L.; supervision, K.-C.L. and B.D.M.; project administration, B.D.M.; funding acquisition, B.D.M. All authors have read and agreed to the published version of the manuscript.

Funding: This work was supported by project SERICS (PE00000014), under the MUR NRRP funded by the EU—NextGenerationEU.

Data Availability Statement: No new data were created.

Conflicts of Interest: The authors declare no conflicts of interest.

References

1. Ometov, A.; Molua, O.L.; Komarov, M.; Nurmi, J. A survey of security in cloud, edge, and fog computing. *Sensors* **2022**, *22*, 927. [CrossRef] [PubMed]
2. Venticinque, S.; Amato, A. A methodology for deployment of IoT application in fog. *J. Ambient Intell. Humaniz. Comput.* **2019**, *10*, 1955–1976. [CrossRef]
3. Venticinque, S.; Nacchia, S. Learning and prediction of E-car charging requirements for flexible loads shifting. In Proceedings of the Internet and Distributed Computing Systems: 12th International Conference, IDCS 2019, Naples, Italy, 10–12 October 2019; pp. 284–293.
4. Liang, W.; Xiao, J.; Chen, Y.; Yang, C.; Xie, K.; Li, K.C.; Di Martino, B. TMHD: Twin-Bridge Scheduling of Multi-Heterogeneous Dependent Tasks for Edge Computing. *Future Gener. Comput. Syst.* **2024**, *158*, 60–72. [CrossRef]
5. Boyles, B. *Virtual Reality and Augmented Reality in Education;* Center For Teaching Excellence, United States Military Academy: West Point, NY, USA, 2017; Volume 67.
6. Gechter, F.; Dafflon, B.; Gruer, P.; Koukam, A. Towards a hybrid real/virtual simulation of autonomous vehicles for critical scenarios. In Proceedings of the Sixth International Conference on Advances in System Simulation (SIMUL 2014), Nice, France, 12–16 October 2014; pp. 14–17.
7. Kumar, U.; Verma, P.; Abbas, S.Q. Bringing edge computing into IoT architecture to improve IoT network performance. In Proceedings of the 2021 International Conference on Computer Communication and Informatics (ICCCI), Coimbatore, India, 27–29 January 2021; pp. 1–5.
8. Krishnasamy, E.; Varrette, S.; Mucciardi, M. Edge Computing: An Overview of Framework and Applications. Technical Report PRACE Aisbl, Bruxelles, Belgium, December. 2020. Available online: https://prace-ri.eu/wp-content/uploads/Edge-Computing-An-Overview-of-Framework-and-Applications.pdf (accessed on 25 September 2024).
9. Zhao, L.; Wang, J.; Liu, J.; Kato, N. Optimal edge resource allocation in IoT-based smart cities. *IEEE Netw.* **2019**, *33*, 30–35. [CrossRef]
10. Churchill, E.F.; Snowdon, D. Collaborative virtual environments: An introductory review of issues and systems. *Virtual Real.* **1998**, *3*, 3–15. [CrossRef]
11. Rekimoto, J. Transvision: A hand-held augmented reality system for collaborative design. In Proceedings of the Virtual Systems and Multimedia, Hiroshima, Japan, 17–23 June 1996; Volume 96, pp. 18–20.
12. Schiffeler, N.; Stehling, V.; Haberstroh, M.; Isenhardt, I. Collaborative augmented reality in engineering education. In *Proceedings of the Cyber-physical Systems and Digital Twins: Proceedings of the 16th International Conference on Remote Engineering and Virtual Instrumentation 16*; Springer: Berlin/Heidelberg, Germany, 2020; pp. 719–732.

13. Wang, X. Augmented reality in architecture and design: Potentials and challenges for application. *Int. J. Archit. Comput.* **2009**, *7*, 309–326. [CrossRef]
14. Hajirasouli, A.; Banihashemi, S. Augmented reality in architecture and construction education: State of the field and opportunities. *Int. J. Educ. Technol. High. Educ.* **2022**, *19*, 39. [CrossRef]
15. Cao, J.; Lam, K.Y.; Lee, L.H.; Liu, X.; Hui, P.; Su, X. Mobile augmented reality: User interfaces, frameworks, and intelligence. *ACM Comput. Surv.* **2023**, *55*, 1–36. [CrossRef]
16. Huo, K.; Wang, T.; Paredes, L.; Villanueva, A.M.; Cao, Y.; Ramani, K. SynchronizAR: Instant Synchronization for Spontaneous and Spatial Collaborations in Augmented Reality. In Proceedings of the UIST, Berlin, Germany, 14–17 October 2018; pp. 19–30.
17. Weigert, T.; Garlan, D.; Knapman, J.; Møller-Pedersen, B.; Selic, B. Modeling of architectures with UML: Panel. In Proceedings of the International Conference on the Unified Modeling Language, York, UK, 2–6 October 2000; pp. 556–569.
18. Di Martino, B.; Esposito, A.; Pezzullo, G.J.; Weng, T.H. Evaluating machine and deep learning techniques in predicting blood sugar levels within the E-health domain. *Connect. Sci.* **2023**, *35*, 2279900. [CrossRef]
19. Bradski, G.; Kaehler, A. *Learning OpenCV: Computer Vision with the OpenCV Library*; O'Reilly Media, Inc.: Sebastopol, CA, USA, 2008.
20. Hardikar, S.; Ahirwar, P.; Rajan, S. Containerization: Cloud computing based inspiration Technology for Adoption through Docker and Kubernetes. In Proceedings of the 2021 Second International Conference on Electronics and Sustainable Communication Systems (ICESC), Coimbatore, India, 4–6 August 2021; pp. 1996–2003.
21. Sazonov, I.; Magiluk, D.; Mikhailova, A. Analysis of Modern Tools for a Mobile Apps Development Running on Android and IOS; Редакционная коллегия: Алл-Руссиан Сциенце-Працтицал Цонференце оф Студенц, Постградуатес анд Ыоунг Сциентисц (Керч, Април 22, 2019); п. 269. Available online: https://elibrary.ru/item.asp?id=41600678 (accessed on 25 September 2024).
22. Chougale, P.; Yadav, V.; Gaikwad, A.; Vidyapeeth, B. Firebase-overview and usage. *Int. Res. J. Mod. Eng. Technol. Sci.* **2021**, *3*, 1178–1183.
23. Kalaitzidou, A.; Senechal, N.; Dimitriou, P.; Chandran, K.; Mcginity, M. "E-WAFE"-A Full Body Embodied Social Exergame. In Proceedings of the Extended Abstracts of the 2022 Annual Symposium on Computer-Human Interaction in Play, Bremen, Germany, 2–5 November 2022; pp. 286–290.
24. Grzejszczak, T.; Kawulok, M.; Galuszka, A. Hand landmarks detection and localization in color images. *Multimed. Tools Appl.* **2016**, *75*, 16363–16387. [CrossRef]
25. Sharma, A.; Pathak, J.; Prakash, M.; Singh, J. Object detection using OpenCV and python. In Proceedings of the 2021 3rd International Conference on Advances in Computing, Communication Control and Networking (ICAC3N), Greater Noida, India, 7–18 December 2021; pp. 501–505.
26. Chandan, G.; Jain, A.; Jain, H. Real time object detection and tracking using Deep Learning and OpenCV. In Proceedings of the 2018 International Conference on Inventive Research in Computing Applications (ICIRCA), Coimbatore, India, 11–12 July 2018; pp. 1305–1308.
27. Linowes, J. *Augmented Reality with Unity AR Foundation: A Practical Guide to Cross-Platform AR Development with Unity 2020 and Later Versions*; Packt Publishing Ltd.: Birmingham, UK, 2021.
28. Chaudhry, T.; Juneja, A.; Rastogi, S. AR foundation for augmented reality in unity. *Int. J. Adv. Eng. Manag. (IJAEM)* **2021**, *3*, 662–667.
29. Suryono, R.R.; Purwandari, B.; Budi, I. Peer to peer (P2P) lending problems and potential solutions: A systematic literature review. *Procedia Comput. Sci.* **2019**, *161*, 204–214. [CrossRef]
30. Potdar, A.M.; Narayan, D.; Kengond, S.; Mulla, M.M. Performance evaluation of docker container and virtual machine. *Procedia Comput. Sci.* **2020**, *171*, 1419–1428. [CrossRef]
31. Ritsos, P.D.; Mearman, J.; Jackson, J.; Roberts, J.C. Synthetic visualizations in web-based mixed reality. In Proceedings of the Immersive Analytics: Exploring Future Visualization and Interaction Technologies for Data Analytics: Workshop, IEEE Conference on Visualization (VIS), Phoenix, AZ, USA, 1–6 October 2017; Available online: https://groups.inf.ed.ac.uk/vishub/immersiveanalytics/papers/IA_1189-paper.pdf (accessed on 25 September 2024).
32. Ahmed, T.; Singh, Y. Analytic study of load balancing techniques using tool cloud analyst. *Int. J. Eng. Res. Appl.* **2012**, *2*, 1027–1030.
33. Goyal, T.; Singh, A.; Agrawal, A. Cloudsim: Simulator for cloud computing infrastructure and modeling. *Procedia Eng.* **2012**, *38*, 3566–3572. [CrossRef]
34. Kumar, R.; Sahoo, G. Cloud computing simulation using CloudSim. *arXiv* **2014**, arXiv:1403.3253.

future internet

MDPI

Article

Securing the Edge: CatBoost Classifier Optimized by the Lyrebird Algorithm to Detect Denial of Service Attacks in Internet of Things-Based Wireless Sensor Networks

Sennanur Srinivasan Abinayaa [1], Prakash Arumugam [2], Divya Bhavani Mohan [3], Anand Rajendran [4], Abderezak Lashab [5], Baoze Wei [5,*] and Josep M. Guerrero [5]

1 Department of Electronics and Communication Engineering, Dr. NGP Institute of Technology, Coimbatore 641048, India; abinayaa.s@drngpit.ac.in
2 Karnavati School of Research, Karnavati University, Gujarat 382422, India; prksh830@gmail.com
3 United World School of Computational Intelligence, Karnavati University, Gujarat 382422, India; divyamohan2009@gmail.com
4 Department of Electrical and Electronics Engineering, Amrita School of Engineering, Amrita Vishwa Vidyapeetham, Bengaluru 560035, India; r_anand@blr.amrita.edu
5 Department of Energy Technology, Aalborg University, 9220 Aalborg, Denmark; abl@et.aau.dk (A.L.); joz@energy.aau.dk (J.M.G.)
* Correspondence: bao@energy.aau.dk

Abstract: The security of Wireless Sensor Networks (WSNs) is of the utmost importance because of their widespread use in various applications. Protecting WSNs from harmful activity is a vital function of intrusion detection systems (IDSs). An innovative approach to WSN intrusion detection (ID) utilizing the CatBoost classifier (Cb-C) and the Lyrebird Optimization Algorithm is presented in this work (LOA). As is typical in ID settings, Cb-C excels at handling datasets that are imbalanced. The lyrebird's remarkable capacity to imitate the sounds of its surroundings served as inspiration for the LOA, a metaheuristic optimization algorithm. The WSN-DS dataset, acquired from Prince Sultan University in Saudi Arabia, is used to assess the suggested method. Among the models presented, LOA-Cb-C produces the highest accuracy of 99.66%; nevertheless, when compared with the other methods discussed in this article, its error value of 0.34% is the lowest. Experimental results reveal that the suggested strategy improves WSN-IoT security over the existing methods in terms of detection accuracy and the false alarm rate.

Keywords: wireless sensor networks (WSNs); intrusion detection (ID); CatBoost classifier (Cb-C); lyrebird optimization algorithm (LOA); WSN-DS dataset; machine learning (ML)

1. Introduction

Emerging as a game-changing technology, Wireless Sensor Networks (WSNs) have the ability to revolutionize numerous industries and applications. The "sensor nodes" that comprise these networks are small autonomous devices that can detect, process, and transmit data wirelessly. Wherever conventional wired networks are too costly or impossible to implement, WSNs have found use, including in environmental monitoring, healthcare, industrial computerization, military shadowing, and many more. One major advantage of WSNs is their ability to gather data from inaccessible or harsh locations. Dense networks formed by several sensor nodes can provide detailed, real-time data about the monitored area. Efficiency and safety can be enhanced in a variety of applications with the use of these data for decision-making, monitoring, and control. Despite all the benefits, WSNs still have a long way to go before they can reach their maximum potential. Problems arise, for example, when the processing and data transfer capacities of individual sensor nodes are inadequate. Energy efficiency is a major concern in WSNs since sensor nodes' batteries have limited capacity, and it is impossible to charge or replace them frequently in many deployment situations. The necessity for efficient and reliable communication protocols is another obstacle with WSNs. The design of the protocols that let sensor nodes communicate with one another and with a central base station is a key factor in the network's overall success. Verifying the dependability and efficiency of communication in WSNs requires fixing problems with routing, data aggregation, and congestion control. A lot of work has gone into improving the efficiency and dependability of WSNs in recent years. Data processing using machine learning algorithms, optimization methods for reduced energy consumption, and new communication protocols for enhanced network efficiency are all examples of what is meant here. When these problems are solved and these innovations are used, WSNs could change data collection, processing, and usage for many different things.

Figure 1 represents the basic structure of an IoT-based WSN. The integration of the Internet of Things (IoT) and WSNs has revolutionized the field of sensing, communication, and data collection in various industries. By combining IoT with WSNs, the communication capabilities of these networks can be enhanced, making them more intelligent and efficient in a wide range of applications including smart cities, healthcare, agriculture, and industrial automation. IoT-based WSNs play a critical role in modern technological ecosystems, particularly in the context of smart environments, industry 4.0, and automation. These networks consist of spatially distributed autonomous sensors that monitor physical or environmental conditions such as temperature, humidity, pressure, and motion, and transmit the data to a central hub for processing. The integration of WSNs with the IoT extends their functionality beyond simple data collection to include remote monitoring, control, and decision-making capabilities. This enables real-time interaction between physical and digital systems across various domains, such as healthcare, agriculture, smart cities, and industrial automation. IoT-based WSNs leverage various communication protocols, including Wi-Fi, Bluetooth, Zigbee, and LoRa, to ensure seamless connectivity and data transfer across devices, even in remote or challenging environments. The scalability and flexibility of these systems allow for the integration of a wide range of sensors and actuators, making them adaptable to diverse applications. However, challenges such as energy efficiency, security, and data privacy remain critical considerations. The limited battery life of sensor nodes requires the development of energy-harvesting techniques or optimized communication protocols to extend network longevity. Additionally, security threats like unauthorized access and data tampering must be addressed through robust encryption and authentication protocols. Despite these challenges, IoT-based WSNs are pivotal in driving innovation across various sectors, fostering greater efficiency, automation, and data-driven decision-making, thereby shaping the future of interconnected systems.

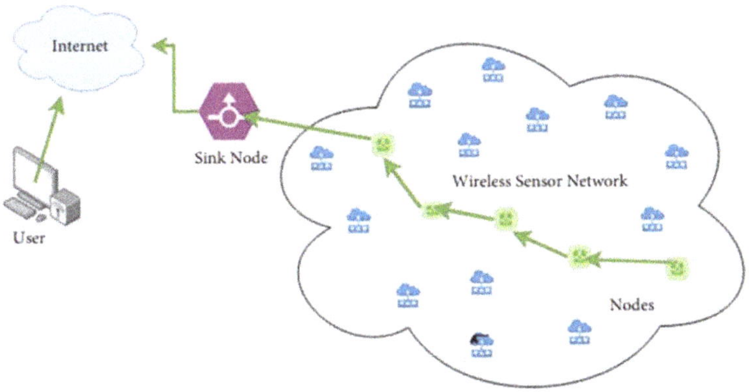

Figure 1. IoT-based Wireless Sensor Network—the basic structure [1].

The structure of this research article is as follows. A comprehensive literature review is presented in Section 2; the contributions of this research article are delineated in Section 3; the proposed methodology is elucidated in Section 4; the performance metrics and simulation results are provided in Sections 5 and 6; the discussion is contained in Section 7; the complexity analysis is elaborated on in Section 8; and the conclusion and future research are presented in Sections 9 and 10, respectively.

2. Literature Review

Many different ML algorithms for WSN ID have been studied recently. In this section, we summarize and analyze a large body of literature on optimization techniques, deep learning methods, machine learning models, and their combined applications. In order to detect different types of attacks successfully, a groundbreaking MBOLT (MegaBAT optimized Long Short-Term Memory)-IDS for WSNs was created and introduced. Using this method to fine-tune deep LSTM's hyperparameters led to better performance with less computational overhead. The proposed ID was tested with the use of the publicly available WSN-DS datasets. Normalizing the data, changing the letters to numbers, and adding multi-class labelling to better attack identification are all steps in the pre-processing that boost classification performance [2]. By grouping the SN using the DFFF algorithm, the study suggested a way to gather data throughout the WSN and ID stages. The data were organized in the pre-processing step, and the matrix values were reduced using ELDA (entropy-based linear discriminant analysis). The QN3 (Quasi-Newton Neural Network) classifier inspects the data for signs of assault or normalcy after matrix reduction and sorts them into DoS, R2L, and U2R categories [3]. In order to implement ID in IoT-WSN, one research study developed and implemented a BCOA-MLID (Binary Chimp Optimization Algorithm with Machine Learning-based Intrusion Detection). To protect the IoT-WSN, this method makes an effort to differentiate between different kinds of attacks. The BCOA-MLID method outperformed XGBoost and KNN (K-Nearest Neighbor)-AOA in terms of accuracy (99.36 percent) in experimental findings conducted on the Kaggle invasion dataset [4]. The FA with SVM was employed for the classification of attacks, where GWO (Grey Wolf Optimizer) optimizes the parameter 'a' that linearly decreases the value from 2 to 0 during the iterations, where a is given by $a = 2 - (\frac{2}{T}\ x\ t)$, where 'T' is the total number of iterations and 't' is the current iteration. Simulations of FA-SVM use the NSL-kDD dataset with 99.34% accuracy. The kNN-PSO and XGBoost models had lower accuracies of 96.42% and 95.36%, respectively [5]. The authors presented a number of potential hybrid intrusion detection systems (IDSs) for SAT-IDSs that made use of feature selection in conjunction with ML or DL models. The methods utilized were ANN, GRU, LSTM, and RF for SFS. The proposed SAT-IDSs were placed through their paces with STIN on satellite networks and UNSW-NB15 on land networks [6].

To detect the numerous assaults documented in the IoT-IDS dataset, one study employed the GWDTO (Grey Wolf Dipper Throated Optimization) and contrasted it with other approaches found in previous research. In the fields of statistics and signal processing, SVD finds use in data partitioning, feature extraction, matrix approximation, and pattern recognition [7]. An ensemble model was suggested in another research study that uses the recursive feature reduction technique with RF assistance to enhance the IDS's prediction capabilities. To extract meaningful information from the datasets, the writers employed a data normalization strategy and a wrapper-based feature removal method. With the goal of generating attack class probabilities through majority voting, a hybrid stacking ensemble was constructed by merging RF-RFE, MLP, RF, and SVM for classification [8]. The CMPRO (Chimp social incentive-based Mutated Poor Rich Optimization) algorithm was used for optimal cluster head selection. Blockchain was deployed on optimal cluster heads and a base station for storage and computational resources [9]. In another research article, a CRNN (convolutional recurrent neural network) model along with MSO for optimal hyperparameter selection was presented with the aim of improving the classifier model's performance. The investigational results of the MSODL-ID (Moth Search Optimizer with

Deep Learning Enabled Intrusion Detection) method were analyzed on the WSN-DS with 374,661 samples. The MSODL-ID approach accurately recognized different types of attacks by providing outstanding results [10]. Geometric SMOTE was used to generate different rare-class attack data while keeping sample feature similarity using the enhanced kernel density estimation algorithm. Soft-voting ensemble learning was used to detect multi-class anomalies in balanced and dimensionally reduced data [11].

In another article, an ID based on DL for IoT networks, employing a four-layered deep FC network architecture, was used to detect malicious traffic. The proposed system was implemented in Python using the TensorFlow library and was tested using the CNS and COS. The suggested system updates on classifier-discovered features. The feature extractor module intercepts data packets and extracts features such as Id, Tr, Rr, and TRR, where Id refers to 'identifier', Tr refers to 'Transmission Ratio', Rr refers to 'Reception Ratio', and TRR refers to 'Transmission Reception Ratio' [12]. The authors of another article chose OBPNN to monitor sensor data and assess health, optimizing the SVM with the FSA. The suggested automated health status evaluation removes outliers using kernel density estimation, determines the appropriate bandwidth for typical data, simulates normality using OBPNN, and calculates the health score based on the decision function and distance from the separation hyperplane [13]. An effective and smart NIDS built on DL was suggested in another article. The model's performance was evaluated using various classification techniques and achieved a 100% and 99.64% accuracy rate when trained and tested with the datasets, respectively [14]. Another study presented an AutoML model that uses Bayesian optimization to automatically choose an ML model and adjust its hyperparameters, where 'k' barriers are needed for accurate detection and prevention of intrusion. The ML models considered in the study included various regression techniques along with bagging, ensemble, and boosting ensemble learning [15]. In another study, a decision tree was built using the CSA, and the selected features were represented by the terminal nodes of the decision tree. The proposed IDS was compared to other techniques using the CIC-IDS2018 benchmark dataset. The suggested approach is a hybrid decision-making framework for classification and feature extraction using a decision tree with a maximum information gain ratio. The KDDCup 99 dataset was used for training and testing the proposed methodology [16].

In another study, a hybrid method that combines the RF model with the Pearson correlation coefficient was devised for efficient and effective feature selection. The categorical features were transformed into numerical values using an encoding approach. When tested in actual network settings, the decision tree algorithm proved to be the most effective and accurate method for ID [17]. In order to identify network intrusions using a multi-model ID system, the paper presented a method based on feature selection and majority vote. Six distinct ML methods were used for training and assessment. A multi-model categorization system was developed using the Majority Voting approach [18]. An effective ML-based approach for WSN routing and clustering was presented in the article. In order to transmit data, identify nodes, detect faults, and conduct analyses, WSNs employ ML algorithms such as the RF algorithm, MLPNN (Multi-Layer Perceptron Neural Network), and RBFNN [19]. In another study, ML-based IDS was implemented to keep an eye on traffic in vehicular ad hoc networks (VANETs) and spot any questionable behavior using streaming engines for big data analytics. Using RF as the data classifier during training and including real-time data management, visualization, and collection, the IDS framework attained maximum accuracy. Additionally, it assessed the effect of the IDS on network throughput, showing that it is a resource-efficient solution [20]. In order to identify attacks on the MQTT-based protocol, the authors of another study introduced a DNN and evaluated its efficacy in comparison to other popular ML techniques. The authors evaluated the ID system's efficacy using evaluation measures like recall, accuracy, precision, and the F1 measure and then computed the information gain using entropy [21].

Using ML techniques for the purpose of detecting previously unseen attacks, another article suggested a multi-layer ID architecture for WSNs. In the initial detection layer, network edge sensors used an NB classifier to make decisions about real-time packet inspection [22]. Another research study used a systematic literature review approach to pick papers to examine. The study provided a taxonomy of ID algorithms based on individual DL methods. The research examined and contrasted the ID systems under study in terms of the simulation metrics, settings, languages, software, datasets, and feature extraction approaches that were employed [23]. Another article presented an ID model that combines TVP-IPSO (Time-Varying Parameter-Improved Particle Swarm Optimization), PCA (Principal Component Analysis), and SVM (Support Vector Machines), specifically PCA, with other popular methods. To reduce energy, PCA was utilized to decrease data dimensions, while SVM was used for high detection accuracy. To improve detection accuracy and convergence speed, the TVP-IPSO method was used to find the optimal parameters for the SVM algorithm and optimize them [24]. Another research study presented a novel method for improving the setup of a lightweight DL-HIDS model using parameters supplied by an IoT device. Memory consumption and inference timing were among the many parameters considered by the authors when they optimized the devices used. The article explored the proposed method for deploying the DL-HIDS in a real-world Internet of Things environment [25]. Another study combined the kNN and SCA (Sine Cosine Algorithm), which allowed a lightweight ID model for WSN to enhance classification accuracy while decreasing false alarm rates. The proposed model made up for the optimization accuracy loss with PM, and a CSCA reduced space and time for calculations [26].

One research study looked at several data mining techniques for an effective IDS in detecting DoS assaults. It used a specialized dataset named WSN-DS and performed a thorough empirical analysis. Prior to and following the use of a feature selection algorithm, the detection accuracy and computational cost of those methods were assessed [27]. Another paper explored the use of DNNs to develop an effective IDS for detecting and classifying cyberattacks in real time. DNNs outperformed other ML classifiers on several publicly available benchmark datasets, according to the study [28]. The authors of another study used the WSN-DS dataset to detect the attack using an RF model. They compared the entails by dividing the WSN-DS dataset into training and testing sets, developing an RF algorithm to learn the training data, and utilizing the RF classifier to predict DoS assaults on the testing set [29]. The paper employed various CNN techniques to discover DoS attacks in WSNs. NN algorithms were trained and assessed on the WSN-DS dataset with diverse DoS attacks [30]. GSWO was proposed in another paper, which combines a GA and a modified WOA. This hybrid approach aimed to enhance feature selection and hyperparameter tuning for intrusion detection systems in WSNs. GSWO is specifically applied for feature selection, where it identifies the most relevant features from datasets. The algorithm uses a fitness function that balances classification error and the number of features retained, promoting efficient model performance. The performance of the proposed methods was evaluated using various metrics, including accuracy, precision, recall, and F1-score. Additionally, ROC curves were utilized to visualize the model's performance across different thresholds [31]. The core of Kitsune's approach is the use of an ensemble of autoencoders, which are NNs designed to learn efficient representations of data. This ensemble method allows for collective differentiation between normal and abnormal traffic patterns, making it effective for anomaly detection in real-time scenarios. Kitsune includes a feature extraction component that efficiently tracks the behavior of all network channels. This framework is crucial for obtaining relevant features from network traffic, which helps in accurately identifying anomalies. One paper discussed the evaluation of Kitsune's performance in terms of detection accuracy and runtime efficiency. The results indicated that Kitsune can perform comparably to traditional batch algorithms, even on low-power devices like Raspberry Pi, showcasing its efficiency and practicality [32]. Another paper demonstrated that denoising autoencoders can significantly improve the accuracy of NIDS. By reconstructing inputs from partial observations, these autoencoders helped distinguish between benign and malicious traffic more effectively. The paper discussed the importance of feature vectors in both packet-based and flow-based NIDS. It highlighted that the way features are extracted can significantly impact detection rates, especially for certain types of attacks [33]. Another paper adopted a deep learning architecture for unsupervised anomaly detection in IoT, evaluating multiple design choices on the IoT-23 and Kitsune datasets. The results demonstrated enhanced performance and robustness, particularly in the face of Label-Flipping poisoning attacks, compared with existing baselines [34]. Table 1 summarizes the recent works carried out in the field of ID in WSNs.

Table 1. Some recent studies related to intrusion detection in WSNs.

Year	Author Names	Model Used	Dataset	Accuracy	Computational Efficiency	Energy Efficiency
2024	Karthikeyan, M.; Manimegalai, D.; Raja Gopal, K. [5]	FA with ML	Not mentioned	95%	High (Complex Optimization)	Moderate
2023	Gautami, A.; Shanthini, J.; Karthik, S. [3]	QNNN	Not mentioned	91%	Medium	High
2023	Aljebreen, M.; Ahmed, M.; Ahmad, M. [4]	BCO	IoT-WSN	93.5%	High	Low
2023	Azar, A.T.; Shehab, E.; Mattar, A.M. [6]	DL-HIDS	Satellite Networks	98%	High	Low
2023	Alhasan, R.A.; Hamza, E.K. [7]	CNN with Dimensionality Reduction	WSN Dataset	97%	High	Moderate
2023	Abbas, Q.; Hina, S. [8]	Hybrid Ensemble Model	Secure Systems	92%	Medium	High
2023	Darla, S.; Naveena, C. [9]	Optimized DL	Blockchain Sensor Systems	94%	High	Moderate
2023	Murugesh, C.; Murugan, S. [10]	MSO	Not mentioned	95%	High	Moderate
2023	Yang, Y.; Gu, Y.; Yan, Y. [11]	ML for Rare-Class Attacks	Not mentioned	90%	Moderate	High
2023	Awajan, A. [12]	Deep learning IDS for IoT	IoT Networks	92%	High	Moderate
2023	Mandala, V.; Senthilnathan, T. [13]	BPNN	Sensor Data	96%	High	Moderate
2023	Hnamte, V.; Hussain, J. [14]	DCNNBiLSTM	WSN	97%	High	Moderate
2023	Balobaid, A.S.; Ahamed, S.B. [19]	NN Clustering	WSN	94%	Moderate	High
2023	Salmi, S.; Oughdir, L. [30]	DL Techniques for DoS Detection	WSN	92%	High	Moderate
2022	Singh, A.; Amutha, J. [15]	AutoML-ID	WSN Dataset	94%	High	Moderate
2022	Karthika, J.; Loganathan, S. [16]	Hybrid ML Feature Selection	NIDS	91%	Medium	High
2022	Patil, D.R.; Pattewar, T.M. [18]	Majority Voting and Feature Selection	Not mentioned	89%	Medium	High

Table 1. *Cont.*

Year	Author Names	Model Used	Dataset	Accuracy	Computational Efficiency	Energy Efficiency
2022	Idrissi, I.; Azizi, M. [25]	Optimized DL-based IDS	Edge IoT	93%	Medium	High
2021	Zang, M.; Yan, Y. [20]	ML for Big Data Analytics	VANET	95%	High	Moderate
2021	Khan, M.A.; Jan, M.A. [21]	DL-IDS	MQTT-Enabled IoT	96%	High	Moderate
2021	Alruhaily, N.M.; Ibrahim, D.M. [22]	Multi-Layer ML IDS	WSN	93%	Moderate	High
2021	Pan, J.S.; Fan, F. [26]	Lightweight IDS	WSN	94%	Moderate	High
2024	Abinayaa, S.S. et al.	LOA-Cb-C	WSN-DS	99.66%	Low (Optimized)	High

The reviewed research articles demonstrate a growing interest in utilizing ML algorithms for ID in WSNs. However, the existing methods often face challenges such as high false alarm rates and limited adaptability to dynamic network environments. By leveraging advanced optimization techniques, such as the LOA, there is a clear opportunity to develop more effective classifiers for WSNs. These optimized classifiers have the capability to enhance the accuracy and efficacy of attack detection significantly, thus addressing the shortcomings of current approaches.

3. Contributions of This Research Article

- The suggested LOA helps to optimize the hyperparameters of the Cb-C.
- The proposed Cb-C incorporates an efficient classification technique for enhancing the prediction capabilities of various attacks.
- This study mainly focuses on integrating the LOA and Cb-C, hence called LOA-Cb-C, which helps in the effective prediction of the maximum number of samples in each category of attack, thus enhancing the accuracy, true positive rate, and F1-score and reducing the error rate.

4. Proposed Methodology

4.1. General Structure of the Proposed Methodology

(i) Dataset collection

The dataset used in this study is the WSN-DS dataset obtained from Prince Sultan University, Saudi Arabia. This dataset contains instances of various types of attacks in WSNs, making it suitable for our classification task.

(ii) Data Splitting

Eighty percent of the dataset was reserved for training purposes, while the remaining twenty percent was used for testing. The holdout method was used to divide the data in this way so that the proposed model could be trained on a large enough portion of the data while retaining a separate set for evaluation. The robustness of the suggested optimization-based classifier (LOA-Cb-C) was evaluated on the mentioned dataset consisting of 374,661 samples. Table 2 displays the breakdown of the total sample size.

(iii) Model Selection and Optimization

We chose the Cb-C for its effectiveness in handling categorical features and its ability to handle imbalanced datasets. The hyperparameters of the Cb-C were optimized using the LOA. This algorithm is known for its efficiency in finding optimal hyperparameters, which can considerably increase the classifier's performance.

(iv) Training athe Cb-C for its effectiveness in handling categorical features nd Prediction

The optimized Cb-C was trained on the training dataset to learn the patterns in the data related to diverse attacks. After training, the model was applied to the testing dataset for prediction purposes. Several metrics were utilized to evaluate the model's performance, including accuracy, precision, recall, and F1-score.

Table 2. Breakdown of WSN-DS dataset.

	Normal	Blackhole	Grayhole	Flooding	TDMA	Total
No. of testing samples (20%)	67,979	2030	2943	618	1363	74,933
No. of training samples (80%)	272,087	8019	11653	2694	5275	299,728
% of proportion	90.77	2.68	3.9	0.88	1.77	374,661

4.2. The WSN-DS Dataset

The WSN-DS dataset used in this study is a comprehensive dataset collected from real-world sensor networks, specifically designed for evaluating IDS. The dataset was obtained from Prince Sultan University, Saudi Arabia, and consists of a vast collection of sensor readings and network traffic data. The dataset can be accessed at https://www.kaggle.com/datasets/bassamkasasbeh1/wsnds accessed on 19 June 2024. The types of attacks and the total number of samples are detailed below.

WSN-DS comprises various types of attacks that can occur in WSNs, including the following:

- Blackhole Attacks: A blackhole attack is a type of security threat where a malicious node in the network selectively drops or discards data packets, without sending them to their anticipated terminal. The purpose of a blackhole attack is to disrupt communication within the network by making the malicious node appear as an attractive route for data traffic.
- Greyhole Attacks: A grayhole attack is a type of security threat where a malicious node selectively drops or modifies data packets, rather than dropping all packets like in a blackhole attack. The goal of a grayhole attack is to disrupt communication in the network while remaining stealthy and difficult to detect.
- Flooding Attacks: A flooding attack is a type of Denial of Service (DoS) attack where an attacker deliberately sends a large volume of packets or messages to the network with the intention of overwhelming its resources. The goal of a flooding attack is to consume the network's bandwidth, energy, or processing capabilities, leading to a disruption in communication and potentially causing legitimate messages to be dropped or delayed.
- TDMA/Scheduling: TDMA/scheduling is a channel access method used to allocate time slots to nodes for transmitting and receiving data. TDMA is a scheduling algorithm that divides the communication channel into time slots, with each node assigned a specific time slot during which it can transmit or receive data.

There are a total of 374,661 samples in the WSN-DS dataset. Out of 374,661 instances, there are 340,066 normal nodes; 10,049 blackhole attacks; 14,596 grayhole attacks; 6638 TDMA/scheduling attacks; and 3312 flooding attacks. The dataset description can be accessed from [30] and its feature importance can be found in [35–37].

The dataset utilized in this investigation was carefully inspected to check for null values, missing values, and value ranges. It was discovered that the dataset was clean and devoid of any missing or null values. This indicated that the dataset was suitable for direct use in the classification task without the need for any specific data pre-processing techniques. The range of values in the dataset was also inspected to ensure that all values fall within the expected range for each feature, which further confirmed the value and appropriateness of the dataset for analysis.

4.3. Lyrebird Optimization Algorithm (LOA)

This section discusses a new population-based metaheuristic algorithm and its mathematical model. Lyrebirds are native to Australia, with the superb lyrebird and Albert's lyrebird as its species. They are primarily recognized for the startling beauty of the enormous tail of the male bird when it is spread out in a mating display, as well as for their exceptional ability to reproduce both manufactured and natural noises that are present in their habitat. Lyrebirds are among the most well-known native birds in Australia. They are distinguished by their distinctive plumes of feathers with a neutral coloration. The females of the superb lyrebird species measure between 74 and 84 cm in length, while the males measure between 80 and 98 cm. To put that into perspective, the female of Albert's lyrebird species can grow to a maximum size of 84 cm, while the males can grow to a maximum size of 90 cm. Although the lyrate feathers of Albert's lyrebird species are smaller and less remarkable than those of the superb lyrebird, the two species are generally comparable. Superb lyrebirds weigh approximately 0.97 kg, which is somewhat more than the average weight of 0.93 kg. When a lyrebird detects the presence of potential danger, one of its behavioral features immediately becomes obvious. A bird's response to this situation is to take a moment to gather its thoughts, survey its immediate area, and then take flight or find a safe haven. The flowchart of LOA is shown in Figure 2.

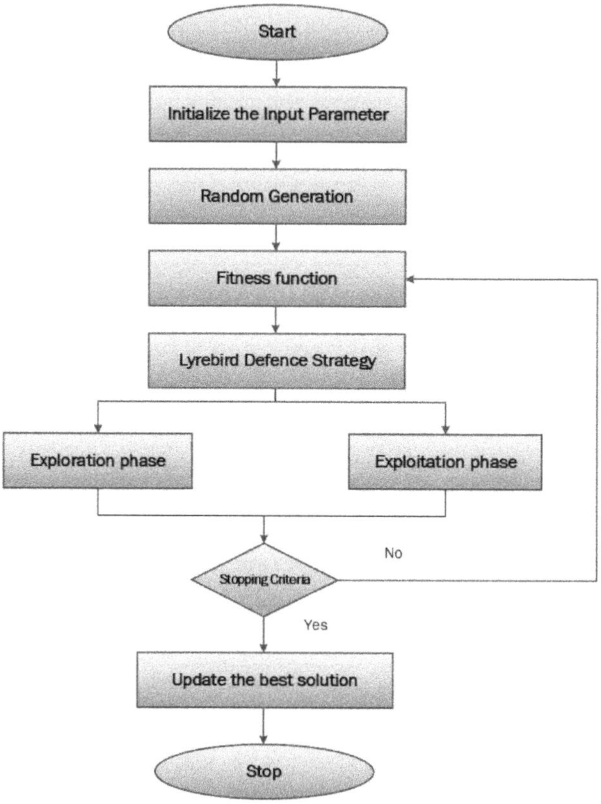

Figure 2. Flowchart of the LOA.

(i) Different phases of the LOA.

The LOA approach is an iterative technique in which the members are updated based on every iteration when lyrebirds sense danger. Based on the situation, the population is updated in two different phases, viz., (a) escaping and (b) hiding.

(ii) Escape strategy (exploration phase).

In the exploration phase, the simulation is carried out in such a way that the birds move from a dangerous spot to a safe place, and then the population member's location in the search space is rationalized accordingly. Relocating a lyrebird to a secure spot causes it to drastically alter its position and scan other regions of the problem-solving space, which expresses the capability of the algorithm in the overall search. As part of the LOA design, each population member's safe zones are defined as the locations of other population members with higher objective function values.

(iii) Hiding strategy (exploitation phase).

Each population member's search space position is updated using the lyrebird's modeling strategy for hiding in its safe area during exploitation. The lyrebird's ability to scan its environment accurately and move cautiously in quest of a suitable hiding place demonstrates the LOA's exploitative skills in the local search since it makes little but noticeable movements. In the LOA design, every member of the flock is given a new position according to the lyrebird's predicted flight path to a nearby hiding place.

4.4. Lyrebird Optimization Algorithm for Intrusion Detection in WSNs

This section describes the fitness function and the parameters that will adapt to reflect the specific optimization goals (e.g., minimizing attack detection errors and energy consumption or maximizing the detection rate).

(a) Fitness function (objective):
In the proposed work, the objective is to minimize false positives and maximize detection accuracy. The fitness function is based on metrics such as accuracy, precision, recall, and F1-score.
The fitness function is defined as

$$Fitness(P_i) = w_1 \cdot Accuracy + w_2 \cdot \text{Precision} + w_3 \cdot \text{Recall} - w_4 \cdot FPR \tag{1}$$

where the weights for balancing the metrics are given by w_1, w_2, w_3, w_4 and FPR is the false positive rate.

(b) Exploration and exploitation phases:
The exploration and exploitation phases are the same as in general optimization, but the updated positions of the solutions reflect the search for optimal network parameters that maximize detection accuracy or minimize energy consumption. The equation for exploration is as follows:

$$P_i^{new} = P_i + \beta\ x\ (r - 0.5) \tag{2}$$

(c) Termination:
The termination criterion are based on reaching a desired detection threshold (e.g., achieving a minimum F1-score) or after a certain number of iterations

$$F1(P_i) \geq Threshold\ or\ Iterations = MaxIter \tag{3}$$

where F1 is the F1-score for attack detection.

4.5. CatBoost Classifier (Cb-C) for WSN Attack Detection

The CatBoost Classifier (Cb-C) is a gradient boosting library-based, open-source, non-linear, tree-based ML approach. It outperforms more sophisticated boosting techniques, including Light GBM, XG Boost, and others, and delivers optimal results even during initial runs. The Cb-C exhibits equivalent performance across a wider variety of data types. The Cb-C was implemented in this pipeline to classify the pre-processed data. By implementing this classifier, the data were categorized with enhanced precision and increased speed without requiring additional time for processing. The Cb-C classifier was supplied with the data for the purpose of classifying the data during the training and testing phases. Each weight was initially established as identical. Figure 3 depicts the flow diagram Cb-C classifier.

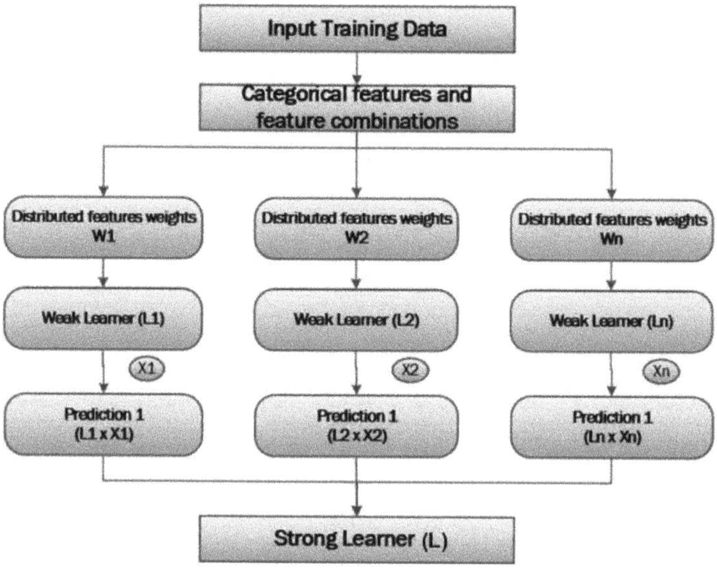

Figure 3. Flowchart of the CatBoost classifier.

(a) Objective function (loss function):
The objective function is a classification loss function, and the base equation for distinguishing between the normal traffic and attack traffic in WSN is given by

$$L(y, \hat{y}) = \sum_{i=1}^{n} y_i \log(\hat{y}_i) + (1 - y_i) \log(1 - \hat{y}_i) \tag{4}$$

where y_i = 1 for attack traffic (DoS) and y_i = 0 for normal traffic. $\hat{y}_i$ is the predicted probability that sample 'i' is an attack.

(b) Handling categorical data in WSNs:
CatBoost's ordered target statistics help in managing the categorical data present in the WSN-DS dataset, and this prevents leakage and overfitting. The equation for the ordered target statistics is given by

$$TS(c) = \frac{\sum_{i=1}^{n-1} y_i}{n - 1} \tag{5}$$

where c is the categorical feature (attack type) and y_i represents the attack labels.

(c) **Prediction of attack likelihood:**
After building the trees iteratively, the final prediction for a given instance is

$$\hat{y}_i = \sum_{m=1}^{M} \eta \cdot h_m(X_i) \tag{6}$$

where $\hat{y}_i$ is the predicted likelihood of an attack on the i-th instance of sensor data and X_i represents features like the packet size, transmission rate, and node energy level.

4.6. CatBoost Classifier (Cb-C) Optimized by the Lyrebird Optimization Algorithm (LOA)

The Cb-C optimized by the LOA has shown promising results in detecting DoS attacks in IoT-based WSNs. The flow diagram of the proposed LOA- Cb-C is presented in Figure 4. The benefits of this approach include the following:

- Improved Accuracy: The CatBoost classifier's ability to differentiate between normal and malicious attack can be enhanced by hyperparameter optimization.
- Robustness: Improved detection of DoS attacks is a result of the enhanced CatBoost classifier's increased resilience to changes in IoT data.
- Efficiency: Because of its improved computing efficiency, the optimized classifier is well-suited for WSNs to identify DoS assaults in real time.

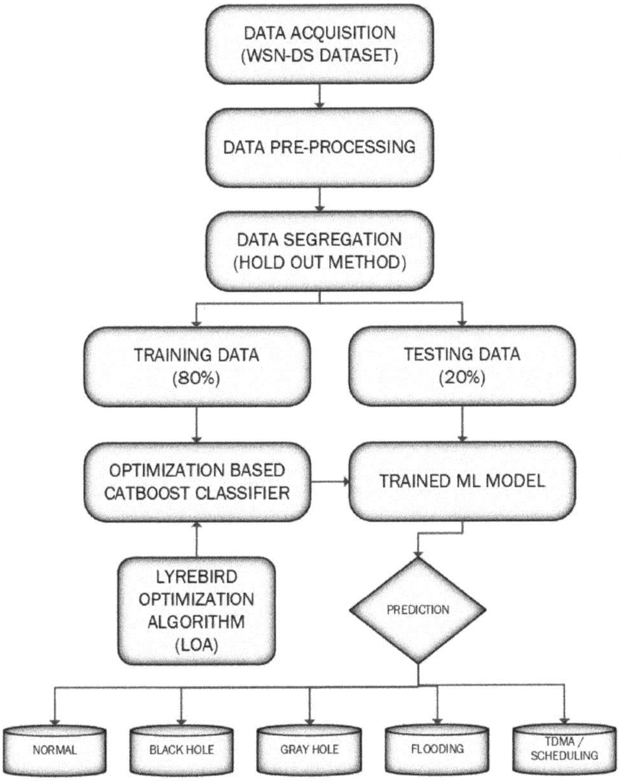

Figure 4. Flow diagram of the proposed LOA-Cb-C.

5. Performance Metrics

The following are the parameters considered for analysis.

True Positive Rate: The ratio of actual positive cases to the sum of true positive and false negatives that are correctly identified by a classifier.

$$TPR = \frac{TP}{TP + FN} \quad (7)$$

False Positive Rate: The proportion of actual negative cases to the sum of true negative and false positives that are incorrectly classified as positive by a classifier.

$$FPR = \frac{FP}{FP + TN} \quad (8)$$

Precision: The fraction of positive instances that a classifier accurately predicts out of all positive instances.

$$Precision = \frac{TP}{TP + FP} \quad (9)$$

Recall: The fraction of correctly predicted positive instances among all actual positive instances.

$$Recall = \frac{TP}{TP + FN} \quad (10)$$

F1-score: The harmonic mean of precision and recall, providing a balance between the two metrics.

$$F1\_Score = 2 \times \frac{(Precison \times Recall)}{(Precison + Recall)} \quad (11)$$

Accuracy: The ratio of correctly classified instances (true positives and true negatives) among all instances.

$$Accuracy = \frac{TP + TN}{overall\ samples} \times 100 \quad (12)$$

Error: The ratio of incorrectly classified instances (both false positives and false negatives) among all instances.

$$Error = \frac{FP + FN}{overall\ samples} \quad (13)$$

6. Simulation Results

The suggested Cb-C was implemented in Python on an Intel(R) Core(TM) i7 processor running Microsoft Windows 11 with a 3.40 GHz central processing unit and 16 GB of random access memory under the Google Collaboratory environment. Table 3 lists the hyperparameters and the values selected for the proposed classifier.

Table 3. Hyperparameters of the proposed classifier.

Parameter	Input Values
Defining search space for hyper parameters	
iterations	range (100, 1000, 100)
depth	range (4, 11)
learning rate	[0.01, 0.05, 0.1, 0.5]
optimizer	lyrebirdOptimizer(param_space)
best_params	optimizer.optimize(X_train, y_train)
model=	Catboost-Classifier(best_params)

The proposed classifier was executed with a learning rate of 0.01, 0.05, 0.1, and 0.5 with 100 iterations. Table 3 provides the values obtained by the proposed classifier on 20% of the testing data.

Table 4 shows that the proposed classifier achieved an average TP rate of 0.99, recall, precision, f1 measure, and ROC, with an FP rate of 0.01.

Table 4. Performance of proposed classifier on test data.

Class	TP Rate	FP Rate	Precision	Recall	F1_Measure	ROC
Normal	0.99	0.02	0.99	0.99	0.99	1.00
Flooding	0.97	0.00	0.94	0.97	0.96	0.99
TDMA	0.93	0.00	1.00	0.93	0.96	0.95
Grayhole	0.97	0.00	0.98	0.97	0.98	1.00
Blackhole	0.99	0.00	0.98	0.99	0.98	1.00
Weighted Average	0.99	0.01	0.99	0.99	0.99	0.99

Table 5 shows that out of 74,932 instances, 74,676 were correctly classified and 256 were incorrectly classified. Therefore, the accuracy is 99.66% and the misclassification cost is 0.34. From Table 6, it is inferred that MAE is 0.0025 and RMSE is 0.034. The kappa statistics value is 0.98, which is very close to 1. This shows that the proposed Cb-C tuned by the LOA fits best in predicting more samples as true positives, which produces better accuracy than the other reported techniques.

Table 5. Confusion matrix of the proposed LOA-Cb-C on test data.

Class	Normal (a)	Flooding (b)	TDMA (c)	Grayhole (d)	Blackhole (e)
Normal (a)	67,914	37	0	31	3
Flooding (b)	16	663	0	0	0
TDMA (c)	93	0	1249	1	0
Grayhole (d)	33	0	0	2798	33
Blackhole (e)	0	0	0	9	2052

Table 6. Output of the proposed LOA-Cb-C.

Metrics	Output
Accuracy	99.66
Error	0.34
Kappa Statistic	0.98
MAE (Mean Absolute Error)	0.0025
RMSE (Root Mean Squared Error)	0.034
Total number of instances	74,932

Table 7 shows the comparative analysis of the performance metrics obtained by the proposed classifier with the other reported models in this article. The accuracy obtained by LOA-Cb-C is 99.66%, which is 0.06% less than Gboost, 0.16% less than MVFS, 0.46% less than DLDM, 0.87% less than CNN, 0.87% less than SVM, 1.66% less than RF, 2.01% less than MLML, 2.62% less than DNN, 2.8% less than CNN+RNN, 3.18% less than RNN, 5.06% less than NB, 6.26% less than LR, 6.66% less than NNC-PSOR, 7.7% less than ANN, and 15.86% less than KNN. The error obtained by LOA-Cb-C is 0.34, which is 0.06 times less than Gboost, 0.16 times less than MVFS, 0.46 times less than DLDM, 0.87 times less than CNN, 0.94 times less than SVM, 1.66 times less than RF, 2.01 times less than MLML, 2.62 times less than DNN, 2.8 times less than CNN+RNN, 3.18 times less than RNN, 5.06 times less than NB, 6.26 times less than LR, 7.0 times less than NNC-PSOR, 7.7 times less than ANN, and 15.86 times less than KNN. The value of precision, recall and F1-score obtained by proposed classifier is 0.99, but the value obtained by ANN is 1.00.

Table 7. LOA-Cb-C comparison with other reported techniques.

Algorithm/Model	Performance Metrics				
	Accuracy	Error	Precision	Recall	F1-Score
LOA-Cb-C (Proposed model)	99.66	0.34	0.99	0.99	0.99
Gboost [36]	99.60	0.40	-	-	0.98
MVFS [18]	99.50	0.50	0.97	0.96	0.96
DLDM [37]	99.20	0.80	-	-	-
CNN [30]	98.79	1.21	0.94	0.92	0.93
SVM [35]	98.72	1.28	-	-	-
RF [28]	98.00	2.00	0.99	0.96	0.97
MLML [22]	97.65	2.35	0.94	0.96	0.93
DNN [30]	97.04	2.96	0.82	0.82	0.82
DT [28]	97.00	3.00	0.94	0.95	0.95
CNN + RNN [30]	96.86	3.14	0.85	0.85	0.82
RNN [30]	96.48	3.52	0.85	0.69	0.75
NB [28]	94.60	5.40	0.32	0.76	0.45
LR [28]	93.40	6.60	0.88	0.77	0.82
NNC-PSOR [19]	93.00	7.00	0.93	0.92	0.92
ANN [29]	91.96	8.04	1.00	1.00	1.00
KNN [28]	83.80	16.20	0.69	0.66	0.68

7. Discussion

The combined use of the LOA and Cb-C for detecting DoS attacks in IoT-based WSNs demonstrates significant improvements over traditional unimodal and hybrid algorithms. The LOA's ability to balance exploration and exploitation during the search process enhances the algorithm's adaptability to dynamic WSN environments. Unlike unimodal algorithms that struggle with local optima, the LOA's population-based approach ensures robust convergence toward optimal solutions, making it well-suited for the detection of complex attack patterns. Additionally, the LOA's iterative process allows for more effective detection of diverse attack types, resulting in improved classification accuracy.

The Cb-C, known for its fast, high-performance gradient boosting technique, further strengthens the detection mechanism. Its unique symmetric tree structure accelerates prediction times and reduces overfitting, which is crucial for maintaining high accuracy in real-time environments like IoT-based WSNs. By leveraging an advanced ordered target statistics method for handling categorical data, CatBoost mitigates issues related to target leakage and enhances model generalization. This is particularly important in the context of intrusion detection, where the correct classification of network traffic and attack types is critical for system security.

In comparison to other hybrid algorithms, the LOA-Cb-C combination delivers superior results in terms of detection accuracy, computational efficiency, and adaptability to real-time network changes. While some challenges remain, such as managing computational complexity in resource-constrained WSN environments, the method's scalability and flexibility in addressing diverse attack vectors present strong advantages. Future work can extend this approach to detect a broader range of attacks, while also exploring further optimization techniques to improve computational efficiency.

8. Complexity Analysis of the Proposed Approach

A detailed complexity analysis is presented in this section. The complexity of the LOA depends on the following parameters: population size (N), number of iterations (T), and fitness evaluation (F) for each individual in the population.

a. **Lyrebird Optimization Algorithm:**
   (i) **Time Complexity:**
   - **Population Initialization:** Randomly generating an initial population requires O(N), where N is the population size.
   - **Fitness Calculation:** For each iteration, the fitness of each individual is evaluated. Let the fitness evaluation take O (F). So, for each iteration, it takes O (N × F).
   - **Exploration and Exploitation (Search Process):** For each iteration, the algorithm applies search mechanisms (exploitation and exploration) on the population. Since each individual is updated per iteration, it contributes to an additional O (N) per iteration.
   - **Overall Time Complexity of the LOA:** O (T × N × F), where T is the number of iterations, N is the population size, and F is the time complexity for fitness calculation.

   (ii) **Space Complexity of the LOA:**
   - Population storage: Each individual in the population is stored, so the space complexity is O (N).

b. **CatBoost Classifier:**
   The complexity of CatBoost depends on the following:
   Number of trees (T), maximum depth of trees (D), number of data points (n), and number of features (f).
   (i) **Time Complexity of CatBoost:**
   - **Tree Construction:** The complexity of building one tree in CatBoost is O(n × f × D), where n-n is the number of data points, f-f is the number of features, and D is the maximum depth of the trees.
   - **Total Time Complexity:** With T trees, the overall time complexity for CatBoost is O(T × n × f × D).

   (ii) **Space Complexity of CatBoost:**
   - **Model Storage:** CatBoost needs to store the trees, so the space complexity is O(T × n × D).

To ensure the efficiency of the proposed approach, let us compare the computational complexity with Gboost [31]. Let us breakdown the time and space complexity of GBoost and investigate how CatBoost improves on it in terms of reducing overfitting, using ordered target statistics, and its balanced tree structure.

The time complexity of Gboost is given by O (T × n × f × log n), where T is the number of trees in the model; n is the number of data points or samples; f is the number of features or columns in the dataset; and log n represents the complexity of sorting the data at each node split. XGBoost builds decision trees iteratively. At each split of the decision tree, the algorithm selects the best feature that minimizes a loss function (like mean squared error for regression tasks). The process of finding the best feature and its splitting point requires sorting the feature values for each node in the tree, which costs O (log n). Since XGBoost builds T trees, and for each tree, it looks through all n data points and f features to find the best split, and the total time complexity becomes O (T × n × f × log n). The space complexity of Gboost is given by O (T × n × D), where D is the maximum depth of the trees. Each tree stores information for all n samples, and since XGBoost constructs T trees, the overall space required for storing the tree structure and the data associated with each node is O (T × n × D).

c. **Lyrebird Optimization Algorithm–CatBoost Classifier (LOA-Cb-C):**

LOA-Cb-C offers a competitive time complexity of O(T × N × F +T × n × f × D), which is efficient because of the robust optimization provided by the LOA and the fast training and inference of CatBoost.

Thus, the LOA-Cb-C combination strikes a favorable balance between computational efficiency and classification performance, making it a suitable choice for large-scale, real-time IoT-based WSN applications.

9. Conclusions

In this study, a novel approach is developed and implemented for detecting and classifying attacks in WSNs using LOA-Cb-C. The experiments reveal that our classifier is highly successful, with 99.66 percent accuracy and 0.34 error. These results outperform the existing models reported in the literature, highlighting the superiority of our approach. Furthermore, our proposed classifier achieves challenging results for key performance metrics such as precision, recall, and F1-score. This indicates that our classifier not only accurately detects attacks but also minimizes false negatives and false positives, making it highly reliable for practical applications in WSNs. Overall, our study demonstrates the effectiveness of using LOA-Cb-C for ID in WSNs. Future work could focus on further enhancing the classifier's performance by exploring additional features or refining the optimization process.

10. Future Research Directions

a. **Enhancing the LOA's Adaptability for Complex IoT Environments:** While the LOA demonstrates strong capabilities in balancing exploration and exploitation, future research could focus on improving its adaptability to more complex, multi-modal attack scenarios. Enhancing the LOA's ability to adjust its exploration parameters dynamically based on the characteristics of the evolving network environment could further improve the accuracy of attack detection. Incorporating adaptive or self-tuning parameters within the LOA could be a significant improvement in achieving optimal performance in dynamic IoT environments.

b. **Integration of Real-Time Constraints and Resource Optimization:** IoT-based WSNs often operate in resource-constrained environments where energy efficiency, memory, and computational power are limited. Future work could focus on optimizing the combination of the LOA and Cb-C to function effectively within these constraints. This may involve integrating energy-aware strategies, low-power communication protocols, or lightweight versions of the algorithm that minimize resource consumption while maintaining high detection accuracy.

c. **Expanding Detection to a Wider Range of Attack Types and Datasets:** The current approach is primarily designed for detecting DoS attacks; however, future research could explore expanding the detection capabilities to cover a broader spectrum of IoT-based WSN attack types, such as routing attacks, Sybil attacks, and blackhole attacks. Testing the LOA-Cb-C framework on more diverse datasets and real-world environments could further validate its generalizability and effectiveness. Moreover, integrating multi-class classification approaches within CatBoost for more granular identification of attack subtypes could lead to deeper insights into network vulnerabilities.

d. **Hybrid Approaches and Deep Learning Integration:** To further improve detection performance, combining LOA with deep learning techniques or other advanced optimization methods (e.g., particle swarm optimization, genetic algorithms) could be explored. Hybrid approaches could capitalize on the strengths of different algorithms and lead to more robust and accurate IDS. Additionally, real-time learning and adaptation, such as online learning techniques, could be integrated to continuously improve the classifier's performance as new threats emerge.

By addressing these research directions, the combination of the LOA and Cb-C could evolve into an even more powerful tool for securing IoT-based WSNs against a wide array of cyber threats.

Author Contributions: Conceptualization, S.S.A. and P.A.; Methodology, P.A.; Software, D.B.M.; Validation, P.A., A.R. and A.L.; Formal analysis, S.S.A.; Investigation, D.B.M.; Resources, P.A.; Data curation, D.B.M.; Writing—original draft preparation, S.S.A.; Writing—review and editing, A.R.; Visualization, B.W.; Supervision, P.A.; Project administration, J.M.G.; Funding acquisition, J.M.G. All authors have read and agreed to the published version of the manuscript.

Funding: This research received no external funding.

Data Availability Statement: The original data presented in the study are openly available in kaggle at https://www.kaggle.com/datasets/bassamkasasbeh1/wsnds, accessed on 15 October 2024.

Conflicts of Interest: The authors declare no conflict of interest.

Abbreviation

Acronym	**Expansion**
ANN	Artificial Neural Network
BCOA-MLID	Binary Chimp Optimization Algorithm with Machine Learning-based Intrusion Detection
Cb-C	Catboost classifier
CMPRO	Chimp social incentive-based Mutated Poor Rich Optimization
CNN	Convolutional Neural Network
CNS	Cooja Network Simulator
COS	Contiki Operating System
CRNN	convolutional recurrent neural network
CSA	Crow Search Algorithm
CSCA	Compact Sine Cosine Algorithm
DFFF	Distance-based Fruit Fly Fuzzy
DL	deep learning
DL-HIDS	deep learning-based host intrusion detection
DoS	Denial of Service
ELDA	entropy-based linear discriminant analysis
FA	Firefly Algorithm
FC	Fully Connected
FSA	fish swarm algorithm
GA	genetic algorithm
GRU	Gated Recurrent Unit
GSWO	Genetic Sacrificial Whale Optimization
GWDTO	Grey Wolf Dipper Throated Optimization
GWO	Grey Wolf Optimizer
ID	intrusion detection
IDS	intrusion detection system
IoT	Internet of Things
LOA	Lyrebird Optimization Algorithm
LSTM	long short-term memory
MBOLT-IDS	MegaBAT optimized Long Short-Term Memory
ML	machine learning
MLP	Multi-Layer Perceptron
MLPNN	Multi-Layer Perceptron Neural Network
MSO	Moth Search Optimizer
MSODL-ID	Moth Search Optimizer with Deep Learning Enabled Intrusion Detection
NIDS	Network ID System
NSL	National Security Laboratory
OBPNN	Optimized Back Propagation Neural Network
PCA	Principal Component Analysis
PM	Polymorphic Mutation
PSO	particle swarm optimization

QN3	Quasi-Newton Neural Network
RBFNN	Radial Basis Function Neural Network
RF	Random Forest
RF-RFE	Random Forest-Recursive Feature Elimination
SFS	Sequential Forward Selection
SMOTE	Synthetic Minority Oversampling Technique
SNs	sensor nodes
SVD	Singular Value Decomposition
SVM	Support Vector Machine
TVP-IPSO	Time-Varying Parameter-Improved Particle Swarm Optimization
WOA	Whale Optimization Algorithm
WSN	Wireless Sensor Network

References

1. Avinash, B.; Manmohan, S.; Ajay Shriaram, K.; Shilpa, S.; Hussien Sobahi, M. Nonlinear Energy Optimization in the Wireless Sensor Network through NN-LEACH. *Math. Prob. Eng.* **2023**, *2023*, 5143260.
2. Nagalalli, G.; Ravi, G. A Novel MegaBAT Optimized Intelligent Intrusion Detection System in Wireless Sensor Networks. *Intell. Autom. Soft Comput.* **2023**, *35*, 475–490. [CrossRef]
3. Gautami, A.; Shanthini, J.; Karthik, S. A Quasi-Newton Neural Network Based Efficient Intrusion Detection System for Wireless Sensor Network. *Comput. Syst. Sci. Eng.* **2023**, *45*, 427–443. [CrossRef]
4. Aljebreen, M.; Ahmed, M.; Ahmad, M.; Abbas, M.; Khan, A.; Alqahtani, S.; Hussien, M.A. Binary Chimp Optimization Algorithm with ML Based Intrusion Detection for Secure IoT-Assisted Wireless Sensor Networks. *Sensors* **2023**, *23*, 4073. [CrossRef]
5. Karthikeyan, M.; Manimegalai, D.; RajaGopal, K. Firefly Algorithm Based WSN-IoT Security Enhancement with Machine Learning for Intrusion Detection. *Sci. Rep.* **2024**, *14*, 231. [CrossRef]
6. Azar, A.T.; Shehab, E.; Mattar, A.M.; Hameed, I.A.; Elsaid, S.A. Deep Learning Based Hybrid Intrusion Detection Systems to Protect Satellite Networks. *J. Netw. Syst. Manag.* **2023**, *31*, 767–788. [CrossRef]
7. Alhasan, R.A.; Hamza, E.K. A Novel CNN Model with Dimensionality Reduction for WSN Intrusion Detection. *Rev. d'Intell. Artif.* **2023**, *37*, 1121–1131. [CrossRef]
8. Abbas, Q.; Hina, S.; Sajjad, H.; Zaidi, K.S.; Akbar, R. Optimization of Predictive Performance of Intrusion Detection System Using Hybrid Ensemble Model for Secure Systems. *PeerJ Comput. Sci.* **2023**, *9*, e1552. [CrossRef]
9. Darla, S.; Naveena, C. An Optimized Deep Learning Based Malicious Nodes Detection in Intelligent Sensor-Based Systems Using Blockchain. *J. Adv. Inf. Technol.* **2023**, *14*, 1037–1045. [CrossRef]
10. Murugesh, C.; Murugan, S. Moth Search Optimizer with Deep Learning Enabled Intrusion Detection System in Wireless Sensor Networks. *SSRG Int. J. Electr. Electron. Eng.* **2023**, *10*, 77–90. [CrossRef]
11. Yang, Y.; Gu, Y.; Yan, Y. Machine Learning-Based Intrusion Detection for Rare-Class Network Attacks. *Electronics* **2023**, *12*, 3911. [CrossRef]
12. Awajan, A. A Novel Deep Learning-Based Intrusion Detection System for IoT Networks. *Computers* **2023**, *12*, 34. [CrossRef]
13. Mandala, V.; Senthilnathan, T.; Suganyadevi, S.; Gobhinath, S.; Selvaraj, D.S.; Dhanapal, R. An Optimized Back Propagation Neural Network for Automated Evaluation of Health Condition Using Sensor Data. *Meas. Sens.* **2023**, *29*, 100846. [CrossRef]
14. Hnamte, V.; Hussain, J. DCNNBiLSTM: An Efficient Hybrid Deep Learning-Based Intrusion Detection System. *Telemat. Inform. Rep.* **2023**, *10*, 100053. [CrossRef]
15. Singh, A.; Amutha, J.; Nagar, J.; Sharma, S.; Lee, C.C. AutoML-ID: Automated Machine Learning Model for Intrusion Detection Using Wireless Sensor Network. *Sci. Rep.* **2022**, *12*, 9074. [CrossRef]
16. Karthika, J.; Loganathan, S.; Vanathi, M. A Hybrid Machine Learning Based Feature Selection Technique for Attack Detection in NIDS. *J. Phys. Conf. Ser.* **2022**, *2335*, 012033. [CrossRef]
17. Hidayat, I.; Ali, M.Z.; Arshad, A. Machine Learning-Based Intrusion Detection System: An Experimental Comparison. *J. Comput. Cogn. Eng.* **2022**, *2*, 88–97. [CrossRef]
18. Patil, D.R.; Pattewar, T.M. Majority Voting and Feature Selection Based Network Intrusion Detection System. *EAI Endorsed Trans. Scalable Inf. Syst.* **2022**, *22*, e173780. [CrossRef]
19. Balobaid, A.S.; Ahamed, S.B.; Shamsudheen, S.; Balamurugan, S. Neural Network Clustering and Swarm Intelligence-Based Routing Protocol for Wireless Sensor Networks: A Machine Learning Perspective. *Comput. Intell. Neurosci.* **2023**, *2023*, 4758852. [CrossRef]
20. Zang, M.; Yan, Y. Machine Learning-Based Intrusion Detection System for Big Data Analytics in VANET. In Proceedings of the IEEE 93rd Vehicular Technology Conference 2021, Helsinki, Finland, 25–28 April 2021. [CrossRef]
21. Khan, M.A.; Jan, M.A.; Alam, M.M.; Khalid, A.; Ahmad, M.; Manzoor, S.; Rodrigues, J.J.P.C.; Rodrigues, O. A Deep Learning-Based Intrusion Detection System for MQTT Enabled IoT. *Sensors* **2021**, *21*, 7016. [CrossRef]
22. Alruhaily, N.M.; Ibrahim, D.M. A Multi-Layer Machine Learning-Based Intrusion Detection System for Wireless Sensor Networks. *Sensors* **2021**, *12*, 281–288. [CrossRef]

23. Lansky, J.; Dobias, P.; Sahula, V.; Kremen, P. Deep Learning-Based Intrusion Detection Systems: A Systematic Review. *IEEE Access* **2021**, *9*, 101574–101599. [CrossRef]
24. Zhang, T.; Han, D.; Marino, M.D.; Wang, L.; Li, K.C. An Evolutionary-Based Approach for Low-Complexity Intrusion Detection in Wireless Sensor Networks. *Wirel. Pers. Commun.* **2021**, *126*, 2019–2042. [CrossRef]
25. Idrissi, I.; Azizi, M.; Moussaoui, O. A Lightweight Optimized Deep Learning-Based Host-Intrusion Detection System Deployed on the Edge for IoT. *Int. J. Comput. Digit. Syst.* **2022**, *11*, 209–216. [CrossRef]
26. Pan, J.S.; Fan, F.; Chu, S.C.; Zhao, H.Q.; Liu, G.Y. A Lightweight Intelligent Intrusion Detection Model for Wireless Sensor Networks. *Secur. Commun. Netw.* **2021**, *2021*, 5540895. [CrossRef]
27. Almomani, I.; Alenezi, M. Efficient Denial of Service Attacks Detection in Wireless Sensor Networks. *J. Inf. Sci. Eng.* **2018**, *34*, 977–1000. [CrossRef]
28. Vinayakumar, R.; Alazab, M.; Soman, K.P.; Poornachandran, P.; Al-Nemrat, A.; Venkatraman, S. Deep Learning Approach for Intelligent Intrusion Detection System. *IEEE Access* **2019**, *7*, 41525–41550. [CrossRef]
29. Le, T.T.H.; Park, T.; Cho, D.; Kim, H. An Effective Classification for DoS Attacks in Wireless Sensor Networks. In Proceedings of the 2018 Tenth International Conference on Ubiquitous and Future Networks (ICUFN), Prague, Czech Republic, 3–6 July 2018; pp. 689–692. [CrossRef]
30. Salmi, S.; Oughdir, L. Performance Evaluation of Deep Learning Techniques for DoS Attacks Detection in Wireless Sensor Network. *J. Big Data* **2023**, *10*, 17. [CrossRef]
31. Nguyen, T.M.; Hanh Hong-Phuv, V.; Yoo, M. Enhancing Intrusion Detection in Wireless Sensor Networks Using a GSWO-CatBoost Approach. *Sensors* **2024**, *24*, 3339. [CrossRef]
32. Mirsky, Y.; Doitshman, T.; Elovici, Y.; Shabtai, A. Kitsune: An Ensemble of Autoencoders for Online Network Intrusion Detection. In Proceedings of the Network and Distributed Systems Security (NDSS)Symposium 2018, San Diego, CA, USA, 18–21 February 2018. [CrossRef]
33. Mohammad Hashemi, J.; Eric, K. Enhancing Robustness Against Adversarial Examples in Network Intrusion Detection Systems. In Proceedings of the 2020 IEEE Conference on Network Function Virtualization and Software Defined Networks (NFV-SDN), Leganes, Spain, 10–12 November 2020; pp. 1–7. [CrossRef]
34. Bovenzi, G.; Aceto, G.; Ciuonzo, D.; Montieri, A.; Persico, V.; Pescape, A. Network anomaly detection methods in IoT environments via deep learning: A Fair comparison of performance and robustness. *Comput. Secur.* **2023**, *128*, 103167. [CrossRef]
35. Deshpande, S.; Gujarathi, J.; Chandre, P.; Nerkar, P. A Comparative Analysis of Machine Deep Learning Algorithms for Intrusion Detection in WSN. *Stud. Syst. Decis. Control* **2021**, *341*, 173–193. [CrossRef]
36. Wazirali, R.; Ahmad, R. Machine Learning Approaches to Detect DoS and Their Effect on WSNs Lifetime. *Comput. Mater. Contin.* **2022**, *70*, 4921–4946. [CrossRef]
37. Premkumar, M.; Sundararajan, T.V.P. DLDM: Deep Learning-Based Defense Mechanism for Denial of Service Attacks in Wireless Sensor Networks. *Microprocess. Microsyst.* **2020**, *79*, 103278. [CrossRef]

future internet

MDPI

Article

Internet of Things Adoption in Technology Ecosystems Within the Central African Region: The Case of Silicon Mountain

Godlove Suila Kuaban [1], Valery Nkemeni [2], Onyeka J. Nwobodo [3], Piotr Czekalski [3] and Fabien Mieyeville [4,*]

[1] Institute of Theoretical and Applied Informatics, Polish Academy of Sciences, Baltycka 5, 44-100 Gliwice, Poland; gskuaban@iitis.pl
[2] Laboratory of Electrical Engineering and Computing, University of Buea, Buea P.O. Box 63, Cameroon; nkemeni.valery@ubuea.cm
[3] Department of Computer Graphics, Vision and Digital Systems, Silesian University of Technology, Akademicka 2A, 44-100 Gliwice, Poland; onyeka.nwobodo@polsl.pl (O.J.N.); piotr.czekalski@polsl.pl (P.C.)
[4] University de Lyon, Université Claude Bernard Lyon 1, Ecole Centrale de Lyon, INSA Lyon, CNRS, Ampère, F-69621 Villeurbanne, France
* Correspondence: fabien.mieyeville@univ-lyon1.fr

Abstract: The Internet of Things (IoT) has emerged as a transformative technology with the potential to revolutionize various sectors and industries worldwide. Despite its global significance, the adoption and implementation of IoT technologies in emerging technology ecosystems within the Central African region still need to be studied and explored. This paper presents a case study of the Silicon Mountain technology ecosystem, located in Fako division of the southwest region of Cameroon, focusing on the barriers and challenges to adopting and integrating IoT technologies within this emerging tech ecosystem. Through a survey-based approach, we investigate the factors influencing IoT adoption in the Silicon Mountain tech ecosystem, including technological, economic, social, and regulatory factors. Our study reveals key insights into the current state of IoT adoption, opportunities for growth and innovation, and IoT adoption challenges. Key among the challenges identified for impeding IoT uptake were issues related to standardization and financial resources, labor shortage in the industry, educational and knowledge gaps, market challenges, government policies, security and data privacy concerns, and inadequate power supply. Based on our findings, we provide recommendations for policymakers, industry stakeholders, and academic institutions to promote and facilitate the widespread adoption of IoT technologies in Silicon Mountain and the Central African region at large.

Keywords: Internet of Things; IoT adoption; IoT adoption barriers; technology ecosystems; Silicon Mountain; Central African region

1. Introduction

The Internet of Things (IoT) has revolutionized the way we interact with technology, creating a network of interconnected devices that communicate and share data to optimize various processes and services [1]. IoT applications span numerous sectors, including healthcare [2], agriculture [3], smart cities [4], industrial automation [5], home automation [6], etc., driving efficiency, innovation, and economic growth [7]. In healthcare, the IoT enables remote patient monitoring [8] and telemedicine [9], improving patient outcomes and reducing healthcare costs. In agriculture, the IoT facilitates precision farming through the use of sensors and data analytics, leading to higher crop yields and sustainable farming practices [10,11]. Smart cities leverage the IoT to enhance urban management, from traffic control and waste management to energy consumption and public safety [12–14]. The potential of the IoT to revolutionize various sectors and industries has led to its adoption worldwide.

While the IoT is present in everyday life in developed countries, its expansion and implementation in different regions of the world differ. In the African context, studies on IoT adoption have been carried out in West Africa, East Africa, and South Africa. For instance, Iwayemi [15] examined the challenges of IoT implementation in Nigeria, identifying key barriers such as cybersecurity threats, privacy concerns, and inadequate infrastructure. Similarly, Dosumu et al. [16] highlighted the shortage of skilled labor and the lack of educational programs focused on the IoT as significant impediments to its adoption in Rwanda, while Moeti et al. [17] highlighted the cost, knowledge gap, perceived value, and risk as some of the factors influencing the adoption of the IoT in South Africa. These studies provide valuable insights but are often limited to specific regions or sectors, making it difficult to generalize their findings across the diverse landscapes of the African continent.

The Central African sub-region [18], comprising countries such as Cameroon, Chad, the Central African Republic, Equatorial Guinea, Gabon, and the Republic of Congo, presents a unique context for IoT adoption. Despite its rich natural resources and strategic geographic location, the region faces numerous challenges, including political instability [19,20], underdeveloped infrastructure [21], and limited access to advanced technologies [22]. In addition, while East and West Africa have attracted substantial investment and developed thriving tech ecosystems, the Central African region has struggled to establish itself in this rapidly evolving landscape. These factors may have hindered the widespread adoption of the IoT in the region. Finally, the limited amount of research focusing on this region and its distinct socio-economic and political conditions makes insights and recommendations from studies conducted in other African regions or countries not directly applicable to the region.

Cameroon, the leading economy in the Central African sub-region, has the most advanced tech ecosystems in the sub-region, with the largest number of tech hubs and startups [23]. The country also leads the region in female representation in the tech sector, running approximately 75 to 80 female-focused programs [24]. The major technology ecosystems in Cameroon include Silicon Mountain, Silicon Wouri, and Silicon River and are concentrated in the cities of Buea, Douala, and Yaoundé, respectively.

Silicon Mountain [25], a sprouting technology ecosystem located in Buea, Fako division of the southwest region of Cameroon, is the most popular tech ecosystem in Cameroon and thus offers an ideal case study for investigating IoT adoption in tech ecosystems within the Central African region. The origin of Silicon Mountain can be traced back to 2006 when young web developers in Buea began exploring technology and building a community. Its prominence grew in 2015, following the graduation of the first batch of engineering and technology students from the University of Buea in December 2014 and the inaugural Silicon Mountain Conference held in June 2015. The University of Buea has played a pivotal role in establishing Silicon Mountain as Cameroon's leading technology hub, as many of these tech entrepreneurs first connected during their studies at the university. Known for its vibrant tech community and innovative startups, Silicon Mountain is home to a growing number of tech enthusiasts, developers, and entrepreneurs who are leveraging technology to address local and global challenges. The ecosystem's unique blend of higher education institutions, tech hubs, developer communities, tech-focused startups, etc., creates a conducive environment for exploring the potential and challenges of IoT adoption.

The objective of this study is to examine the barriers and opportunities for IoT adoption in the Silicon Mountain technology ecosystem and, by extension, the Central African region. This research aims to provide a comprehensive understanding of the factors influencing IoT adoption and to propose actionable recommendations for stakeholders to foster a more conducive environment for IoT implementation.

This study provides the following contributions:

- Identifying the key challenges for IoT adoption in the Silicon Mountain technology ecosystem and, by extension, the Central African region.

- Providing empirical data and insights specific to Silicon Mountain, which can serve as a benchmark for similar ecosystems in the region.
- Proposing strategies to overcome the identified barriers and to enhance the adoption of the IoT in the Silicon Mountain technology ecosystem and, by extension, the Central African region.
- Highlighting the role of educational institutions, government policies, and private sector initiatives in promoting IoT adoption.

The remainder of the paper is organized as follows: Section 2 presents a review of related works, Section 3 presents the methodology adopted, Section 4 presents the results and discussion, and Section 5 concludes the paper.

2. Review of Related Works

Studies on IoT adoption have been conducted globally across various geographic regions and technological domains. Geographically, these studies cover regions such as Europe, the United States, and Asia, as well as Eastern, Western, and Southern Africa. Technologically, the focus of these studies spans sectors like education, healthcare, agriculture, governance, and construction. Table 1 provides a summarized review of the related literature on IoT adoption, highlighting the diverse application areas and demonstrating the broad versatility of IoT technologies. Each sector encounters distinct challenges and opportunities in adopting the IoT, shaped by its specific technological, economic, and regulatory contexts. The following section synthesizes the findings by categorizing the studies based on their application areas: smart cities, education, healthcare, e-government, smart agriculture, and construction.

IoT adoption studies focusing on smart cities emphasize the role of the IoT in improving urban infrastructure management. In India, Mishra et al. [26] identified barriers such as privacy concerns, regulatory gaps, and high operational costs in smart city waste management. Similarly, in Europe, Padyab et al. [27] examined IoT adoption across multiple smart city applications, including autonomous driving and smart agriculture, identifying trust, privacy, and cost as key barriers. These findings highlight that while the IoT can significantly enhance urban services, concerns over data security and financial sustainability continue to hinder its widespread adoption.

In the educational sector, IoT adoption has been explored in both African and international contexts. The studies of Ajigini et al. [28], conducted in South Africa and Evwiekpaefe et al. [29], conducted in Nigeria, found that performance expectancy, effort expectancy, facilitating conditions, and social influence positively impact behavioral intentions to adopt the IoT in higher education institutions (HEIs). Another study in Nigeria [15] points to infrastructure issues, such as power supply shortages and the fear of cyber attacks, as major challenges. These studies reveal that while the IoT holds the potential to transform education, especially in resource-constrained environments, the success of its adoption largely depends on improving infrastructure and addressing security concerns.

The healthcare sector presents a unique opportunity for IoT adoption, particularly in improving patient care and health management. Al-rawashdeh et al. [30] conducted a systematic review of factors influencing medical professionals to adopt the IoT in healthcare, highlighting perceived usefulness, privacy risks, and financial costs as key determinants. The findings suggest that the IoT can bring significant benefits to healthcare, but issues related to privacy and financial feasibility must be addressed to encourage wider adoption by medical professionals.

Table 1. Review of related works on IoT adoption.

Ref	Geography Focus	Technological Focus	Research Objectives	Methodology	Identified Factors Influencing or Hindering IoT Adoption
[26]	India	Smart cities	Investigate the impact of IoT barriers for smart city waste management	An analytic approach involving a hybrid multi-attribute decision-making model applied to 15 IoT barriers identified from the literature and expert opinions	Security and privacy issues, lack of regulatory norms and policies, operational costs and extended payback periods, etc.
[28]	South Africa	Education	Investigate and identify the determinants of IoT adoption by higher educational institutions (HEIs) within the South African setting	A quantitative (empirical) method involving a survey of 250 respondents selected randomly from some tertiary institutions and the use of exploratory factor analysis (EFA) and regression analysis to determine factors affecting IoT adoption in HEIs	Behavioral intention to use the IoT was positively influenced by performance expectancy, social influence, and effort expectancy.
[30]	N.A.	Healthcare	Analyze and statistically classify existing knowledge about the factors that influence medical professionals to adopt IoT applications in the healthcare sector.	Systematic review of relevant IoT adoption studies from 2015 to 2021 carried out on nine major scientific databases and leading to 22 articles being selected as per the inclusion criteria	Social influence, attitude, and personal inattentiveness; perceived usefulness, perceived ease of use, performance expectancy, and effort expectations; perceived privacy risk, perceived severity and perceived health risk; financial cost; and facilitating conditions
[31]	Pakistan	E-government	Explore the success factors of IoT service orchestration to create public value in smart government.	A quantitative method for data collection involving a field survey conducted through online and paper-based questionnaires administered to 87 respondents. Partial least squares structural equation modeling was used for data analysis	Decision transparency, government trust, service collaboration, service effectiveness, service transparency, public engagement, perceived ease of use, public trust, and perceived usefulness are valid success measures of e-gov IoT service orchestration
[17]	South Africa	Smart Agriculture	Identify factors that may determine the adoption and use of IoT within the agricultural sector in Limpopo province.	A quantitative approach involving data collected via interviews, observations, and document reviews. Thematic analysis was used for data analysis	Organizational support, cost, knowledge gap, security, policy, monitoring and control, and perceived value and risk

Table 1. *Cont.*

Ref	Geography Focus	Technological Focus	Research Objectives	Methodology	Identified Factors Influencing or Hindering IoT Adoption
[32]	China	Construction	Investigate factors influencing the adoption of the IoT by construction companies in China.	Review of the related literature, adoption theories, semi-structured expert interviews, and a survey via questionnaires were used for data collection and regression analysis was used for analyzing the data	External environmental pressure, perceived benefit, top management support, company resource readiness, adoption intention, and perceived compatibility
[16]	Rwanda	Construction	Investigate the adoption, application and challenges of IoT technologies in the Rwandan construction industry.	Descriptive survey research method using a questionnaire with closed- and open-ended questions. Data analysis carried out using frequencies, mean scores, and Student's t-tests	Lack of training centers, lack of IoT awareness, lack of expertise, poor internet connectivity, etc.
[27]	Europe	Smart cities, autonomous driving, wearables and smart agriculture	Explore IoT adoption barriers in four large-scale pilots in Europe.	Literature review, workshops, and interviews were used to determine relevant IoT adoption barriers	Trust, cost, perceived value, privacy, and security
[33]	US	Agriculture	Explore IoT adoption barriers in precision agriculture practices in the Midwestern (Indiana) region of the US.	Focus group interview sessions conducted with eighteen subject matter experts (SME) in IoT-based precision agriculture practices	Cost, data latency, data scalability, data storage, data interoperability, type of sensors, type of wireless communication, type of precision agriculture application, and power consumption
[29]	Nigeria	Education	Investigate the behavioral intentions of students and staff at tertiary institutions in Kaduna metropolis to adopt IoT technology for educational purposes.	A quantitative method for data collection involving a field survey conducted through online questionnaires administered to 300 respondents. Partial least squares structural equation modeling was used for data analysis	Performance expectancy, effort expectancy, and facilitating condition positively influence behavioral intentions to use IoT technology
[15]	Nigeria	Education	Review IoT implementation challenges in Nigeria.	Literature review and survey via the use of questionnaires	Fraud, lack of power supply, religion, technical know-how, cost of implementing IoT, government policy, cyber attacks, privacy, security, and fear of loss of jobs

The IoT in e-government services has the potential to enhance public value through service efficiency and transparency. In Pakistan, Chohan and Hu [31] explored the success factors for IoT service orchestration in smart government, identifying decision transparency, public trust, and service effectiveness as critical factors. The study emphasizes the importance of public engagement and ease of use in achieving successful IoT implementation in government services. However, fostering trust between the government and citizens remains a key challenge in driving IoT adoption in e-government initiatives.

The agricultural sector, particularly in developing regions, has also embraced IoT applications to improve productivity and resource management. In South Africa, Moeti et al. [17] explored factors such as organizational support and knowledge gaps that influence IoT adoption in smart agriculture. Similarly, Hundal et al. [33] in the US identified technical barriers such as data latency, scalability, and sensor compatibility. These studies indicate that the IoT can play a transformative role in agriculture, but addressing technological constraints and improving farmer awareness and training are essential for successful adoption.

The construction industry offers another unique application area for the IoT, with the potential to improve efficiency and safety in construction projects. In China, Zhao et al. [32] investigated factors influencing IoT adoption by construction companies, identifying external environmental pressure and top management support as significant factors. In Rwanda, Dosumu et al. [16] found that a lack of IoT awareness and poor internet connectivity were major challenges in the construction industry. Both studies emphasize the importance of leadership support and infrastructure development in driving IoT adoption in construction.

The review of related works across these application areas reveals common themes in IoT adoption, such as concerns over privacy, security, and infrastructure. However, the specific challenges vary by sector and region, with industries like healthcare and education focusing on trust and usability, while sectors like agriculture and construction emphasize technological readiness and organizational support. These insights emphasize the need for sector-specific strategies to address the barriers to IoT adoption and fully leverage its potential across different industries and market segments.

While the IoT has attracted significant attention as a transformative technology across various sectors, existing studies primarily focus on sector-specific IoT adoption in areas such as smart cities, education, healthcare, and agriculture, often in more developed regions. Despite these insights, there remains a critical gap in the literature concerning IoT adoption within emerging technology ecosystems, particularly in the underexplored Central African region.

No comprehensive study has examined the factors influencing IoT adoption in technology ecosystems within the Central African region, particularly within innovation clusters like Silicon Mountain. This gap is critical, as the region presents unique barriers (e.g., infrastructure limitations, skill gaps, and regulatory challenges) that are distinct from those found in more developed ecosystems. Understanding these region-specific factors is essential for fostering IoT innovation and growth, yet the absence of targeted research on IoT adoption in Central African technology ecosystems leaves policymakers, industry stakeholders, and academic institutions without the necessary data to inform strategic decision-making. While global studies, including those from international organizations such as the World Bank, Internation Telecommunications Union (ITU), and African Development Bank, have provided valuable insights into the challenges of IoT adoption in developing regions, such as sub-Saharan Africa, there remains a critical need for region-specific studies that address the distinct socio-economic, infrastructural, and regulatory conditions of Central African ecosystems like Silicon Mountain. For example, the World Bank and ITU reports have highlighted common barriers, such as inadequate infrastructure, skill gaps, and regulatory challenges, that are relevant to many African regions [34,35]. However, these global frameworks and findings often provide macro-level data that may not fully capture the unique nuances of smaller technology ecosystems in Central Africa.

This study aims to build upon these global insights by narrowing the focus to the Silicon Mountain technology ecosystem, a hub that has yet to be extensively explored in IoT-specific research. Silicon Mountain presents distinct challenges, such as the limited technological infrastructure and regulatory frameworks that differ from those in better-documented ecosystems, like Kenya's Silicon Savannah [36]. By investigating IoT adoption specifically within the Silicon Mountain context, this study contributes localized insights that complement the broader body of research, helping to address the knowledge gap specific to this underexplored region.

3. Methodology

The methodology employed in this study follows a systematic process to investigate the factors influencing IoT adoption within the Silicon Mountain technology ecosystem. A quantitative survey-based research method, commonly used in management sciences, was applied. This methodology is structured into five key steps: conducting a literature review, designing the survey instrument, sampling and data collection, data validation, and data analysis.

3.1. Literature Review

A comprehensive review of existing studies on IoT adoption, particularly in developing regions, was conducted as presented in Section 2. This helped in formulating the research questions and designing the survey instrument.

3.2. Survey Design and Development

Based on the literature review, a 42-item questionnaire was developed (refer to Appendix A, Table A2). The questions were structured using a 5-point Likert scale and divided into five sections: demographics, IoT awareness, IoT applications, challenges to IoT adoption, and strategies for enhancement. The Likert scale used to assess the challenges to IoT adoption was configured as follows: 1 for "not serious", 2 for "less serious", 3 for "moderate", 4 for "more serious", and 5 for "very serious".

3.3. Sampling and Data Collection

The target population for this study included tech-focused startups, technology hubs, higher education institutions (HEIs), and developer communities located in Buea, all affiliated with the Silicon Mountain technology ecosystem. The ecosystem currently has over fifty registered and active startups, seven tech hubs, five developer communities, and seven tech-focused HEIs. Startups were defined as businesses operating for fewer than five years. A simple random sampling method was used to select 200 participants for the study. Questionnaires were distributed to these participants both online and offline, with data collected through Google Forms and printed forms.

3.4. Data Validation

To ensure face validity, the questionnaire was first reviewed by a data analyst to confirm that the constructs were measured accurately. Data from the field survey were manually coded, except for the data collected online using Google Forms. To ensure the integrity of the data, a series of data verification steps were undertaken. Data collected via online platforms such as Google Forms were checked for any unusual response patterns or inconsistencies that might suggest automation or AI involvement. To ensure data validity and accuracy, responses were manually reviewed and subjected to item analysis using Cronbach's Alpha to assess internal consistency [37]. Construct validity was evaluated through the reliabilities of individual factors [38], also measured using Cronbach's Alpha coefficient and through Exploratory Factor Analysis (EFA) [39].

3.5. Data Analysis

The cleaned and refined data were analyzed using IBM SPSS version 25.0 software. Exploratory Factor Analysis (EFA) and Principal Component Analysis (PCA) with Varimax Rotation [40] were applied to extract key factors influencing IoT adoption. The scale was refined by removing items with low cross-loadings, low factor loadings, and low communalities, improving the interpretability of the factor structure, as recommended by [41]. Challenges with an average seriousness score below 3.5 were excluded from further analysis, as they did not constitute significant barriers to IoT adoption.

4. Results and Discussion

This section presents the findings from the analysis of questionnaires distributed to respondents within the Silicon Mountain technology ecosystem. Out of the 200 questionnaires administered, 160 responses were received, resulting in an 80% response rate, with 146 of these deemed usable for the study.

4.1. Respondent's Demographics

Among the 146 participants who completed the questionnaire, the majority were male (94 or 64.4%), while 52 (35.6%) were female. This result is representative of the field. The tech ecosystem in Cameroon, similar to that of sub-Saharan Africa, is predominantly male-dominated, with most startups being founded and led by men. As of 2020, 85% of co-founders or C-level executives in Africa were male [25]. This can be attributed to cultural practices in the region which significantly contribute to the underrepresentation of women in technical fields. These practices shape societal expectations, gender roles, and access to education, which together create barriers for women [42,43]. The age distribution showed that most respondents were between 21 and 30 years old (69 or 47.3%), followed by those aged 31 to 40 years (30 or 20.5%), with the smallest group being those aged 51 and above. The mean age of the respondents was 30.98 years. This result is representative of the field.

Figure 1 presents the composition of the respondent's affiliation in the Silicon Mountain technology ecosystem obtained from the field survey. The data indicate that 56 respondents (38.4%) are associated with the academic sector within the Silicon Mountain technology ecosystem. Start-up firms comprise 22 respondents (15.1%), developer communities include 15 respondents (10.3%), and incubators account for 18 respondents (12.3%). Furthermore, 4 respondents (2.7%) represent SMEs utilizing IT systems, 16 respondents (11.0%) are technology promoters or enthusiasts, 6 respondents (4.1%) are NGOs involved in technology promotion, 4 respondents (2.7%) are government agencies, and the remaining 5 respondents (3.4%) fall into other categories. This result is representative of the field.

The majority of respondents, 99 (67.8%), held entry-level positions (students, interns, administrative assistants, etc.) in their respective organizations. Additionally, 18 (12.3%) held managerial positions (head of departments, operations managers, product managers, etc.), 15 (10.3%) were co-founders, and the remaining 14 (9.6%) held junior-level positions (junior software developers and marketers).

Figure 2 presents the fields of specialization of the respondents. The majority, 49 (33.6%), were from the telecommunications sector, followed by 38 (26.0%) from software development. Additionally, 13 (8.9%) were from health sciences and computer science, 12 (8.2%) were from the field of computer networks, 7 (4.8%) were from computer maintenance, and the smallest group, 4 (2.7%), were from agriculture. This indicates that within the Silicon Mountain technology ecosystem, the telecommunications sector has the highest representation, while the agricultural field has the lowest. This result is representative of the field.

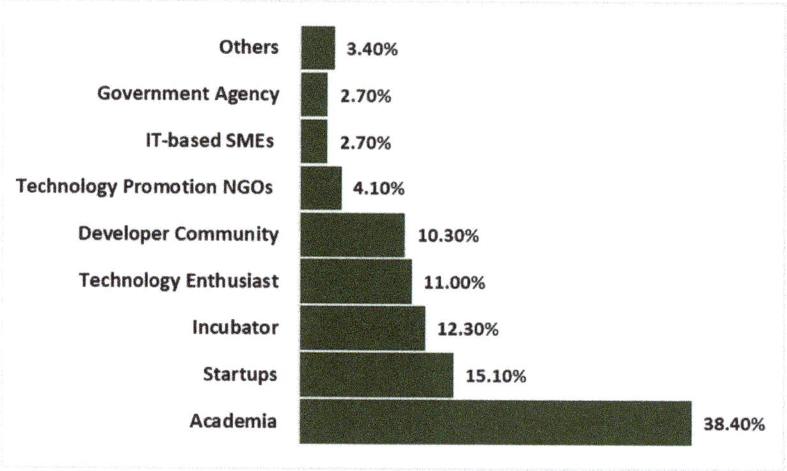

Figure 1. Respondents' affiliation within the Silicon Mountain technology ecosystem.

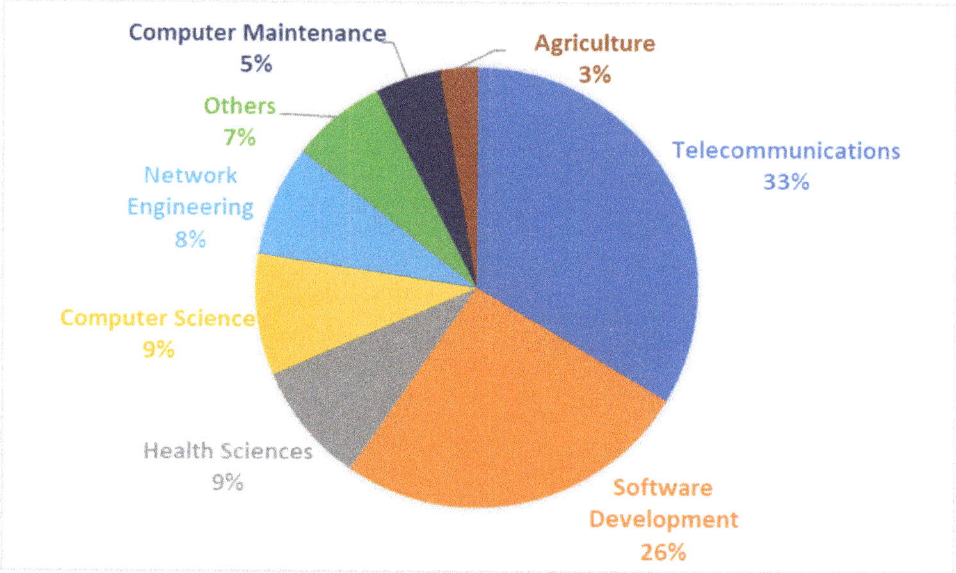

Figure 2. Respondents' field of specialization.

4.2. Reliability Analysis

Evaluating the questionnaire and its individual questions is essential to ensure the consistency of each question group supporting the respective variables and the relevance of the selected questions [44]. Reliability testing was conducted using Cronbach's Alpha statistic [45], and construct validity was assessed through the reliabilities of the individual factors, measured using Cronbach's Alpha coefficient and Exploratory Factor Analysis (EFA).

The reliability testing yielded an overall Cronbach's Alpha value of 0.821, which is considered acceptable as it surpasses the minimum acceptable threshold of 0.7 [46,47]. The Cronbach's Alpha coefficients for all five factors on the questionnaire were satisfactory, as they exceeded the recommended value of 0.7. Furthermore, the results of construct validity from EFA indicated no cross-loading constructs, leading to the identification of seven main barriers for IoT adoption. According to Park and Kim [48], factor analysis typically requires a sample size of 100 or more, but it can be performed with a minimum of 50 samples. This study's sample size exceeded that threshold.

4.3. Awareness and the Level of Knowledge About IoT in the Silicon Mountain Technology Ecosystem

When asked about their knowledge of the IoT and their sources of information, the results show that out of 146 respondents, 122 (83.6%) were familiar with the term IoT, with information acquired from various sources such as the media (59 or 81.9%), books (47 or 38.5%), and others including courses (12 or 9.8%), workshops (3 or 2.4%), and articles (1 or 0.8%). This indicates that most respondents were versed in the concept of the IoT and likely had sufficient knowledge of the challenges related to IoT adoption within the Silicon Mountain technology hub in Buea. Furthermore, more than half of the respondents, 96 (65.8%), rated their understanding of the IoT as good, 14 (9.6%) rated their knowledge as excellent, 22 (15%) had average knowledge, and 14 (9.6%) considered their knowledge of the IoT to be poor.

4.4. Potential Areas for the Implementation of Internet of Things of in the Central African Sub-Region

This study also aimed to identify potential areas and benefits of the IoT within the Central African sub-region. As illustrated in Figure 3, the results indicate that the majority of respondents (121 or 82.9%) advocated for the adoption of the IoT in smart health applications. Similarly, there was considerable support for applying the IoT to the agricultural sector (105 or 71.9%). The findings also highlighted significant interest in implementing the IoT for security and safety (74 or 50.7%), smart metering, and smart cities (99 or 67.8%). The least favored area for IoT adoption was intelligent transport systems and logistics (50 or 34.2%). Additionally, other potential areas for IoT application included environmental and weather monitoring, flexible manufacturing or industry, control of factory physical systems, and smart logistics and businesses.

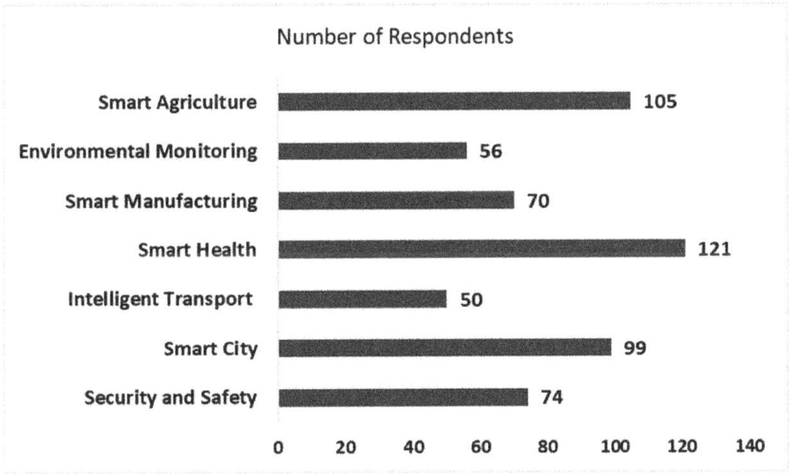

Figure 3. Respondents' identification of potential areas for the implementation of the Internet of Things in the Central African sub-region.

These results align closely with the literature on IoT adoption. For instance, data published in 2018 by IoT Analytics [49], a leading provider of market insights and strategic business intelligence for Industry 4.0 and IoT, reveal the growing importance of the IoT in sectors such as healthcare and agriculture, noting that these areas are frequently highlighted as high-potential domains for IoT applications [50]. The significant interest in smart health and agriculture observed in this study corroborates their findings, emphasizing the global trend towards leveraging the IoT for enhancing healthcare delivery and optimizing agricultural processes [51]. Furthermore, the interest in the IoT for security and safety, smart metering, and smart cities reflects the broader industry focus on urban management and infrastructure development, which has been well-documented in previous studies [52].

Other sectors (such as education, transportation, and manufacturing) also offer significant opportunities for IoT adoption in the Central African region. In higher education, the IoT can play a crucial role in smart campuses, improving operational efficiency and safety [53]. IoT sensors can optimize energy usage, monitor building security, track equipment usage, estimate room occupation, and determine student classroom attendance, leading to cost savings for educational institutions. Furthermore, the IoT can be leveraged to support research initiatives, providing real-time data collection for various academic fields. In the transportation sector, the IoT can transform public transportation by providing real-time updates on bus or train schedules and optimizing routes based on current traffic conditions to enhance commuting experience. In logistics, the IoT can streamline supply chains by enabling fleet management systems to monitor vehicle locations, fuel consumption, and cargo conditions in real time, improving efficiency and reducing costs [54]. In manufacturing, the IoT can help optimize supply chain management, tracking raw materials and finished products throughout the production and distribution processes [55]. This will lead to improved inventory management, faster response times, and enhanced coordination between suppliers, manufacturers, and distributors. The adoption of automation and robotics powered by the IoT can also improve product consistency and quality control, driving competitiveness for local manufacturers in the global market. Thus, as the Central African region seeks to improve its educational system, modernize its transportation sector, and expand its industrial base, adopting the IoT will play a key role in achieving these goals.

4.5. Challenges Impeding IoT Adoption Within the Silicon Mountain Technology Ecosystem

Table 2 presents the challenges impeding IoT adoption within the Silicon Mountain technology ecosystem. Respondents were asked to evaluate the seriousness of each challenge using the following scale: Very Serious (VS), More Serious (MS), Moderate (M), Less Serious (LS), and Not Serious (NS).

Table 2. Challenges impeding IoT adoption within the Silicon Mountain technology ecosystem.

Items	VS	MS	M	LS	NS
Poor internet connectivity and high cost of internet data	28 19.2%	5 3.4%	9 6.2%	28 19.2%	76 52.1%
Insufficient power supply and high energy costs	30 20.5%	12 8.25	5 3.4%	27 18.5%	72 49.3%
Lack of skilled labor in the field of IoT	56 40.4%	28 19.2%	36 24.7%	11 7.5%	12 8.2%
Adoption of new technologies requires an updated educational curriculum	45 30.8%	43 29.5%	33 22.3%	16 11.0%	9 6.2%
Insufficient financial resources	48 32.2%	41 28.1%	37 25.3%	13 8.9%	6 4.1%
Lack of standardization in IoT	39 26.7%	43 29.5%	40 27.4%	20 13.7%	4 2.7%
Concerns regarding data confidentiality, integrity, authentication, and ownership	33 22.6%	37 25.3%	36 24.7%	29 19.9%	11 7.5%
Potential damage resulting from a successful IoT attack	29 19.9%	38 26.0%	46 31.5%	25 17.1%	8 5.5%
Inadequate security mechanisms within IoT systems	24 16.4%	44 30.1%	45 30.8%	25 17.1%	8 5.5%

Table 2. *Cont.*

Items	VS	MS	M	LS	NS
Lack of legal recognition and a comprehensive policy framework for IoT	38 26.0%	37 25.3%	40 27.4%	24 16.4%	7 4.8%
Government interference and bureaucratic obstacles in Cameroon	25 17.1%	48 32.9%	35 24.0%	25 17.1%	13 8.9%
Conflicting and overlapping policies	46 31.5%	42 28.6%	33 22.6%	21 14.4%	4 2.7%
Increased tax burden resulting from changes in tax policy	37 25.3%	40 27.4%	44 30.1%	14 9.6%	11 7.5%
Ambiguity and lack of rigor in existing policies	47 32.2%	52 35.6%	24 16.4%	15 10.3%	8 5.5%
Prevalence of favoritism and corruption in policy implementation	47 32.2%	39 26.7%	33 22.6%	16 11.0%	11 7.5%
Potential clients are hesitant to adopt the IoT due to the need for significant infrastructure setup and upgrades	52 36.6%	42 28.8%	27 18.5%	14 9.6%	11 7.5%
Lack of understanding of commercial practices and market regulations	41 28.1%	45 30.8%	45 30.8%	11 7.5%	4 2.7%
The cost of IoT solutions and the associated payback period hinder adoption	35 24.0%	40 27.4%	42 28.8%	18 12.3%	0 00%
Difficulty in establishing cooperation with local distribution networks	25 17.1%	49 33.6%	41 28.1%	24 16.4%	7 4.8%
The high cost of marketing IoT solutions makes it difficult for startups to afford	45 30.8%	49 33.6%	31 21.2%	13 8.9%	8 5.5%
Ongoing economic crises in the country	40 27.4%	58 39.7%	33 22.6%	11 7.5%	4 2.7%
Organizations often lack understanding of the benefits of the IoT and are generally not motivated to invest in it	58 39.7%	43 29.5%	23 15.8%	16 11.0%	6 4.1%

NS = Not Serious, LS = Less Serious, M = Moderate, MS = More Serious, VS = Very Serious.

The results are as follows:

- Poor Internet Connectivity: This is not considered a serious challenge, with 52.1% of respondents rating it as "Not Serious".
- Power Supply and High Energy Costs: Similarly, these issues are not seen as significant barriers, with 49.3% of respondents rating them as "Not Serious".

Conversely, several factors are identified as serious challenges:

- Insufficient Skilled Labor: The lack of skilled professionals in technological areas such as data science, cybersecurity, IoT development, agriculture, etc., is considered a significant challenge by 40.4% of respondents who rated it as "Very Serious".
- Inadequate Financial Resources: Challenges such as difficulty securing loans and limited funding support are rated as "Very Serious" by 32.2% of respondents.
- Lack of Standardization: The absence of uniform standards in IoT hardware, software, and communication protocols makes interoperability difficult. This was rated as "More Serious" by 29.5% of respondents.

Other significant challenges include the following:

- Sub-Standard Curriculum: The outdated educational curricula in most of Silicon Mountain's academic institutions, which fail to keep up with advancements in technology, were rated as "Very Serious" by 30.8% of respondents.
- Data Security Concerns: Issues related to data confidentiality, integrity, and authentication are considered a challenge, with 30.8% rating these concerns as "Moderate".
- Risk of IoT Attacks: The potential damage from IoT attacks, such as the 2016 IoT botnet attack, is seen as a significant risk, rated as "More Serious" by 26% of respondents.
- Inadequate Security Mechanisms: The perception of the IoT as the "Internet of Threats" due to insufficient security measures is also considered a barrier.

In terms of legal and regulatory issues, the following were stated:

- Lack of Legal Recognition and Policy Framework: The absence of a clear legal and policy framework is rated as "More Serious" by 51.2% of respondents.
- Government Interference and Bureaucracy: Overlapping and conflicting policies, increased tax burdens, and corruption are significant deterrents, with 52.7% rating tax policy changes as "More Serious" and 58.9% identifying favoritism and corruption as barriers.

Market-related challenges include the following:

- Reluctance to Adopt IoT: Potential client reluctance to invest in IoT due to the need for infrastructure upgrades and new business models was rated as "More Serious" by 64.4% of respondents.
- Lack of Understanding of Market Practices: Poor understanding of commercial practices and market regulations was also a notable challenge, rated as "More Serious" by 58.9% of respondents.
- IoT Costs and Payback Period: The high costs associated with IoT implementation and the difficulty in establishing local distribution networks were rated as significant barriers by 51.4% of respondents.

Improvement strategies for addressing the challenges in IoT adoption are detailed in Table 3. The findings were as follows:

- Tax Policy Reforms: Rated as highly influential by 87 respondents (59.6%), improving tax policies is seen as a significant factor in enhancing IoT adoption among businesses in the Silicon Mountain.
- Network Connectivity and Internet Data Costs: Improving network connectivity and reducing internet data costs were also deemed crucial, with 43.8% of respondents highlighting their importance.
- Reduction in IoT Device Prices: Lowering the costs of IoT devices was rated as a highly influential factor by 95 respondents (65.1%), which could significantly boost IoT adoption.
- Enhanced Energy Availability: Improving the availability of energy to businesses was similarly recognized as an important factor.

Table 3. Proposed improvement strategies to the challenges identified.

Improvement Strategies	GTE	GE	M	LE	NE
Improvement in tax policies to encourage the adoption of IoT businesses	60 41.1%	27 18.5%	33 22.6%	14 9.6%	12 8.2%
Enhance network connectivity and reduce internet data costs	38 26.0%	26 17.8%	20 13.7%	39 26.7%	23 15.8%
Reduction in the prices of IoT devices	64 43.8%	31 21.2%	26 17.8%	14 9.6%	11 7.5%
Enhance the availability and reliability of energy supply	65 44.5%	46 31.5%	19 13.0%	11 7.5%	5 3.4%
Enhance the security mechanisms for IoT systems	61 41.8%	52 35.6%	27 18.5%	6 4.1%	0 00%
Organize IoT workshops, seminars, and meet-ups and incorporate IoT-related courses into the curriculum to enhance skilled labor in the IoT	62 42.5%	47 32.2%	26 17.8%	9 6.2%	2 1.4%
Provide access to funding, loans, and IoT research grants for academic institutions and incubators	57 39.0%	37 25.3%	40 27.4%	12 8.2%	0 0.0%

NE = Not at all, LE = Lesser Extent, M = Moderate, GE = Great Extent, GTE = Greater Extent.

Additionally, several other strategies were proposed to improve IoT adoption:

- Enhanced IoT Security Mechanisms: Strengthening security measures for IoT systems is considered essential for fostering adoption.
- Educational Initiatives: Organizing IoT workshops, seminars, and meetups, as well as integrating IoT-related courses into academic curricula, is expected to address the skills gap and increase labor proficiency.
- Access to Funding: Providing access to funding, loans, and IoT research grants for academic institutions and incubators is identified as a key strategy to support IoT development and adoption.

4.6. *Verification of the Hypothesis of the Study*

In this study, Exploratory Factor Analysis (EFA) was conducted using the Principal Components Analysis (PCA) method with Varimax Rotation to investigate the challenges to IoT adoption in the Silicon Mountain technology ecosystem. To enhance the interpretability of the factor structure, the scale was refined by removing items with low cross-loadings, low factor loadings, and low communalities, following the recommendations of [41].

4.6.1. Factor Analysis

To determine if the data captured in this study were appropriate for factor analysis, we used the Kaiser–Meyer–Olkin (KMO) and Bartlett's Test of Sphericity. From the literature, a KMO value > 0.6 is acceptable for a sample size < 100, while a KMO value between 0.5 and 0.6 is acceptable for sample sizes between 100 and 200 [39,56]. In this study, the KMO measure of sampling adequacy was 0.706, and Bartlett's Test of Sphericity was significant (Sig = 0.000), with a Chi-square value of 785.296 and 231 degrees of freedom (df). Table 4 presents the results generated from the SPSS software for KMO and Bartlett's Test of Sphericity. These results demonstrate that the data set is not an identity matrix with zero correlations (i.e., the variables are indeed correlated), thereby confirming the appropriateness of applying factor analysis.

Table 4. Kaiser–Meyer–Olkin and Bartlett's Test of Sphericity.

Kaiser–Meyer–Olkin Measure of Sampling Adequacy		0.706
Bartlett's Test of Sphericity	Approx. Chi-Square	785.296
	df	231
	Sig.	0.000

determinant = 0.003.

In study, we measured 22 items related to the challenges of IoT adoption in the Silicon Mountain tech ecosystem, using a five-point Likert scale to gauge their level of seriousness. The averages of these items were calculated to provide an overview of how respondents rated the different challenges. To focus the analysis on the most significant barriers, we applied a cutoff threshold of 3.5, which allowed us to identify the factors perceived by respondents as serious impediments to IoT adoption in the Silicon Mountain tech ecosystem. After applying this threshold, 13 out of the 22 factors emerged as critical barriers to IoT adoption, and these are displayed in Table 5 along with their average ratings (mean values).

Table 5. Major factors affecting IoT adoption in the Silicon Mountain technology ecosystem.

Major Factors that Affect the Adoption of Internet of Things	Mean
Organizations often lack an understanding of the benefits of IoT and are generally not motivated to invest in it	3.8973
Ongoing socio-economic crises in the country	3.8151

Table 5. *Cont.*

Major Factors that Affect the Adoption of Internet of Things	Mean
Inadequate financial resources, difficulty in securing loans, and limited funding support from the government and other sponsors	3.8014
The loose nature of policies	3.7877
Insufficient skilled labor in the IoT, data science, and agriculture	3.7603
Potential clients are hesitant to adopt IoT due to the necessity of setting up or upgrading infrastructure and adopting new business models, which may result in a limited market	3.7534
The high cost of marketing IoT solutions poses a significant challenge, as many startups are unable to afford these expenses	3.7534
Lack of understanding of commercial practices and market regulations related to the IoT	3.7397
The mass movements of graduates from STEM (Science, Technology, Engineering and Mathematics) fields for greener pastures	3.7260
Overlapping and conflicting policies	3.7192
Lack of updated educational curricula with many academic institutions lacking dynamic curricula that integrate the latest advancements in hardware, software, and communication technologies	3.6781
Favoritism and corruption	3.6507
Lack of standardization in IoT as each vendor develops its own hardware, software, and communication protocols without adhering to common standards, making it challenging to integrate devices from different manufacturers into a cohesive IoT application	3.6370

Table 5 reveals the primary challenges to IoT adoption in the Silicon Mountain based on the mean averages. The major challenges identified include the following:

- Lack of Understanding and Motivation: organizations typically do not grasp the benefits of the IoT and are often unwilling to invest in it, with a mean score of 3.8973.
- Socio-economic Crises: the ongoing socio-economic crises in the country pose a significant barrier, scoring 3.8151.
- Inadequate Financial Resources: the inability to secure loans and the lack of funding support from the government and other sponsors are major issues, with a mean score of 3.8014.
- Loose Policies: the loose nature of policies is a critical challenge, reflected in a mean score of 3.7877.
- Insufficient Skilled Labor: there is a shortage of skilled labor in the IoT, data science, and agriculture, scoring 3.7603.
- Client Reluctance: potential clients are hesitant to adopt the IoT due to the need for infrastructure upgrades and new business models, scoring 3.7534.
- High Marketing Costs: the cost of marketing IoT solutions is high, making it unafford-able for startups, with a mean score of 3.7534.
- Lack of Commercial Understanding: there is a lack of understanding of commercial practices and market regulation, scoring 3.7397.
- Brain Drain: the mass movement of graduates from Science, Technology, Engineering, and Mathematics (STEM) fields seeking better opportunities is a significant barrier, scoring 3.7260.
- Conflicting Policies: overlapping and conflicting policies also pose a challenge, with a mean score of 3.7192.
- Outdated Educational Curricula: many academic institutions lack dynamic curricula to equip students with the latest developments in IoT technologies, scoring 3.6781.
- Favoritism and Corruption: these issues also constitute serious barriers, with a mean score of 3.6507.

- Lack of Standardization: the lack of standardization in the IoT, where each vendor develops their hardware, software, and communication protocols independently, is a hindrance, scoring 3.6370.

These challenges highlight significant barriers to the adoption of IoT in the Silicon Mountain area, as indicated by the mean scores derived from the survey.

4.6.2. Principal Component Analysis of IoT Adoption Challenges in the Silicon Mountain Technology Ecosystem

The Principal Component Analysis (PCA) method was employed, and the eigenvalues associated with each linear component (factor) before extraction, after extraction, and after rotation are presented in Table 6. Initially, 22 linear components were identified within the data set. Among these, seven primary components were extracted based on their eigenvalues, with only factors having eigenvalues greater than 1 being considered. These seven factors accounted for approximately 60.449% of the variance in the challenges to IoT adoption within the Silicon Mountain technology ecosystem. This percentage is deemed satisfactory, as it exceeds the minimum threshold of 50%. It is recommended that the proportion of the total variance explained by the retained factors should be at least 50% [39]. Consequently, about 39.551% of the variance is attributable to other challenges to IoT adoption that were not considered.

Table 6. Determination of primary components based on total variance.

Total Variance Explained									
Component	Initial Eigenvalues			Extraction Sums of Squared Loadings			Rotation Sums of Squared Loadings		
	Total	% of Variance	Cumulative %	Total	% of Variance	Cumulative %	Total	% of Variance	Cumulative %
1	4.789	21.770	21.770	4.789	21.770	21.770	2.981	13.548	13.548
2	1.788	8.127	29.897	1.788	8.127	29.897	2.173	9.878	23.426
3	1.716	7.799	37.696	1.716	7.799	37.696	1.754	7.975	31.401
4	1.396	6.344	44.040	1.396	6.344	44.040	1.752	7.963	39.364
5	1.353	6.148	50.188	1.353	6.148	50.188	1.608	7.311	46.674
6	1.176	5.345	55.533	1.176	5.345	55.533	1.520	6.910	53.585
7	1.081	4.916	60.449	1.081	4.916	60.449	1.510	6.864	60.449
8	0.948	4.310	64.759						
9	0.889	4.040	68.799						
10	0.824	3.747	72.546						
11	0.719	3.267	75.813						
12	0.711	3.232	79.044						
13	0.681	3.094	82.138						
14	0.633	2.878	85.016						
15	0.564	2.565	87.581						
16	0.543	2.467	90.048						
17	0.463	2.106	92.154						
18	0.448	2.035	94.189						
19	0.402	1.828	96.016						
20	0.352	1.599	97.615						
21	0.312	1.417	99.032						
22	0.213	0.968	100.000						

Extraction Method: Principal Component Analysis.

Table 7 provides a classification of the various challenges under the seven identified components. This classification facilitates the regrouping of the primary challenges affecting the adoption of the IoT in the Silicon Mountain technology ecosystem, as illustrated in Table 8. The categorization helps in understanding the underlying factors and how they interrelate, thereby offering a clearer perspective on the main obstacles to IoT adoption in the Silicon Mountain tech ecosystem.

Table 7. The rotated component matrix and the reclassification of components.

Rotated Component Matrix [a]							
	Component						
	1	2	3	4	5	6	7
Loose nature of policies	0.798						
Overlapping and conflicting policies	0.654						
Favoritism and corruption	0.651						
Cameroon government interference and bureaucracy	0.631						
Increase in tax burden due to changes in tax policy	0.604						
Potential clients are reluctant adopt the IoT	0.500						
The damage that can result from a successful IoT attack		0.770					
Inadequate security mechanisms for IoT systems means that the IoT is viewed as the "Internet of Threats" despite its potential benefits		0.720					
Data confidentiality, integrity, authentication, data ownership, etc., are major concerns		0.545					
Lack of legal recognition and policy framework		0.496					
Inadequate financial resources, inability to secure loans, and little or no funding support from government and other sponsors		0.092	0.769				
Organizations do not usually understand the benefits of the IoT and are often not motivated to pay for it			0.652				
Lack of standardization in the IoT as each and every vendor is developing its hardware, software, and communication protocol without any standardization			0.526				
Ongoing economic crises in the country				0.784			
Difficult to establish cooperation with local distribution network				0.625			
The cost of marketing IoT solutions is high and startups are not able to afford this				0.578			
Technological adoption requires an updated educational curriculum but most academic institutions do not have dynamic educational curricula to equip the students with				0.102	0.844		
Could be a result of mass movements of graduates from STEM (Science, Technology, Engineering and Mathematics) fields for greener pastures.					0.524		
Lack of understanding of commercial practice and market regulation						0.828	
Insufficient power supply and the high cost of energy is one of the challenges to the adoption of IoT						−0.546	
The cost of the IoT and its payback period are a hindrance for adoption						0.444	
Insufficient skilled labor in the area of the IoT, data science, and agriculture							0.792

Extraction Method: Principal Component Analysis. Rotation Method: Varimax with Kaiser Normalization.
[a] Rotation converged in 9 iterations.

Table 8. Subcategorization of challenges to IoT adoption in the Silicon Mountain technology ecosystem.

Main Factors	Challenges to the Adoption of Internet of Things (IoT)	Mean	Global Mean
Government policies	Loose nature of policies	3.788	3.628
	Overlapping and conflicting policies	3.719	
	Favoritism and corruption	3.651	
	Cameroon government interference and bureaucracy	3.322	
	Increase in tax burden due to changes in tax policy	3.534	
	Potential clients are reluctant adopt the IoT	3.753	
Security and data privacy challenges	The damage that can result from a successful IoT attack	3.377	3.399
	Inadequate security mechanisms for IoT systems means that the IoT is viewed as the "Internet of Threats" despite its potential benefits	3.349	
	Data confidentiality, integrity, authentication, data ownership, etc., are major concerns	3.356	
	Lack of legal recognition and policy framework	3.514	
Standardization and Financial Resources	Inadequate financial resources, inability to secure loans, and little or no funding support from government and other sponsors	3.801	3.779
	Organizations do not usually understand the benefits of the IoT and are often not motivated to pay for it	3.897	
	Lack of standardization in the IoT as each and every vendor is developing its hardware, software, and communication protocol with any standardization	3.637	
Market Challenges	Ongoing economic crises in the country	3.815	3.662
	Difficult to establish cooperation with local distribution network	3.418	
	The cost of marketing IoT solutions is high and startups are not able to afford this	3.753	
Educational and knowledge challenges	Technological adoption requires an updated educational curriculum but most academic institutions do not have dynamic educational curricula to equip the students with	3.678	3.702
	The mass movements of graduates from STEM (Science, Technology, Engineering and Mathematics) fields for greener pastures	3.726	
Labor and power supply	Lack of understanding of commercial practice and market regulation	3.740	3.274
	Insufficient power supply and the high cost of energy is one of the challenges to the adoption of the IoT	2.322	
	The cost of the IoT and its payback period are a hindrance for adoption	3.760	
Labor Shortage in the industry	Insufficient skilled labor in the area of the IoT, data science, and agriculture	3.760	3.76

After the rotation of these factors, they were categorized into the following groups: government policies, security and data privacy challenges, standardization and financial resources, market challenges, educational and knowledge challenges, labor and power supply, and labor shortage in the industry.

In Table 8, the government policies category comprised six factors: the loose nature of policies, overlapping and conflicting policies, favoritism and corruption, Cameroon government interference and bureaucracy, increase in tax burden due to changes in tax policy, and reluctance of potential clients to adopt the IoT. This category had a global mean of 3.628.

Similarly, the standardization and financial resources category included inadequate financial resources, inability to secure loans, and minimal funding support from the government and other sponsors. It also encompassed organizations' lack of understanding of IoT benefits and their consequent lack of motivation to invest in it, as well as the lack of standardization in the IoT, with each vendor developing its hardware, software, and communication protocols independently. The mean value for this factor was 3.779.

The global mean of each category presented in Table 8 was used to rank the factors affecting the adoption of IoT in the Silicon Mountain tech ecosystem in order of importance. The results of this ranking are displayed in Table 9. This ranking provides a clear prioritization of the challenges, highlighting which areas require the most immediate attention to improve IoT adoption in the Silicon Mountain technology ecosystem.

Table 9. Mean scores and ranking of factors affecting IoT adoption in the Silicon Mountain technology ecosystem.

Main Challenges to IoT Adoption	Mean	Rank
Standardization and financial resources	3.779	1st
Labor shortage in the industry	3.760	2nd
Educational and knowledge challenges	3.702	3rd
Market challenges	3.662	4th
Government policies	3.628	5th
Security and data privacy challenges	3.399	6th
Labor and power supply	3.274	7th

An analysis of Table 9 shows that the mean scores for all barriers ranged between 3.00 and 4.00. These scores indicate an average level of concern between 'moderate' and 'serious' on the Likert scale. The most significant challenge identified was standardization and financial Resources, with a mean score of 3.779. This was closely followed by labor shortage in the industry, which had a mean of 3.760. The remaining categories, in descending order of severity, were educational and knowledge challenges, market challenges, government policies, security and data privacy challenges, and labor and power supply.

4.7. Discussion

This study identified a range of challenges hindering IoT adoption in the Silicon Mountain technology ecosystem. The challenges were categorized into the following areas:

1. Standardization and Financial Resources: issues related to the lack of standardized protocols and financial constraints.
2. Labor Shortage in the Industry: the shortage of skilled labor in the field.
3. Educational and Knowledge Challenges: inadequate educational curricula and knowledge gaps.
4. Market Challenges: difficulties related to market adoption and commercial practices.
5. Government Policies: issues arising from governmental policies and regulatory frameworks.
6. Security and Data Privacy Challenges: concerns about data security and privacy.
7. Labor and Power Supply: challenges related to the availability of reliable power and labor.

This study found that market challenges significantly impact the adoption of the IoT within the Silicon Mountain technology ecosystem. Key market challenges identified include the ongoing socio-economic crises in the country, difficulties in establishing cooperation with local distribution networks, and the high cost of marketing IoT solutions, which many start-ups cannot afford. These issues were highlighted by a high mean score of 3.662, indicating that they are considered very serious challenges.

Another significant challenge identified was data privacy and security concerns. The proliferation of IoT devices results in the generation, collection, and sharing of vast amounts of data. These data often include sensitive personal information, raising significant concerns around data privacy, including unauthorized access, data breaches, surveillance and tracking, data access and control, etc. In addition, security is also a critical concern for IoT systems due to the sheer number of connected devices, which increases the potential attack surface for cyberattacks. Inadequate security mechanisms can result in severe consequences, such as data breaches, loss of control over critical systems, and the manipulation of physical devices. This study identified security and data privacy as a significant challenge affecting IoT adoption. The results reveal that data security and user privacy are major concerns in IoT applications due to the extensive amount of data shared across platforms, increasing user vulnerability. This aligns with Iwayemi's study in Nigeria [15], which identified fraud, cyber attacks, privacy issues, and security concerns as critical challenges in IoT implementation. The primary security risk of the IoT is linked to its greatest advantage: the connection of physical objects to a global network [57]. Although the IoT has tremendous potential to drive innovation across various sectors in the Silicon Mountain ecosystem, the technical challenges of data privacy and security remain significant barriers to widespread adoption. Before the advent of the IoT, security breaches were primarily concerned with data theft and manipulation of physical entities. However, the IoT introduces the potential for direct control of these physical entities, many of which are part of critical infrastructure. Without adequate security measures, malware such as viruses and ransomware could easily spread through interconnected IoT networks, leading to potentially catastrophic global consequences. Addressing these issues is crucial to ensuring that IoT systems are secure, efficient, and capable of scaling across different industries. To address these challenges and promote IoT adoption, businesses in the Silicon Mountain ecosystem can implement mitigation strategies to minimize data privacy risks (such as end-to-end encryption, anonymization schemes, introspection, blockchain, access control, physical security, edge processing, etc.) and mitigation strategies address the security risks (such as device authentication, regular firmware updates, network segmentation, intrusion detection systems, etc.) [58].

IoT interoperability was also identified as another major challenge impeding IoT adoption in the Silicon Mountain tech ecosystem. Interoperability refers to the ability of different IoT devices and platforms to communicate and work together seamlessly. A lack of standardization in IoT hardware, software, and communication protocols makes it difficult for devices from different manufacturers to interact, posing a major challenge for IoT adoption in Silicon Mountain. The absence of interoperability can lead to fragmentation, high integration cost, and limited scalability [59]. To enhance IoT interoperability within the Silicon Mountain ecosystem, the use of open standards (MQTT, CoAP, Zigbee, etc.) and middleware solutions can be adopted [60].

The development of robust and scalable IoT infrastructure is also crucial for fostering the adoption of IoT technologies in emerging ecosystems like Silicon Mountain. In particular, leveraging innovations such as fog computing can significantly enhance the performance and scalability of IoT systems by processing data closer to the edge, thus reducing latency and improving response times. According to the research by Okafor et al. [61], the Spine-Leaf Network Topology, combined with fog computing, offers an effective approach for managing the scalability challenges of IoT datacenters. This framework facilitates the seamless integration of numerous IoT devices by decentralizing data processing and management, which can be particularly valuable for regions with limited network infrastructure, like Silicon Mountain. Given the infrastructural challenges and connectivity limitations in Central African ecosystems, adopting such scalable IoT solutions could accelerate the deployment of IoT technologies across sectors, including agriculture, healthcare, and urban management.

Digital literacy was also found to be one of the key factors inhibiting IoT adoption in developing countries due to the low-level of digital literacy within the population [62]. In this study, we consider digital literacy as the ability to effectively use digital technologies, including understanding how IoT devices function and how to leverage them for personal, professional, or industrial purposes. Based on this definition, the level of digital literacy in the Silicon Mountain tech ecosystem is low as many individuals in the region lack the necessary skills or understanding to fully engage with IoT technologies. This study identified labor shortage resulting from this low level of digital literacy in the region as a major challenge to IoT adoption, with a mean score of 3.760. This challenge is closely related to inadequate education on the IoT and the absence of specialized university courses in this emerging technology within the region [63]. These findings are consistent with the results of Morrissey [64], who noted that a shortage of skilled labor in the IoT, data science, and other technical fields could contribute to the migration of STEM (science, technology, engineering, and mathematics) graduates seeking better opportunities elsewhere. The scarcity of formal IoT programs in universities exacerbates this issue, as companies are hesitant to adopt new technologies without the assurance of having access to qualified personnel for operation, maintenance, and support. Improving digital literacy is crucial for expanding IoT adoption across sectors such as agriculture, healthcare, transportation, and education. Educational institutions, governments, and private sector stakeholders must collaborate to offer digital literacy training programs tailored to specific industries. Equipping individuals with the necessary skills to understand and interact with IoT technologies will foster greater innovation and lead to more efficient IoT integration across various sectors in the Silicon Mountain tech ecosystem [65]. In addition to the challenges posed by low digital literacy, societal resistance to technology can hinder IoT adoption [27]. Societal resistance is often driven by cultural norms, fear of job displacement, privacy concerns, costs, or skepticism about the benefits of emerging technologies [66]. Although this aspect was not deeply explored in the current paper, we believe that addressing societal resistance will enhance IoT uptake in the ecosystem and the region at large. Addressing societal resistance will require not only community engagement but also public awareness campaigns that demystify IoT and highlight its potential benefits, particularly for economic growth and improved service delivery. Policymakers and business leaders need to actively promote IoT solutions as tools that enhance productivity and job creation, ensuring that public concerns are mitigated through clear communication. Beyond digital literacy and societal resistance, other socio-cultural factors such as language barriers, traditional beliefs, convenience, social influence, habits, etc., will also influence IoT adoption [67].

Government policies also emerged as a significant barrier to IoT adoption. The rotated component factor model revealed that challenges related to government policies—including the loose nature of regulations, overlapping and conflicting policies, favoritism and corruption, government interference and bureaucracy, and increased tax burdens—accounted for 13.55% of the obstacles to IoT implementation in Cameroon. Research by Cole et al. [68] highlights a similar issue across the African continent, where cyber security initiatives are scarce and existing efforts often focus solely on cybercrime legislation with minimal implementation. This lack of supportive legislation and policies impedes technological advancement and scientific research. The high vulnerability of IoT systems, coupled with inadequate regulatory frameworks, may deter many African businesses from adopting the IoT due to perceived risks and potential threats to their systems.

The results of this study indicate that various challenges have impeded the adoption of the IoT within the Silicon Mountain technology ecosystem and the broader Central African region. Nevertheless, several improvement strategies were proposed to address these issues. These strategies include the following:

- Enhancing Tax Policies: revising tax regulations to better support IoT businesses.
- Improving Network Connectivity: expanding network infrastructure and reducing internet data costs.
- Reducing IoT Device Prices: making IoT devices more affordable.

- Increasing Energy Availability: ensuring a more reliable energy supply for IoT operations.
- Strengthening IoT Security: enhancing security mechanisms to protect IoT systems.
- Organizing IoT Workshops and Seminars: hosting events to raise awareness and build expertise in IoT.
- Updating Educational Curricula: integrating IoT-related courses into academic programs to address labor shortages and improve skill levels.

These measures aim to address key barriers such as government policies, labor shortages, and insufficient IoT knowledge, ultimately leveraging the numerous benefits of IoT applications to foster adoption and innovation in the region.

4.8. Future Trends in IoT Adoption in Silicon Mountain and Central Africa

While this study primarily focuses on current challenges in IoT adoption, it is equally important to consider longer-term trends that could significantly influence IoT uptake in the Silicon Mountain tech ecosystem and the broader Central African region. These trends include future technological advancements, evolving workforce skills, and policy changes, all of which are important for shaping the future of the IoT in the region.

The development of technologies such as 5G and edge computing will play a transformative role in enhancing IoT infrastructure and capabilities. In terms of this, 5G will provide the high-speed, low-latency connectivity necessary to support large-scale IoT deployments across sectors such as healthcare, smart cities, and agriculture. Moreover, the advent of artificial intelligence (AI) and machine learning (ML) integration with IoT devices will enable more intelligent automation, predictive analytics, and real-time decision-making, offering immense potential for innovation in sectors like manufacturing and transportation. Edge computing will also mitigate data privacy concerns, thereby positively influencing IoT uptake. Preparing for these advancements will be key to ensuring the successful scaling of IoT applications in the Silicon Mountain tech ecosystem.

One of the significant barriers to IoT adoption in the region identified by this study is the lack of skilled labor in fields such as IoT development, data science, and cybersecurity. However, as IoT technologies continue to evolve, there will be an increasing demand for a workforce proficient in managing and maintaining complex IoT systems. Educational institutions will need to adapt by incorporating the IoT, AI, and data analytics into their curricula, while industry partnerships can play a vital role in providing hands-on training and certifications. Government and private-sector initiatives to foster IoT skill development will be critical to ensure that the workforce is equipped to meet the demands of an IoT-driven economy. This training of next-generation IoT professionals will facilitate IoT uptake.

For IoT adoption to thrive in the Central African region, supportive regulatory frameworks are essential. Governments must develop policies that address data privacy, cybersecurity, and interoperability to create a stable environment for IoT deployment. Additionally, policymakers can incentivize IoT innovation by providing tax breaks, grants, and funding opportunities for startups. The establishment of IoT regulatory bodies to oversee compliance with global standards and to facilitate public–private collaboration will also help accelerate IoT adoption across various industries.

4.9. Limitations and Recommendations for Future Work

This preliminary study on IoT adoption in the Central African sub-region provides valuable insights into the Silicon Mountain ecosystem. However, it is not without limitations. In this sub-section, we discuss some of the study's key limitations and propose areas for future research that could offer more comprehensive insights into the factors influencing IoT adoption in the Central African sub-region.

This study is limited to the Silicon Mountain tech ecosystem, and the sample of 146 usable responses may not fully capture the broader diversity of stakeholders across the Central African region. Consequently, the findings may not be generalizable to all tech ecosystems within the region. Additionally, the high concentration of entry-level positions

(67.8%) and the gender imbalance (64.4% male respondents) may have influenced the results, particularly with respect to gender representation and experience levels. In future research, we plan to extend this study to include a wider range of stakeholders across different tech ecosystems in the Central African region, ensuring a more balanced gender representation and a broader distribution of respondents across various experience levels, including mid-level and senior management roles. This will provide a more comprehensive understanding of the challenges and opportunities related to IoT adoption in the Central African region.

Another limitation of the study is that it relies primarily on questionnaire responses, which may introduce certain biases, resulting from social desirability or limited depth in participants' understanding of complex topics like IoT technology. To address the limitations of self-reported data, we propose the adoption of a mixed-methods approach in future work. Combining quantitative survey data with qualitative methods (e.g., expert interviews, focus groups, or case studies) would allow for triangulation and a more comprehensive exploration of IoT adoption challenges. Additionally, we are developing a smart agriculture Proof of Concept (PoC) that focuses on determining the levels of key macronutrients (Nitrogen, Phosphorus, Potassium) in the soil. This PoC aims to provide farmers in the region with real-time information on soil fertility, enabling them to make informed decisions about crop selection to improve yields. This PoC will address key challenges identified in the study, including infrastructure limitations, regulatory barriers, and skills gaps by testing the feasibility of deploying IoT solutions in the region. These approaches will offer deeper insights into the complex issues that may have been overlooked or simplified in the survey responses.

The study also found the high rating of poor internet connectivity (52.1%) and unreliable power supply (49.3%) as "Not Serious" by respondents to be usual. This is because these are common infrastructural challenges in sub-Saharan Africa that significantly impede IoT uptake in the region, as reported in earlier IoT adoption studies [15,16]. Thus, it is important to note at this point that the "Not Serious" rating for poor internet connectivity and unreliable power supply reflects the perceptions of respondents who are part of the Silicon Mountain technology ecosystem, which benefits from relatively better infrastructure compared to other regions in Cameroon and Central Africa. As a result, these challenges may not have been perceived as immediate barriers for IoT adoption within this specific ecosystem. However, in the broader context of the Central African region, internet connectivity and power supply are indeed significant impediments, especially in more rural areas and less developed tech hubs. Thus, generalizing the findings of this study beyond the Silicon Mountain ecosystem may risk downplaying the severity of these issues. There is need for future research to focus on tech ecosystems within the Central African region where internet connectivity and power supply issues are more acute. A more in-depth analysis of how these infrastructure limitations affect IoT adoption outside of established tech ecosystems will provide a more comprehensive understanding of IoT adoption challenges in the region.

5. Conclusions

This study examined the adoption of the IoT in tech ecosystems within the Central African sub-region, focusing specifically on the Silicon Mountain technology ecosystem. The primary objectives were to identify the potential areas for IoT implementation and to uncover the challenges impeding IoT uptake in the Silicon Mountain tech ecosystem and, by extension, other tech ecosystems in the Central African sub-region. Utilizing a survey research design, the study analyzed data using both descriptive and inferential tools.

The findings suggest significant potential and numerous opportunities for IoT adoption in the Silicon Mountain tech ecosystem. The key areas of benefit identified include intelligent transport systems, smart health facilities, smart metering and smart cities, environmental and weather monitoring, security and safety, flexible manufacturing or industry control, IoT-driven agriculture, logistics, and smart businesses. The study highlighted a substantial market gap, indicating a high potential for the IoT to enhance SME performance, stimulate economic activities, and improve business connectivity in the tech ecosystem.

The study also identified numerous challenges impacting IoT adoption in the Silicon Mountain tech ecosystem. Issues related to standardization and financial resources, labor shortages in the industry, educational and knowledge gaps, market challenges, government policies, security and data privacy concerns, and inadequate labor and power supply were key among these challenges. These obstacles have collectively hindered the adoption of IoT, resulting in a slow uptake rate.

Author Contributions: Conceptualization, G.S.K., V.N. and P.C.; methodology, G.S.K. and V.N.; software, G.S.K. and V.N.; validation, G.S.K. and V.N.; formal analysis, G.S.K. and V.N; writing—original draft preparation, G.S.K. and V.N.; writing—review and editing, G.S.K., V.N., O.J.N., F.M. and P.C.; supervision, F.M. and P.C. All authors have read and agreed to the published version of the manuscript.

Funding: This research received no external funding.

Data Availability Statement: The original contributions presented in the study are included in the article, further inquiries can be directed to the corresponding author.

Conflicts of Interest: The authors declare no conflicts of interest.

Appendix A

Table A1. Measurement scale.

1	2	3	4	5
Not serious Not at all	Less serious Lesser extent	Moderate Moderate	More serious Great Extent	Very serious Greater Extent

Table A2. Questionnaire items.

	Operating Barriers	1	2	3	4	5
1	The implementation of THE IoT requires organizations to upgrade and adopt new business models.					
2	IoT applications need a higher infrastructure to support them, which most business cannot afford.					
3	Fragmentation of standards with new ones evolving every day makes it difficult for IoT practitioners.					
4	Increase in businesses' operating costs.					
5	IoT adoption because most of the services are delivered to mobile users.					
6	Limited skilled workforce in Cameroon as compared to developed countries.					
7	Poor internet connectivity.					
8	Varying accessibility of internet connection across the nation.					
	Information/Security Barriers	1	2	3	4	5
9	Personal privacy issue (data ownership) is a major concern in employing IoT networks as the connected objects and devices can be easily traced and hacked.					
10	Billions of devices are connected through the IoT which necessitates efficient security mechanisms that not only help in protecting the information but also enable data sharing over IoT-based smart city networks.					
11	Lack of knowledge on production costs of IoT systems.					
12	Unsecure provenance data may result in the exposition of sensitive Information.					

Table A2. *Cont.*

	Operating Barriers	1	2	3	4	5
	Legal/Bureaucracy Barriers	1	2	3	4	5
13	Lack of legal recognition and policy framework.					
14	Cameroon government interference and bureaucracy.					
15	Overlapping and conflicting policies.					
16	Increase in tax burden due to changes in tax policy.					
17	Loose nature of policies.					
18	Favoritism and corruption.					
	Market challenges					
19	IoT applications employ a huge number of sensing and actuating devices.					
20	Lack of understanding of commercial practice.					
21	IoT costs and its payback period are a hindrance for adoption.					
22	Difficult to establish cooperation with local distribution network.					
23	Difficulty in locating supply lines for local raw materials.					
24	Ongoing economic crises in the country.					
25	Global misinformation systems.					
	Impact of challenges on IoT adoption	1	2	3	4	5
26	Improvement in tax policies for adoption of IoT businesses.					
27	Increase in network connectivity.					
28	Regularizing prices for materials.					
29	Improvement in information flow and communication systems.					
30	Improvement in the security of information systems.					

References

1. Kopetz, H.; Steiner, W. Internet of Things. In *Real-Time Systems: Design Principles for Distributed Embedded Applications*; Kopetz, H., Steiner, W., Eds.; Springer International Publishing: Cham, Switzerland, 2022; pp. 325–341. [CrossRef]
2. Rejeb, A.; Rejeb, K.; Treiblmaier, H.; Appolloni, A.; Alghamdi, S.; Alhasawi, Y.; Iranmanesh, M. The Internet of Things (IoT) in healthcare: Taking stock and moving forward. *Internet Things* **2023**, *22*, 100721. [CrossRef]
3. Rajak, P.; Ganguly, A.; Adhikary, S.; Bhattacharya, S. Internet of Things and smart sensors in agriculture: Scopes and challenges. *J. Agric. Food Res.* **2023**, *14*, 100776. [CrossRef]
4. Musa, A.A.; Malami, S.I.; Alanazi, F.; Ounaies, W.; Alshammari, M.; Haruna, S.I. Sustainable Traffic Management for Smart Cities Using Internet-of-Things-Oriented Intelligent Transportation Systems (ITS): Challenges and Recommendations. *Sustainability* **2023**, *15*, 9859. [CrossRef]
5. Babayigit, B.; Abubaker, M. Industrial Internet of Things: A Review of Improvements Over Traditional SCADA Systems for Industrial Automation. *IEEE Syst. J.* **2024**, *18*, 120–133. [CrossRef]
6. Orfanos, V.A.; Kaminaris, S.D.; Papageorgas, P.; Piromalis, D.; Kandris, D. A Comprehensive Review of IoT Networking Technologies for Smart Home Automation Applications. *J. Sens. Actuator Netw.* **2023**, *12*, 30. [CrossRef]
7. Edquist, H.; Goodridge, P.; Haskel, J. The Internet of Things and economic growth in a panel of countries. *Econ. Innov. New Technol.* **2021**, *30*, 262–283. [CrossRef]
8. Alasmary, H. ScalableDigitalHealth (SDH): An IoT-Based Scalable Framework for Remote Patient Monitoring. *Sensors* **2024**, *24*, 1346. [CrossRef]
9. Zhong, Y.; Xu, Z.; Cao, L. Intelligent IoT-based telemedicine systems implement for smart medical treatment. *Pers. Ubiquitous Comput.* **2023**, *27*, 1429–1439. [CrossRef]
10. Ali, A.; Hussain, T.; Tantashutikun, N.; Hussain, N.; Cocetta, G. Application of Smart Techniques, Internet of Things and Data Mining for Resource Use Efficient and Sustainable Crop Production. *Agriculture* **2023**, *13*, 397. [CrossRef]
11. Kuaban, G.S.; Czekalski, P.; Molua, E.L.; Grochla, K. An Architectural Framework Proposal for IoT Driven Agriculture. In *Computer Networks*; Gaj, P., Sawicki, M., Kwiecień, A., Eds.; Springer International Publishing: Cham, Switzerland, 2019; pp. 18–33. [CrossRef]
12. Hassebo, A.; Tealab, M. Global Models of Smart Cities and Potential IoT Applications: A Review. *IoT* **2023**, *4*, 366–411. [CrossRef]

13. Szpilko, D.; de la Torre Gallegos, F.A.; Naharro, F.J.; Rzepka, A.; Remiszewska, A. Waste Management in the Smart City: Current Practices and Future Directions. *Resources* **2023**, *12*, 115. [CrossRef]
14. Mishra, P.; Singh, G. Energy Management Systems in Sustainable Smart Cities Based on the Internet of Energy: A Technical Review. *Energies* **2023**, *16*, 6903. [CrossRef]
15. Iwayemi, A. Internet of things: Implementation challenges in Nigeria. *Am. J. Eng. Res.* **2018**, *7*, 105–115.
16. Dosumu, O.S.; Mahame, C.; Niyitegeka, S.; Hahiirwuwambaza, J.A. Applications and Challenges of Adopting the Internet of Things (IoT) in the Rwandan Construction Industry. *J. Constr. Dev. Ctries.* **2023**, *28*, 81–100.
17. Moeti, M.N.; Mokwena, S.N.; Selape, M. Factors influencing the adoption of Internet of Things in the agricultural sector in Limpopo province. *S. Afr. J. Inf. Manag.* **2024**, *26*, 1–8. [CrossRef]
18. Ofori-Amoah, B. The Economic Community of Central African States. In *The African Continental Free Trade Area: Prospects, Problems and Challenges*; Ofori-Amoah, B., Ed.; Springer International Publishing: Cham, Switzerland, 2024; pp. 93–107. [CrossRef]
19. Kewir, K.J. Rethinking Regional Security in Central Africa: The Case of the Central African Republic. *Int. J. Afr. Renaiss. Stud. Multi-, Inter- Transdiscipl.* **2020**, *15*, 115–133. [CrossRef]
20. Rex, E.; Njie, M.J. Explaining the Absence of a Regional Hegemon in the Central African Sub-region. *Cent. Eur. J. Int. Secur. Stud.* **2021**, *15*, 32–47. [CrossRef]
21. Obasa, S.O. Africa's Political Environment and the Challenge of Underdevelopment. *Soc. Sci.* **2020**, *9*, 241. [CrossRef]
22. Fabrice, N.; Bertrand, N.A.S.; Adamou, N. Effects of Information and Communication Technologies on Structural Change in Sub-Saharan Africa. *J. Knowl. Econ.* **2024**, *15*, 2271–2293. [CrossRef]
23. Briter Bridges. 618 Active Tech Hubs in Africa. Briter. Available online: https://briterbridges.com/618-active-tech-hubs (accessed on 23 September 2024).
24. AfriLabs. African Innovation Ecosystem Roundtables: Exploring and Understanding the African Innovation Ecosystem and Its Needs. 2021. Available online: https://www.afrilabs.com/ecosystem-insights/ (accessed on 26 September 2024).
25. Ajadi, S.; Acland, S. Navigating the Tech Ecosystem in Cameroon. Mobile for Development. Available online: https://www.gsma.com/solutions-and-impact/connectivity-for-good/mobile-for-development/gsma_resources/navigating-the-tech-ecosystem-in-cameroon/ (accessed on 1 August 2024).
26. Mishra, A.R.; Rani, P.; Saha, A.; Hezam, I.M.; Pamucar, D.; Marinovic, M.; Pandey, K. Assessing the Adaptation of Internet of Things (IoT) Barriers for Smart Cities' Waste Management Using Fermatean Fuzzy Combined Compromise Solution Approach. *IEEE Access* **2022**, *10*, 37109–37130. [CrossRef]
27. Padyab, A.; Habibipour, A.; Rizk, A.; Ståhlbröst, A. Adoption Barriers of IoT in Large Scale Pilots. *Information* **2019**, *11*, 23. [CrossRef]
28. Ajigini, O.A. Adoption of Internet of Things in the Higher Educational Institutions: Perspectives from South Africa. *Int. J. Emerg. Technol. Learn. (IJET)* **2023**, *18*, 165–181. [CrossRef]
29. Evwiekpaefe, A.E.; Amrevuawho, O.F. Acceptance of IoT Technology among Students and Staff of Tertiary Institutions in Kaduna State, Nigeria. *Dutse J. Pure Appl. Sci.* **2023**, *9*, 117–126. [CrossRef]
30. Al-rawashdeh, M.; Keikhosrokiani, P.; Belaton, B.; Alawida, M.; Zwiri, A. IoT Adoption and Application for Smart Healthcare: A Systematic Review. *Sensors* **2022**, *22*, 5377. [CrossRef]
31. Chohan, S.R.; Hu, G. Success Factors Influencing Citizens' Adoption of IoT Service Orchestration for Public Value Creation in Smart Government. *IEEE Access* **2020**, *8*, 208427–208448. [CrossRef]
32. Zhao, Y.; Hao, S.; Chen, Z.; Zhou, X.; Zhang, L.; Guo, Z. Critical factors influencing the internet of things technology adoption behavior of construction companies: Evidence from China. *Eng. Constr. Archit. Manag.* 2023; *ahead of print*. [CrossRef]
33. Hundal, G.S.; Laux, C.M.; Buckmaster, D.; Sutton, M.J.; Langemeier, M. Exploring Barriers to the Adoption of Internet of Things-Based Precision Agriculture Practices. *Agriculture* **2023**, *13*, 163. [CrossRef]
34. Das, L.; Mangalam, S.; Rasit, M.; Claus, S.; Martin, L. Internet of Things: The New Government to Business Platform—A Review of Opportunities, Practices, and Challenges. World Bank. Available online: https://documents.worldbank.org/en/publication/documents-reports/documentdetail/610081509689089303/Internet-of-things-the-new-government-to-business-platform-a-review-of-opportunities-practices-and-challenges (accessed on 7 October 2024).
35. Garrity, J. *Harnessing the Internet of Things for Global Development*; SSRN: Rochester, NY, USA, 2015. [CrossRef]
36. Akamanzi, C.; Deutscher, P.; Guerich, B.; Lobelle, A.; Ooko-Ombaka, A. Silicon Savannah: The Kenya ICT Services Cluster. *Microecon. Compet.* **2016**, *7*, 36–49.
37. Cheah, J.-H.; Sarstedt, M.; Ringle, C.M.; Ramayah, T.; Ting, H. Convergent validity assessment of formatively measured constructs in PLS-SEM: On using single-item versus multi-item measures in redundancy analyses. *Int. J. Contemp. Hosp. Manag.* **2018**, *30*, 3192–3210. [CrossRef]
38. Hajjar, S.T.E. Statistical Analysis: Internal-Consistency Reliability and Construct Validity. *Int. J. Quant. Qual. Res. Methods* **2018**, *6*, 27–38.
39. Shrestha, N. Factor analysis as a tool for survey analysis. *Am. J. Appl. Math. Stat.* **2021**, *9*, 4–11. [CrossRef]
40. Schreiber, J.B. Issues and recommendations for exploratory factor analysis and principal component analysis. *Res. Soc. Adm. Pharm.* **2021**, *17*, 1004–1011. [CrossRef]

41. Boateng, G.O.; Neilands, T.B.; Frongillo, E.A.; Melgar-Quiñonez, H.R.; Young, S.L. Best Practices for Developing and Validating Scales for Health, Social, and Behavioral Research: A Primer. *Front. Public Health* **2018**, *6*, 149. [CrossRef] [PubMed]
42. Siwale, K.; Mwalemba, G. Societal influences on career decision making: Perspectives of African women pursuing technology-related professions. *Electron. J. Inf. Syst. Dev. Ctries.* **2023**, *89*, e12259. [CrossRef]
43. Hailu, M.F.; Gaete, I.P. Sub-Saharan women in engineering higher education: A literature-informed research tool. *Policy Futures Educ.* **2024**, 147821032412265274. [CrossRef]
44. Wrycza, S.; Marcinkowski, B.; Gajda, D. The Enriched UTAUT Model for the Acceptance of Software Engineering Tools in Academic Education. *Inf. Syst. Manag.* **2017**, *34*, 38–49. [CrossRef]
45. Taber, K.S. The Use of Cronbach's Alpha When Developing and Reporting Research Instruments in Science Education. *Res. Sci. Educ.* **2018**, *48*, 1273–1296. [CrossRef]
46. Lavrakas, P.J. *Encyclopedia of Survey Research Methods*; Sage Publications, Inc.: Thousand Oaks, CA, USA, 2008. [CrossRef]
47. Alnahdi, G.H.; Goldan, J.; Schwab, S. Psychometric Properties and Rasch Validation of the Teachers' Version of the Perception of Resources Questionnaire. *Front. Psychol.* **2021**, *12*, 633801. [CrossRef]
48. Park, C.; Kim, Y. Identifying key factors affecting consumer purchase behavior in an online shopping context. *Int. J. Retail Distrib. Manag.* **2003**, *31*, 16–29. [CrossRef]
49. IoT Analytics. New Research on 1600 Enterprise IoT Projects: Upsurge in Smart City and Connected Building Related IoT Projects. Available online: https://iot-analytics.com/global-overview-1600-enterprise-iot-projects/ (accessed on 6 September 2024).
50. Nižetić, S.; Šolić, P.; González-de-Artaza, D.L.-D.-I.; Patrono, L. Internet of Things (IoT): Opportunities, issues and challenges towards a smart and sustainable future. *J. Clean. Prod.* **2020**, *274*, 122877. [CrossRef]
51. Kautsarina; Kusumawati, D. The Potential Adoption of the Internet of Things in Rural Areas. In Proceedings of the 2018 International Conference on ICT for Rural Development (IC-ICTRuDev), Badung, Indonesia, 17–18 October 2018; pp. 124–130. [CrossRef]
52. López-Vargas, A.; Fuentes, M.; Vivar, M. Challenges and Opportunities of the Internet of Things for Global Development to Achieve the United Nations Sustainable Development Goals. *IEEE Access* **2020**, *8*, 37202–37213. [CrossRef]
53. TFernández-Caramés, M.; Fraga-Lamas, P. Towards Next Generation Teaching, Learning, and Context-Aware Applications for Higher Education: A Review on Blockchain, IoT, Fog and Edge Computing Enabled Smart Campuses and Universities. *Appl. Sci.* **2019**, *9*, 4479. [CrossRef]
54. Tran-Dang, H.; Krommenacker, N.; Charpentier, P.; Kim, D.-S. The Internet of Things for Logistics: Perspectives, Application Review, and Challenges. *IETE Tech. Rev.* **2022**, *39*, 93–121. [CrossRef]
55. Kalsoom, T.; Ahmed, S.; Rafi-Ul-Shan, P.M.; Azmat, M.; Akhtar, P.; Pervez, Z.; Imran, M.A.; Ur-Rehman, M. Impact of IoT on Manufacturing Industry 4.0: A New Triangular Systematic Review. *Sustainability* **2021**, *13*, 12506. [CrossRef]
56. Kaiser, H.F. A second generation little jiffy. *Psychometrika* **1970**, *35*, 401–415. [CrossRef]
57. Chanal, P.M.; Kakkasageri, M.S. Security and Privacy in IoT: A Survey. *Wirel. Pers. Commun.* **2020**, *115*, 1667–1693. [CrossRef]
58. Abdulghani, H.A.; Nijdam, N.A.; Collen, A.; Konstantas, D. A Study on Security and Privacy Guidelines, Countermeasures, Threats: IoT Data at Rest Perspective. *Symmetry* **2019**, *11*, 774. [CrossRef]
59. Albouq, S.S.; Sen, A.A.A.; Almashf, N.; Yamin, M.; Alshanqiti, A.; Bahbouh, N.M. A Survey of Interoperability Challenges and Solutions for Dealing With Them in IoT Environment. *IEEE Access* **2022**, *10*, 36416–36428. [CrossRef]
60. Lee, E.; Seo, Y.-D.; Oh, S.-R.; Kim, Y.-G. A Survey on Standards for Interoperability and Security in the Internet of Things. *IEEE Commun. Surv. Tutor.* **2021**, *23*, 1020–1047. [CrossRef]
61. Okafor, K.C.; Achumba, I.E.; Chukwudebe, G.A.; Ononiwu, G.C. Leveraging Fog Computing for Scalable IoT Datacenter Using Spine-Leaf Network Topology. *J. Electr. Comput. Eng.* **2017**, *2017*, 2363240. [CrossRef]
62. Madni, S.H.H.; Ali, J.; Husnain, H.A.; Masum, M.H.; Mustafa, S.; Shuja, J.; Maray, M.; Hosseini, S. Factors Influencing the Adoption of IoT for E-Learning in Higher Educational Institutes in Developing Countries. *Front. Psychol.* **2022**, *13*, 915596. [CrossRef]
63. Kuaban, G.S.; Nowak, M.; Czekalski, P.; Tokarz, K.; Tangka, J.K.; Siggursson, K.; Nikitenko, A.; Berkolds, K.; Sell, R. An IoT Course Program to Foster the Adoption of IoT Driven Food and Agriculture in Sub-Saharan Africa (SSA). In Proceedings of the 2022 International Conference on Electrical, Computer and Energy Technologies (ICECET), Prague, Czech Republic, 20–22 July 2022; pp. 1–7. [CrossRef]
64. Morrissey, J. *The Energy Challenge in Sub-Saharan Africa: A Guide for Advocates and Policy Makers, Part 2: Addressing Energy Poverty. Oxfam America, 2017.* Available online: https://www.oxfamamerica.org/explore/research-publications/the-energy-challenge-in-sub-saharan-africa/ (accessed on 6 September 2024).
65. Cetindamar, D.; Abedin, B.; Shirahada, K. The Role of Employees in Digital Transformation: A Preliminary Study on How Employees' Digital Literacy Impacts Use of Digital Technologies. *IEEE Trans. Eng. Manag.* **2024**, *71*, 7837–7848. [CrossRef]
66. Pal, D.; Zhang, X.; Siyal, S. Prohibitive factors to the acceptance of Internet of Things (IoT) technology in society: A smart-home context using a resistive modelling approach. *Technol. Soc.* **2021**, *66*, 101683. [CrossRef]

67. Almugari, F.; Bajaj, P.; Tabash, M.I.; Khan, A.; Ali, M.A. An examination of consumers' adoption of internet of things (IoT) in Indian banks. *Cogent Bus. Manag.* **2020**, *7*, 1809071. [CrossRef]
68. Cole, K.; Chetty, M.; LaRosa, C.; Rietta, F.; Schmitt, D.K.; Goodman, S.E. *Cybersecurity in Africa: An Assessment*; Sam Nunn School of International Affairs, Georgia Institute of Technology: Atlanta, GA, USA, 2008. Available online: https://www.academia.edu/57022945/Cybersecurity_in_Africa_An_Assessment (accessed on 6 September 2024).

future internet

MDPI

Article

Optimizing Network Performance: A Comparative Analysis of EIGRP, OSPF, and BGP in IPv6-Based Load-Sharing and Link-Failover Systems

Kamal Shahid [1,†], Saleem Naseer Ahmad [1,†] and Syed Tahir Hussain Rizvi [2,*]

1 Institute of Electrical, Electronics and Computer Engineering, University of the Punjab, Lahore 54590, Pakistan; kamal.ee@pu.edu.pk (K.S.); saleem.naseer@wateen.com (S.N.A.)
2 Department of Electrical Engineering and Computer Science, University of Stavanger, 4021 Stavanger, Norway
* Correspondence: syed.rizvi@polito.it or tahir098@msn.com
† These authors contributed equally to this work.

Abstract: The purpose of this study is to evaluate and compare how well different routing protocols perform in terms of load sharing, link failover, and overall network performance. Wireshark was used for packet-level analysis, VMWare was used for virtualization, GNS3 was used for network simulation, and Iperf3 was used to measure network performance parameters. Convergence time, packet losses, network jitter, and network delay are the parameters that were selected for assessment. To examine the behaviors of Open Shortest Path First (OSPF) and Enhanced Interior Gateway Routing Protocol (EIGRP) routing protocols in a variety of network settings, a simulated network environment incorporating both protocols along with Border Gateway Protocol (BGP) is created for the research. The setup for the experiment entails simulating different network conditions, such as fluctuating traffic loads and connection failures, to track how the protocols function in dynamic situations. The efficiency metrics for OSPF and EIGRP with BGP are measured and evaluated using the data generated by Wireshark and Iperf3. The results of this research show that EIGRP has a better failover convergence time and packet loss percentage as compared to the OSPF.

Keywords: comparative study; routing protocols; IPv6 transition; OSPF; EIGRP; BGP; load sharing; link failover; routing protocols evaluation; network delay; network jitter; packet loss; convergence time; GNS3; VMware; Wireshark; Iperf3

1. Introduction

Corporate networks require a stable connection with internet services and remote branches. Organizations strive to minimize network downtime through link-failover mechanisms. However, a significant limitation of these mechanisms is the idle state of backup links when the primary link remains operational for extended periods, leading to unnecessary costs for unused resources. Additionally, organizations managing both branch-to-branch communication and internet traffic face challenges in handling these traffic types simultaneously. For security reasons, some organizations mandate that data traffic must traverse an overlay network, while internet traffic uses an underlay network. Moreover, organizations seek the flexibility to choose optimal paths for network traffic to enhance performance.

Network engineers often struggle to select the most appropriate routing protocol without a thorough understanding of the strengths and limitations of available options. This knowledge is essential for improving routing infrastructure and ensuring effective traffic distribution. Therefore, a comprehensive solution is needed that efficiently utilizes backup links, manages dual traffic types, secures and optimizes routing paths, and equips network engineers with the necessary insights to choose the best routing protocols for superior network performance.

This study aims to provide valuable insights for researchers and network engineers on the performance of Enhanced Interior Gateway Routing Protocol (EIGRP) and Open Shortest Path First (OSPF) when integrated with Border Gateway Protocol (BGP), particularly in the contexts of load sharing and link-failover strategies. To conduct a thorough evaluation, this work employs simulation tools like Graphical Network Simulator-3 (GNS3) for network topology simulation, VMware for virtualization, and Wireshark and Iperf3 for detailed network analysis. These tools allow us to create realistic network scenarios and assess critical performance metrics such as packet loss, convergence time, network jitter, and delay.

As networks continue to evolve to support new technologies, a robust routing infrastructure becomes increasingly essential. This study contributes to the understanding of how routing protocols perform in modern network environments. By combining BGP, which plays a key role in connecting autonomous systems, with widely used interior gateway protocols like OSPF and EIGRP, our research offers a comprehensive view of routing protocol efficiency in practical settings. This work aims to identify the strengths and weaknesses of OSPF and EIGRP in scenarios involving load sharing and link failures, thereby evaluating their suitability for various networking contexts. Including Internet Protocol version 6 (IPv6) in the analysis ensures that the findings align with the industry's transition to the latest version of the Internet Protocol.

Advanced simulation tools, such as GNS3, facilitate this investigation by enabling the construction of realistic network environments for in-depth analysis. By simulating real-world conditions, we can observe how different routing protocols perform in dynamic and changing network environments. The ultimate goal is to extract actionable insights from the collected data, providing researchers and network engineers with the knowledge needed to make informed decisions about selecting and implementing routing protocols in contemporary networking scenarios. This research aims to enhance network performance, flexibility, and scalability by understanding the intricate dynamics of OSPF and EIGRP in conjunction with BGP, particularly in the context of IPv6. The expected outcomes will serve as a valuable resource for making informed choices, ensuring that routing protocols effectively meet the evolving demands of modern network architectures.

This research makes the following key contributions: (1) Introduces a mechanism that utilizes both primary and secondary links simultaneously, addressing the inefficiency of idle backup links and ensuring cost-effective resource utilization; (2) Focuses on managing two distinct types of traffic: data traffic for branch-to-branch communication and internet traffic for external services; (3) Employs an overlay network for secure data communication and an underlay network for internet traffic, enhancing security and optimizing network resource use; (4) Develops a route-mapping mechanism to manage both data and internet traffic effectively. This mechanism supports load sharing and link failover on the preferred link according to specific needs, ensuring optimal network performance; (5) Compares EIGRP and OSPF based on key network parameters such as delay, jitter, packet loss, and failover convergence time in an IPv6 environment. This comparison provides network engineers and administrators with the information needed to select the most appropriate routing protocol to enhance their routing infrastructure for effective traffic distribution.

The remainder of this paper is structured as follows: Section 2 provides an overview of routing protocols; Section 3 presents a literature review; Section 4 discusses load sharing and link-failover systems; Section 5 highlights the importance of IPv6 in networking; Section 6 details the methodology and performance metrics; Section 7 presents the results and discussion; and Section 8 concludes the paper with a summary and suggestions for future work.

2. Routing Protocols Overview

The performance and stability of network communication heavily rely on the choice and implementation of routing protocols. In business networks, two widely used interior gateway protocols are OSPF (Open Shortest Path First) and EIGRP (Enhanced Interior Gateway Routing Protocol). OSPF uses a link-state routing algorithm, which enables it to make efficient routing decisions based on a comprehensive understanding of the entire network topology. EIGRP, developed by Cisco, is designed to achieve fast convergence and low resource usage by incorporating both distance vector and link-state characteristics.

For scenarios that involve internet access and the need to connect multiple autonomous systems, the exterior gateway protocol BGP (Border Gateway Protocol) plays a crucial role. BGP is essential for routing data between different networks, ensuring stable and reliable communication across diverse and geographically distributed systems.

The study aims to assess the performance of EIGRP and OSPF, particularly in an IPv6 environment, focusing on their effectiveness in handling load sharing and link-failover scenarios. This evaluation could provide insights into how these protocols contribute to network resilience and traffic distribution, offering recommendations for enhancing failover capabilities and load-sharing techniques in IPv6-based systems.

2.1. EIGRP Features and Characteristics

EIGRP (Enhanced Interior Gateway Routing Protocol) significantly enhances the efficiency and flexibility of network operations. Developed by Cisco, EIGRP is a highly effective and proprietary interior gateway protocol that combines elements of both link-state and distance vector protocols. One of its key features is the Diffusing Update Algorithm (DUAL), which enables rapid convergence and efficient use of network resources. EIGRP excels in load-sharing scenarios due to its ability to dynamically distribute traffic across multiple paths, optimizing network efficiency and ensuring a more balanced workload distribution. Additionally, EIGRP's adaptability in quickly responding to changes in network topology makes it well-suited for environments where link failure is a critical concern. In the context of load-sharing and link failover, EIGRP plays a pivotal role by continuously monitoring the network for changes and selecting the best routes based on real-time metrics. When evaluated alongside OSPF and BGP in an IPv6 environment, EIGRP's performance analysis provides a comprehensive understanding of its contribution to enhancing network resilience and efficiency.

Convergence Process of EIGRP

The process begins with the use of Hello packets, which are sent to establish neighbor relationships and share crucial information. Once routers recognize each other, they exchange Update packets containing information about reachable destinations and their associated metrics. These data are essential for constructing and updating topology tables. EIGRP routers then utilize the DUAL algorithm to calculate feasible distances and determine the optimal paths. The continuous exchange of routing information through Update packets ensures that network updates occur in real time, allowing routers to quickly adapt to changes in topology. This combined process enhances EIGRP's responsiveness and reliability, especially in dynamic network environments where conditions are constantly changing. The convergence process of EIGRP is illustrated in Figure 1.

Figure 1 shows the step-by-step process of how EIGRP routers establish neighbor relationships, exchange routing information, calculate optimal paths using DUAL, and update the network topology to ensure efficient routing.

Time	Source	Destination	Protocol	Length	Info
132.018724	fe80::c802:30ff:fe6…	ff02::a	EIGRP	94	Hello
132.035978	fe80::c802:30ff:fe6…	fe80::c801:37ff:fe6…	EIGRP	74	Update
132.036975	fe80::c802:30ff:fe6…	ff02::a	EIGRP	123	Hello
132.036975	fe80::c802:30ff:fe6…	ff02::a	EIGRP	166	Update
132.036975	fe80::c801:37ff:fe6…	fe80::c802:30ff:fe6…	EIGRP	74	Update
133.997139	fe80::c801:37ff:fe6…	fe80::c802:30ff:fe6…	EIGRP	74	Update
134.017135	fe80::c802:30ff:fe6…	fe80::c801:37ff:fe6…	EIGRP	166	Update
134.017135	fe80::c802:30ff:fe6…	fe80::c801:37ff:fe6…	EIGRP	74	Hello (Ack)

Figure 1. EIGRP convergence process.

2.2. OSPF Features and Characteristics

OSPF (Open Shortest Path First) is a link-state routing protocol that enables network routers to maintain a synchronized view of the network topology. By having a comprehensive understanding of the network architecture, OSPF can determine the shortest path to a destination, facilitating efficient and optimal routing decisions. In the context of this study, OSPF is likely employed to facilitate communication between routers within the same autonomous system, particularly in an IPv6 environment. OSPF's role includes load sharing, where it allows traffic to be distributed across multiple paths, thereby enhancing network performance and resource efficiency. Additionally, OSPF contributes to system resilience by supporting efficient link-failover mechanisms, ensuring a seamless transition in the event of network outages. The performance analysis of OSPF, in conjunction with EIGRP and BGP, provides valuable insights into load sharing and link-failover strategies within IPv6-based systems.

Convergence Process of OSPF

The convergence process in OSPF involves several critical phases and the exchange of specific OSPF protocol packets. The process begins with the exchange of Hello packets between neighboring routers, initiating neighbor detection and verification. These Hello packets are essential for establishing and maintaining adjacencies between routers. For proper adjacency formation, routers must match OSPF parameters such as the router ID, area ID, and authentication settings.

Once adjacencies are established, the routers exchange Database Description (DBD) packets, which provide an overview of the router's link-state database. If there are missing entries, Link State Request (LSR) packets are sent to request specific Link State Advertisements (LSAs) that are not present in the recipient's database. Upon receiving the necessary LSAs, the responding router sends out Link State Update (LSU) packets. Finally, to confirm the receipt of LSAs, Link State Acknowledgment (LSAck) packets are exchanged.

This series of OSPF protocol packets ensures that routers share and synchronize their understanding of the network's link-state information, enabling precise and efficient routing decisions. Figure 2 would typically illustrate this convergence process, depicting the step-by-step exchange of packets that leads to the synchronization of network topology information across routers.

Time	Source	Destination	Protocol	Length	Info
41.011275	fe80::c801:37ff:fe6…	fe80::c802:30ff:fe6…	OSPF	82	DB Description
41.011275	fe80::c801:37ff:fe6…	fe80::c802:30ff:fe6…	OSPF	106	LS Request
41.011275	fe80::c801:37ff:fe6…	fe80::c802:30ff:fe6…	OSPF	210	LS Update
41.028966	fe80::c802:30ff:fe6…	fe80::c801:37ff:fe6…	OSPF	82	DB Description
41.028966	fe80::c802:30ff:fe6…	fe80::c801:37ff:fe6…	OSPF	210	LS Update
41.049334	fe80::c802:30ff:fe6…	ff02::5	OSPF	210	LS Update
41.049334	fe80::c801:37ff:fe6…	fe80::c802:30ff:fe6…	OSPF	82	DB Description
41.068065	fe80::c801:37ff:fe6…	fe80::c802:30ff:fe6…	OSPF	130	LS Acknowledge

Figure 2. OSPF convergence process.

Figure 2 shows the stages of OSPF convergence, from the initial Hello packet exchange to the final acknowledgment of LSAs, highlighting how OSPF routers achieve a consistent and accurate view of the network.

2.3. BGP Features and Characteristics

BGP (Border Gateway Protocol) is essential for enabling communication between multiple autonomous systems (ASs) on the internet. As an exterior gateway protocol, BGP is responsible for exchanging routing information and determining the best routes for data and internet traffic across diverse network domains. It must handle complex routing decisions based on policies, such as path attributes and network policies, to optimize traffic flow and ensure efficient load sharing. In the context of the load sharing and link-failover system being studied, BGP plays a critical role by influencing routing decisions that guide traffic between autonomous systems, thereby affecting the overall performance of the network. BGP is divided into two primary types:

1. Internal Border Gateway Protocol (iBGP): iBGP is used for communication between routers within the same autonomous system (AS). It facilitates the distribution of routing information within the boundaries of a single AS, ensuring consistent and effective routing decisions across the internal network. iBGP helps maintain a coherent view of the network's topology, enabling routers within the AS to make informed decisions about traffic routing.
2. External Border Gateway Protocol (eBGP): eBGP is utilized for communication between routers in different autonomous systems. It ensures that networks managed by separate administrative entities can exchange routing information, thereby enabling inter-AS communication. eBGP plays a pivotal role in the broader internet infrastructure by facilitating the exchange of routing data across the global network, allowing data to traverse multiple autonomous systems efficiently.

Both iBGP and eBGP contribute to BGP's ability to manage and optimize the flow of traffic across the internet, making it a crucial protocol for global network connectivity and stability.

3. Literature Review

The research presented in [1] introduces an innovative technique that integrates a backup mechanism directly into the real-time network, enhancing downtime management and maintaining optimal quality at 100%. The simulations demonstrate that the backup process operates smoothly, ensuring network quality remains intact. This study highlights the benefits of a failover system using BGP routing on a single link connection, showing superior performance.

The study in [2] evaluates the effectiveness of merging internal and external routing protocols using GNS3, focusing on parameters such as throughput, jitter, packet loss, and network convergence. To achieve high Quality of Service (QoS), it is essential to minimize levels of throughput, jitter, and packet loss. The findings reveal that the OSPF routing protocol offers the fastest network convergence, while the combination of OSPF and BGP delivers the highest throughput, lowest packet loss, and lowest jitter.

In [3], the research aims to identify the best interior gateway routing protocol for various traffic conditions within a corporate network. The study seeks to determine the most effective protocol for managing and routing network traffic, ensuring efficient communication and performance. The ultimate goal is to provide enterprises with valuable insights into selecting the internal gateway protocol that best meets their specific network requirements.

The research in [4] focuses on comparing various networking characteristics using Cisco's Packet Tracer simulation environment, specifically examining packet drops, routing convergence speed, and end-to-end latency. The study likely assesses the performance of different networking setups or protocols based on these criteria to gain insights into their efficiency and effectiveness in a simulated environment.

The study in [5] analyzes the performance of IPv6, concentrating on the header format, security concerns, and routing protocols, utilizing Packet Tracer for simulations. The emphasis is on evaluating the efficiency and functionality of these elements within the context of IPv6.

The research in [6] investigates the performance of well-known routers, focusing on three IPv6 protocols: EIGRPv6, OSPFv3, and Routing Information Protocol Next Generation (RIPng). Data transmission rates and convergence times are measured using a Cisco simulation platform. Real-time comparisons are made using the ping command to check network connections, with findings collected through Cisco Packet Tracer, offering insights into the efficiency of these protocols in an IPv6 environment.

In [7], the work examines the challenges faced by Internet Service Providers (ISPs) during the transition to IPv6. Issues such as packet traversal difficulties, routing scaling limitations, performance reliability concerns, and the need for enhanced security measures are explored. The study provides a comprehensive overview of the complexities involved in migrating to an IPv6 network.

The fundamental purpose of the research in [8] is to evaluate the performance of specific protocols within simulated network models. The assessment is based on factors such as throughput, jitter, convergence time, end-to-end latency, and packet depletion. The results indicate that the EIGRP routing protocol outperforms OSPF in terms of overall performance, suggesting it is more suitable for real-world applications.

The study in [9] explores multiple Internet Protocol Security (IPsec) transformations in Network Simulator Version 2 (NS2) simulations, using different authentication and encryption techniques. The findings reveal that IPsec overhead is minimal for smaller packet sizes but significantly increases for larger packets, especially when fragmentation is necessary. This information can help network managers make informed decisions about the trade-off between processing costs and the need for larger address spaces when transmitting large IP packets.

In [10], the research compares the performance of three dynamic routing methods and investigates their redistribution mechanisms within a simulated network topology. The performance evaluation focuses on latency, throughput, and packet loss, with the network model comprising three PCs, nine Cisco routers, and four switches.

The study in [11] assesses the performance of system failover connections within a network architecture that utilizes a combination of internal and external routing protocols and various Autonomous System (AS) numbers. Using the GNS3 simulator, the study measures key performance metrics such as throughput, jitter, packet loss, and latency, providing insights into the reliability and effectiveness of failover mechanisms in complex network scenarios.

The research in [12] explores the Intermediate System to Intermediate System (IS–IS) and Open Shortest Path First version 3 (OSPFv3) protocols, including their metric systems, with a focus on simulation outcomes. The study aims to draw conclusions about the efficiency of these protocols when implemented in an IPv6 corporate network.

In [13], the research delves into RIPng and OSPFv3, comparing these protocols within an IPv6 framework. The study discusses simulation findings and seeks to determine which protocol is most effective under various network conditions. The study in [14] evaluates several transition techniques in networking using Cisco Packet Tracer, highlighting that the dual-stack approach performs better than tunneling. The research provides insights into the effectiveness of these processes in managing network transitions and emphasizes the benefits of adopting a dual-stack approach.

The research in [15] compares the performance of an Interior Gateway Routing Protocol (IGRP) with an Exterior Gateway Protocol (EGP), aiming to identify the best protocol combination for complex environments. The study also simulates the Hot Standby Routing Protocol (HSRP) and the Gateway Load Balancing Protocol (GLBP) to evaluate load balancing and redundancy specific to BGP.

The study in [16] investigates the transition and migration processes of IPv6, followed by a performance comparison of IPv4 and IPv6 for both data and voice traffic using Riverbed. The analysis shows that dual-stack is the most effective strategy for transitioning from IPv4 to IPv6, with tunneling as a viable alternative.

In [17], the research builds a network to evaluate the performance of OSPF and OSPFv3 routing protocols in both IPv4 and IPv6 environments. The study compares response times for various applications, such as Database Query, Email, and FTP Download, under OSPF and OSPFv3, measuring traffic dropouts, hop counts, background traffic latency, and Ethernet delay.

The study in [18] reviews multiple research papers on IPv6 deployment and the performance analysis of the OSPFv3 routing protocol. The review provides significant insights for researchers, laying the foundation for future investigation and advancement in the field.

The research in [19] analyzes how different Generic Routing Encapsulation (GRE) tunnel parameters affect the efficiency of real-time application streaming in IP networks. The study examines tunnel depth and the routing methods used within GRE tunnels, offering insights into the limitations and optimal routing schemes for real-time traffic.

The purpose of the research in [20] is to assess the effectiveness of routing protocols within an IPv6 network, particularly RIPng, OSPFv3, and EIGRP. Performance measures such as throughput, jitter, and packet loss are evaluated using GNS3, with the goal of determining the suitability of each routing protocol in an IPv6 context.

This research distinguishes itself by utilizing advanced simulation and virtualization tools like GNS3, VMware, Wireshark, and Iperf3 to evaluate critical metrics such as convergence latency, jitter, and packet loss. Unlike previous studies that often relied on physical network setups with inherent limitations, this study leverages sophisticated tools to create and analyze complex, realistic network environments. This approach allows for a more comprehensive assessment of the effectiveness of IPv6 routing protocols under various conditions, including traffic load sharing and connection failures. By exploring a broader range of scenarios, this research provides deeper insights into the strengths and weaknesses of the selected routing protocols in a complex network environment.

4. Load Sharing and Link-Failover Systems

The study focuses on the load-sharing capabilities and link-failover performance of EIGRP and OSPF, two dynamic routing protocols essential for optimizing network efficiency and reliability.

4.1. Load Sharing Capability of EIGRP and OSPF

Load sharing refers to the distribution of network traffic across multiple pathways to enhance resource utilization and overall network performance. EIGRP and OSPF, both dynamic routing protocols, have distinct mechanisms for managing load sharing.

EIGRP is known for its advanced load-sharing capabilities, which involve a sophisticated system that considers various parameters such as bandwidth, latency, reliability, and line load. EIGRP dynamically calculates composite metrics for multiple routes, enabling it to make informed decisions about how to distribute traffic effectively. This research will delve into the complexities of EIGRP's load-sharing algorithms, evaluating their adaptability to changing network conditions and the efficiency of their traffic distribution strategies.

OSPF, on the other hand, utilizes link costs to determine the shortest path to a destination. OSPF's load-sharing capability is based on Equal Cost Multi-Path (ECMP) routing, which allows it to split traffic across multiple paths with the same cost. The study will explore OSPF's load-sharing methods, examining how it handles traffic distribution when multiple routes have equal costs and the impact this has on overall network performance.

Through a series of experiments simulating various network architectures and traffic flow patterns, this research will compare the load-sharing efficiencies of EIGRP and OSPF.

The results will provide valuable insights into the comparative advantages of each protocol, aiding network administrators and engineers in optimizing their routing infrastructure for efficient traffic distribution.

4.2. Link-Failover Performance of EIGRP and OSPF

Link-failover performance is crucial for maintaining network stability and reliability. EIGRP and OSPF both excel in their ability to reroute traffic swiftly and effectively in the event of a connection failure.

EIGRP utilizes the DUAL (Diffusing Update Algorithm) to determine the best route to a destination. This approach considers both primary and secondary paths, allowing for rapid convergence when a link fails. The feasibility condition in EIGRP, coupled with the DUAL process, enables routers to quickly identify alternative paths and redirect traffic, minimizing downtime and packet loss. This inherent design enhances EIGRP's link-failover performance.

OSPF employs a different method for handling link failures. It uses the Hello protocol to establish neighbor relationships and detect link failures. When a failure occurs, OSPF routers utilize the Shortest Path First (SPF) algorithm to recalculate optimal routes to the affected destinations. Although OSPF may take slightly longer to converge compared to EIGRP, it still provides reliable link-failover capabilities. OSPF's use of designated routers and backup designated routers further improves its ability to respond swiftly to changes in network topology.

Both protocols support route summarization, load balancing, and route redistribution, enhancing overall link-failover performance. The choice between EIGRP and OSPF often depends on factors such as network size, vendor preferences, and specific feature requirements. Ultimately, the effective link-failover performance of these routing protocols is critical for ensuring seamless and efficient communication in dynamic network environments.

5. IPv6 in Networking

IPv6 plays a crucial role in enhancing load-sharing and link-failure systems by providing advanced capabilities that improve network resilience and efficiency. The expanded address space of IPv6 allows for a more extensive allocation of IP addresses, facilitating the distribution of network traffic across multiple servers or routes. This scalability ensures balanced resource utilization, reduces congestion, and enhances overall network performance.

IPv6 also includes features like Stateless Address Auto Configuration (SLAAC) and Duplicate Address Detection (DAD), which are essential for link-failover systems. These features enable devices to automatically configure their IPv6 addresses and detect address conflicts, ensuring smooth transitions between alternative paths during link failures. The flexibility and adaptability of IPv6 contribute to continuous connectivity and efficient resource usage in dynamic network environments.

5.1. Improved Header Format

IPv6 introduces a more streamlined header format compared to its predecessor, IPv4. IPv6's fixed header size of 40 bytes, in contrast to the variable-length header of IPv4, simplifies packet processing and reduces the processing burden on routers and network devices. This streamlined header includes only essential information, omitting unnecessary or rarely used functionalities, which accelerates packet forwarding and enhances network scalability. The improved header format aligns with IPv6's broader goal of providing a more efficient and scalable foundation for the growing network of internet-connected devices.

5.2. Address Space Exhaustion

IPv6 addresses the issue of address space exhaustion, a significant limitation of IPv4. The limited number of IPv4 addresses creates bottlenecks as more devices connect to the network. IPv6's vast address space eliminates these scalability challenges, ensuring that every device participating in load-sharing or link-failure scenarios can be uniquely identified with its IP address. This research emphasizes the practical implications of adopting IPv6 in networks where dynamic and efficient address allocation is critical for seamless operation.

5.3. Support for Quality of Service (QoS)

IPv6's support for Quality of Service (QoS) is vital in optimizing load-sharing and link-failure systems. QoS mechanisms in IPv6 allow for the prioritization of different types of network traffic based on factors like latency, jitter, and bandwidth requirements. In load-sharing scenarios, this ensures that critical applications or services receive priority, preventing congestion and improving overall network performance. Similarly, in link-failover systems, QoS maintains an uninterrupted user experience by prioritizing essential traffic even during link transitions. IPv6's QoS capabilities provide enhanced control over network resource management, creating a more flexible, efficient, and reliable network infrastructure.

5.4. Enhanced Security Features

IPv6 includes built-in security features such as mandatory support for IPsec at the network level. IPsec provides authentication and encryption to secure the confidentiality and integrity of data transmitted across the network. These security mechanisms are particularly important in load-sharing and link-failure scenarios, where secure data transfer and smooth network transitions are critical to maintaining network reliability and confidentiality. IPv6's emphasis on security enhances the overall dependability of load-sharing and link-failure systems, establishing a more secure foundation for modern networking environments.

6. Methodology and Performance Metrics Measurement

The network topology for this study was meticulously designed using GNS3, incorporating thirteen Cisco routers configured with OSPF, EIGRP, and BGP protocols to simulate a complex network environment. Two virtual machines were deployed on VMware to represent end-user devices, all configured with IPv6 to evaluate the latest iteration of the Internet Protocol. Detailed packet-level analysis was performed using Wireshark, which allowed for an in-depth examination of routing protocol behavior. IPerf3 was employed to generate traffic and measure critical performance metrics such as network delay, jitter, and packet loss across various scenarios.

Load-sharing and link-failover mechanisms were configured to assess how OSPF and EIGRP manage traffic distribution and handle link failures. The experiments systematically varied parameters such as network size, traffic load, and link conditions to provide a comprehensive understanding of the strengths and weaknesses of OSPF and EIGRP, particularly in comparison to BGP within an IPv6 framework. The results were meticulously analyzed to evaluate the performance and suitability of each protocol for specific network conditions, offering valuable insights for network administrators and designers in making informed decisions about protocol selection and network architecture.

Performance metrics were carefully measured as follows:

1. Network delay:

The total network delay was calculated by summing propagation, transmission, queuing, and processing delays, as in Equation (1):

$$TotalDelay = d_{prop} + d_{trans} + d_{queue} + d_{proc} \quad (1)$$

where d_{prop} is the propagation delay, d_{trans} is the transmission delay, d_{queue} is the queuing delay, and d_{proc} is the processing delay.

2. Network jitter:

Measured in milliseconds, jitter is represented as the average deviation from the mean delay calculated in Equation (2).

$$J = \sqrt{\frac{1}{N}\sum_{i=1}^{N}(D_i - \bar{D})^2} \quad (2)$$

where J is jitter, $1/N$ is the total number of measured packets, D_i is a delay of the i-th packet, and $\bar{D}$ is the average delay of all the measured packets. The packet loss (P_{loss}) percentage.

3. Packet loss:

The packet loss percentage was calculated using Equation (3):

$$P_{loss} = \frac{Number\ of\ Lost\ Packets}{Total\ Number\ of\ Sent\ Packets} \times 100 \quad (3)$$

4. Convergence Time:

This metric refers to the time taken to detect and recover from a link failure, given by Equation (4):

$$T_{convergence} = Time_{recovery} - Time_{failure} \quad (4)$$

In evaluating these metrics, the study employed a structured experimental setup to simulate various network conditions, load-sharing configurations, and link-failure scenarios. Rigorous testing and statistical analysis were conducted to assess the efficiency of EIGRP and OSPF, providing a comprehensive understanding of their real-world application and performance in load-sharing and link-failover systems. The findings contribute to a better grasp of the strengths and limitations of each protocol, offering guidance for enhancing network efficiency and reliability.

There are three use cases of load-sharing and link-failover systems:

6.1. Normal Condition

In this condition, the initial configuration requires the intelligent distribution of data and Internet traffic between two ISPs called ISP-A and ISP-B, to maximize network resilience and performance. The data traffic is going from the overlay network (Tunnel) and Internet traffic is going from the underlay network. Because of its capacity and speed, ISP-A serves as the primary connection in this system for the majority of data traffic. In addition, ISP-B acts as a backup connection for data flow, guaranteeing load sharing to effectively disperse network traffic. Conversely, internet traffic is routed via ISP-B, which serves as a primary link, making use of its unique benefits, including reduced latency or cost. Automatic failover techniques ensure continuous connectivity and minimize service disruption in the case of a link breakdown or degradation on the major pathways by smoothly redirecting the impacted traffic to the secondary links. The quick and automatic reaction helps to create a more resilient and efficient network architecture by reducing downtime and guaranteeing constant connectivity. This dual-ISP strategy offers a strong failover mechanism, enhancing overall network efficiency and providing a dependable and resilient network architecture.

In this experiment for data traffic, ISP-A is working as a primary link and ISP-B is working as a secondary link. Similarly, for Internet traffic ISP-B is working as a primary link and ISP-A is working as a secondary link. In case of link failure, the traffic shifts to the secondary link accordingly.

6.1.1. EIGRP

In this scenario, EIGRP is configured to use Tunnel-1 as the primary connection and Tunnel-2 as the secondary connection within the overlay network for data traffic. This setup enables load sharing by distributing data flows across both tunnels, optimizing bandwidth utilization. If the primary link (Tunnel-1) experiences a failure, EIGRP dynamically reroutes data traffic to the secondary link (Tunnel-2) to maintain connectivity without interruption. EIGRP continuously monitors the health and status of these tunnels to ensure reliability.

For internet traffic, EIGRP identifies ISP-A as the backup link and ISP-B as the primary link within the underlay network. This configuration facilitates both failover and load sharing for internet-bound traffic. EIGRP continuously assesses the condition of these links, and in the event of an issue with the primary link (ISP-B), it automatically redirects internet traffic to the secondary link (ISP-A). This dynamic routing capability of EIGRP ensures optimal use of network resources and enhances network resilience in the face of link failures. The overall network performance and reliability are significantly improved through this adaptive approach, which effectively balances data and internet traffic across multiple channels. The EIGRP topology with dual ISPs is illustrated in Figure 3.

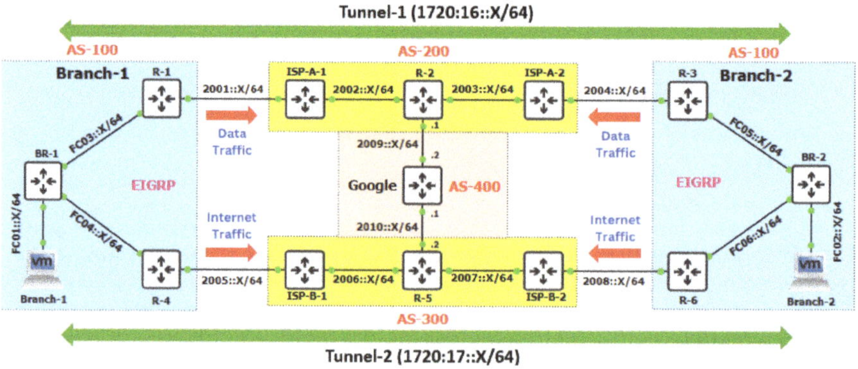

Figure 3. EIGRP normal topology.

The traceroute results for data and internet traffic originating from Branch-1 in the EIGRP-enabled network architecture are depicted in Figure 4. As shown in the diagram, internet traffic is routed through the underlay network via ISP-B, while data traffic from Branch-1 to Branch-2 is transmitted via the primary tunnel in the overlay network connected to ISP-A. This approach ensures an efficient distribution of both incoming and outgoing traffic, effectively balancing the load between the two ISP connections.

```
C:\Users\Branch-1>tracert FC02::2

Tracing route to fc02::2 over a maximum of 30 hops

  1    67 ms    64 ms    16 ms  fc01::1
  2   537 ms   305 ms   467 ms  1720:16::2
  3   548 ms   286 ms   456 ms  fc02::2

Trace complete.

C:\Users\Branch-1>tracert 2001:4860:4860::8888

Tracing route to 2001:4860:4860::8888 over a maximum of 30 hops

  1     5 ms    23 ms    16 ms  fc01::1
  2    40 ms   113 ms    69 ms  fc04::2
  3   102 ms   104 ms   105 ms  2005::2
  4   188 ms   243 ms   189 ms  2006::2
  5   134 ms   253 ms   236 ms  2001:4860:4860::8888

Trace complete.
```

Figure 4. Traceroute from Branch-1.

Similarly, the traceroute results for data and internet traffic from Branch-2 using EIGRP in the network architecture are presented in Figure 5. The findings indicate that internet traffic is directed through the underlay network via ISP-B, while data traffic between Branch-2 and Branch-1 travels through the primary tunnel in the overlay network connected to

ISP-A. This method allows for load sharing by equally distributing both incoming and outgoing traffic across the two ISP connections.

```
C:\Users\Branch-2>tracert FC01::2

Tracing route to fc01::2 over a maximum of 30 hops

  1    20 ms    17 ms    78 ms  fc02::1
  2   335 ms   436 ms   328 ms  1720:16::1
  3   351 ms   646 ms   433 ms  fc01::2

Trace complete.

C:\Users\Branch-2>tracert 2001:4860:4860::8888

Tracing route to 2001:4860:4860::8888 over a maximum of 30 hops

  1    51 ms    30 ms    54 ms  fc02::1
  2    83 ms   135 ms    77 ms  fc06::1
  3    92 ms    75 ms   120 ms  2008::1
  4   153 ms   153 ms   154 ms  2007::1
  5   184 ms   181 ms   180 ms  2001:4860:4860::8888

Trace complete.
```

Figure 5. Traceroute from Branch-2.

6.1.2. OSPF

OSPF plays a critical role in enabling flexible and efficient routing decisions within the network. As a dynamic routing protocol, OSPF is particularly effective in disseminating routing information across an autonomous system involving multiple connections. In the current configuration, OSPF is responsible for directing data traffic along the most efficient paths. The data traffic traverses the overlay network (Tunnel), while internet traffic is managed by the underlay network. Tunnel-1 serves as the primary connection for data traffic, with Tunnel-2 acting as the backup. Additionally, OSPF manages internet traffic by designating ISP-B as the primary connection and ISP-A as the backup. This arrangement facilitates load sharing, provides link-failover capabilities, and optimizes network performance by distributing traffic across multiple links. In the event of a primary link failure, OSPF dynamically redirects traffic to the secondary link, thereby minimizing downtime and ensuring uninterrupted connectivity. The responsive and adaptive routing capabilities of OSPF enable the load-sharing and link-failover system to effectively utilize network resources while maintaining stable connectivity for both data and internet traffic. Figure 3 illustrates the EIGRP topology with dual ISPs, and Figure 6 presents the OSPF topology with dual ISPs under normal operating conditions.

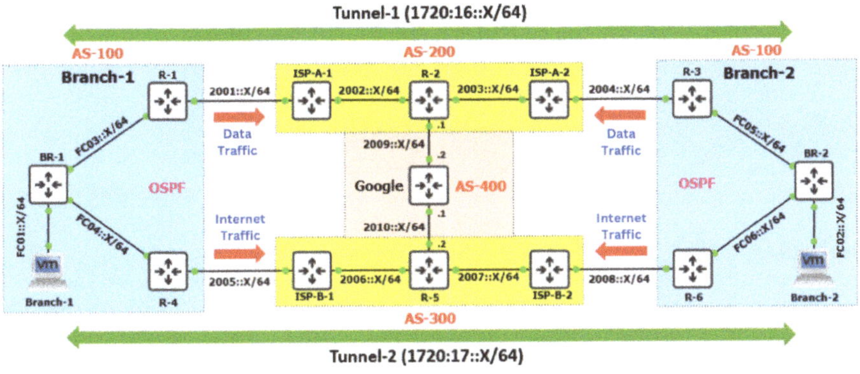

Figure 6. OSPF normal topology.

The traceroute results for data and internet traffic originating from Branch-1 with OSPF enabled in the topology are shown in Figure 7. A closer inspection reveals that internet traffic is routed via ISP-B, while data traffic from Branch-1 to Branch-2 is transmitted through the primary tunnel assigned to ISP-A. This approach ensures efficient load sharing by distributing both incoming and outgoing traffic across the two ISP connections.

```
C:\Users\Branch-1>tracert FC02::2

Tracing route to fc02::2 over a maximum of 30 hops

  1    21 ms    18 ms    29 ms  fc01::1
  2   499 ms   403 ms   778 ms  1720:16::2
  3  1330 ms   512 ms   551 ms  fc02::2

Trace complete.

C:\Users\Branch-1>tracert 2001:4860:4860::8888

Tracing route to 2001:4860:4860::8888 over a maximum of 30 hops

  1    12 ms    69 ms    25 ms  fc01::1
  2   115 ms   107 ms    99 ms  fc04::2
  3   213 ms   163 ms   215 ms  2005::2
  4   140 ms   165 ms   219 ms  2006::2
  5   259 ms   417 ms   296 ms  2001:4860:4860::8888

Trace complete.
```

Figure 7. Traceroute from Branch-1.

The traceroute results for data and internet traffic originating from Branch-2 while OSPF is active in the topology are depicted in Figure 8. The results show that data traffic from Branch-2 to Branch-1 is routed through the primary tunnel assigned to ISP-A, while internet traffic is directed via ISP-B. This configuration effectively distributes both incoming and outgoing traffic across the two ISP connections, optimizing network resource utilization.

```
C:\Users\Branch-2>tracert FC01::2

Tracing route to fc01::2 over a maximum of 30 hops

  1    21 ms    26 ms    31 ms  fc02::1
  2   413 ms   656 ms   373 ms  1720:16::1
  3   454 ms   418 ms   535 ms  fc01::2

Trace complete.

C:\Users\Branch-2>tracert 2001:4860:4860::8888

Tracing route to 2001:4860:4860::8888 over a maximum of 30 hops

  1    58 ms    58 ms    62 ms  fc02::1
  2    94 ms    44 ms   142 ms  fc06::1
  3   125 ms   157 ms   106 ms  2008::1
  4   123 ms   135 ms   333 ms  2007::1
  5   416 ms   322 ms   270 ms  2001:4860:4860::8888

Trace complete.
```

Figure 8. Traceroute from Branch-2.

6.2. When Link Failure Occurs in EIGRP

When a network link failure occurs on the primary connection, such as Tunnel-1 from the overlay network established by ISP-A for data traffic, EIGRP quickly detects the issue using its rapid convergence mechanisms. EIGRP then reroutes the data traffic to the alternative connection, Tunnel-2, which is established by ISP-B. EIGRP routers are equipped with various timers and protocols that enable them to promptly identify network changes. Upon detecting a fault, the affected router initiates the Diffusing Update

Algorithm (DUAL), which recalculates the routing table to find an alternate path. This transition is facilitated by the exchange of routing information among routers, ensuring that all routers within the EIGRP domain are updated on the changes in network topology. Additionally, precomputed backup routes, or viable successor routes, further reduce convergence time.

For Internet traffic, when ISP-B is the primary connection and ISP-A is the backup, EIGRP manages a link failure on the primary connection by redirecting traffic to the secondary connection from the underlay network. This seamless failover between primary and secondary connections ensures continuous connectivity and minimizes interruptions during link failures. Figure 9 illustrates the link failure through ISP-A while EIGRP is operational in the network topology.

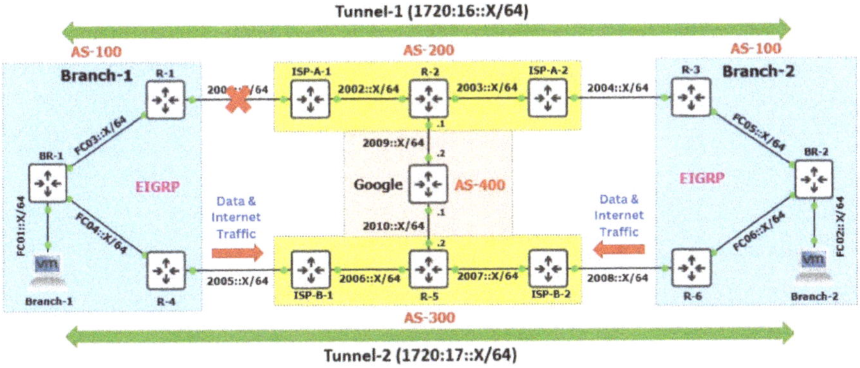

Figure 9. ISP-A failure.

Traceroute results for data and Internet traffic from Branch-1 with EIGRP enabled are shown in Figure 10. When a link failure occurs between Branch-1 and ISP-A, the system smoothly transitions data traffic to the backup connection, reducing network disruptions and ensuring uninterrupted data connectivity. Consequently, if the primary tunnel (Tunnel-1) via ISP-A fails, data traffic quickly shifts to the secondary tunnel (Tunnel-2) via ISP-B. Internet traffic, which is already routed through ISP-B, continues smoothly. This setup enables ISP-B to efficiently manage both data and Internet traffic, maintaining a stable network flow.

```
C:\Users\Branch-1>tracert FC02::2

Tracing route to fc02::2 over a maximum of 30 hops

  1     2 ms    48 ms    40 ms  fc01::1
  2   228 ms   353 ms   245 ms  1720:17::2
  3   291 ms   264 ms   387 ms  fc02::2

Trace complete.

C:\Users\Branch-1>tracert 2001:4860:4860::8888

Tracing route to 2001:4860:4860::8888 over a maximum of 30 hops

  1    16 ms    38 ms    13 ms  fc01::1
  2   107 ms   114 ms    37 ms  fc04::2
  3    88 ms    80 ms   376 ms  2005::2
  4   187 ms   188 ms   283 ms  2006::2
  5   222 ms   232 ms   181 ms  2001:4860:4860::8888

Trace complete.
```

Figure 10. Traceroute from Branch-1.

If the primary Internet link connecting Branch-1 to ISP-B fails, as shown in Figure 11, the secondary link, which connects Branch-1 to ISP-A, takes over to maintain Internet connectivity from the underlay network. This failover mechanism ensures that Internet traffic is seamlessly redirected through ISP-A, preserving network operation during a primary link failure. Thus, both data and Internet traffic are routed via ISP-A, ensuring minimal downtime for Internet services. For Branch-2, data traffic continues through Tunnel-1 via ISP-A, and Internet traffic is routed through ISP-B. This configuration enhances network resilience, ensuring minimal downtime in the event of a link failure.

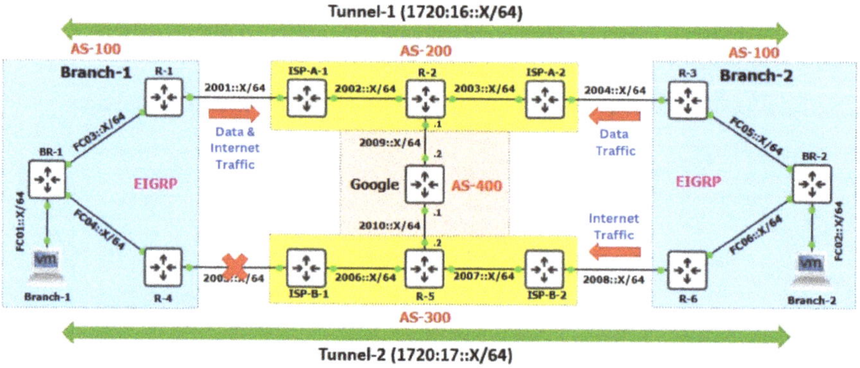

Figure 11. ISP-B failure.

Traceroute findings for data and Internet traffic from Branch-1, when ISP-B fails, are shown in Figure 12. The failover mechanism activates, efficiently redirecting Internet traffic to the backup link, ISP-A, to avoid network disturbances and maintain uninterrupted connectivity. As a result, if the primary connection for Internet traffic via ISP-B becomes unavailable, traffic is automatically rerouted through ISP-A. Data traffic, already routed through ISP-A, ensures that both data and Internet traffic are effectively managed, maintaining network stability.

```
C:\Users\Branch-1>tracert FC02::2

Tracing route to fc02::2 over a maximum of 30 hops

  1    12 ms    64 ms    26 ms  fc01::1
  2   258 ms   336 ms   307 ms  1720:16::2
  3   324 ms   527 ms   425 ms  fc02::2

Trace complete.

C:\Users\Branch-1>tracert 2001:4860:4860::8888

Tracing route to 2001:4860:4860::8888 over a maximum of 30 hops

  1     6 ms    69 ms    13 ms  fc01::1
  2    88 ms   104 ms   129 ms  fc03::2
  3   118 ms   124 ms    86 ms  2001::2
  4   124 ms   149 ms   165 ms  2002::2
  5   274 ms   257 ms   255 ms  2001:4860:4860::8888

Trace complete.
```

Figure 12. Traceroute from Branch-1.

A similar failover scenario occurs at Branch-2, where ISP-A is the primary link for data traffic and ISP-B is the backup, while ISP-B is the primary link for Internet traffic and ISP-A is the backup. In the event of a link failure, EIGRP's failover mechanism automatically shifts traffic to the secondary link, ensuring continuous network connectivity.

This transition is crucial for maintaining stable and uninterrupted network services for businesses and organizations.

6.3. When Link Failure Occurs in OSPF

As a link-state routing protocol, OSPF continually exchanges routing information between routers to maintain an up-to-date map of the network. In this setup, OSPF ensures that data traffic primarily uses Tunnel-1 via ISP-A when it is operational, as it is designated the primary connection. If Tunnel-1 fails, OSPF dynamically reroutes data traffic to Tunnel-2 via ISP-B, enhancing network resilience. For Internet traffic, when ISP-B is the primary link and ISP-A is the secondary link, OSPF adjusts the routing based on real-time network conditions and link statuses. This dynamic adaptability is a key advantage of OSPF, improving network performance and ensuring optimal use of available resources. Figure 13 illustrates the link failure through ISP-A while OSPF is functioning.

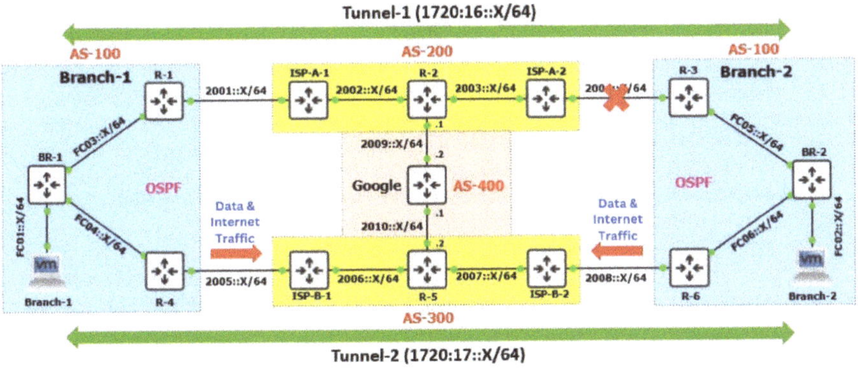

Figure 13. ISP-A failure.

Traceroute results for data and Internet traffic from Branch-2 are shown in Figure 14. When connectivity between Branch-2 and ISP-A fails, the system smoothly reroutes data traffic to the backup link, avoiding network disturbances and ensuring continuous data connectivity. If Tunnel-1 via ISP-A fails, data traffic automatically shifts to Tunnel-2 via ISP-B, while Internet traffic continues through ISP-B from the underlay network. Consequently, both data and Internet traffic are routed through the backup link via ISP-B, maintaining reliable network performance.

```
C:\Users\Branch-2>tracert FC01::2

Tracing route to fc01::2 over a maximum of 30 hops

  1    18 ms    53 ms    61 ms  fc02::1
  2   159 ms   388 ms   264 ms  1720:17::1
  3   371 ms   227 ms   295 ms  fc01::2

Trace complete.

C:\Users\Branch-2>tracert 2001:4860:4860::8888

Tracing route to 2001:4860:4860::8888 over a maximum of 30 hops

  1    10 ms    59 ms    48 ms  fc02::1
  2    93 ms    70 ms    65 ms  fc06::1
  3    67 ms    95 ms   105 ms  2008::1
  4   118 ms   140 ms   122 ms  2007::1
  5   126 ms   244 ms   195 ms  2001:4860:4860::8888

Trace complete.
```

Figure 14. Traceroute from Branch-2.

When the primary Internet connection between Branch-2 and ISP-B fails, the network quickly reroutes Internet traffic to the secondary connection through ISP-A. This automatic transition allows for a swift response to connection failures, ensuring uninterrupted Internet access despite the outage of the primary link. This failover strategy enhances network reliability and stability by dynamically adapting to changing conditions and maintaining connectivity for critical services. For Branch-1, data traffic uses Tunnel-1 via ISP-A and Internet traffic is routed through ISP-B from the underlay network. Figure 15 shows the link failure through ISP-B with OSPF in operation.

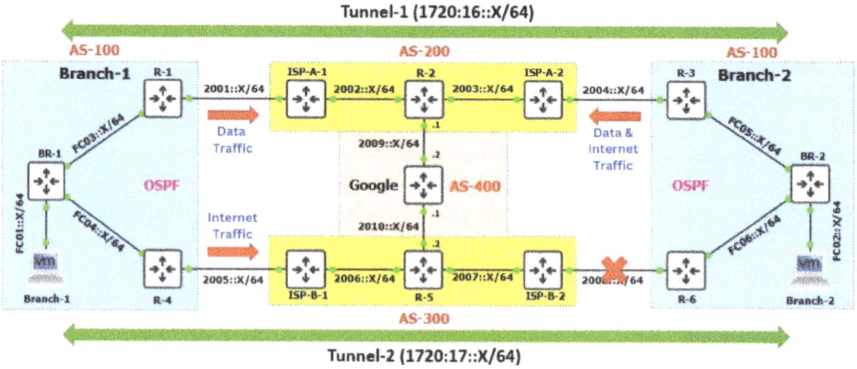

Figure 15. ISP-B failure.

Traceroute results for data and Internet traffic from Branch-2 are shown in Figure 16. When the primary Internet connection through ISP-B fails, the system automatically reroutes Internet traffic through the secondary connection via ISP-A. Data traffic continues through Tunnel-1 via ISP-A. This configuration ensures that both data and Internet traffic are routed through ISP-A, effectively mitigating the impact of the primary connection failure and supporting a stable network design.

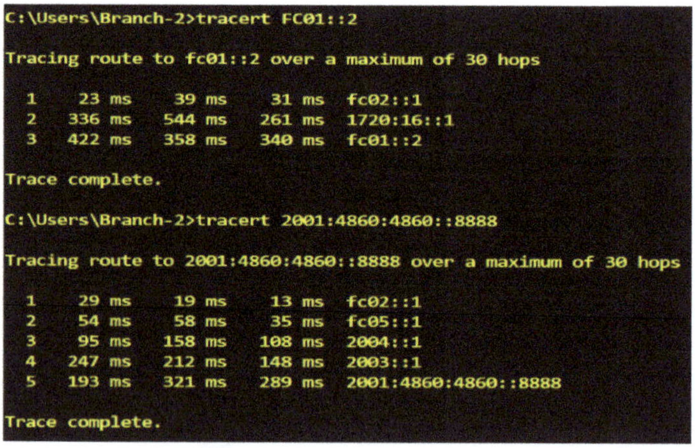

Figure 16. Traceroute from Branch-2.

A similar scenario applies to Branch-1, where ISP-A is the primary link for data traffic from the overlay network and ISP-B is the secondary link. Conversely, ISP-B is the primary link for Internet traffic from the underlay network, and ISP-A is the secondary link. In the event of a link failure, OSPF's failover mechanism automatically shifts traffic to the secondary link, reducing downtime and maintaining continuous communication. This redundancy approach enhances network resilience, minimizes the impact of connection failures, and ensures efficient traffic rerouting, thereby improving overall network stability and efficiency.

7. Results and Discussion

The evaluation of network performance in this study focused on key metrics such as network latency, network jitter, packet loss, and convergence time. The findings indicate that both EIGRP and OSPF have distinct strengths and weaknesses in terms of load sharing and link failover. Specifically, EIGRP demonstrated effective load-sharing capabilities, which helped reduce network latency and packet loss. On the other hand, OSPF excelled in convergence time, especially under link-failure conditions. The integration of BGP further enhanced the system's resilience, making it more robust.

The tools used, such as Wireshark and IPerf3, provided deep insights into packet-level dynamics, offering a thorough understanding of protocol behavior. This research serves as a valuable resource for network managers and engineers seeking to optimize IPv6 performance and resilience by making informed decisions about protocol selection and parameter adjustments.

7.1. Network Delay

Without authentication, EIGRP exhibited delays ranging from 30.21 to 30.39 s, while OSPF delays ranged from 30.24 to 30.35 s. With authentication, EIGRP delays varied between 30.40 and 30.48 s, and OSPF delays ranged from 30.31 to 30.46 s. These results indicate that authentication introduces some variability in the delay levels of both EIGRP and OSPF. Figure 17 provides a detailed graph illustrating the network delay differences with and without authentication.

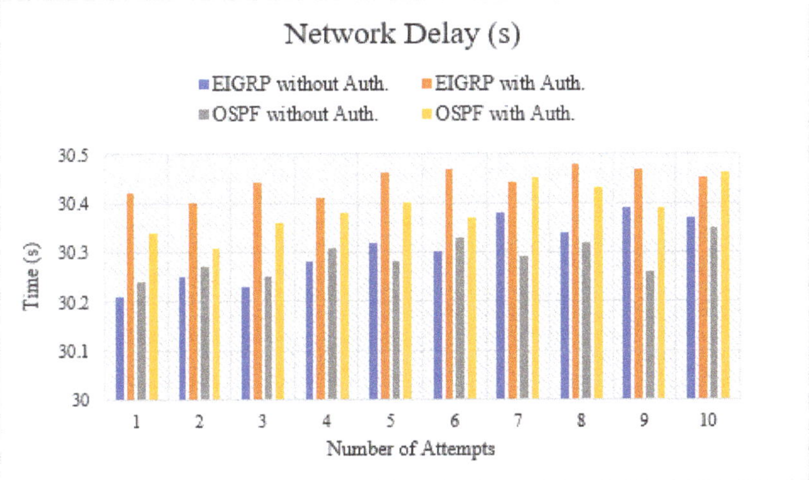

Figure 17. Network delay using 13 Routers—EIGRP vs. OSPF.

7.2. Network Jitter

Without authentication, EIGRP jitter values ranged from 35.66 to 44.11 ms, while OSPF jitter values varied between 37.01 and 45.64 ms. With authentication enabled, EIGRP jitter ranged from 35.96 to 45.05 ms, and OSPF jitter ranged from 35.91 to 45.14 ms. The inclusion of authentication slightly increased jitter in both routing protocols. Figure 18 shows a comprehensive graph of network jitter for visual analysis. Network jitter, which can be calculated as the variance in network delay, is also depicted in the graph.

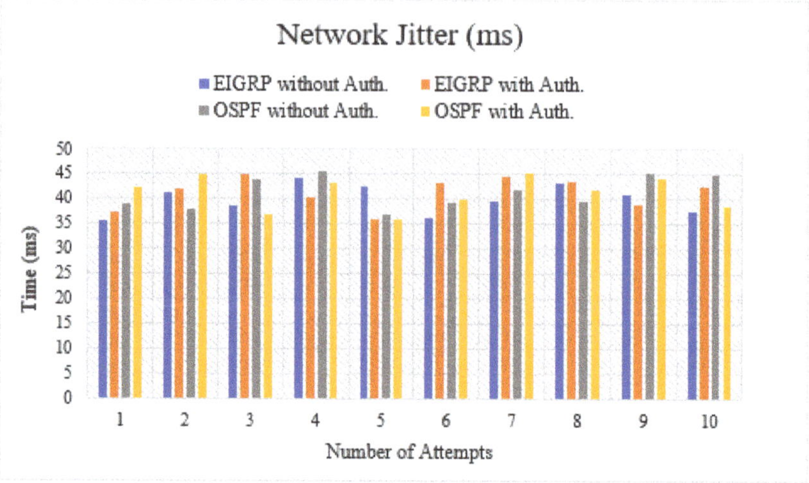

Figure 18. Network jitter using 13 routers—EIGRP vs. OSPF.

7.3. Packet Loss

Packet loss was minimal, which is an indicator of good network performance. The experiment was repeated multiple times, with packet losses observed using the IPerf3 tool. For EIGRP, the packet loss rate was 5%, while OSPF experienced a slightly higher packet loss rate of 5.4%. Though the difference is minor, it suggests that OSPF may face more challenges in maintaining data integrity and reliable communication. This difference in packet loss could lead to retransmissions and increased delay, potentially compromising the reliability of OSPF. Figure 19 presents the packet loss data for both protocols.

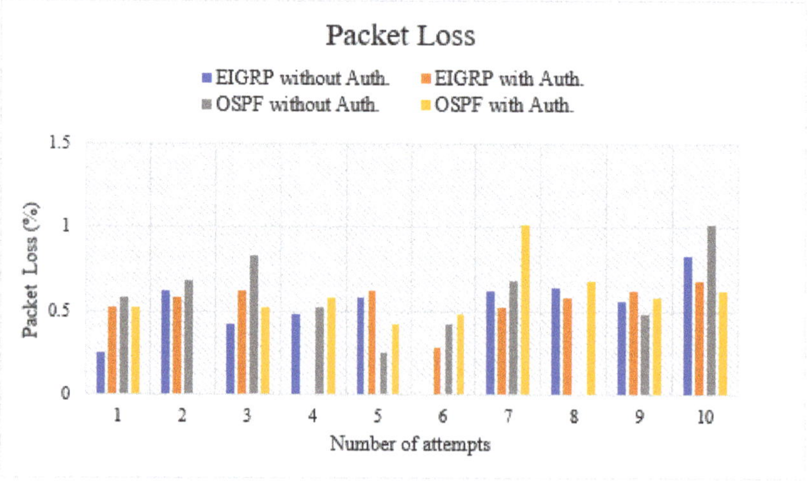

Figure 19. Packet loss using 13 routers—EIGRP vs. OSPF.

7.4. Convergence Time

Convergence time is critical for network resilience, stability, and performance. During a link failure between Branch-1 and Branch-2 via the primary provider (ISP-A), an alternative route through a secondary provider (ISP-B) was established. The goal was to measure how quickly the network responded to the link loss and rerouted traffic through the new connection.

Without authentication, EIGRP took between 125 and 140 s to establish an alternate path, while OSPF required 150 to 170 s. On average, EIGRP recovered from a link failover in 134.2 s, whereas OSPF needed 159.1 s. This demonstrates that EIGRP outperforms OSPF in backup path determination and link-failure recovery under these conditions. Figure 20 illustrates the convergence time without authentication.

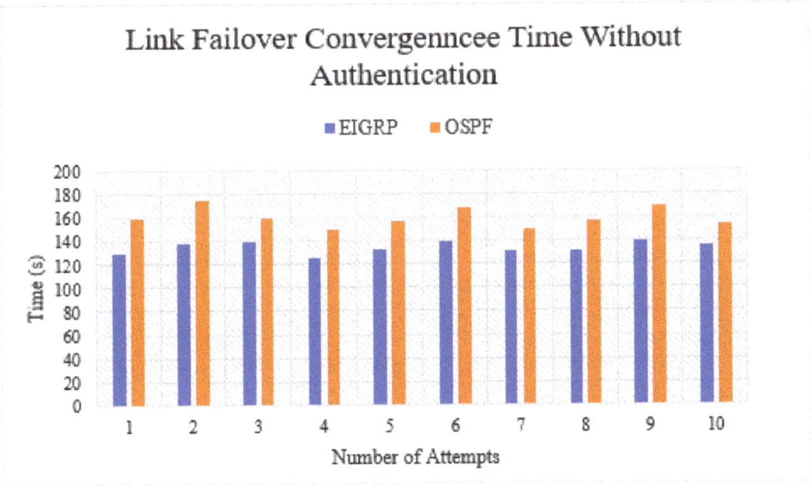

Figure 20. Convergence time without authentication.

With authentication, EIGRP required 13 to 15 s to generate an alternate path, while OSPF needed 20 to 27 s. On average, EIGRP recovered in 14.3 s, compared to 24.3 s for OSPF. These results further highlight EIGRP's superiority in handling backup path determination and link-failure recovery with authentication enabled. Figure 21 presents the convergence time data with authentication.

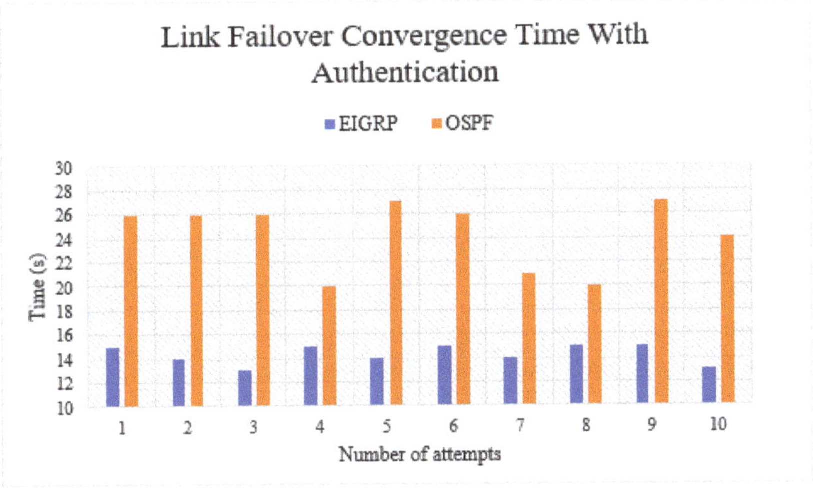

Figure 21. Convergence time with authentication.

Additionally, the study notes that a relatively short hold time in BGP, particularly less than 10 s, can lead to frequent disconnections, causing network instability. To mitigate this, a hold time of at least 10 s or more is recommended to ensure a stable and continuous BGP connection, thereby enhancing network efficiency.

8. Conclusions and Future Work

This research highlights the distinct advantages of EIGRP over OSPF, particularly in terms of packet loss and link-failure convergence time when operating in an IPv6 environment. While both protocols exhibited minimal differences in network latency and jitter, the absence of authentication led to lower network latency for both. However, the introduction of authentication introduced variability in delay levels. EIGRP consistently demonstrated superior performance in link-failover scenarios, whether authentication was enabled or not, recovering faster than OSPF. Additionally, the lower packet loss rate observed with EIGRP suggests its better capability in handling network challenges, contributing to more reliable data transmission.

The importance of selecting an appropriate routing protocol is underscored by the significant impact that even minor variations in performance metrics can have on overall network performance and reliability. This study provides a comprehensive approach, expanding the focus beyond traditional link-failure scenarios to include a more holistic strategy that addresses both connection failover and load sharing across various traffic types in an IPv6 context. This research fills a crucial gap in existing literature, offering valuable insights for network managers and engineers seeking to optimize their networks through intelligent protocol selection and parameter tuning.

The future work of this study aims to further enhance network resilience by incorporating hardware failover techniques. By integrating hardware failover options, the research seeks to bolster the network's defenses against potential hardware failures, ensuring continuous connectivity with minimal disruption to data and internet traffic. This expanded module will conduct an in-depth analysis of how the combination of EIGRP, OSPF, and BGP, when paired with hardware failover mechanisms, impacts critical performance metrics such as network latency, jitter, packet loss, and link-failure convergence time within an IPv6 environment.

By pursuing this avenue of research, the goal is to develop a more robust and resilient network infrastructure that can withstand both software and hardware challenges, ultimately leading to more reliable and efficient communication systems.

Author Contributions: Conceptualization, K.S. and S.N.A.; methodology, K.S.; software, S.N.A.; validation, K.S., S.N.A. and S.T.H.R.; formal analysis, K.S.; investigation, K.S.; resources, S.T.H.R.; data curation, S.N.A. and S.T.H.R.; writing—original draft preparation, K.S. and S.N.A.; writing—review and editing, K.S. and S.N.A.; visualization, K.S. and S.T.H.R.; supervision, K.S. and S.T.H.R.; project administration, K.S. and S.T.H.R.; funding acquisition, S.T.H.R.. All authors have read and agreed to the published version of the manuscript.

Funding: This research received no external funding.

Data Availability Statement: The datasets presented in this article are not readily available because the data are part of an ongoing study.

Acknowledgments: The authors would like to acknowledge Syed Zohair Raza at Wateen Telecom, for his assistance in developing the network topology.

Conflicts of Interest: The authors declare no conflicts of interest.

References

1. Simanjuntak, I.U.V.; Rochendi, A.D.; Silalahi, L.M. Simulation and Analysis of Link Failover Using Routing Border Gateway Protocol (BGP) Multi-Protocol Label Switching (MPLS) Networks. In Proceedings of the 2023 International Conference on Radar, Antenna, Microwave, Electronics, and Telecommunications (ICRAMET), Bandung, Indonesia, 15–16 November 2023; pp. 341–346.
2. Masruroh, S.U.; Fiade, A.; Iman, M.F. Performance evaluation of routing protocol RIPv2, OSPF, EIGRP with BGP. In Proceedings of the 2017 International Conference on Innovative and Creative Information Technology (ICITech), Salatiga, Indonesia, 2–4 November 2017; pp. 1–7.
3. Athira, M.; Abrahami, L.; Sangeetha, R. Study on network performance of interior gateway protocols—RIP, EIGRP and OSPF. In Proceedings of the 2017 International Conference on Nextgen Electronic Technologies: Silicon to Software (ICNETS2), Chennai, India, 23–25 March 2017; pp. 344–348.
4. Hossain, M.A.; Islam, M.M.; Majumder, M.N.U. Comparative Analysis of Two Prominent Routing Protocols in IPv6 Network: OSPFv3 & EIGRPv6. *Int. J. Comput. (IJC)* **2016**, *22*, 79–89.
5. Hossain, M.A.; Podder, D.; Jahan, S.; Hussain, M. Performance analysis of three transition mechanisms between IPv6 network and IPv4 network: Dual Stack, Tunneling and Translation. *Int. J. Comput. (IJC)* **2016**, *20*, 217–228.
6. Akter, M.S.; Hossain, M.A. Analysis and comparative study for developing computer network in terms of routing protocols having IPv6 network using cisco packet tracer. *Softw. Eng.* **2019**, *7*, 16–29.
7. Ashraf, S.; Muhammad, D.; Aslam, Z. Analyzing challenging aspects of IPv6 over IPv4. *J. Ilm. Tek. Elektro Komput. Dan Inf.* **2020**, *6*, 54–67. [CrossRef]
8. Karna, H.; Baggan, V.; Sahoo, A.K.; Sarangi, P.K. Performance Analysis of Interior Gateway Protocols (IGPs) using GNS-3. In Proceedings of the 2019 8th International Conference System Modeling and Advancement in Research Trends (SMART), Moradabad, India, 22–23 November 2019; pp. 204–209.
9. NuraYusuf, M.; Ya'u, I. A Comparative Analysis of Additional Overhead Imposed by Internet Protocol Security (IPsec) on IPv4 and IPv6 Enabled Communication. *Int. J. Eng. Res. Technol.* **2016**, *6*, 13–19.
10. Sudha, R.; Macedo, R.D. Distribution of Dynamic Routing Protocols (Is-Is, EIGRP, OSPF) in IPv6 Network and Their Performance Analysis. *Int. J. Eng. Res. Technol.* **2020**, *8*, 38–44.
11. Fiade, A.; Agustian, M.A.; Masruroh, S.U. Analysis of Failover Link System Performance in OSPF, EIGRP, RIPV2 Routing Protocol with BGP. In Proceedings of the 2019 7th International Conference on Cyber and IT Service Management (CITSM), Jakarta, Indonesia, 6–8 November 2019; Volume 7, pp. 1–7.
12. Sharma, K.; Sharma, B.; Saini, R. Comparative Analysis of IS-IS and OSPFV3 with IPV6. *Int. J. Adv. Res. Comput. Sci. Softw. Eng.* **2016**, *6*, 316–320.
13. Kumari, N.; Sharma, E.B.; Saini, R. Comparative Study of RIPng and OSPFV3 with IPV6. *Int. J. Adv. Res. Comput. Sci. Softw. Eng.* **2016**, *6*, 321–325.
14. Singalar, S.; Banakar, R. Performance analysis of IPv4 to IPv6 transition mechanisms. In Proceedings of the 2018 Fourth International Conference on Computing Communication Control and Automation (ICCUBEA), Pune, India, 16–18 August 2018; pp. 1–6.
15. Ali, A.B.; Tabassum, M.; Mathew, K. A comparative study of IGP and EGP routing protocols, performance evaluation along load balancing and redundancy across different AS. In Proceedings of the International MultiConference of Engineers and Computer Scientists, Hong Kong, China, 16–18 March 2016; Volume 2, pp. 487–967.
16. Ahmed, M.R.A.; Shaikhedris, S.S.A. Network migration and performance analysis of IPv4 and IPv6. In Proceedings of the 2020 International Conference on Computer, Control, Electrical, and Electronics Engineering (ICCCEEE), Khartoum, Sudan, 26 February–1 March 2021; pp. 1–6.
17. Jain, N.; Payal, A. Comparison between IPv4 and IPv6 using OSPF and OSPFv3 on riverbed modeler. In Proceedings of the 2019 IEEE International Conference on Advanced Networks and Telecommunications Systems (ANTS), Goa, India, 16–19 December 2019; pp. 1–7.
18. Javid, S.R.; Dubey, S.K. A systematic review of performance analysis and implementation of OSPFv3 in IPv6 network. In Proceedings of the 2016 3rd International Conference on Computing for Sustainable Global Development (INDIACom), New Delhi, India, 16–18 March 2016; pp. 4051–4057.
19. El Idrissi, D.; Elkamoun, N.; Lakrami, F.; Hilal, R. Study of the impact of routing and the profoundness of GRE tunnels on the performance of the transmission of real time applications in IP networks. *IJCSNS* **2018**, *18*, 76.
20. Masruroh, S.U.; Robby, F.; Hakiem, N. Performance evaluation of routing protocols RIPng, OSPFv3, and EIGRP in an IPv6 network. In Proceedings of the 2016 International Conference on Informatics and Computing (ICIC), Mataram, Indonesia, 28–29 October 2016; pp. 111–116.

future internet

MDPI

Article

Developing a Secure Service Ecosystem to Implement the Intelligent Edge Environment for Smart Cities †

Gayathri Karthick [1,*] and Glenford Mapp [2,*]

1 Department of Data Science and Computer Science, York St John University, Export Building, 1 Clove Cres, London E14 2BA, UK
2 Faculty of Science and Technology, Middlesex University, The Burroughs, London NW4 4BT, UK
* Correspondence: g.karthick@yorksj.ac.uk (G.K.); g.mapp@mdx.ac.uk (G.M.)
† This paper is an extension of Building an Intelligent Edge Environment to Provide Essential Services for Smart Cities, originally presented at the Workshop on Mobility in Evolving Internet Architecture (MobiArch 2023), Madrid, Spain, 6 October 2023.

Abstract: In the future, smart cities will provide key services including seamless communication, intelligent transport systems, advanced healthcare platforms, urban and infrastructure management, and digital services for local and regional government. Therefore, a new service and networking paradigm, called the Intelligent Edge Environment, has been specified. As a key part of this system, a new secure service ecosystem must be developed to provide the secure real-time movement of services on different High-Performance Edge Cloud Systems. This paper explores these issues by introducing the following mechanisms: a Resource Allocation Algorithm, a Resource Allocation Secure Protocol and finally a Secure Service Protocol. These systems were integrated into the Basic Capability System Library and a multithreaded FUSE client connected to the Service Management Framework. Docker was used as the migration mechanism. A prototype was developed and implemented using a FUSE-Network Memory System in which the Network Memory Server was migrated as users moved around. The result shows that this approach was safe and could be used to develop new applications and services for smart cities.

Keywords: intelligent edge environment; secure service ecosystem; capabilities; FUSE; docker

1. Introduction

Smart cities need to leverage advanced technologies such as Mobile Edge Computing (MEC), Internet of Things (IoT), AI, Machine Learning (ML), and fast communication networks, for example 5G/6G, to deliver efficient, sustainable, high-quality services, thus improving the overall quality of life for their citizens. These technologies can be combined to produce a new computing and service paradigm, called the Intelligent Edge Environment (IEE), in which services are run and managed from the edge of the network by default. As shown in Figure 1, the IEE is composed of these 7 layers: Heterogeneous Networking Layer, Data Management Layer, the High-Performance Edge Cloud Systems, Service Management Framework, Microservices Layer, Application Framework Layer, and Application Layer. The details of the IEE have been explored in [1].

Intelligent Edge Environment Layers

The layers of the IEE are shown in Figure 2 and are briefly described below:

- Layer 1: Heterogeneous Networking Layer (HNL): This layer provides connections using various wireless technologies such as 4G, 5G, WiFi, and Cellular.
- Layer 2: Data Management Layer (DML): This layer plays a crucial role in handling vast amounts of data generated by edge devices such as Connected and Autonomous Vehicles (CAVs) and uses many structures such as blocks, files, databases, and ML algorithms to manage data.

- Layer 3: High-Performance Edge Cloud Systems (HPECS): This layer supports various cloud architectures and cloud types, including private, public, hybrid, and community clouds (AWS, Hadoop, etc.) using Virtual Machines (VMs) including VMware and Citrix ecosystems as well as video streaming, augmented and virtual reality, and autonomous systems.
- Layer 4: Service Management Framework (SMF): This layer manages services and servers within the system. It offers mobile service support by migrating and replicating services using various migration techniques such as Docker (containerization), KVM (virtualization), and Unikernels (specialized single-purpose virtual machines).
- Layer 5: Microservices Layer (MSL): This layer supports microservices and is responsible for independently deployable services. These services should be fast and small in order to be easily migrated.
- Layer 6: Application Framework Layer (AFL): This layer uses the Microservices Layer below to provide Applications Frameworks (AFs) to build applications for different environments such as Mobile Communications, Vehicular Networking, and IoT Smart Grids.
- Layer 7: Application Layer (AL): This layer allows applications that have been built using the Application Framework Layer to be installed on the system and made available to users. Through this layer, users get applications that use all the resources of the IEE.

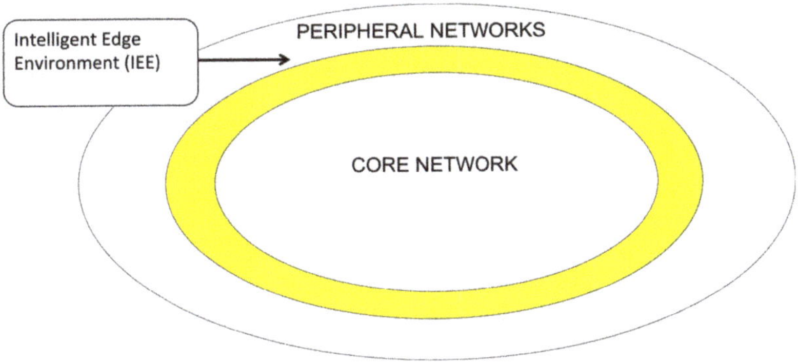

Figure 1. Intelligent Edge Environment.

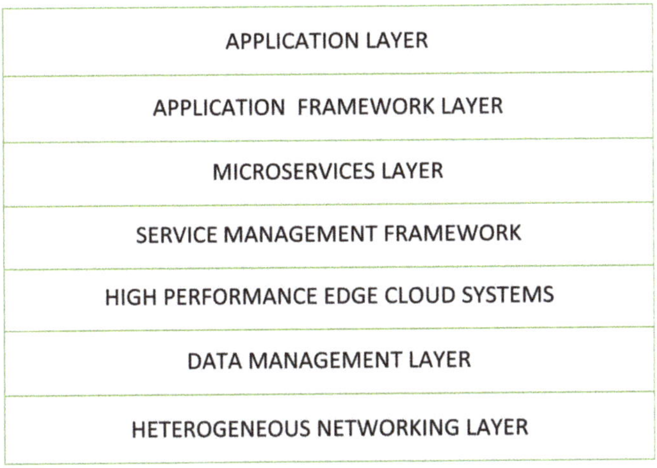

Figure 2. Intelligent Edge Environment layers.

A key part of the IEE is the development of a Secure Service Ecosystem (SSE) in which services can be securely moved between different commercial Cloud Systems. As shown in Figure 2, the SSE, therefore, encompasses the three core layers of the IEE which are the HPECS, SMF, and MSL layers.

This paper explores how to build an SSE and the contributions of the work are detailed below:

- A new simple Resource Allocation Algorithm (RAA) is developed to enable mobile services. This algorithm has to be simple and fast.
- A new secure transfer protocol called the Resource Allocation Secure Protocol (RASP) is detailed. This will involve the use of cryptographic protocol verifiers such as ProVerif to show that the transfer protocol is safe.
- A secure access control system using capabilities to provide the Authentication, Authorization, Accounting (AAA).
- The development of a new Service Management Framework (SMF) which can be used to manage applications and services in the IEE.
- These mechanisms are combined to develop a capability-based Secure Service Protocol (SSP) to provide a complete SSE for the IEE. The SSP is shown to be safe using Proverif.
- The implementation of a prototype SSE system using a Network Memory Server (NMS) to provide backing storage for a FUSE file system in a vehicular network is detailed.

The rest of this paper is organized as follows: Section 2 reviews the Related Work. Section 3 details the Simple Resource Allocation Algorithm, while Section 4 explores the RASP Protocol using ProVerif. In Section 5, a capability system for IEE is investigated, and in Section 6, the SSP Protocol is proposed and tested using ProVerif. Section 7 covers the prototype implementation. Finally, Section 8 concludes the paper.

2. Related Work

2.1. Mobile Edge Computing (MEC)

MEC was originally developed as an offloading mechanism to provide more computing resources at the edge of the network. As shown in [2] there has been a lot of work done in MEC. Two recent projects are EDGELESS [3] and CODECO [4]. EDGELESS is an ongoing EU project that is developing a secure edge-cloud platform that can dynamically adjust itself to ensure a high Quality of Service (QoS) for applications. Although the IEE shares some of these goals, there are significant differences. Unlike EDGELESS, the IEE will manage and run services at the edge of the network by default to support real-time applications with very tight requirements for low latency and high bandwidth; thus, in the IEE there will be no central Cloud platform. The CODECO project is enhancing the container orchestration platform, Kubernetes, with a cognitive edge-cloud management framework that provides support for real-time industrial applications. While CODECO is looking at a software solution to provide real-time support for Kubernetes, the IEE is committed to providing end-to-end low latency using smart networks, caching, and prefetching algorithms as well as low-latency data access and processing via fast hardware, AI and Unikernels.

2.2. Vehicular Networks

The last decade has seen a revolution in transport based on the emergence of Connected and Autonomous Vehicles (CAVs). Several research testbeds have been built [5]. This has spurred more research into Intelligent Transport Systems (ITS) which will result in smaller journey times, less congestion and a reduction in the number of road accidents. Vehicular networks pose serious challenges as they require reliable, low latency, high bandwidth communication as well as the ability to process data in real-time. These challenges can only be met by moving data processing and services to the edge of the network.

The convergence of the automotive industry with cognitive computing, forming the Industrial Cognitive Internet of Vehicles (CIoV), is a rapidly evolving field with significant implications for the QoS and security in vehicular networks. This convergence is driven by the increasing impact of social media on automotive services and the need for advanced edge computing solutions to reduce latency and enhance reliability. As explored by the author in [6], offloading cognitive computing tasks to the network edge using methods like 88 CQP, which employs Canopy and K-medoids clustering along with a non-dominated sorting 89 genetic algorithm III, can optimize edge server (ES) quantification and placement, thereby improving the QoS by 90%.

2.3. Virtualization and Service Management in Future Internet

Cloud Systems are now used by many companies to provide services to their clients. These systems use virtualisation techniques and enable service migration through Docker, KVM, LXD, and Unikernels mechanisms. Mobile services therefore are a key requirement for future networks. The authors in [7,8], investigated the communication dynamics necessary for seamless connectivity and service migration in vehicular edge environments. The authors in [9] attempted to address the development of a secure commercial advertising scheme for vehicular networks. They proposed a scheme called "Business discovery (BUY)" that presents the concept of the beaconing market using a vehicular network. However, these endeavours also underscore the need for resource management algorithms and secure transport mechanisms to enable mobile services for highly mobile networks.

2.4. Research Gap

Though all these efforts are useful and have led to the development of the IEE platform, new mechanisms and techniques are needed to fully realise this proposed framework. The most pressing of which is the need to develop a secure service ecosystem to allow services to be managed and run from the edge of the Internet by default. This includes a simple and fast resource management algorithm to allow services to migrate using different Edge Clouds, a secure service transfer mechanism, and providing Authentication, Authorisation, and Accounting (AAA) for the new environment. This paper addresses these issues.

3. Simple Resource Algorithm

Resource management [10] is the process of distributing available resources, such as CPU, Memory, Network and Storage, among various tasks in an efficient manner as it helps to deliver high performance in Cloud infrastructure to achieve a high QoS. Cloud systems use virtualization to replicate and share resources. Several algorithms are used to manage this allocation effectively. There are two types of resource algorithms, Static and Dynamic algorithms. However, when services are moved between Clouds, we must use dynamic algorithms which must be simple and fast because it is a highly mobile environment. This algorithm is shown in Figure 3.

The roles in the RAA are specified as follows:

1. Advertising Cloud (CA, CB, CC... etc.): Each Cloud Service Provider (CSP) has a finite set of resources available for services and servers. A Cloud System broadcasts its available resources (CPU, Memory, Network, and Storage) to the Receiving Servers.
2. Receiving Servers (SA, SB, SC... etc.): These servers can choose to migrate their services to the Advertising Clouds based on their hosting requirements.
3. Resource Allocation Server (RAS): A trusted party responsible for verifying the resources of Advertising Clouds and the hosting requirements of Receiving Servers. Table 1 shows the information held by the RAS.

The first stage of the RASP protocol uses the Resource Allocation Algorithm (RAA) for cloud advertisements. Each Cloud System actively advertises its free resources in each round and uses mathematical formulations to determine if a service can be securely migrated to an Advertising Cloud (AC). The formulation below demonstrates how Cloud CB advertises its resources and Receiving Server SA obtains the resources it needs to run on the AC.

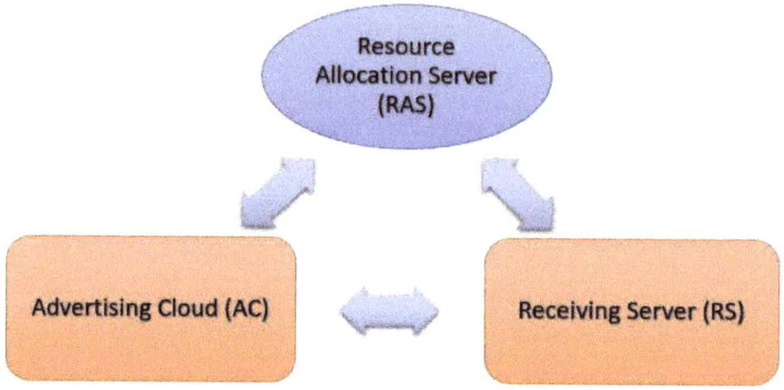

Figure 3. Simple resource allocation design.

Table 1. RAS Table.

Resource Allocation Server	Adverting Cloud (CA)	Adverting Cloud (CB)	Adverting Cloud (N)
Receiving Server (SA)	CPU, Memory, Network, and Storage	CPU, Memory, Network and Storage	CPU, Memory, Network, and Storage
Receiving Server (SB)	CPU, Memory, Network, and Storage	CPU, Memory, Network, and Storage	CPU, Memory, Network, and Storage
Receiving Server (N)	CPU, Memory, Network, and Storage	CPU, Memory, Network, and Storage	CPU, Memory, Network, and Storage

3.1. Advertising Cloud Formulation

The variables indicate the number of CPUs, Memory, Storage, and Network resources respectively. These values help in determining the resource availability and allocation for secure service migration. At each round, each provider will use the mathematical formulation below: Step 1 of the RASP protocol and general notations is as follows:

- **Stage 1** 1. CB $\rightarrow$ SA: Advc (CB, ResCB) [CB $\rightarrow$ SA: Advertising Cloud (CB) sends an advertisement (Advc) to the Receiving Server (SA), detailing its free resources (ResCB)].
    - Maximum Resource of Cloud (MAX_Cm) = [CPU (Cmc), Memory (Cmm), Storage (Cms), Network (Cmn)],
    - Allocated Resource of Cloud ($ALLOC\_Ca$) = [CPU (Cac), Memory (Cam), Storage (Cas), Network (Can)],
    - Free Resource of Cloud ($FREE\_Cf$) = [CPU (Cfc), Memory (Cfm), Storage (Cfs), Network (Cfn)]

  Cloud CB Formulation Algorithm 1 in detail,

Algorithm 1 Cloud CB Formulation

Resources(r) $\in$ {Cpu(c), Network(n), Memory(m), and Storage(s)}
$MAX\_Cm\ (Cmr) = \{Cmc, Cmm, Cms, Cmn\}$
$ALLOC\_Ca\ (Car) = \{Cac, Cam, Cas, Can\}$ &
$FREE\_Cf\ (Cfr) = \{Cfc, Cfm, Cfs, Cfn\}$
$Cfr \longleftarrow Cfr \cup$ Resources(r)
If $Cfr \leftarrow (Cmr - Car) > 0$ then
Send Advc of Cfr and wait for response;
else $Cfr \leq \phi$ then
wait for $Cfr > 0$;
End if

- **Step 1**: The resources in consideration are categorized as CPU (c), Network (n), Memory (m), and Storage (s).
- **Step 2–4**: These steps define the maximum capacity for each type of resource (Cmr), current allocation of resources (Car), and the available (free) resources (Cfr) in the AC.
- **Step 5–10**: Condition Check and Advertisement: The condition checks if there are any free resources (Cfr). If there are free resources, the AC sends an advertisement of these resources and waits for a response. If there are no free resources, the system waits until resources become available, i.e., when (Cfr) is greater than 0.

3.2. Receiving Servers Formulation

Receiving Servers (RS) receive an advertisement from the Advertising Cloud (AC) and its free resources. A server that needs to use a cloud has variables that detail its requirements. If the free resources of AC, Cfc, Cfm, Cfs, Cfn are larger than Receiving Server requirements, it can forward the request to the Resource Allocation Server (RAS) also known as the Registry (R). The required resources of the server are given by (Req_Res of SA (SAreqr)). If we assume the requested resources a less than the free resources of the AC and all requested resources are valid, then and only then, it sends the request to RAS. Step 2 of the RASP protocol is as follows:

- **Stage 2** 2. SA $\rightarrow$ R : (SA, CB, ResCB)pkR [SA $\rightarrow$ R: Receiving or Requested Servers (SA) send a message to the Registry to verify the identity and free resources (Res freeCB) of the Advertising Cloud, CB].
  - Requested Resource of Server (Req_Res of SA ($SAreqr$)) = $\{Src, Srm, Sms, Srn\}$ CPU (Src), Memory (Srm), Storage (Sms), Network (Srn)]

Server SA Formulation Algorithm 2 in detail,

Algorithm 2 Server SA Formulation

```
1: Resources(r) ∈ {Cpu(c), Network(n), Memory(m), and Storage(s)}
2: Req_Res (SAreqr) = {Src, Srm, Sms, Srn}
3: SAreqr ⟵ SAreqr ∪ Req_Resources
4: If SAreqr > 0 then
5: Search for Resource Migration;
6: If SAreqr ← (Cf − SAreqr) > 0 then
7: Accept Cf and send a message to RAS;
8: Else ignore the request;
9: End if
```

- **Step 1**: The resources CPU, Networks, Memory, Storage are members of resources(r).
- **Step 2–3**: Server SA's Requested resources are declared as a set of elements and is given by SAreqr resources.
- **Step 4–5**: If the Requested resources are greater than 0, the server can look to migrate the service to the Advertising Cloud.
- **Step 6–9 Condition check before resource Migration**: It checks if the AC has sufficient free resources to meet the Receiving Server's request. If sufficient resources are available, then the request is granted, and the details are sent to the RAS for verification and processing, else Server SA ignores the advertisement.

3.3. Resource Allocation Server

The Resource Allocation Server (RAS) plays a crucial role in the resource allocation process. It is a trusted Party responsible for confirming the registration of Cloud Providers and certifying the capacity of their resources. The RAS ensures that only valid and adequately resourced Clouds participate in service migrations. Function of RAS in the Algorithm are:

- **Registration and Certification:** The RAS confirms the registration of Cloud Providers and certifies the capacity of resources available with the registered Cloud Providers.

- **Request Verification:** When a request for resources is received from a Receiving Server (SA), the RAS verifies the resources based on specific criteria before approving the migration.

Stage 2 of the RASP protocol therefore provides verification and certification. Once it receives the request from SA requested resources (SAreqr), the RAS verifies the resources based on the Algorithm below:

- 3. R → SA: sign((CB, pkC, ResCB), pkS) [R → SA: The Registry approves the advertisement (Advc) and sends a message to the Receiving Servers (SA), detailing the free resources (ResCB) with its signature].

Server RAS Formulation Algorithm 3 in detail:

Algorithm 3 RAS_CB

```
1: If Cf = Valid Cloud and RAS ← (Cf > SAreqr) ≠ 0 then
2: Accept and send an authenticated message;
3: Else
4: Reject the request;
5: End if
```

- **Step 1–2 Verify Validity**: The RAS server verifies whether the CB is a valid cloud and if its Cloud resources are greater than the requested resources. If either condition is false, then it rejects the request and updates Server SA that CB is an invalid cloud.
- **Step 2–5 Pass Conditions:** If the above conditions pass, then it sends an authenticated message to SA. This message confirms the approval of the resource migration.

Server RAS Algorithm 4 Formulation in detail,

Algorithm 4 RAS_SA

```
1: If SAreqr = valid server and RAS ← (Cf>SAreqr ) ≠ 0 then
2: Accept and send an authenticated message;
3: Else
4: Reject the request;
5: End if
```

- **Step 1–2**: RAS server verifies whether it is a valid server and if Cloud resources are greater than the requested resources which is not equalt 0. If either conditions are false, then it rejects the request and updates SA that its an invalid Cloud.
- **Step 2–5**: If the above conditions pass, then it sends an authenticated message to SA.

The RAS is essential for ensuring the integrity and efficiency of resource allocation in Cloud environments. It validates Cloud Providers, certifies their resources, and manages requests from Receiving Servers, ensuring only valid and adequately resourced Clouds participate in service migrations. This multi-step verification process helps maintain a secure and reliable resource allocation framework.

4. RASP Protocol—An Overview

This protocol has three roles: Server SA on Cloud CA, Cloud CB, and Registry. The Resource Allocation Security protocol (RASP) is broken into four stages. In the first stage, it uses the Resource Allocation Algorithm to manage cloud advertisements [11]. In addition, the proposed protocol was tested by ProVerif. The protocol is shown in Figure 4 as follows: Stage 1 corresponds to step 1 of the protocol; Stage 2 corresponds to steps 2–7; Stage 3 corresponds to steps 8–11, and finally, Stage 4 corresponds to step 12. The RASP protocol is followed in exactly the same way as outlined below and shows the steps for Cloud-to-Cloud migration of services.

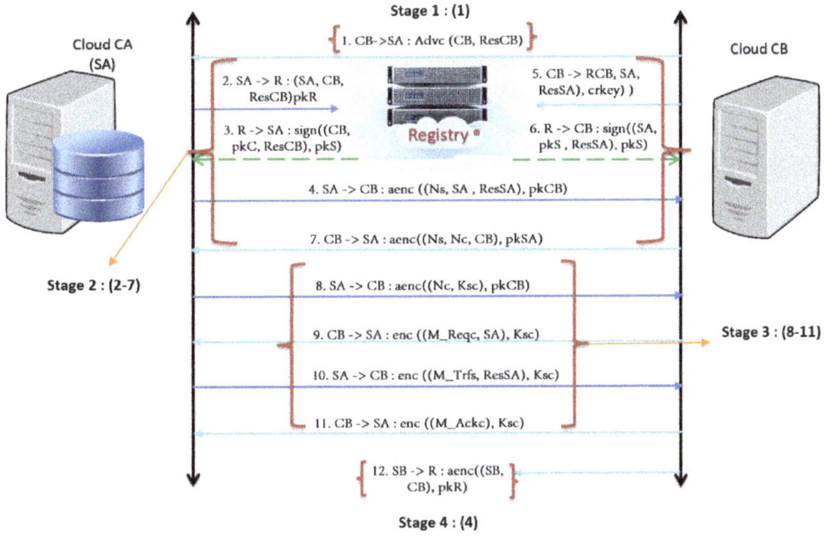

Figure 4. Migration between SA to CB.

4.1. General Notations

Table 2 shows the parameters used in the RASP protocol.

Table 2. RASP Table.

Notation	Explanation
CA, CB, SA and SB	Cloud and Server Identities
pkC/skC, pkS/skS, pkR/skR	public and private key pairs of Cloud CB, Server SA & Registry
M_Reqc, M_Trfs, M_Ackc	Request for migration, transfers and acknowledgement
sign	Signature/signed by the Registry
aenc	Asymmetric Encryption
enc	Symmetric Encryption
Ksc	Symmetric session key
Ns, Nc	Nonce of SA and CB
ResSA, ResCB	Requested Resources of SA & CB

1. **Stage 1: Advertisement** :
   Server SA receives advertisements from Cloud CB advertising its resources.
   1. CB → SA: Advc (CB, ResCB)
2. **Stage 2: Authentication of SA and CB as well as migration request and response**:
   Server SA first requests the RAS/Registry to authenticate Cloud CB and its resources. In Step 3, the Registry (R) authenticates Cloud CB. In Step 4, Server SA sends a migration request to Cloud CB. In Step 5, Cloud CB sends a request to the Registry to verify that Server SA's request for resources is valid. In Step 6, the Registry replies to Cloud CB. In Step 7, Cloud CB sends the migration response back to Server SA.
   2. SA → R: (SA, CB, ResCB)pkR
   3. R → SA: sign((CB, pkC, ResCB), pkS)
   4. SA → CB: aenc ((Ns, SA, ResSA), pkC)
   5. CB → R: (CB, SA, ResSA)pkR
   6. R → CB: sign((SA, pkS, ResSA), pkC)
   7. CB → SA: aenc((Ns, Nc, CB), pkS)

3. **Stage 3: Migration transfer**:
   In Step 8, Server SA generates the session key (Ksc) to start the migration. In Step 9, Cloud CB sends the migration initialization request. In Step 10, Server SA performs the migration transfer. In Step 11, Cloud CB sends an acknowledgment to Server SA.
   8. SA → CB: aenc((Nc, Ksc), pkC)
   9. CB → SA: enc ((M_Reqc, SA), Ksc)
   10. SA → CB: enc ((M_Trfs, ResSA), Ksc)
   11. CB → SA: enc ((M_Ackc), Ksc)
4. **Stage 4: Update of New service location to the Registry**:
   In Step 12, the service on Cloud CB (SB) updates the Registry on its new location. The new service SB is now running on Cloud CB and informs the Registry that it has been successfully migrated.
   12. SB → R: aenc((SB, CB), pkR)

4.2. ProVerif an Overview

ProVerif [12] is a formal verification and highly automated tool used for analyzing the security properties of cryptographic protocols. It employs applied calculus to model concurrent systems and their interactions. The tool comprehends the protocol's abstraction, including how messages are exchanged between parties and the use of cryptographic primitives such as encryption, decryption, and signatures. ProVerif verifies the service migration mechanism's secrecy, authentication, and key exchange. Another strength of this tool is that it performs symbolic analysis, aiding in understanding attack scenarios. ProVerif provides attack traces [13] if it finds any violations of a security property.

The output of the Query attacker() query function results as "True", indicating that the security property cannot be accessed by the attacker. This validates the attacker's lack of knowledge and ensures the secrecy of data authentication between parties or multiple roles for securely transferring data and authenticated across an unlimited number of sessions using unbounded data. If the outcome of the attacker() function is "False", the security property value is accessible to the attacker. Finally, the result displays any attack trace and indicates whether the attacker() query returns TRUE or FALSE.

ProVerif Results

The results shown in Table 3 indicate that RASP can preserve the secrecy, authentication and key exchange of the service migration mechanism.

- **Nonces are secured and not derived by the attacker:** specific nonces (SNs, SNc, CNs, CNc) used in the protocol are not derivable by an attacker, ensuring their confidentiality. Each line indicates that the respective nonce cannot be compromised (is true).
- **Session key:** Results confirm that the session key (Ksc) and associated bitstrings (SNk, CNk) are secure from the attacker. The line "RESULT not attacker_bitstring (SNk []) is true" with Ksc also specifies the conditions under which this key is secure.
- **Private keys:** Results confirm that the session key (Ksc) and associated bitstrings (SNk, CNk) are secure from the attacker. The line "RESULT not attacker_bitstring (CNk []) is true" with Ksc also specifies the conditions under which this key is secure.
- **Authentication:** It validates the mutual authentication between SA and CB. The use of inj-event indicates that the protocol verifies injective correspondence, meaning each event endSparam (or endCparam) has a matching beginSparam (or beginCparam), ensuring that both parties authenticate each other correctly.

By using a symmetric session key (Ksc), the requested service is transferred to the new location CB. This section has explored the development of a new resource allocation and secure service migration framework that encompasses the computing resources to migrate services in cloud environments.

Table 3. Query attacker Results

Security Properties	Server SA Event	Cloud CB Event
Session key	True	True
Private keys	True	True
Nonces	True	True
Event begin	True	True
Requested resources	True	-
Advc Resources	-	False (Not encrypted)

5. Capabilities

Capabilities are critical for system security, providing a robust mechanism for access control through unforgeable tokens. It plays a crucial role in identifying objects and their properties within a system. It is essential to manage and protect these capabilities diligently to prevent unauthorized generation or alteration. Proper management is vital to maintaining system integrity and security, ensuring that only authorized users can access specific objects and perform actions according to their assigned capabilities. This careful oversight helps safeguard the system against potential security breaches and misuse. The data structure contains two pieces of data and functionality.

- **Data:** Unique Object Identification and Access Rights.
- **Functionality:** Capabilities can provide Role-Based Access Control (RBAC) access for users. Some capabilities are not directly assigned to users; instead, they are assigned to roles, and roles are then assigned to users. These are known as role-based capabilities. This structure supports RBAC, ensuring that users have access based on their roles within an organization.
- **IPv6 Address Space and Capability ID System:** Utilizes a modified Location/ID split based on the work of [14]. This enables the creation of a capability ID-based system for people, applications, and cloud infrastructure.

5.1. Capabilities in the IEE

Intelligent Edge Environment (IEE) capabilities are crucial for secure and efficient access control. By utilizing role-based capabilities and advanced addressing systems like IPv6, the IEE can ensure robust access management and resource allocation while maintaining high levels of security and integrity. The IEE is a dynamic environment where security challenges are significantly higher than those in traditional computing environments. Traditional AAA (Authentication, Authorization, and Accounting) mechanisms, such as using RADIUS servers, are no longer effective solutions in this context. Given the scalability requirements of large systems, it was decided that AAA should be based on the subject or user rather than the object. This approach is more scalable and suitable for modern, complex environments. Consequently, capabilities are used to provide AAA for the IEE, ensuring that security and access control mechanisms are effective and adaptable to the unique demands of edge computing [15].

Capabilities Structure

In the Intelligent Edge Environment (IEE), every object and its properties are identified using capabilities. These capabilities must be carefully managed and protected to prevent unauthorized creation or modification, and they should be easily revocable. The format of the capability-based system is shown in Figure 5, and its structure is explained below:

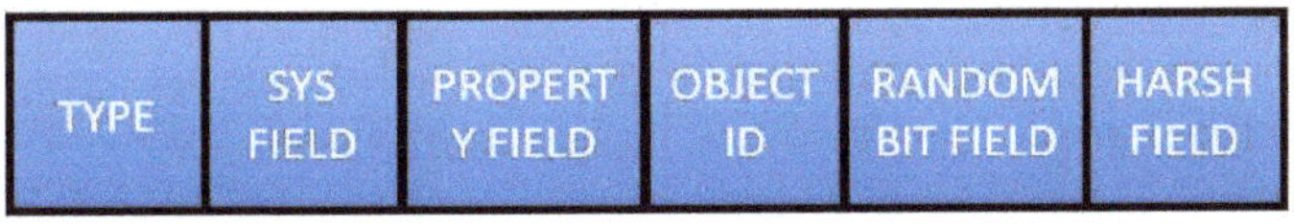

Figure 5. Capability structure.

- **Type Field (8 bits):** This field specifies the type of object capability being used, such as users, digital assets, facilities, etc.
- **SYS Field (4 bits):** This field helps manage capabilities. The four bits within the SYS field are explained below.
- **Property Field (12 bits):** This field defines the properties of the object associated with the capability. It relates to the properties or functions of the object that the capability refers to.
- **Object ID (72 bits):** This field uniquely identifies the object in the system. It includes a EUI-64 identification field to identify the object and an 8-bit netadmin field to manage the object on a network.
- **Random Bit Field (16 bits):** This field provides unforgeability and helps uniquely identify the object. This field is generated after the type field, SYS field, property field, and Object ID field are created. When proxy certificates are created, a new random field is generated. This field also allows for easy revocation of capabilities by simply changing the random field and recomputing the hash field, hence revoking previous versions.
- **Hash Field (16 bits):** This field detects the tampering of capabilities. When a capability is created, the type field, SYS field, property field, and Object ID field are first generated, followed by the random bit field. These fields are then used to generate a SHA-1 hash, which is placed in the Hash Field of the capability.

As shown in Figure 6, the SYS field consists of the following bits:

- **Private or P bit:** Restricts the list of people holding the capability. With a public capability, only the capability for the object must be presented, allowing anyone to hold it without needing the identification of the subject, the person holding the capability. With a private capability, both the object's capability and the subject's capability must be presented to ensure the subject has the right to invoke the object.
- **System or S bit:** Indicates whether the object involved was created by the system or by an application or user. A system capability cannot be modified or deleted by users or applications.
- **Master or M bit:** Indicates that the capability was created by a Certificate Authority (CA). The master capability is usually created when the object is created. If this bit is not set, it means this is a proxy capability. Proxy capabilities are derived from master capabilities and cannot be derived from other proxy capabilities.
- **Change or C bit:** Indicates whether this capability can be changed. If this bit is set, proxy capabilities can be derived from the master capability. If this bit is not set, the capability cannot be modified, and proxy capabilities cannot be generated.

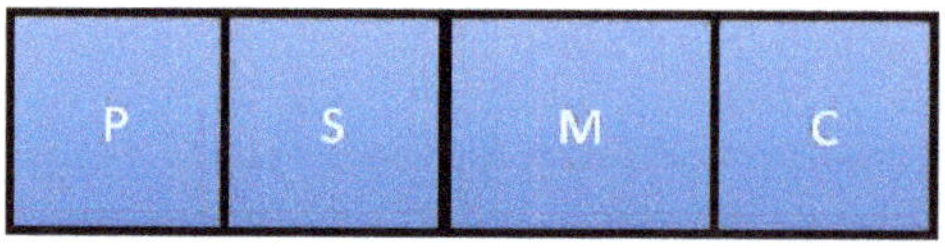

Figure 6. Capability structure—SYS FIELD.

By adhering to these principles, Intelligent Edge Environments can maintain a high level of security and efficiency, ensuring that resources are managed effectively and that unauthorized access is prevented.

6. The Secure Service Protocol (SSP)

The advancement of highly mobile technologies such as Vehicular Adhoc Networks (VANETs), MEC, AI, ML, and IoT systems requires multiple interfaces to seamlessly connect and provide optimal performance for mobile users. As discussed in the Introduction, MEC facilitates moving services closer, minimizing the need for data processing on remote servers, reducing delays, and increasing network bandwidth. However, in order to allow services to run from the edge of the network, it is essential to enable service migration to support these networks, allowing services to migrate as mobile users move around. Figure 7 is a visual representation of the change needed. In the old environment, the service provider had to manage the scaling and migration of services. In the new environment, these functions are now managed by the Service Management Framework (SMF).

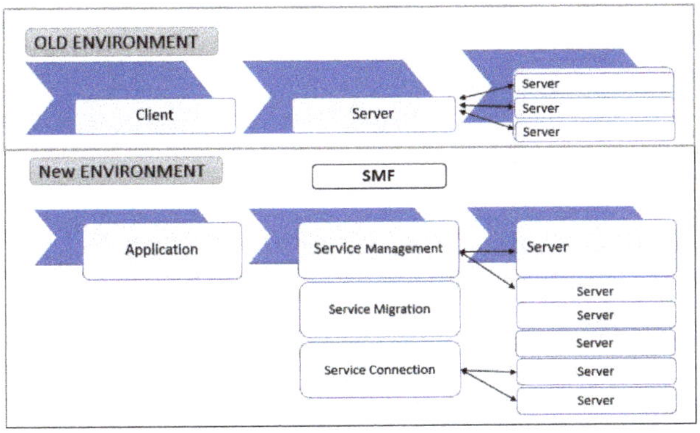

Figure 7. Effect of introducing SMF in the client–server environment.

A new SMF for mobile services has been developed, as shown in Figure 8 and detailed in [16].

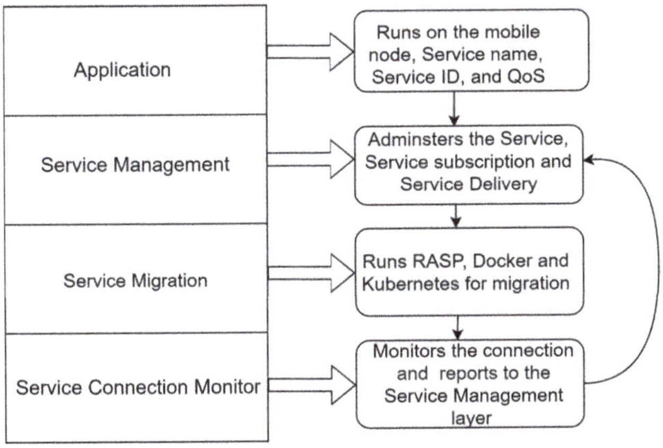

Figure 8. Service Migration Prototype (SMP).

6.1. SMP Layers in Detail

- The Application Layer (AL) is the first layer of the SMF. It runs on the mobile node and calls the service through the Service Management Layer (SManL). AL provides the service name, Service ID, and the required QoS of the service it requires such as delay time, latency, bandwidth, reliability, and security. When a service first registers with the SMF, it is given a unique ID for identification and a service name which indicates the type of service being provided, and the resources such as CPU, Memory, or Storage needed to run the service.
- The Service Management Layer (SManL) is responsible for administering the mobile service, managing service subscriptions, and overseeing service delivery for the layers below it. Service subscription includes managing Service-Level Agreements (SLAs) and billing. Service delivery entails determining how and when services should move

from one location to another. When this layer determines that a service should be migrated, it forwards this information to the Service Migration Layer (SML).

- The Service Migration Layer (SML) manages migration requests from SManL and employs RASP to securely execute the migration process. RASP, as described in [17], utilizes standard migration mechanisms like Docker, KVM, LXD, and Unikernels for the actual migration. Upon completion, SML informs SManL.
- Service Connection Layer (SCL): This layer monitors the connections between the mobile node and the server. It reports to the SManL when the mobile node is no longer available due to handover to another network.

6.2. SSP Protocol—An Overview

Capabilities can be flexibly used to provide AAA in many environments. Furthermore, by combining capabilities, SMF, and RASP techniques, it is possible to design a Secure Service Protocol (SSP) that can protect any service. The SSP protcol has been developed to ensure that the proposed service protocol is secure and can be applied to any service. It is broken down into five stages to clarify the necessary operations in secure service migration. The interaction between an application, the Service Management Framework (SMF), and services supported by the SMF are shown in Table 4 and Figure 9. The SSP protocol is defined in the same way as the RASP protocol outlined above.

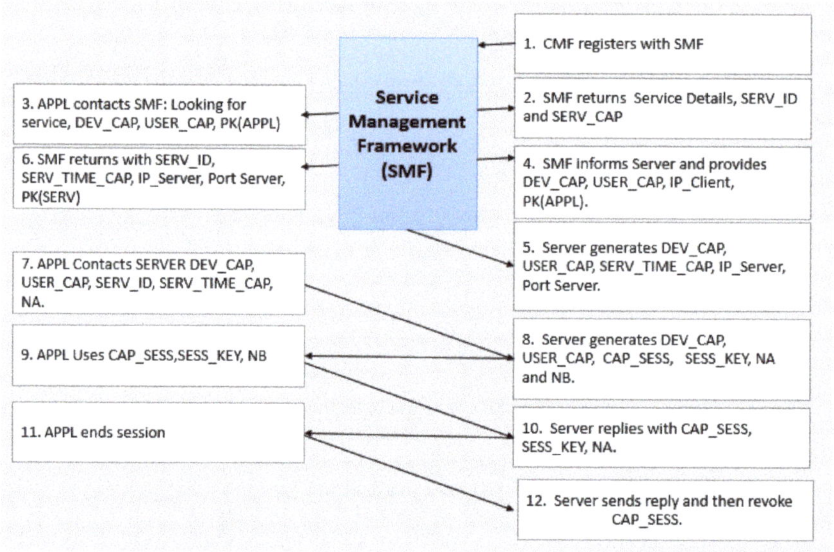

Figure 9. Secure service protocol.

Table 4. General Notations.

Notations	Explanation
CMS	Cloud Management System
SMF	Service Management Framework
APPL	Applications
Chosen Server	The SMF chooses a server of that service
PK(SMF)/PK(APPL)/PK(SERV)	Public key of SMF/APPL/Server
SK(SMF)/SK(APPL)/SK(SERV)/	Private key of SMF/APPL/Server
SESS KEY	Session key

Table 4. *Cont.*

Notations	Explanation
NA and NB	Nonce of NA and NB
Register Service	CMS contacts to Register the Service
Service Details	Servers, keys, and running services.
Service Registered	The SMF registers the Service
SERV ID	Service ID
SERV CAP	Service Capability
DEV CAP	The Capability for the Device
Request service	Request to an appropriate server
USER CAP	User capability
CAP SESS	Session capability
Service Name	Name of the service
Service Version	Service Version
IP Client	IP address of Client
SERV TIME CAP	proxy capability
IP Server	IP address of Server
Port Server	TCP or UDP Port of Service
Usage request	SMF contacts the server
Usage request accepted	The Server accepts the request
Request service accepted	SMF returns all the server details
Session Start Request	Time capability sends start request
Service request	The application requests service
Service request done	The application gets service
Request Details	Details of APPL request
Result Details	Details of Chosen Server result
Session End Request	The application terminates the session
Session End Req accepted	Server terminates session

- **Stage 1: Registration of the Service with the SMF:** In Stage 1, the Cloud Management System (CMS) registers the service with the SMF. This involves providing a list of servers and their public keys that will be running the service. After this, in step 2, the SMF registers the service and returns the Service ID (SERV ID) and the Service Capability (SERV CAP). Following this, the CMS initiates the servers to implement the Service on different machines and passes the Service ID and the Service Capability.
  1. CMS → SMF: (Register Service (Service Details), (PK(SMF)))
  2. SMF → CMS: (Service Registered (Service Details, SERV ID, SERV CAP), (PK(CMS)))
- **Stage 2: The Application interacts with the SMF to get a server that implements the Service:** In Stage 2, the Application interacts with the SMF to obtain a server that provides the service. To utilize a service, an application must request the SMF to locate a suitable server. In step 3, the Application provides the Device Capability (DEV CAP), User Capability (USER CAP), Service Name, Service Version, and the Application's public key running on the machine. In step 4, the SMF selects a server for that Service and contacts it using its public key, passing the Client's DEV CAP, USER CAP, and IP address. In the subsequent step, the Chosen Server accepts the request. It generates a timed capability from the service capability, which expires

in 60 s if the Application does not connect to the server. This SERV TIME CAP is a private proxy capability derived from the Service Capability and cannot be altered; only the USER CAP and DEV CAP can utilize the capability. The Chosen Server also provides its IP address and the TCP port of the Service using the public key of the SMF. In the final step of Stage 2, the SMF returns to the Application with DEV CAP, USER CAP, timed capability, the Server's IP address, Service Port number, and public keys of the Chosen Server, enabling the Application to connect to the server.

3. APPL → SMF: (Request service (Service Name, Service Version, DEV CAP, USER CAP, PK(APPL)), (PK(SMF))
4. SMF Chosen → Server: (Usage request (DEV CAP, USER CAP, IP Client), (PK(SERV))).
5. Chosen Server → SMF: SMF (Usage request accepted (DEV CAP, USER CAP, SERV TIME CAP, IP Server, Port Server), (PK(SMF)))
6. SMF → APPL: (Request service accepted (DEV CAP, USER CAP, SERV TIME CAP, IP Server, Port Server, PK(SERV)), (PK(APPL)))

- **Stage 3: The Application sets up a secure session with the Server:** During Stage 3, the Application initiates a secure session with the Server by sending a session start request. This request includes the DEV CAP (device capability), USER CAP (user capability), SERV ID (server ID), a unique random number called Nonce of A (NA), the Server's public key, and the SERV TIME CAP (server time capability). Nonce (NA) ensures that the session is unique on the Application side. In response, the Server sends back a session capability (CAP SESS), DEV CAP, USER CAP, NA, NB (another unique random number for the Server side), and a session key (SESS KEY). The SESS KEY is a symmetric key used in a single communication session.

7. APPL → Chosen Server: (Session Start Request (DEV CAP, USER CAP, SERV ID, SERV TIME CAP, NA)), (PK(SERV)).
8. Chosen Server → APPL: (Session Start Request Accepted DEV CAP, USER CAP, CAP SESS, SESS KEY, NA, NB), (PK(APPL)).

- **Stage 4: The Application gets service by using the CAP SESS key and encrypts using the SESS KEY:** In Stage 4 of the process, the application uses the CAP SESS key to access a service and encrypts data using the SESS KEY. The application sends a service request to the chosen server with the CAP SESS, Nonce (NB), and uses the SESS KEY. The server responds by sending CAP SESS, NA, and detailed results using the SESS KEY. NA ensures that the session is unique on the application side.

9. APPL → Chosen Server: (Service Request (CAP SESS, NB, Request Details) (SESS KEY))
10. Chosen Server → APPL: (Service Request Done (CAP SESS, NA, Result Details) (SESS KEY))

- **Stage 5: The Application is finished and terminates the session:** In Stage 5, the application terminates the session by sending an end request to the Chosen Server with CAP SESS, nonce (NB), and the session end indication using the session key. The server then terminates the session and revokes the CAP SESS capability to prevent replay attacks.

11. APPL → Chosen Server: (Session End Request Accepted (CAP SESS, Nonce (A), Session End)(SESS KEY)).

6.3. *ProVerif Results*

The SSP protocol was designed using the ProVerif tool, and the results show that the system is "safe". In Stage 4, the application gets service by using the capability session key and encrypts using the Session key to the Chosen server. The query attacker of function to "Session key" (Ksappl) is TRUE.

The private keys of Cloud Management System (CMS), Service Management Framework (SMF), Application (Appl), and Chosen Server(S) results as True. In Stage 3 and

Stage 4, nonces are used between the chosen Server and the Application to prevent replay attacks. The output of nonce is "True" from Server sessions. The Cloud Management System (CMS), which supports a number of services, contacts the SMF to register the service. We applied the "event begin and end function" to verify whether the sessions started before the SMF started or not, and the result is "True". In the same way, the event begin and end functions are used to verify the server sessions.

Table 5 shows that the SSP protocol is working fine. The results from ProVerif are displayed in Figure A1 in the Appendix A. Hence, this is a more secure mechanism for capability-based services.

Table 5. QUERY ATTACKER Results using ProVerif

Security Properties	CMF	SMF	SERVER	APPL
Private Keys	True	True	True	True
Session Key	-	-	True	True
Nonces	-	-	True	-
Event Begin()	True	-	-	-
Event end()	True	-	-	-
inj-event begin()	-	-	True	-
inj-event-end()	-	-	True	-

6.4. *Queries for Private Keys*

Queries for Private keys of Application, Cloud Management System, Service Management Framework and Server : *query attacker(sksmf); query attacker(skcms); query attacker(skappl); query attacker(skS);*

- RESULT not attacker_*skey(sksmf[])* is true.
- RESULT not attacker_*skey(skcms[])* is true.
- RESULT not attacker_*skey(skappl[])* is true.
- RESULT not attacker_*skey(skS[])* is true.

6.4.1. Queries for nonces

Queries for nonce between Server and application: *query attacker(SERVERNA); attacker(SERVERNB); attacker(APPLNB); attacker(APPLNA):*

- RESULT not attacker_bitstring_*(SERVERNA[])* is true.
- RESULT not attacker_bitstring_*(SERVERNB[])* is true.

6.4.2. Queries for Symmetric key

Queries for Symmetric key : *query attacker(Ksappl); query attacker(SERVERk)*

- RESULT not attacker_key *(Ksappl[m7 = v_10131,m4 = v_10132,!1 = v_10133])* is true.
- RESULT not attacker_bitstring *(SERVERk[[]])* is true.

6.4.3. Queries for authentication of Server event and CMS event

Queries for Symmetric key : *query attacker(Ksappl); query attacker(SERVERk)*

- RESULT inj-event(endSERVERparam(x_24696)) → inj-event(beginSERVERparam(x_24696)) is true.
- RESULT inj-event(endCMSparam(x_38772)) → inj-event(beginCMSparam(x_38772)) is true.
- RESULT event(endCMSparam(x_42655)) → event(beginCMSparam(x_42655)) is true.

7. Prototype Implementation

Using new mechanisms such as Capabilities, and a new Service Management Framework, this research has proposed a new Secure Service Protocol, which can be used to protect any service. The protocol has been verified using ProVerif. In this section, we explore the building of a prototype system.

7.1. Basic Capability System Library (BCSL)

We developed our prototype system using the Basic Capability System Library (BCSL) as our foundation. This library, depicted in Figure 10, is part of the Base Layer of the Implementation Framework. It supports the creation of users, devices, and services and allows servers to be added to services. Each component has its capability, which is used to access other objects, such as files. Services are created and registered with the Service Management Layer (SManL). The BCSL created by the ALERT Team of Middlesex University, London, is a primary system that makes users, devices, services, and servers. These types are identified as CAP USER, CAP DEVICE, and CAP SERVICE as their Capability types, respectively.

The middle layer is responsible for enhancement, tuning, mapping layers, and updates while the top layer focuses on system implementation. In this layer, our primary goal is to improve the Service Management Framework (SMF), so that it can securely replicate and migrate services.

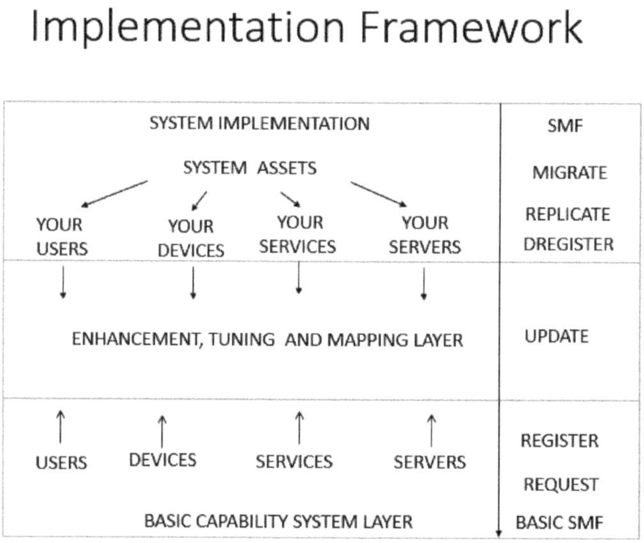

Figure 10. Basic Capability System Library (BCSL).

7.2. Make Fuxfs Multithreaded

The FUSE and NMS servers store and manage the system's data. The NMS provides networked block storage. When a client moves to another network, the NMS is migrated to the new network to improve performance. In this scenario, the client is referred to as "fuxfs", and the server is called "fuxfs server", and they communicate using normal communication protocols.

7.3. The NMS Server

The NMS server is a simple program that provides networked block storage; so should be easy to migrate between networks. This NMS server is working with the FUSE system. Hence this executable was called the Fuxfs_server.

7.4. The FUSE Client

This is the client side of the FUSE code and runs on the mobile node. The executable was called "Fuxfs" and interacts with the Fuxfs_server to manage and store data.

7.5. NMS Part of FUSE as a Service

This framework can be used to implement microservices in vehicular environments. Microservices are faster to migrate and hence can be used to maintain QoS in these networks. As our first use case, we consider a FUSE file system that is a user space file system commonly employed in the Linux environment. The setup, which is shown in Figure 11, provides a storage platform for mobile users as the NMS provides block network storage to FUSE clients which run on mobile phones. If a mobile user moves to another network then the NMS is migrated in order to achieve better performance. In order to test the Service Management Framework, the NMS will be migrated from one cloud server to another. In this paper, we show how to implement the NMS in the Docker's private repository and migrate it to a new location. We installed Docker on a Linux Ubuntu 20.04 machine and set up a private repository to store our services. This allows us to use computing resources for migrating to cloud environments.

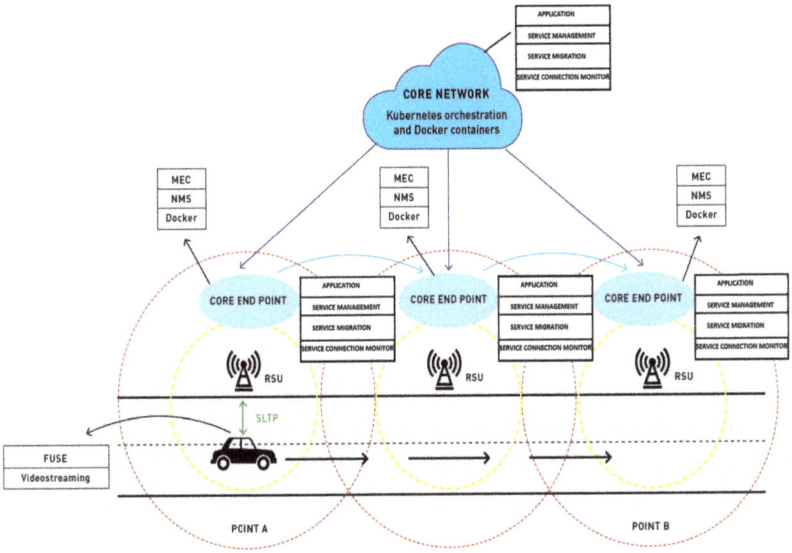

Figure 11. Implementation scenario: FUSE architecture with NMS.

7.6. Requirements Table

Table 6 explains the requirements for the prototype implementation to do a successful migration.

Table 6. Requirements table for Prototype.

Name	Details
Docker private repository	Secure Migration
NMS	Microservices
RASP	Migration Protocol
SMF	Service Management Framework
Fuse Client	Uses NMS as Backing Store
Capabilities	Users, Devices, Service, Servers

7.7. Make Fuxfs Multithreaded

In order to develop the prototype, it was decided to make the client (i.e., the fuxfs program) multithreaded. One thread called SMF_THREAD was used to manage the interaction with the SMF as shown in Figure 12. In this prototype, the FUSE client was used to tell the SMF to migrate the service.

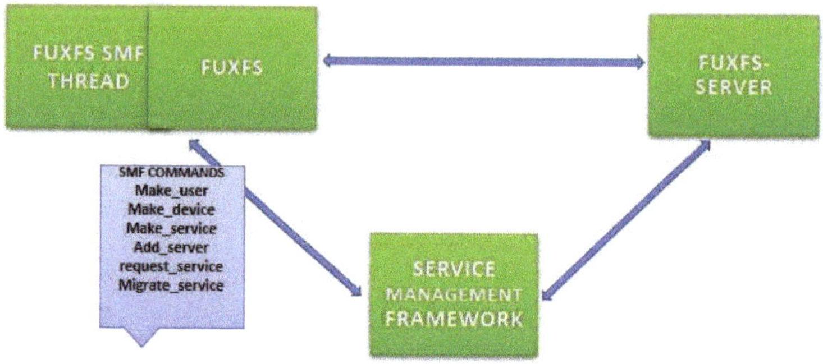

Figure 12. Fuxfs Multithread.

7.8. SMF Commands

The SMF was developed to manage services and migrate and replicate services in a secure environment. To check secure migration on the Service Management Framework (SMF), we developed C programs on the Ubuntu 20.04 platform. We used a private Docker [18] repository to migrate our service and tested them in our local environment. The SMF provides the following functions:

- **Register Service:** The function allows the service to be registered with the SMF. It collects information on the service, including the service name, the description of the service, the version of the service (i.e., 0 is the latest version), the TCP/UDP port number, and the service capability. Once the service has been successfully registered with the SMF, the SMF generates the global_id. The local_id is generated by the CMS.
- **Register User:** This function helps the new user register with the SMF. It collects information about the user, including the first name, surname, role, rank, and specialisation, as well as the capability of the user to register. Once the user has been successfully registered with the SMF, the SMF will generate their global user ID.
- **Register Device:** This register device function allows the devices to register with SMF. To register a device, the name of the device, the first name and surname of the device owner, and the device capability are also collected once the device is registered. Each device will have a unique local device ID and a global device ID.
- **Add Server:** This function helps a server be added to the required service. It also collects details about the server, including the server global ID given by the NMS, the server's name, the server location using its IPv4 address, and the server's maximum load.
- **Request Service:** Once a service is registered with the SMF, the service can be requested by users who want to use it. Servers should provide this service to the requesting applications. This function allows an application to request service. After the application sends a service request to SManL, SManL will provide the necessary parameters for the application to contact the server that runs the requested service.
- **Migrate Service:** This function allows the services to migrate to the required servers. It also collects details about the global service ID, the global user ID, and the global device ID and will set up the migration using Docker container technology. Once the migration is successful, a successful result will be returned to the caller.

7.9. FUSE Server Migration Using Docker

In the source code compilation, using the command prompt, compile the Fuse server (fuxfs_server.c). The next step is to run Docker, build the Docker image and check the built image. To secure the service migration, we have created a private repository in Docker for the migration. As we know that the SMF supports the following functions: Register the service, register the user, register the device, add a server, request and migrate the service. It was compiled and executed using the below commands to start the functions. Figure A2 in the Appendix A shows that the SMF has successfully started.

- Compile command: gcc -o smf smf.c
- Run command: ./smf

7.9.1. Fuxfs Server Start-Up from Dockers Private Repository

After the SMF started, the Source code of "Fuxfs_server.c" compiled and was executed as shown in Figure A3 in the Appendix A, which highlights that the Fuxfs server was started from the Docker Repository.

- Compile command: gcc -o Fuxfs server Fuxfs server.c
- Run command: ./Fuxfs server 0.0.0.0.
- docker run command: gayuinfy/gkprivate:v1

This Fuxfs server derives from Docker private container, we used the docker run command:gayuinfy/gkprivate:v1 and the container ID:ff0fa32d3036 as shown in Figure A4 in the Appendix A.

7.9.2. Fuxfs Client Start-Up

After the Fuse server, the fuse client (Fuxfs.c) was compiled and executed as shown in Figure A5 in the Appendix A.

- Compile command : gcc -Wall fuxfs.c 'pkg-config fuse –cflags –libs' -o fuxfs -w -lpthread
- Run command: ./fuxfs /tmp/fuse 0.0.0.0

7.9.3. NMS Service Added

The NMS is an example of block storage service, registered with the SMF. The "Add server" command from SMF allows servers to be added including Server name, type, Server IP address, TCP and UDP port details has shown in Figure A6 in the Appendix A.

Once the service was successfully added to the server, the service was requested by the FUSE client using the SMF command Request service. The FUSE client then requested that the NMS was migrated to a different machine. The service is then successfully migrated as shown in Figure A7 in the Appendix A. Figure A8 in the Appendix A shows all the components of the working prototype.

8. Conclusions and Future Work

This research has focused on the development of the Secure Service Ecosystem (SSE) to implement the Intelligent Edge Environment for smart cities. This effort looked at three layers of the IEE and developed key mechanisms to help implement the SSE including a new Resource Allocation Algorithm, a new Resource Allocation Secure Protocol and finally a new Secure Service Protocol. Using these mechanisms along with capabilities, ProVerif was used to show that this system was safe. The SSE was then used to support a FUSE-NMS system in which the NMS was migrated as the users moved around.

Though the prototype demonstrated was basic, it showed that it was possible to build an SSE that could be used to develop new services for smart cities. We therefore believe that this approach will allow services for smart cities to be developed and deployed in a much shorter time frame as these services will be automatically managed by the Service Management Framework not by the developers of the service.

For future work, we need to explore how we use this architecture to support a number of microserivces for the vehicular environment including vehicle health monitoring and remote navigation and control systems.

Author Contributions: Formal analysis, algorithms, and software implementation, G.K.; protocols, BCSL, and software implementation, G.M. writing, review, and editing, G.K. and G.M. All authors have read and agreed to the published version of the manuscript.

Funding: This research received no external funding.

Data Availability Statement: The original contributions presented in the study are included in the article, further inquiries can be directed to the corresponding authors.

Acknowledgments: The authors would like to thank Florian Kammueller and Mahdi Aiash for their help and guidance during this effort. We would also like to thank the Department for Transport (DfT) for funding the Middlesex Connected Vehicle testbed which was the motivational starting point for this research.

Conflicts of Interest: The authors declare no conflicts of interest.

Appendix A

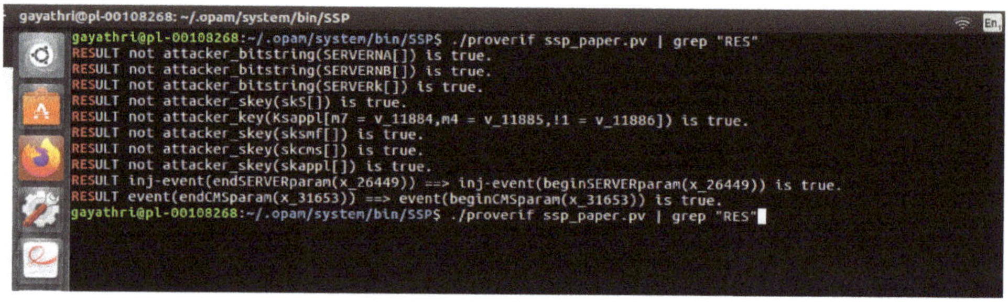

Figure A1. SSP protocols results.

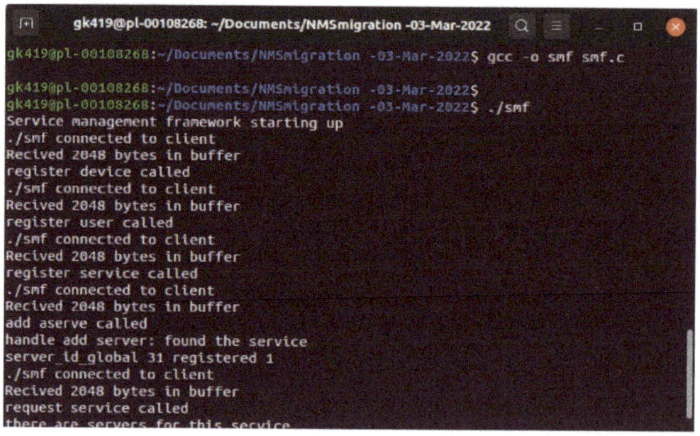

Figure A2. SMF running successfully.

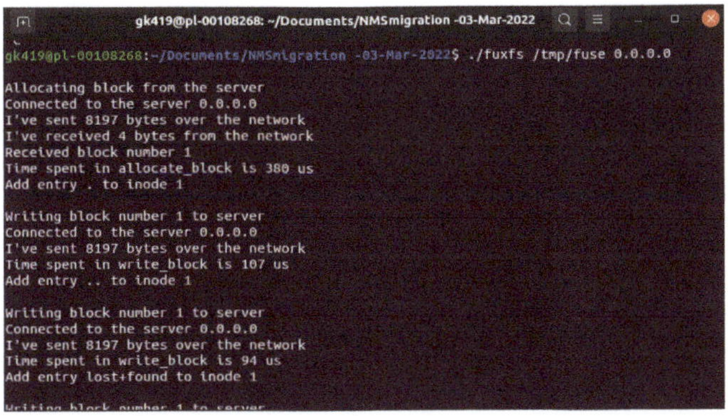

Figure A3. Fuxfs server start-up.

Figure A4. Fuxfs server start-up from Docker's private repository.

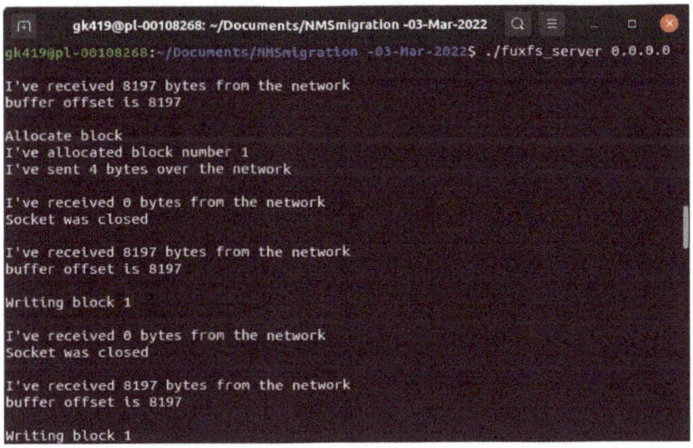

Figure A5. Fuxfs client start-up.

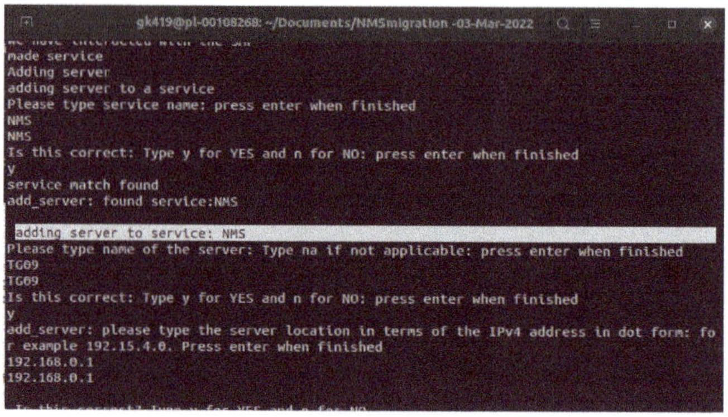

Figure A6. A Server is added to the NMS Service.

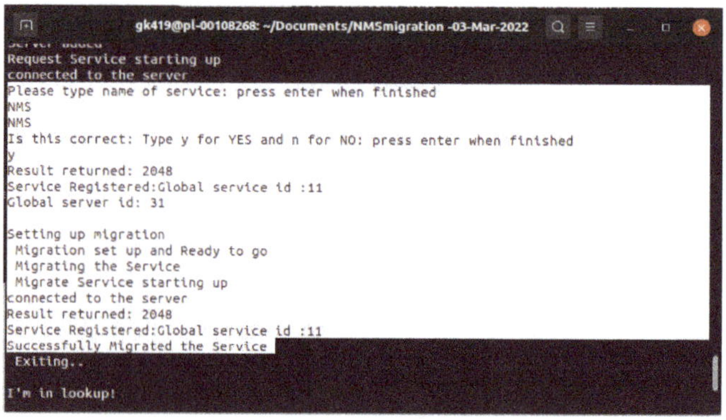

Figure A7. NMS service migrated.

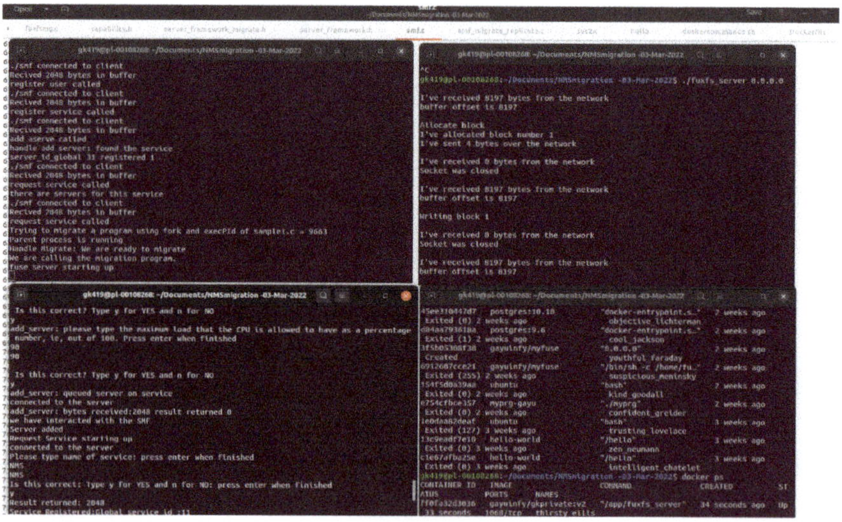

Figure A8. SMF (**top left**), FUSE Client (**bottom left**), NMS (**top right**), and Docker Status (**bottom right**): NMS running at a different location using the SMF.

References

1. Gayathri, K.; Glenford, M.; Jon, C. Building an Intelligent Edge Environment to Provide Essential Services for Smart Cities. In Proceedings of the MobiArch '23, Madrid , Spain, 6 October 2023; pp. 13–18. [CrossRef]
2. Pavel, M.; Zdenek, B. Mobile edge computing: A survey on architecture and computational offloading. *IEEE Commun. Surv. Tutor.* **2017**, *19*, 1628–1656. [CrossRef]
3. Edgeless: Cognitive Edge-Cloud with Serverless Computing. Available online: https://edgeless-project.eu/ (accessed on 18 July 2024).
4. CODECO: A Novel Edge-Cloud Orchestration Framework, Focusing on Data-Compute-Network. Available online: https://he-codeco.eu/ (accessed on 18 July 2024).
5. Paranthaman, V.V.; Ghosh, A.; Mapp, G.; Iniovosa, V.; Shah, P.; Nguyen, H.X.; Gemikonakli, O.; Rahman, S. Building a Prototype VANET Testbed to Explore Communication Dynamics in Highly Mobile Environments. In *Testbeds and Research Infrastructures for the Development of Networks and Communities. TridentCom 2016*; Guo, S., Wei, G., Xiang, Y., Lin, X., Lorenz, P., Eds.; Lecture Notes of the Institute for Computer Sciences, Social Informatics and Telecommunications Engineering; Springer: Cham, Switzerland, 2017; Volume 177. [CrossRef]
6. Xiaolong, X.; Bowen, S.; Xiaochun, Y.; Mohammad, R.; Khosravi, H. Edge Server Quantification and Placement for Offloading Social Media Services in Industrial Cognitive IoV. *IEEE Trans. Ind. Inform.* **2021**, *17*, 2910–2918. [CrossRef]
7. Onyekachukwu, A.E.; Gayathri, K.; Glenford, M.; Ramona, T. Exploring the Provision of Reliable Network Storage in Highly Mobile Environments. In Proceedings of the 2020 13th International Conference on Communications (COMM), Bucharest, Romania, 18–20 June 2020; pp. 255–260. [CrossRef]
8. Chen, S.; Zhou, M. Evolving container to unikernel for edge computing and applications in process industry. *Processes* **2021**, *9*, 351. [CrossRef]
9. Kifayat, U.; Luz, M.S.; Joao, B.R.; Edson, D.M. A lightweight beaconing-based commercial services advertisement protocol for vehicular ad hoc network. In Proceedings of the International Conference on Ad-Hoc Networks and Wireless, Lille, France, 4–6 July 2016; Springer: Berlin/Heidelberg, Germany, 2016; pp. 279–293.
10. Jennings, B.; Stadler, R. Resource management in clouds: Survey and research challenges. *J. Netw. Syst. Manag.* **2015**, *23*, 567–619. [CrossRef]
11. Karthick, G.; Mapp, G.; Kammueller, F.; Aiash, M. Formalization and Analysis of a Resource Allocation Security Protocol for Secure Service Migration. In Proceedings of the IEEE/ACM International Conference on Utility and Cloud Computing Companion (UCC Companion), Zurich, Switzerland, 17–20 December 2018; pp. 207–212. [CrossRef]
12. ProVerif: Cryptographic Protocol Verifier in the Formal Model. Available online: https://bblanche.gitlabpages.inria.fr/proverif/ (accessed on 18 July 2024).
13. Blanchet, B. Modeling and Verifying Security Protocols with the Applied pi Calculus and Proverif. *Found. Trends® Priv. Secur.* **2016**, *1*, 148. Available online: https://ieeexplore.ieee.org/document/8186937 (accessed on 18 July 2024).
14. Mapp, G.; Aiash, M.; Guardia, H.C.; Crowcroft, J. Exploring Multi-homing Issues in Heterogeneous Environments. In Proceedings of the 2011 IEEE Workshops of International Conference on Advanced Information Networking and Applications, Singapore, 22–25 March 2011; pp. 690–695. [CrossRef]
15. Vithanwattana, N.; Karthick, G.; Mapp, G.; George, C.; Samuels, A. Securing future healthcare environments in a post-COVID-19 world: Moving from frameworks to prototypes. *J. Reliab. Intell. Environ.* **2022**, *8*, 299–315. [CrossRef] [PubMed] [PubMed Central]
16. Jose, R.; Onyekachukwu, A.E.; Gayathri, K.; Ramona,T.; Glenford, M. A New Service Management Framework for Vehicular Networks. In Proceedings of the 2020 23rd Conference on Innovation in Clouds, Internet and Networks and Workshops (ICIN), Paris, France, 24–27 February 2020; pp. 162–164. [CrossRef]
17. Karthick, G.; Mapp, G.; Kammueller, F.; Aiash, M. Modeling and verifying a resource allocation algorithm for secure service migration for commercial cloud systems. *Comput. Intell.* **2022**, *38*, 811–828. [CrossRef]
18. Docker: Containerize Your Applications. Available online: https://www.docker.com/ (accessed on 18 July 2024).

future internet

MDPI

Article

TRUST-ME: Trust-Based Resource Allocation and Server Selection in Multi-Access Edge Computing

Sean Tsikteris, Aisha B Rahman, Md. Sadman Siraj and Eirini Eleni Tsiropoulou *

Department of Electrical and Computer Engineering, University of New Mexico, Albuquerque, NM 87131-0001, USA; stsikteris1@unm.edu (S.T.); arahman3@unm.edu (A.B.R.); mdsadmansiraj96@unm.edu (M.S.S.)
* Correspondence: eirini@unm.edu

Abstract: Multi-access edge computing (MEC) has attracted the interest of the research and industrial community to support Internet of things (IoT) applications by enabling efficient data processing and minimizing latency. This paper presents significant contributions toward optimizing the resource allocation and enhancing the decision-making process in edge computing environments. Specifically, the TRUST-ME model is introduced, which consists of multiple edge servers and IoT devices, i.e., users, with varied computing tasks offloaded to the MEC servers. A utility function was designed to quantify the benefits in terms of latency and cost for the IoT device while utilizing the MEC servers' computing capacities. The core innovation of our work is a novel trust model that was designed to evaluate the IoT devices' confidence in MEC servers. This model integrates both direct and indirect trust and reflects the trustworthiness of the servers based on the direct interactions and social feedback from other devices using the same servers. This dual trust approach helps with accurately gauging the reliability of MEC services and ensuring more informed decision making. A reinforcement learning framework based on the optimistic Q-learning with an upper confidence bounds action selection algorithm enables the IoT devices to autonomously select a MEC server to process their computing tasks. Also, a multilateral bargaining model is proposed for fair resource allocation of the MEC servers' computing resources to the users while accounting for their computing demands. Numerical simulations demonstrated the operational effectiveness, convergence, and scalability of the TRUST-ME model, which was validated through real-world scenarios and comprehensive comparative evaluations against existing approaches.

Keywords: multi-access edge computing; Internet of things; reinforcement learning; game theory

1. Introduction

The rise of new technologies, such as artificial intelligence, real-time video analytics, and virtual reality, has increased the expectations for the computing power, energy efficiency, and responsiveness of mobile devices within the Internet of things (IoT). Due to constraints in storage, computing capabilities, and battery life, IoT devices face significant challenges in locally handling demanding tasks. Multi-access edge computing (MEC) has emerged as a promising solution, enabling users to shift their computationally intensive tasks away from mobile devices to MEC servers by exploiting wireless connections [1].

However, the proliferation of IoT devices, including smartphones, tablets, and smart vehicles, which are driven by advancements in smart cities and intelligent transportation systems, has dramatically increased the volume of computation-intensive applications [2]. Thus, there has been a corresponding surge in workload and network traffic within MEC servers. In this paper, we propose the TRUST-ME model, which is a novel framework that enables users to autonomously choose an optimal MEC server for processing their computational tasks by considering their trust levels of the servers' quality of service (QoS), communication capabilities, and computing characteristics. Additionally, the TRUST-ME model facilitates the MEC servers in efficiently allocating their computing resources to meet the users' latency constraints in a fair and computationally effective manner.

1.1. Related Work and Motivation

Several recent research works focused on the problem of *resource allocation and/or server selection* in MEC environments. A non-orthogonal multiple access or NOMA-based vehicle edge computing network model was designed in [3] and consists of several heuristic algorithms to jointly optimize the task offloading and MEC resource assignment to minimize the overall system's costs while ensuring delay tolerance for vehicular user equipment. An efficient D2D-assisted MEC computation offloading framework based on attention communication deep reinforcement learning (ACDRL) is introduced in [4] to enhance a system's performance by facilitating resource sharing and reducing the latency. An efficient algorithm for optimizing the energy consumption in an NOMA-enabled MEC system with strict latency requirements is designed in [5] to address both the resource allocation and the subchannel assignment through decomposition and optimization methods. A similar approach is followed in [6] by focusing on the energy-efficient and low-latency task execution for IoT devices through the joint sparse code multiple access (SCMA) codebook assignment, power allocation, CPU frequency scheduling, and task offloading policy optimization.

Optimization techniques and heuristics algorithms were designed to address the problem of resource allocation and/or server selection in MEC environments [7]. The joint task offloading and resource allocation problem in cooperative MEC server scenarios was studied in [8] by targeting the efficiency and fairness of the resource allocation process through a two-level algorithmic approach. A computationally efficient repeated auction model is proposed in [9] by utilizing a modified generalized second price algorithm to manage the resource allocation in the competitive MEC offloading service market while considering varying server workloads. Given the plurality of IoT devices in several applications supported by unmanned aerial vehicles (UAVs), an innovative alternative optimization approach for integrating UAV systems as both remote base stations and mobile edge servers using NOMA is proposed in [10] to minimize the latency and optimize the resource allocation. An MEC framework for IoT applications in air–ground-integrated wireless networks was analyzed in [11] with the aim to minimize the service latency while meeting the learning accuracy requirements and reducing the energy consumption through an optimized deep neural network (DNN) model decision, computation, communication resource allocation, and UAV trajectory control. A collaborative multi-UAV-assisted MEC system integrated with a terrestrial base station is proposed in [12] in order to minimize the total latency for IoT devices by optimizing the offloading decisions and resource allocations under the IoT devices' energy constraints. An MEC framework that jointly optimizes the caching, offloading, deployment, and resource allocation was analyzed in [13] to minimize the latency and energy costs.

Game theory has been extensively adopted in the recent literature to deal with the distributed optimization problem of resource allocation in MEC environments [14]. A task-offloading scheme for MEC environments is proposed in [15] to optimize the users' utility by leveraging potential games. A scheme based on the double deep Q-network (DDQN) to optimize service caching, resource allocation, and computation offloading in a MEC system is analyzed in [16] to reduce the delay and energy consumption costs. Focusing on the MEC system's effective resource utilization, the authors in [17] introduce a joint bandwidth and computing frequency allocation mechanism based on the Stackelberg games. A two-level bargaining-based incentive mechanism for task offloading and collaborative computing in MEC-enabled networks was analyzed in [18] to ensure the optimal resource allocation and load balance. An iterative algorithm that minimizes the latency in digital twin-aided MEC systems for industrial IoT was formulated in [19] to optimize the resource allocation through an alternating optimization approach combined with an inner convex approximation. A game-theoretic approach to optimize multiuser computing task offloading in a device-enhanced MEC environment is presented in [20] with the aim to maximizing the aggregate offloading benefits by jointly optimizing the heterogeneous (i.e., communication and computing) resource allocation. A similar approach was followed in [21] based on a multistage Stackelberg game, where in the first stage, a contract-based incentive mechanism was introduced to motivate the IoT nodes to share idle resources, and in the second stage, the optimal pricing strategies are derived to optimize the IoT nodes' utilities.

Moreover, an energy-efficient game-theoretic approach to support the resource allocation for the IoT nodes in a MEC environment is proposed in [22] with the aim to optimize the IoT nodes' task offloading decisions based on their personal latency and energy consumption constraints. A similar decentralized game-theoretic approach was followed in [23] with the aim to optimally allocate mobile devices to nearby MEC servers to minimize the latency and communication interference of the IoT devices. The latter approach was further extended in [24] to address the interference-aware software-as-a-service user allocation problem in MEC environments by demonstrating the effectiveness and efficiency of a decentralized algorithm to find its Nash equilibrium. A decentralized-edge-node-grouping algorithm in MEC networks was investigated in [25] by addressing the system uncertainties and proving the convergence to a unique Nash equilibrium with high performance. A fair and efficient mechanism for multi-resource allocation in MEC environments was studied in [26] and guarantees a Nash equilibrium in polynomial time and satisfies various fairness criteria.

Given the distributed nature of the decision-making process regarding the resource allocation in MEC environments, the principles of *reinforcement learning (RL)* have been widely adopted in the recent literature [27]. A deep-reinforcement-learning-based approach to optimize computation offloading and resource allocation in NOMA-MEC systems is proposed in [28] in order to significantly reduce the computational overhead. The authors in [29] integrated artificial intelligence into UAV data offloading in a multi-server MEC environment using game theory and reinforcement learning principles to enhance the efficiency and effectiveness. Various optimization algorithms for managing resources in a MEC environment were studied in [30], and the authors demonstrated their similar performances and highlighted the adaptability of deep-RL-based approaches to changing conditions. A software-defined network or SDN-based MEC system is introduced in [31] using a stochastic game-based resource allocation algorithm to effectively reduce energy consumption and processing latency in IoT systems. A novel AI-based mechanism using RL and Bayesian reasoning for autonomous MEC server activation was analyzed in [32] to enhance the system's reputation and manage computing costs while ensuring the users' quality of experience. An RL-based strategy for efficient task offloading and resource allocation in multi-edge server collaboration is presented in [33] to jointly optimize the task latency, the user service numbers, and the energy consumption. An RL-based approach and an enhanced deferred acceptance algorithm are discussed in [34] to jointly optimize the virtual network functions' (VNFs') placement, routing, and scheduling, and significantly reduce the service latency and resource consumption in MEC environments. A strategy for joint task type and vehicle speed-aware task offloading and resource allocation in vehicular MEC environments is proposed in [35] to optimize the energy costs and processing revenue while meeting the task delay constraints. A Q-learning-based reinforcement learning solution for optimizing dynamic resource allocation in 5G radio access network slicing supporting MEC systems is presented in [36] by significantly improving the network utility compared with myopic, random, and first-come-first-served approaches. A distributed framework using autonomous MEC servers and stochastic learning automata in IoT networks to optimize server activation, device–server associations, and transmission power for QoS satisfaction is presented in [37].

Additionally, a Markov-decision-process-based task offloading strategy in a vehicular edge-cloud computing network is introduced in [38] based on a dueling actor–critic reinforcement learning approach to effectively manage the resource allocation and minimize the task completion times. Similarly, a shared offloading strategy using deep reinforcement learning (DRL) for vehicular edge computing (VEC) is discussed in [39] to reduce the delay and energy consumption by allowing vehicles to share computing results and adaptively select optimal offloading modes in complex IoT environments. Also, a hierarchical vehicular edge computing architecture is designed in [40] to enhance the global task computing efficiency by allowing neighboring regions to share idle resources. The authors of [41] analyzed and compared value-based, policy-based, and hybrid deep reinforcement learning algorithms in order to address the task-offloading challenges in edge computing environments, and they provided a thorough discussion regarding their respective strengths, weaknesses, and future research directions. A dynamic offloading decision algorithm combined with DRL was analyzed in [42] to optimize the task offloading and resource allocation in an MEC environment, and it significantly improved the energy efficiency and task completion time under varying wireless conditions. A novel offloading algorithm that combines meta-reinforcement learning with DRL is proposed in [43] to efficiently generate near-optimal task-offloading decisions in resource-constrained IoT environments. A DRL-based computation offloading scheme for virtual reality video transmission in MEC networks was analyzed in [44] in order to optimize the task management through a deep deterministic policy gradient algorithm. Similarly, a DRL-based computation-offloading scheme for UAV-enabled MEC environments is proposed in [45] with the aim to reduce the task execution delay, energy consumption, and overall offloading cost compared with conventional methods. Moreover, an autonomous partial offloading system for delay-sensitive tasks in multiuser IoT MEC environments is introduced in [46] and is based on Q-learning and deep deterministic policy gradient strategies to significantly reduce the devices' delay and enhance their quality of service. A meta-RL task-offloading algorithm was designed in [47] based on graph neural networks and enhances the adaptability and robustness in dynamic MEC environments by effectively managing the task dependencies and optimizing the sampling efficiency.

1.2. Contributions

Though significant research efforts have been devoted in the recent literature to deal with the joint problem of MEC server selection and resource allocation in MEC environments consisting of multiple IoT devices, the study of these problems remains highly fragmented, meaning that the recent research works either focus on the problem of MEC server selection or on the problem of resource allocation in a separate manner. Additionally, assessing the trustworthiness of the MEC servers' computing capabilities in order to meet the IoT devices' latency constraints has been largely overlooked. To address these research gaps, we propose the TRUST-ME model, which enables the autonomous selection of edge servers by the IoT devices for task offloading while considering the MEC servers' trustworthiness in delivering quality of service to the IoT devices. Furthermore, we introduce a distributed resource allocation framework based on the multilateral bargaining games to facilitate the fair allocation of the MEC servers' computing resources to the IoT devices based on the computing demands of the latter ones.

The main contributions of this research work are summarized below:

1. Initially, the TRUST-ME model is presented as consisting of multiple edge servers and multiple IoT devices, where the latter ones are characterized by different computing tasks to be fully offloaded to the MEC servers for further processing. The communications and computing characteristics of the IoT devices are presented and a utility function is designed to capture the IoT devices' benefit by the experienced latency and cost from utilizing the computing capacity of the selected MEC server.
2. A novel trust model of the IoT devices to the MEC servers' computing capabilities was designed and consisted of the direct and indirect trust of the devices, where the latter one was derived from the social ties between the IoT devices that have used the same MEC server to process their computing tasks. A reinforcement learning approach based on optimistic Q-learning with an upper bound confidence action

selection algorithm is presented to enable the IoT devices to autonomously select an MEC server.

3. A multilateral bargaining model is presented for resource allocation, enabling the MEC servers to allocate their computing capacity to the IoT devices' tasks by taking into account their computing demand and the fairness in service provision between the devices.
4. A detailed set of simulation-based experiments was performed to demonstrate the operational efficacy and performance convergence of the TRUST-ME model in terms of the MEC server selection and resource allocation. Moreover, a real-world scenario was analyzed by considering different types of computing applications requested by the IoT devices to demonstrate the TRUST-ME model's applicability. A thorough scalability analysis also quantified its efficiency and robustness. A detailed comparative evaluation against alternative MEC server selection and resource allocation approaches quantified the superiority of the TRUST-ME model over current state-of-the-art methods.

1.3. Outline

The remainder of this paper is organized as follows. Section 2 presents the TRUST-ME model, and Section 3 analyzes the IoT devices' trust model and the autonomous RL-based MEC server selection. Section 4 provides the analysis for the multilateral bargaining resource allocation of the MEC servers' computing capacity, and Section 5 provides a detailed simulation-based evaluation of the TRUST-ME model. Finally, Section 6 concludes the paper.

2. TRUST-ME System Model

We consider a multi-access edge computing (MEC) environment with a group of users $\mathcal{N} = \{1, \ldots, n, \ldots, N\}$ and a set of MEC servers $\mathcal{S} = \{1, \ldots, s, \ldots, S\}$. Each user has a computing task represented by $A_n = (B_n, C_n, \phi_n, T_n, e_n)$, where B_n [bits] is the total data size, and C_n [CPU-cycles] is the required processing cycles, which is defined as $C_n = \phi_n B_n$, with ϕ_n $[\frac{CPU-cycles}{bits}]$ denoting the computation intensity. Additionally, T_n [sec] and e_n [J] represent the user's latency and energy constraints, respectively. The users fully offload their data B_n to MEC server s. Each MEC server has a computing capacity F_s $[\frac{CPU-cycles}{sec}]$ and allocates its capacity among the users offloading to it. The allocation vector is denoted by $\mathbf{f_s} = [f_{s,1}, \ldots, f_{s,n}, \ldots, f_{s,N}]$ $[\frac{CPU-cycles}{sec}]$, satisfying $\sum\limits_{\forall n \in \mathcal{N}} f_{s,n} = F_s$.

User n offloads its data to MEC server s using the non-orthogonal multiple access (NOMA) technique, with the successive interference cancellation (SIC) implemented at the MEC server (receiver). Assuming the users' channel gains are sorted as $G_1 \leq \cdots \leq G_n \leq \cdots \leq G_{N_s}$, where N_s is the number of users offloading their computing tasks to server s, the throughput for each user n is given by the following equation [48]:

$$R_{n,s} = W \log_2 \left(1 + \frac{P_n G_n}{I_0 + \sum\limits_{n'=1}^{n-1} G_{n'} P_{n'}}\right) \tag{1}$$

where W [Hz] denotes the bandwidth, P_n [watts] denotes the transmission power, and G_n denotes the channel gain. It is noted that for simplicity in the notation, we considered that the users N_s associated with MEC server s have a corresponding channel gain and we denote the channel gain of user n as G_n. The corresponding set of users selecting server s is denoted as $\mathcal{N}_s\{a, \ldots, n, \ldots, N_s\}$. Also, I_0 denotes the power spectral density of zero-mean additive white Gaussian noise (AWGN).

User n's time overhead consists of the overhead to transmit and process its data and it is given as follows:

$$t_n = \frac{B_n}{R_{n,s}} + \frac{C_n}{f_{s,n}} \tag{2}$$

Based on the experienced latency and the cost to utilize the computing resources of the MEC server, each user experiences a utility by processing its computing task using the MEC server, which is given as follows:

$$u_n = \frac{\frac{1}{t_n}}{\frac{1}{\max\limits_{n \in \mathcal{N}}\{t_n\}}} - \beta_n \cdot \frac{\mathcal{C}_s f_{s,n}}{\mathcal{C}_s \max\limits_{s \in \mathcal{S}}\{F_s\}} \tag{3}$$

where t_n [sec] is the user's experienced latency to transmit and process its computing task, as given by Equation (2); $\mathcal{C}_s$ $[\frac{\$}{CPU-cycles}]$ is the MEC server's announced computing price to process the users' data; $f_{s,n}$ $[\frac{CPU-cycles}{sec}]$ is the amount of computing resources allocated by MEC server s to the user n's computing task; and β_n is a weight factor. It is noted that the user's utility u_n is unitless and the normalization is performed for demonstration purposes in order to capture the pure differences between the users.

3. Trust-Based Reinforcement-Learning-Enabled MEC Server Selection

The users evaluate the reliability (i.e., trust levels) of the MEC servers based on the quality of service that they provide for processing the offloaded computing tasks in order to ultimately identify the most dependable MEC server. The trust of the users to the MEC servers is assessed by considering both the direct trust $dtr_{s,n}$ and the indirect trust $itr_{s,n}$. The direct trust stems from the users' previous interactions with the MEC servers, while the indirect trust, or reputation and reliability, is built on the collective experiences of other users. This dual-trust approach improves the users' understanding of the service quality offered by the MEC servers, especially in the case where the direct interactions of the users with the MEC servers are infrequent.

3.1. Influencers' Direct Trust

The level of direct trust a user places in an MEC server depends on whether the MEC server meets the user's minimum utility threshold, which is symbolized as U_n, and its latency constraint T_n [sec]. This is measured through the ratings $\tilde{r_1}_{s,n} \in [0,1]$ and $\tilde{r_2}_{s,n} \in [0,1]$, respectively, which the user assigns to the MEC server based on the computing capacity that the latter one offers. The user's ratings are evaluated under two distinct conditions:

Case 1: If the user's requirements are satisfied, meaning $U_n \leq u_n$ and $T_n \geq t_n$, the MEC server receives a perfect satisfaction rating of 1 for the computing capacity service. Thus, the final rating given to the MEC server is $\tilde{r}_{s,n} = \hat{r}_{s,n}$.

Case 2: If the computing capacity service provided by the MEC server does not meet the user's utility and latency constraints, the user's satisfaction rating will reflect the gap between the actual utility received and the minimum required utility, and the latency constraint gap, respectively.

The ratings provided under the two cases considering the experienced utility and latency are given in Equation (4) and Equation (5), respectively:

$$\tilde{r_1}_{s,n} = \begin{cases} \hat{r}_{s,n} & ,\text{if } U_n \leq u_n \\ \frac{u_n - U_n}{U_n} & ,\text{if } U_n > u_n \end{cases} \tag{4}$$

$$\tilde{r_2}_{s,n} = \begin{cases} \hat{r}_{s,n} & , \text{if } T_n \geq t_n \\ \frac{T_n}{t_n} - 1 & , \text{if } T_n < t_n \end{cases} \quad (5)$$

By combining the two ratings in an overall rating $\tilde{r}_{s,n}$ provided by the user to the MEC server, the corresponding overall rating is derived as follows by considering that the user considers the satisfaction of its utility and latency constraints to be equally important:

$$\tilde{r}_{s,n} = 0.5 \cdot \tilde{r_1}_{s,n} + 0.5 \cdot \tilde{r_2}_{s,n} \quad (6)$$

In Case 1, the ratings $\tilde{r_1}_{s,n}$ and $\tilde{r_2}_{s,n}$ are non-negative and are both set to 1. In Case 2, the ratings for both variables are negative and within the range of $[-1, 0)$. To address this, we employed the min–max normalization technique, which is a common method for data normalization, to transform the piecewise rating function from $[-1, 1]$ to $[0, 1]$, as demonstrated below:

$$r_{s,n} = \frac{\tilde{r}_{s,n} - \min_{\forall i \in \mathcal{N}_{n,s}}\{\tilde{r}_{s,n}\}}{\max_{\forall i \in \mathcal{N}_{n,s}}\{\tilde{r}_{s,n}\} - \min_{\forall i \in \mathcal{N}_{n,s}}\{\tilde{r}_{s,n}\}} = \frac{\tilde{r}_{s,n} + 1}{2} \quad (7)$$

where $\mathcal{N}_{n,s}$ refers to the set of computing service times provided to user n by MEC server s.

The expression $f(t_i)$ captures the time decay factor, which reflects how the user's earlier ratings lose their relevance over time in terms of impacting the user's trust in an MEC server, and is defined as follows:

$$f(t_i) = \exp(-\lambda(t - t_i)) \quad (8)$$

where λ, t, and t_i are the rate of decay, current service time, and historical service time, respectively. The decay rate λ is used in the time decay function to reduce the impact of older feedback on the current trust value. If λ is high, then the older feedback will decay faster, and thus, the recent interactions will significantly influence the trust metric. This can be beneficial in dynamic environments where recent performance is more indicative of future behavior. On the other hand, if λ is low, then the feedback decays slowly, and thus, more weight is given to historical data. This can stabilize the trust metric in environments where performance is consistent over time.

Based on the above analysis, user n's direct trust $dtr_{s,n}$ of MEC server s is defined as follows:

$$dtr_{s,n} = \frac{\sum_{i \in \mathcal{N}_{n,s}} r_{s,n} \cdot f(t_i)}{\sum_{i \in \mathcal{N}_{n,s}} f(t_i)} \quad (9)$$

where the denominator $\sum_{i \in \mathcal{N}_{n,s}} f(t_i)$ incorporates the exponential decay function for normalization purposes.

3.2. *Influencers' Indirect Trust*

In an edge computing environment, the users establish a variety of social connections, which are represented as $\mathcal{C} = \{1, \ldots, c, \ldots, C\}$ and include friendships, familial bonds, and acquaintances with strangers. The strength of the social connection c between any two users is indicated by η_c, where $\eta_c > 0$ for all $c \in \mathcal{C}$. The relationship vector between user n and user n' is denoted by $\mathbf{\Lambda}_{n,n'} = \{\Lambda_{n,n',1}, \ldots, \Lambda_{n,n',c}, \ldots, \Lambda_{n,n',C}\}$. If $\Lambda_{n,n',c} = 1$, it means that the users n and n' have a relationship of type c; otherwise, $\Lambda_{n,n',c} = 0$.

For a user n, the trustworthiness of MEC server s is influenced by recommendations from other users with whom the user has several social connections. Generally, the users who are reliable provide truthful recommendations, while the users with malicious intent provide deceptive feedback. The reliability factor $rl_{n,n'}$ serves as a weight for these recommendations provided by other users n' to user n, which reflects how trustworthy the other users' feedback is. This factor is based on both the degree of their social relationship and the similarity between user n and user n', which is calculated as follows:

$$rl_{n,n'} = \frac{\eta_c \cdot \Lambda_{n,n',c} \cdot SIM_{n,n'}}{\max\limits_{c \in \mathcal{C}} \eta_c} \tag{10}$$

Let $\text{SIM}_{n,n'}$ denote the similarity score between the users n and n'. To standardize these scores, we used the normalization factor $\max\limits_{c \in \mathcal{C}} \eta_c$. In general, the users with more similar ratings will have a higher similarity score, which is calculated using the Pearson correlation coefficient. This coefficient measures the degree of similarity between the users n and n' by analyzing their ratings on the MEC servers that they both have been served from. The similarity score is given by

$$SIM_{n,n'} = \frac{\sum\limits_{s \in \mathcal{S}_{n,n'}} (r_{s,n} - \bar{r}_n)(r_{s,n'} - \bar{r}_{n'})}{\sqrt{\sum\limits_{s \in \mathcal{S}_{n,n'}} (r_{s,n} - \bar{r}_n)^2} \sqrt{\sum\limits_{s \in \mathcal{S}_{n,n'}} (r_{s,n'} - \bar{r}_{n'})^2}} \tag{11}$$

where $\bar{r}_n$ and $\bar{r}_{n'}$ represent the average ratings given by user n and user n', respectively. The set $\mathcal{S}_{n,n'}$ includes all the MEC servers that have provided computing services to both users n and n'.

From this analysis, the indirect trust $itr_{s,n}$ can be expressed as follows:

$$itr_{s,n} = \frac{\sum\limits_{n,n' \in \mathcal{N}_s, n \neq n'} rl_{n,n'} \cdot dtr_{s,n'}}{\sum\limits_{n,n' \in \mathcal{N}_s, n \neq n'} rl_{n,n'}} \tag{12}$$

where $\mathcal{N}_s$ denotes the set of users being served by MEC server s.

Different types of social connections, such as friendships and familial bonds, can significantly impact the strength of the social connection η_c of the indirect trust in an MEC environment. Friendships often imply a higher degree of trust and regular interaction. Recommendations from friends are typically considered reliable because friends are likely to share similar standards and expectations regarding service quality. Friends often interact frequently, which means they have a richer history of shared experiences with MEC servers. This historical data enhances the accuracy of the trust metric, as the feedback is based on multiple interactions over time. Familial bonds are usually the strongest social connections. Recommendations from family members are highly reliable because the family members generally prioritize each other's best interests and provide honest feedback. Acquaintances have a weaker social connection compared with friendships and familial bonds. Recommendations from acquaintances are considered less reliable, but still valuable, as they provide additional perspectives. Finally, recommendations from strangers carry the least weight due to the lack of a personal connection and historical interaction.

3.3. *Influencers' Overall Trust*

The users combine their direct trust (Equation (9)) and their indirect trust (Equation (12)) in order to form their overall trust in MEC server s, which is given as follows:

$$tr_{s,n} = \begin{cases} \kappa \cdot dtr_{s,n} + (1-\kappa) itr_{s,n}, & \text{if } N_{n,s} \neq 0 \\ 0.5 & \text{otherwise} \end{cases} \tag{13}$$

where $N_{n,s}$ denotes the number of times that MEC server s has provided services to user n, and the weight factor κ is defined as follows:

$$\kappa = \frac{1 - \exp(-N_{n,s})}{1 + \exp(-N_{n,s})} \tag{14}$$

The role of the weight factor κ is to balance the impact of the direct and indirect trust into the overall trust score. Higher values of κ give priority to the users' personal experiences, while lower values allow the overall trust score to incorporate broader feedback for comprehensive trust evaluation.

In our proposed research work, the robustness of the direct and indirect trust metrics against varying network conditions and user behaviors is a critical aspect of the multi-access edge computing (MEC) environment's operation. The direct and indirect trust leverage (1) the users' historical interactions and (2) the collective experiences of other users to evaluate the trustworthiness of the MEC servers. It is noted that the direct trust is influenced by the user's previous interactions with the server, while accounting for the satisfaction (or not) of the user's utility and latency requirements. On the other hand, the indirect trust incorporates the recommendations provided by other socially connected users. By jointly considering the direct and indirect trust, the evaluation of the trust level of each user to the MEC servers is improved, even under scenarios where individual interactions are infrequent or the network conditions fluctuate. The main network conditions that can influence the users' trust are the bandwidth, channel gain conditions, and service load of the MEC servers. Focusing on the bandwidth, if the bandwidth varies, then the users' experienced throughput is affected. However, the direct trust metric takes into account the experienced latency and utility, which can reflect changes due to the bandwidth fluctuations. Focusing on the users' channel gains, which can also vary due to the users' mobility or even due to environmental factors, the direct trust metric adjusts to the channel gain conditions' variations as it incorporates the real-time performance of the MEC server. Focusing on the MEC server's load, which can vary depending on the users' offloaded tasks, the computing capacity allocated to each user can vary and ultimately affect the processing time. The indirect trust metric includes the feedback from other users, who may experience different server loads. Thus, the proposed approach helps in adjusting the trust score based on the server's performance under varying loads. Focusing on the users' behavior, the users who interact infrequently with the MEC servers depend on the input stemming from the indirect trust metric. The indirect trust aggregates the collective experiences of other users and provides a reliable trust score, even with limited direct interactions. For example, new users can trust servers with high indirect trust scores based on the feedback from established users. The indirect trust also accounts for potential malicious behavior by weighing the reliability of the feedback from other users. Specifically, recommendations from users with strong social connections and similar behavior patterns are given more weight, and thus, filter out unreliable or deceptive feedback from potentially malicious users.

3.4. Reinforcement-Learning-Based MEC Server Selection

The objective for the users is to independently choose an MEC server to efficiently handle their computational tasks. In this scenario, the users function as reinforcement learning (RL) agents that evaluate the potential reward $\rho_{n,a_s}^{(ite)}$ associated with each action a_s at each iteration ite of the RL algorithm. This process continues until they reach a stable and optimal MEC server selection. The possible actions available to the users are represented by the set $\mathcal{A} = \{a_1, \ldots, a_s, \ldots, a_S\}$. The reward $\rho_{n,a_s}^{(ite)}$ for a user depends on several factors, i.e., the computational capacity $f_{s,n}$ provided by the chosen MEC server s, the user's confidence in the quality of service offered by the MEC server, the proximity of the user to the MEC server (which affects the user's communication latency), and the MEC server's overall computing capacity. By combining all these factors, the reward experienced by user n when offloading its computing task to MEC server s is given as follows:

$$\rho_{n,a_s}^{(ite)} = w_1 \frac{f_{s,n}}{F_s} + w_2 tr_{s,n} + w_3 \frac{x}{d_{s,n}} + w_4 \frac{F_s}{\sum\limits_{\forall s \in \mathcal{S}} F_s} \tag{15}$$

where the trust level $tr_{s,n} \in [0,1]$ quantifies how much user n trusts MEC server s; $d_{s,n}$ [m] denotes the distance between MEC server s and user n; x [m] represents the closest distance of a user to the selected MEC server; and the weights satisfy the following conditions: $w_1 + w_2 + w_3 + w_4 = 1$, where $w_1, w_2, w_3, w_4 \in \mathbb{R}^+$. A higher value of w_1 increases the importance of the computational capacity ratio and gives priority to servers with higher available capacity relative to their total capacity. In this case, the users tend to prefer the servers with better computational resources more in order to optimize the task processing speed. A higher value of w_2 emphasizes the trust level, and thus, MEC servers with higher trust scores are preferred. In this case, the reliability and security of the task offloading process are improved, as the users are more likely to choose trusted servers. A higher value of w_3 increases the importance of proximity, and thus, the users tend to prefer closer servers to offload their tasks. In this case, the communication latency is decreased and the users' experience and system responsiveness are improved. Finally, a higher value of w_4 emphasizes the overall computing capacity and promotes the selection of servers with a larger total capacity. In this case, a balance of the load across the network is achieved, and the servers' overloading is prevented.

The optimistic Q-Learning with upper bound confidence (OQ-UCB) action selection RL algorithm is introduced for the users to autonomously choose an MEC server. According to the experienced reward $\rho_{n,a_s}^{(ite)}$ at the iteration ite of the OQ-UCB algorithm, each user updates its expected reward $Q_{a_s}^{(ite)}$ to select an MEC server in the next iteration, which is defined as follows:

$$Q_{a_s}^{(ite)} = Q_{a_s}^{(ite-1)} + \gamma(\rho_{n,a_s}^{(ite)} - Q_{a_s}^{(ite-1)}) \tag{16}$$

where $\gamma \in (0,1)$ represents the learning rate of the OQ-UCB algorithm. Every user chooses an MEC server based on their anticipated reward and uncertainty regarding the outcome, which can be described as follows:

$$a_s^{(ite)} = \arg\max_{a_s^{(ite)}} [Q_{a_s}^{(ite)} + c \cdot \sqrt{\frac{\ln(ite)}{N_{a_s}^{(ite)}}}] \tag{17}$$

where $c \in \mathbb{R}^+$ represents the confidence level and $N_{a_s}^{(ite)}$ denotes the number of times action a_s has been selected up to iteration ite. Equation (17) incorporates two main components. The first addresses the uncertainty related to the user's selection of an MEC server, where a consistent choice reduces the uncertainty, while variability in terms of choosing different actions encourages the exploration for an optimal server selection. The convergence of the OQ-UCB algorithm is achieved when the expected reward $Q_{a_s}^{(ite)} \geq \epsilon$, where $\epsilon = 95\%$ for at least one MEC server a_s. By utilizing the OQ-UCB algorithm, the users are enabled to autonomously determine their preferred MEC server choice to offload their computing tasks.

4. Multilateral Bargaining Resource Allocation

The proposed mechanism for the reinforcement-learning-based edge server selection enables each user to independently choose an MEC server for offloading their data computing tasks. This process allows the MEC servers to dynamically adjust their resource allocation (i.e., computing capacity) based on the number of users requiring service while considering the sequence of service requests and data-processing volumes requested by the users. The users engage in a competition between each other to access a larger share of the selected MEC server's computing capacity F_s to meet their latency constraints $T_n, \forall n \in \mathcal{N}$, and satisfy their minimum utility requests U_n.

This competitive interaction between the users who select the same MEC servers $\mathcal{N}_s$ can be modeled as a *multilateral bargaining game*. In this game, the users negotiate between each other to share the common pool of resources F_s available at the selected MEC server. The computing capacity allocated to each user is denoted as $f_{s,n}$. The bargaining operator for an individual user n is defined by the matrix $\mathcal{B}_n$, where $b_{n'n'} = \hat{t}_{n'}$; $\forall n \neq n', b_{nn'} = 1 - \hat{t}_{n'}$; and $\forall n \neq n', b_{nn} = 1$, with $\hat{t}_n = \frac{B_n}{\sum_{n \in \mathcal{N}_s} B_n}$. In the matrix $\mathcal{B}_n, B_n$ represents the bargaining power of user n, which is determined relative to the total bargaining power of all the users selecting the same MEC server F_s:

$$\mathcal{B}_n = \begin{bmatrix} \hat{t}_1 & 0 & \dots & 0 & 0 & 0 & \dots & 0 \\ 0 & \hat{t}_2 & \dots & 0 & 0 & 0 & \dots & 0 \\ \vdots & \vdots & \dots & \vdots & \vdots & \vdots & \dots & \vdots \\ 1-\hat{t}_1 & 1-\hat{t}_2 & \dots & 1-\hat{t}_{n-1} & 1 & 1-\hat{t}_{n+1} & \dots & 1-\hat{t}_{N_s} \\ \vdots & \vdots & \dots & \vdots & \vdots & \vdots & \dots & \vdots \\ 0 & 0 & \dots & 0 & 0 & 0 & \dots & \hat{t}_{N_s} \end{bmatrix} \tag{18}$$

Let the bargaining operator in the multilateral bargaining game be denoted by $\mathcal{B} = \mathcal{B}_1\mathcal{B}_2 \dots \mathcal{B}_{N_s}$, its corresponding characteristic polynomial be given by $c(\lambda) = \det(\lambda I - \mathcal{B})$, and each individual bargaining operator be partitioned as follows:

$$\mathcal{B}_n = \begin{bmatrix} \mathcal{B}_{11}^{(n)} & \mathcal{B}_{12}^{(n)} \\ \mathcal{B}_{21}^{(n)} & \mathcal{B}_{22}^{(n)} \end{bmatrix} \tag{19}$$

where $\mathcal{B}_{11}^{(n)}$ is a scalar matrix, and $\mathcal{B}_{22}^{(n)}$ is a matrix with dimensions $(N_s - 1) \times (N_s - 1)$.

A similar partition is performed for the bargaining operator of the overall multilateral bargaining game, as follows:

$$\mathcal{B} = \begin{bmatrix} \mathcal{B}_{11} & \mathcal{B}_{12} \\ \mathcal{B}_{21} & \mathcal{B}_{22} \end{bmatrix} \tag{20}$$

Based on the above analysis and following the principles of bargaining game theory [49,50], the share function of each user is given as follows:

$$\begin{aligned} &\mathbb{S}_n(\hat{t}_{n+1}, \dots, \hat{t}_{N_s}, \hat{t}_1, \dots, \hat{t}_{n-1}) \\ &= \det(I - \mathcal{B}_{22}^{(n)} \dots \mathcal{B}_{22}^{(N_s)} \mathcal{B}_{22}^{(1)} \dots \mathcal{B}_{22}^{(n-1)}) = \det(I - \mathcal{B}_{22}) \end{aligned} \tag{21}$$

and each user's optimal share of the F_s computing resource of the selected MEC server is derived below:

$$f_{s,n} = \frac{\hat{t}_n^{n-1} \cdot \mathbb{S}_n(\hat{t}_{n+1}, \dots, \hat{t}_{N_s}, \hat{t}_1, \dots, \hat{t}_{n-1})}{\frac{\partial c(\lambda)}{\partial \lambda}|_{\lambda=1}} F_s \tag{22}$$

A detailed flowchart of the TRUST-ME model is presented in Figure 1.

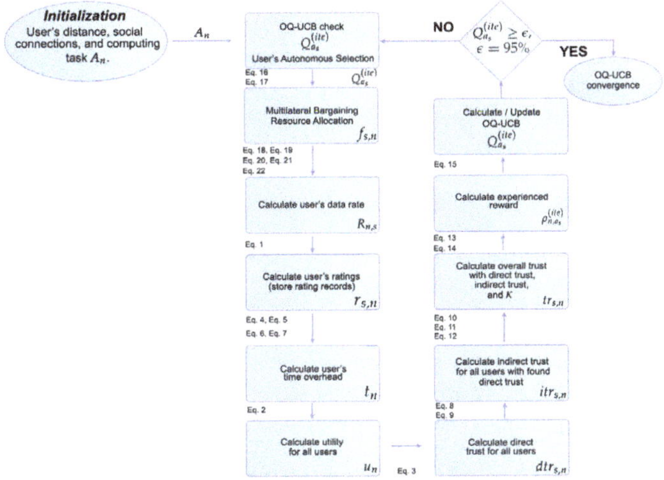

Figure 1. TRUST-ME flowchart.

5. Numerical Evaluation

In this section, the results are given of a detailed simulation-based numerical evaluation that was performed in order to demonstrate the operational characteristics and the priority of the TRUST-ME model. Specifically, its pure operation and performance are presented in Section 5.1 and a real-world application scenario of implementing the TRUST-ME model is discussed in Section 5.2. A detailed scalability analysis is performed in Section 5.3 in order to demonstrate the robustness and superiority of the TRUST-ME model. A thorough comparative evaluation is presented in Section 5.4 by considering different approaches in terms of enabling the users to select an MEC server and in terms of allocating the MEC servers computing resources.

The following simulation parameters were used in the rest of the analysis: $N = 12$, $S = 3$, $c = 1.5$, $\lambda = 2$, $\gamma = 0.8$, $w_1 = 0.05$, $w_2 = 0.85$, $w_3 = 0.05$, $w_4 = 0.05$, $\phi_n = 1$ $[\frac{CPU-cycles}{bits}]$, $e_n = 10^{-9}$ J, $f_c = 73.5$ GHz, $I_0 = 10 \cdot 10^{-22}$, $W = 5$ GHz, $P_n = 0.2$ W, $F_s = [3, 2, 1]$ $[\frac{GCPU-cycles}{sec}]$, $T_n = [20, 24, 27, 31, 34, 38, 42, 45, 49, 53, 56, 60]$ msec, $B_n = [2.00, 1.92, 1.84, 1.75, 1.67, 1.59, 1.51, 1.43, 1.34, 1.26, 1.18, 1.10]$ Mbits, $U_n = [90.0, 82.7, 75.5, 68.2, 60.9, 53.6, 46.4, 39.1, 31.8, 24.5, 17.3, 10.0]$, $C_s = 0.007$ $[\frac{\$}{CPU-cycles}]$, $\beta_n = 10^{-1}$, $d_{1,n} = [14.14, 20.75, 28.20, 35.96, 43.88, 51.88, 59.93, 68.01, 76.11, 84.23, 92.36, 100.50]$ m, $d_{2,n} = [31.62, 35.08, 39.94, 45.75, 52.21, 59.09, 66.27, 73.66, 81.20, 88.85, 96.59, 104.40]$ m, and $d_{3,n} = [50.99, 53.20, 56.52, 60.77, 65.77, 71.36, 77.41, 83.82, 90.52, 97.44, 104.55, 111.80]$ m, unless otherwise explicitly stated.

5.1. *Operation and Performance of the* TRUST-ME *Model*

For this section, our goal was to present the pure operation and performance of the TRUST-ME model. Specifically, we considered an indicative setup that consisted of 12 users and three MEC servers, where the users with higher IDs were characterized by relaxed latency constraints, as they requested the processing of a smaller amount of data and imposed a smaller constraint in terms of the expected achieved utility. Figure 2a–d demonstrate the users' allocated computing capacity, their achieved data rate, and their experienced latency and utility while considering the selected MEC server following the optimistic Q-learning with the upper bound confidence action selection reinforcement learning algorithm. The results demonstrate that more users tended to select the MEC server that was characterized by a higher computing capacity, i.e., MEC servers with lower IDs. Furthermore, the results show that the users with lower IDs that entered into the the bargaining process early and are characterized by a computing task that requires higher computing capacity resulted in being allocated a corresponding higher computing capacity by the selected MEC server. Furthermore, considering that the users resided relatively closer to the MEC server with higher computing capacity, they achieved a corresponding higher data rate, while also considering that users with lower IDs were in general closer to the MEC servers. By combining the two previous observations, we concluded that the users with lower IDs experienced lower corresponding latency by considering the selected MEC server, as they were allocated a higher computing capacity and they achieved a better data rate. The latter observation resulted in higher experienced utility for users with lower IDs relative to the corresponding selected MEC server given that the users who selected the same MEC server competed for its computing resources. Furthermore, Figure 3 illustrates the number of users associated with each MEC server and the corresponding total trust score accumulated by all the users who selected the corresponding MEC server. The results indicate a clear preference among the users for selecting the MEC server with a greater computing capacity. This preference correlated with an increased trust score for the service given the superior quality of service experienced when using higher-capacity MEC servers.

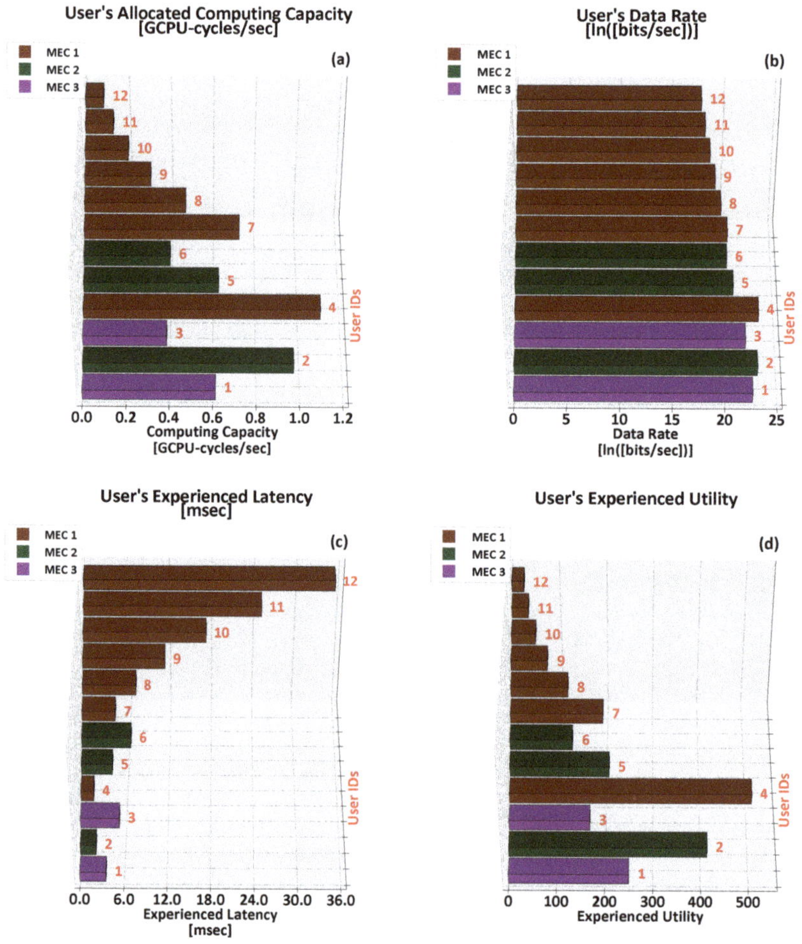

Figure 2. (**a**) Allocated computing capacity, (**b**) data rate, (**c**) experienced latency, and (**d**) experienced utility for the users and their respective MEC selected server.

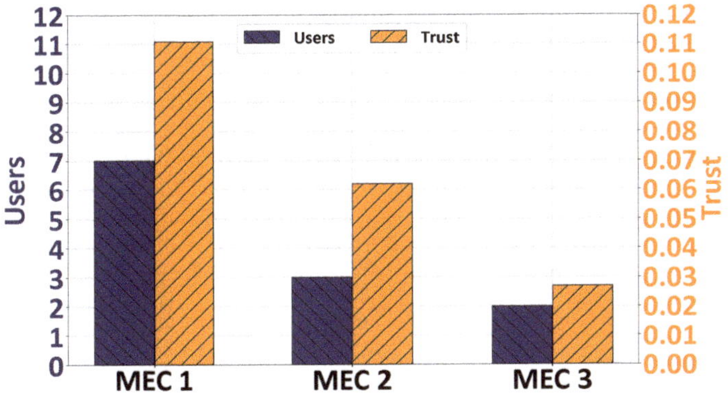

Figure 3. Trust analysis.

The convergence of the optimistic Q-learning with the upper bound confidence action selection reinforcement learning algorithm was also studied. Figure 4a,b demonstrate the OQ-UCB reward (Equation (15)) and the corresponding experience expected reward (Equation (16)) for all the users regarding their corresponding finally selected action over the iterations of the OQ-UCB algorithm, where different colors are used for the corresponding finally selected MEC servers by each user. The results demonstrate that the OQ-UCB algorithm converged fast (in less than 200 iterations, corresponding to a few milliseconds) to a stable action selection and the corresponding expected reward, i.e., Q-value, achieved values above 95% for all the users. Moreover, the results show that the users with lower IDs experienced a higher OQ-UCB reward given the higher trust that they created with respect to the corresponding MEC server, their proximity to the MEC servers, and the higher computing capacity that they were allocated by the selected MEC server.

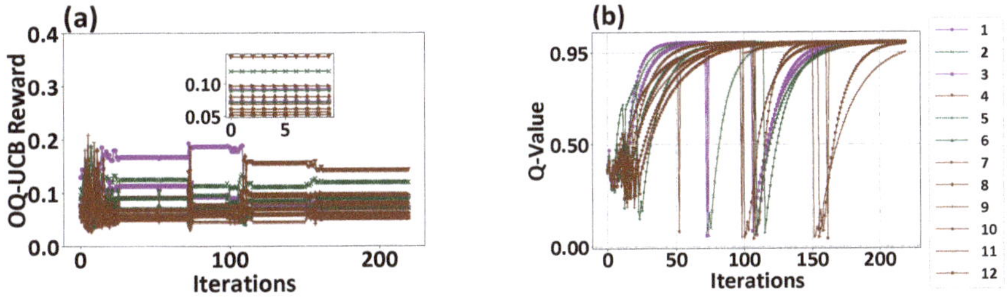

Figure 4. Convergence analysis: (**a**) Reward and (**b**) Q-value convergence.

5.2. A Real-World Application Scenario

As discussed in this section, we examined three representative applications requested by the users, with each one characterized by different levels of computing demand and data-processing requirements of the MEC servers. Specifically, we considered three distinct user groups, with each one consisting of four users that requested applications for augmented reality, real-time data analytics, and content caching. These applications represented high, medium, and low computing demands, respectively, in terms of the amount of data processed at the MEC servers. The augmented reality applications required significant computational resources for real-time image processing, object recognition, and overlay rendering. These applications were latency-sensitive and demanded quick responses to ensure a seamless user experience. The users that ran the augmented reality applications offloaded tasks such as image processing and rendering to the MEC servers, which allocated substantial computing capacity to meet the high processing requirements. Real-time data analytics involved processing streaming data for insights and decision making. These applications required moderate computational resources and were moderately latency sensitive. Content caching applications involved storing and retrieving frequently accessed data to improve the access speed and reduce the latency. These applications required relatively low computational resources and were less latency sensitive.

Figure 5a illustrates the convergence of the OQ-UCB reward for the final action selected by the users with high, medium, and low computing demands. Figure 5b shows the average computing capacity allocated to the users by the selected MEC servers. The results indicate that the users that requested applications with higher computing demands experienced a higher OQ-UCB reward, as the servers allocated greater computing capacity to handle their computationally intensive tasks.

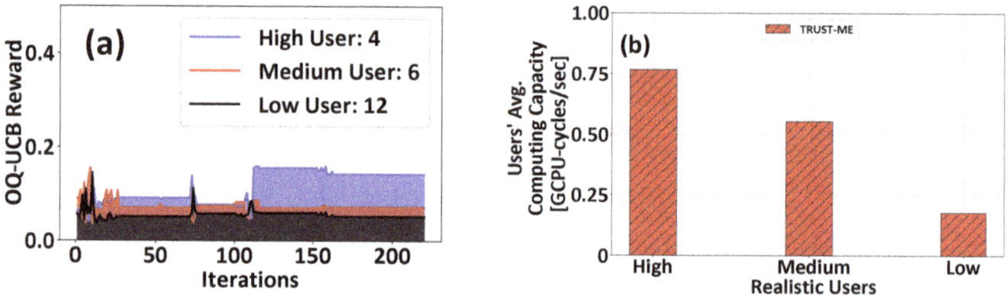

Figure 5. (**a**) Convergence of the OQ-UCB reward for the final action selected by users with high, medium, and low computing demands. (**b**) Average computing capacity allocated to users by the selected MEC servers.

5.3. Scalability Analysis

As discussed in this section, we analyzed the scalability of the proposed TRUST-ME model by varying the number of MEC servers and users. Figure 6a–c show the average computing capacity allocated to each user, the corresponding experienced average user's utility, and the resulting average latency experienced as the number of MEC servers and users changed. The results reveal that as the number of users increased and the number of MEC servers remained constant, the average computing capacity available to each user decreased, and thus, this caused an increased latency. This phenomenon occurred due to the finite computing capacity of the MEC servers, which when divided between more users, led to greater utilization of the MEC servers' resources, and thus, ultimately increased the users' experienced latency.

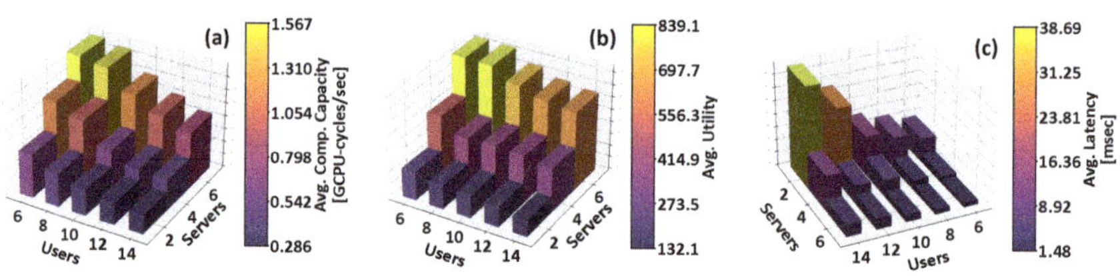

Figure 6. Scalability analysis.

5.4. Comparative Evaluation

As discussed in this section, we performed a comparative analysis of the proposed TRUST-ME model against two alternative scenarios:

- **Without trust:** the users selected an MEC server without considering the trust levels related to the services provided, and the resource allocation followed the multilateral bargaining game.

- **Proportional fair:** the users selected an MEC server using the proposed OQ-UCB algorithm, and the MEC servers' resources were allocated based on the proportional fairness by taking into account the users' data-processing needs, i.e., B_n.

Figure 7a–c show the percentage of the computing capacity allocated by the selected MEC servers to the three user groups (high, medium, and low computing demand), where in total, we considered a set of 12 users. Figure 8a–c show the average computing capacity allocation, the experienced average users' utility, and the corresponding latency experienced by users under each scenario.

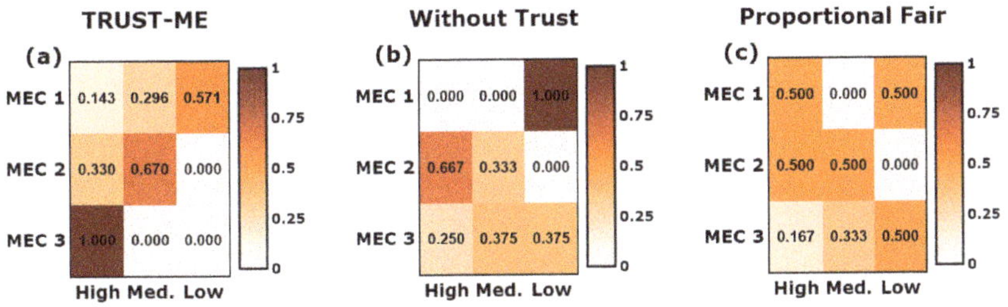

Figure 7. Comparative heat distribution plots showing the percentage allocations of the computing capacity by the selected MEC servers to high, medium, and low computing demand user groups.

The results reveal that the proposed TRUST-ME model achieved a more balanced distribution of the users across the MEC servers. The users with higher computing demands tended to select the MEC servers with lower capacities in order to dominate them and be allocated a large portion of their computing capacity. In the without trust scenario, the users with high computing demands predominantly chose the server with the medium computing capacity (MEC server 2), leaving the users with lower computing demands to utilize the higher-capacity server (Figure 7b). In the proportional fair scenario, the users with higher computing demands often selected the MEC servers with the high computing capacity, allowing them to dominate these servers and secure a larger share of its resources. Thus, the users with lower computing demands were distributed between the servers to capture their remaining computing capacities. The results also show that the without trust and proportional fairness resource allocation scenarios inadequately addressed the users' computing demands, where they experienced higher latencies due to insufficient and unbalanced resource allocation (Figure 8c).

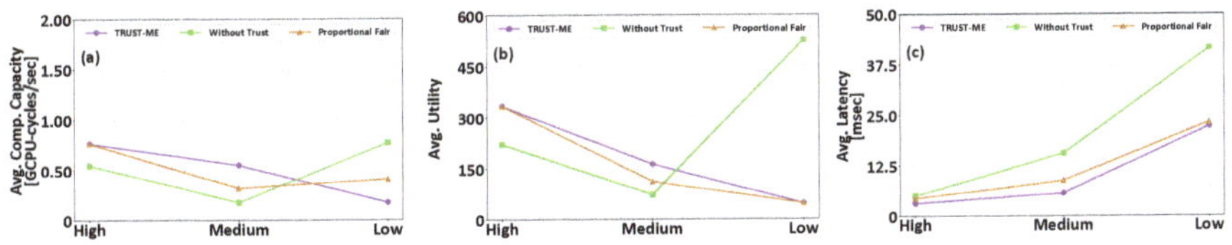

Figure 8. Comparative evaluation showing the (**a**) average computing capacity allocation, (**b**) average users' utility, and (**c**) latency experienced by users across different scenarios.

The proportional fairness (PF) strategy, while it allocated the resources based on the users' data processing needs, tended to allow users with high computing demands to dominate high-capacity servers. This approach can result in suboptimal resource utilization, where low-demand users do not receive sufficient resources. Also, the PF strategy did not account for the dynamic and often fluctuating network conditions as effectively as TRUST-ME. The users could experience varying levels of service quality due to the bandwidth fluctuations, server loads, and channel gain conditions. Moreover, it should be noted that although the latency was only slightly higher by following the PF strategy, this approach did not fully address the need for adaptive and efficient resource allocation under varying demands and conditions. Additionally, the users with higher demands experienced better performance at the expense of those with lower demands under the PF strategy. On the other hand, the TRUST-ME model provided a more robust evaluation of the MEC server performance by jointly considering the direct and indirect trust. This adaptability ensured consistent and reliable service quality, even under fluctuating network conditions. Also, it should be noted that the execution time of the TRUST-ME model was very low (few msec), as discussed in Section 5.1, and TRUST-ME ensured lower latency by effectively balancing the resource allocation and adapting to real-time network conditions and user behaviors. The integration of trust metrics allowed for a more comprehensive assessment of the servers' performance and it led to more informed and efficient resource allocation decisions. This resulted in a consistent reduction in latency, as presented in Figure 8c. Moreover, TRUST-ME enhanced the overall user experience by providing a balanced and fair distribution of resources. Specifically, the users with varying demands could rely on the trust-based allocation to receive sufficient resources and ensure a satisfactory quality of service.

6. Conclusions

In this paper, the TRUST-ME model is presented by considering a multi-MEC servers multi-users edge computing environment, where the users are characterized by diverse computing tasks routed to the MEC servers for processing. A novel trust model is introduced for the users to assess the MEC servers' computing capabilities, integrating both direct and indirect trust mechanisms derived from the social interactions among the users using the same servers. A reinforcement learning approach based on the optimistic Q-learning with the upper confidence bound action selection algorithm is introduced to enable the autonomous MEC server selection by the users. A multilateral bargaining model was designed to support the resource allocation of the MEC servers' computing capacity to the associated users to ensure a fair distribution of the MEC servers' computing capacities based on the users' computing demands. Numerical simulations demonstrated the operational efficiency, convergence, and scalability of the TRUST-ME model, which were validated through real-world scenarios and simulations. Comparative evaluations against existing approaches quantified the superior performance of the TRUST-ME model in terms of the MEC server selection and resource allocation strategies.

Part of our current and future work includes the extension of the proposed trust model to incorporate dynamic trust updates based on real-time performance feedback from the MEC servers and the users, as well as adaptive learning mechanisms. Also, our goal is to implement the proposed model in an industrial IoT environment to support the users, i.e., IoT nodes, with real-time decision making in industrial IoT applications.

Author Contributions: Conceptualization and writing, S.T., A.B.R. and M.S.S.; methodology and supervision, E.E.T. All authors read and agreed to the published version of this manuscript.

Funding: The research of Tsiropoulou and Tsikteris was partially supported by the National Sciemca Foundation, USA, Awards #2219617 and #2319994.

Data Availability Statement: The original contributions presented in the study are included in the article, further inquiries can be directed to the corresponding author.

Conflicts of Interest: The authors declare no conflicts of interest.

References

1. Liu, Y.; Zhong, P.; Yang, Z.; Li, W.; Li, S. Computation Offloading Based on a Distributed Overlay Network Cache-Sharing Mechanism in Multi-Access Edge Computing. *Future Internet* **2024**, *16*, 136. [CrossRef]
2. Kochetkova, I.; Leonteva, K.; Ghebrial, I.; Vlaskina, A.; Burtseva, S.; Kushchazli, A.; Samouylov, K. Controllable Queuing System with Elastic Traffic and Signals for Resource Capacity Planning in 5G Network Slicing. *Future Internet* **2023**, *16*, 18. [CrossRef]

3. Du, J.; Sun, Y.; Zhang, N.; Xiong, Z.; Sun, A.; Ding, Z. Cost-Effective Task Offloading in NOMA-Enabled Vehicular Mobile Edge Computing. *IEEE Syst. J.* **2023**, *17*, 928–939. [CrossRef]
4. Li, K.; Wang, X.; He, Q.; Yang, M.; Huang, M.; Dustdar, S. Task Computation Offloading for Multi-Access Edge Computing via Attention Communication Deep Reinforcement Learning. *IEEE Trans. Serv. Comput.* **2023**, *16*, 2985–2999. [CrossRef]
5. Liu, L.; Sun, B.; Tan, X.; Tsang, D.H.K. Energy-Efficient Resource Allocation and Subchannel Assignment for NOMA-Enabled Multiaccess Edge Computing. *IEEE Syst. J.* **2022**, *16*, 1558–1569. [CrossRef]
6. Liu, P.; An, K.; Lei, J.; Zheng, G.; Sun, Y.; Liu, W. SCMA-Based Multiaccess Edge Computing in IoT Systems: An Energy-Efficiency and Latency Tradeoff. *IEEE Internet Things J.* **2022**, *9*, 4849–4862. [CrossRef]
7. Yang, W.; Shi, L.; Liang, H.; Zhang, W. Trusted Mobile Edge Computing: DAG Blockchain-Aided Trust Management and Resource Allocation. *IEEE Trans. Wirel. Commun.* **2024**, *23*, 5006–5018. [CrossRef]
8. Zhou, J.; Zhang, X. Fairness-Aware Task Offloading and Resource Allocation in Cooperative Mobile-Edge Computing. *IEEE Internet Things J.* **2022**, *9*, 3812–3824. [CrossRef]
9. Habiba, U.; Maghsudi, S.; Hossain, E. A Repeated Auction Model for Load-Aware Dynamic Resource Allocation in Multi-Access Edge Computing. *IEEE Trans. Mob. Comput.* **2024**, *23*, 7801–7817. [CrossRef]
10. Do-Duy, T.; Huynh, D.V.; Garcia-Palacios, E.; Cao, T.V.; Sharma, V.; Duong, T.Q. Joint Computation and Communication Resource Allocation for Unmanned Aerial Vehicle NOMA Systems. In Proceedings of the 2023 IEEE 28th International Workshop on Computer Aided Modeling and Design of Communication Links and Networks (CAMAD), Edinburgh, UK, 6–8 November 2023; pp. 290–295. [CrossRef]
11. Deng, C.; Fang, X.; Wang, X. UAV-Enabled Mobile-Edge Computing for AI Applications: Joint Model Decision, Resource Allocation, and Trajectory Optimization. *IEEE Internet Things J.* **2023**, *10*, 5662–5675. [CrossRef]
12. Tun, Y.K.; Dang, T.N.; Kim, K.; Alsenwi, M.; Saad, W.; Hong, C.S. Collaboration in the Sky: A Distributed Framework for Task Offloading and Resource Allocation in Multi-Access Edge Computing. *IEEE Internet Things J.* **2022**, *9*, 24221–24235. [CrossRef]
13. Liu, B.; Liu, C.; Peng, M. Computation Offloading and Resource Allocation in Unmanned Aerial Vehicle Networks. *IEEE Trans. Veh. Technol.* **2023**, *72*, 4981–4995. [CrossRef]
14. Chen, Y.; Wu, J.; Han, J.; Zhao, H.; Deng, S. A Game-Theoretic Approach-Based Task Offloading and Resource Pricing Method for Idle Vehicle Devices Assisted VEC. *IEEE Internet Things J.* **2024**, *11*, 21954–21969. [CrossRef]
15. Niu, Z.; Liu, H.; Ge, Y.; Du, J. Distributed Hybrid Task Offloading in Mobile-Edge Computing: A Potential Game Scheme. *IEEE Internet Things J.* **2024**, *11*, 18698–18710. [CrossRef]
16. Wang, L.; Zhang, G. Joint Service Caching, Resource Allocation and Computation Offloading in Three-Tier Cooperative Mobile Edge Computing System. *IEEE Trans. Netw. Sci. Eng.* **2023**, *10*, 3343–3353. [CrossRef]
17. Jiang, J.; Xin, P.; Wang, Y.; Liu, L.; Chai, Y.; Zhang, Y.; Liu, S. Computing Resource Allocation in Mobile Edge Networks Based on Game Theory. In Proceedings of the 2021 IEEE 4th International Conference on Electronics and Communication Engineering (ICECE), Xi'an, China, 17–19 December 2021; pp. 179–183. [CrossRef]
18. Chen, G.; Chen, Y.; Mai, Z.; Hao, C.; Yang, M.; Du, L. Incentive-Based Distributed Resource Allocation for Task Offloading and Collaborative Computing in MEC-Enabled Networks. *IEEE Internet Things J.* **2023**, *10*, 9077–9091. [CrossRef]
19. Van Huynh, D.; Nguyen, V.D.; Khosravirad, S.R.; Sharma, V.; Dobre, O.A.; Shin, H.; Duong, T.Q. URLLC Edge Networks With Joint Optimal User Association, Task Offloading and Resource Allocation: A Digital Twin Approach. *IEEE Trans. Commun.* **2022**, *70*, 7669–7682. [CrossRef]
20. Fang, T.; Yuan, F.; Ao, L.; Chen, J. Joint Task Offloading, D2D Pairing, and Resource Allocation in Device-Enhanced MEC: A Potential Game Approach. *IEEE Internet Things J.* **2022**, *9*, 3226–3237. [CrossRef]
21. Li, Y.; Yang, B.; Wu, H.; Han, Q.; Chen, C.; Guan, X. Joint Offloading Decision and Resource Allocation for Vehicular Fog-Edge Computing Networks: A Contract-Stackelberg Approach. *IEEE Internet Things J.* **2022**, *9*, 15969–15982. [CrossRef]
22. Irtija, N.; Anagnostopoulos, I.; Zervakis, G.; Tsiropoulou, E.E.; Amrouch, H.; Henkel, J. Energy Efficient Edge Computing Enabled by Satisfaction Games and Approximate Computing. *IEEE Trans. Green Commun. Netw.* **2022**, *6*, 281–294. [CrossRef]
23. Cui, G.; He, Q.; Chen, F.; Zhang, Y.; Jin, H.; Yang, Y. Interference-Aware Game-Theoretic Device Allocation for Mobile Edge Computing. *IEEE Trans. Mob. Comput.* **2022**, *21*, 4001–4012. [CrossRef]
24. Cui, G.; He, Q.; Xia, X.; Lai, P.; Chen, F.; Gu, T.; Yang, Y. Interference-Aware SaaS User Allocation Game for Edge Computing. *IEEE Trans. Cloud Comput.* **2022**, *10*, 1888–1899. [CrossRef]
25. Li, Q.; Ma, X.; Zhou, A.; Luo, X.; Yang, F.; Wang, S. User-Oriented Edge Node Grouping in Mobile Edge Computing. *IEEE Trans. Mob. Comput.* **2023**, *22*, 3691–3705. [CrossRef]
26. Meskar, E.; Liang, B. MAGIKS: Fair Multi-Resource Allocation Game Induced by Kalai-Smorodinsky Bargaining Solution. *IEEE Open J. Commun. Soc.* **2022**, *3*, 797–810. [CrossRef]
27. Li, Z.; Ju, H.; Ren, Z. A Learning Game-Based Approach to Task-Dependent Edge Resource Allocation. *Future Internet* **2023**, *15*, 395. [CrossRef]
28. Shang, C.; Sun, Y.; Luo, H.; Guizani, M. Computation Offloading and Resource Allocation in NOMA–MEC: A Deep Reinforcement Learning Approach. *IEEE Internet Things J.* **2023**, *10*, 15464–15476. [CrossRef]
29. Fragkos, G.; Kemp, N.; Tsiropoulou, E.E.; Papavassiliou, S. Artificial Intelligence Empowered UAVs Data Offloading in Mobile Edge Computing. In Proceedings of the ICC 2020—2020 IEEE International Conference on Communications (ICC), Dublin, Ireland, 7–11 June 2020; pp. 1–7. [CrossRef]

30. Poltronieri, F.; Stefanelli, C.; Tortonesi, M.; Zaccarini, M. Reinforcement Learning vs. Computational Intelligence: Comparing Service Management Approaches for the Cloud Continuum. *Future Internet* **2023**, *15*, 359. [CrossRef]
31. Wu, G.; Wang, H.; Zhang, H.; Zhao, Y.; Yu, S.; Shen, S. Computation Offloading Method Using Stochastic Games for Software-Defined-Network-Based Multiagent Mobile Edge Computing. *IEEE Internet Things J.* **2023**, *10*, 17620–17634. [CrossRef]
32. Fragkos, G.; Lebien, S.; Tsiropoulou, E.E. Artificial Intelligent Multi-Access Edge Computing Servers Management. *IEEE Access* **2020**, *8*, 171292–171304. [CrossRef]
33. Shi, B.; Wu, Y. Task Offloading and Resource Allocation Strategies Among Multiple Edge Servers. *IEEE Internet Things J.* **2024**, *11*, 14647–14656. [CrossRef]
34. Abouaomar, A.; Cherkaoui, S.; Mlika, Z.; Kobbane, A. Service Function Chaining in MEC: A Mean-Field Game and Reinforcement Learning Approach. *IEEE Syst. J.* **2022**, *16*, 5357–5368. [CrossRef]
35. Huang, X.; He, L.; Chen, X.; Wang, L.; Li, F. Revenue and Energy Efficiency-Driven Delay-Constrained Computing Task Offloading and Resource Allocation in a Vehicular Edge Computing Network: A Deep Reinforcement Learning Approach. *IEEE Internet Things J.* **2022**, *9*, 8852–8868. [CrossRef]
36. Shi, Y.; Sagduyu, Y.E.; Erpek, T. Reinforcement Learning for Dynamic Resource Optimization in 5G Radio Access Network Slicing. In Proceedings of the 2020 IEEE 25th International Workshop on Computer Aided Modeling and Design of Communication Links and Networks (CAMAD), Pisa, Italy, 14–16 September 2020; pp. 1–6. [CrossRef]
37. Apostolopoulos, P.A.; Tsiropoulou, E.E.; Papavassiliou, S. Game-theoretic Learning-based QoS Satisfaction in Autonomous Mobile Edge Computing. In Proceedings of the 2018 Global Information Infrastructure and Networking Symposium (GIIS), Thessaloniki, Greece, 23–25 October 2018; pp. 1–5. [CrossRef]
38. Binh, T.H.; Son, D.B.; Vo, H.; Nguyen, B.M.; Binh, H.T.T. Reinforcement Learning for Optimizing Delay-Sensitive Task Offloading in Vehicular Edge–Cloud Computing. *IEEE Internet Things J.* **2024**, *11*, 2058–2069. [CrossRef]
39. Peng, X.; Han, Z.; Xie, W.; Yu, C.; Zhu, P.; Xiao, J.; Yang, J. Deep Reinforcement Learning for Shared Offloading Strategy in Vehicle Edge Computing. *IEEE Syst. J.* **2023**, *17*, 2089–2100. [CrossRef]
40. Hou, Y.; Wei, Z.; Zhang, R.; Cheng, X.; Yang, L. Hierarchical Task Offloading for Vehicular Fog Computing Based on Multi-Agent Deep Reinforcement Learning. *IEEE Trans. Wirel. Commun.* **2024**, *23*, 3074–3085. [CrossRef]
41. Abdulazeez, D.H.; Askar, S.K. Offloading Mechanisms Based on Reinforcement Learning and Deep Learning Algorithms in the Fog Computing Environment. *IEEE Access* **2023**, *11*, 12555–12586. [CrossRef]
42. Fang, J.; Qu, D.; Chen, H.; Liu, Y. Dependency-Aware Dynamic Task Offloading Based on Deep Reinforcement Learning in Mobile-Edge Computing. *IEEE Trans. Netw. Serv. Manag.* **2024**, *21*, 1403–1415. [CrossRef]
43. Zhang, Z.; Wang, N.; Wu, H.; Tang, C.; Li, R. MR-DRO: A Fast and Efficient Task Offloading Algorithm in Heterogeneous Edge/Cloud Computing Environments. *IEEE Internet Things J.* **2023**, *10*, 3165–3178. [CrossRef]
44. Xu, X.; Song, Y. A Deep Reinforcement Learning-Based Optimal Computation Offloading Scheme for VR Video Transmission in Mobile Edge Networks. *IEEE Access* **2023**, *11*, 122772–122781. [CrossRef]
45. Huda, S.M.A.; Moh, S. Deep Reinforcement Learning-Based Computation Offloading in UAV Swarm-Enabled Edge Computing for Surveillance Applications. *IEEE Access* **2023**, *11*, 68269–68285. [CrossRef]
46. Deng, X.; Yin, J.; Guan, P.; Xiong, N.N.; Zhang, L.; Mumtaz, S. Intelligent Delay-Aware Partial Computing Task Offloading for Multiuser Industrial Internet of Things Through Edge Computing. *IEEE Internet Things J.* **2023**, *10*, 2954–2966. [CrossRef]
47. Li, Y.; Li, J.; Lv, Z.; Li, H.; Wang, Y.; Xu, Z. GASTO: A Fast Adaptive Graph Learning Framework for Edge Computing Empowered Task Offloading. *IEEE Trans. Netw. Serv. Manag.* **2023**, *20*, 932–944. [CrossRef]
48. Diamanti, M.; Charatsaris, P.; Tsiropoulou, E.E.; Papavassiliou, S. Incentive Mechanism and Resource Allocation for Edge-Fog Networks Driven by Multi-Dimensional Contract and Game Theories. *IEEE Open J. Commun. Soc.* **2022**, *3*, 435–452. [CrossRef]
49. Rubinstein, A. Perfect equilibrium in a bargaining model. *Econom. J. Econom. Soc.* **1982**, *50*, 97–109. [CrossRef]
50. Jin, Y.; Zhang, J. A closed form characterization of the stationary outcome in multilateral bargaining. *Front. Econ. China* **2013**, *8*, 272–287.

future internet

Article

Active Queue Management in L4S with Asynchronous Advantage Actor-Critic: A FreeBSD Networking Stack Perspective

Deol Satish, Jonathan Kua * and Shiva Raj Pokhrel

IoT & Software Engineering Research Lab, School of Information Technology, Deakin University, Geelong, VIC 3220, Australia; deol.satish@deakin.edu.au (D.S.); shiva.pokhrel@deakin.edu.au (S.R.P.)
* Correspondence: jonathan.kua@deakin.edu.au

Abstract: Bufferbloat is one of the leading causes of high data transmission latency and jitter on the Internet, which severely impacts the performance of low-latency interactive applications such as online streaming, cloud-based gaming/applications, Internet of Things (IoT) applications, voice over IP (VoIP), real-time video conferencing, and so forth. There is currently a pressing need for developing Transmission Control Protocol (TCP) congestion control algorithms and bottleneck queue management schemes that can collaboratively control/reduce end-to-end latency, thus ensuring optimal quality of service (QoS) and quality of experience (QoE) for users. This paper introduces a novel solution by experimentally integrate the low latency, low loss, and scalable throughput (L4S) architecture (specified by the IETF in RFC 9330) in FreeBSD framework with the asynchronous advantage actor-critic (A3C) reinforcement learning algorithm. The first phase involves incorporating a modified dual-queue coupled active queue management (AQM) system for L4S into the FreeBSD networking stack, enhancing queue management and mitigating latency and packet loss. The second phase employs A3C to adjust and fine-tune the system performance dynamically. Finally, we evaluate the proposed solution's effectiveness through comprehensive experiments, comparing it with traditional AQM-based systems. This paper contributes to the advancement of machine learning (ML) for transport protocol research in the field. The experimental implementation and results presented in this paper are made available through our GitHub repositories.

Keywords: active queue management; L4S; FreeBSD; deep learning; experience-driven; DualPI2

1. Introduction

Network routers use buffers to improve routing performance and overall throughput by absorbing sudden bursts of packets and minimizing packet loss, ultimately boosting network efficiency. However, the trend of using large buffers due to more affordable memory has led to "bufferbloat", particularly when dealing with congestion [1].

In response, researchers have turned to active queue management (AQM) techniques to manage buffers in routers. These AQM algorithms control queue length by selectively dropping or marking packets when the buffer becomes full or the queue delay exceeds a certain threshold. An early implementation of this was the random early detection (RED) algorithm [2], which utilized queue length to predict congestion. However, configuring these types of AQMs can be challenging, and they may not perform well in certain scenarios.

Modern AQMs like controlled delay (CoDel) and proportional integral controller enhanced (PIE) have been developed to address these challenges. These algorithms utilize queue delay rather than queue length to detect congestion. These AQMs aim to maintain low latency even under a high network load by focusing on delay.

The next advancement in AQMs involved developing hybrid schemes such as flow queue CoDel (FQ-CoDel) and flow queue proportional integral controller enhanced (FQ-

PIE), which combined the merits of CoDel and PIE with a modified deficit round robin (DDR) scheduler.

In FQ-CoDel, flows are assigned to a pool of internal queues, each managed independently by an instance of CoDel for buffer management. The DDR scheduler shares the outbound link capacity among the active queues, ensuring a fair allocation of resources. Likewise, the hybrid strategy "FQ-PIE" amalgamates the FlowQueuing aspect of FQ-CoDel with the PIE queue management. Both algorithms have shown exemplary capacity sharing between competing flows while achieving high throughput and low queuing delay.

Despite their efficacy in throughput and queuing delay reduction, these delay-based algorithms are insufficient for the growing demand for low-latency and low-loss data transmission required for applications such as online gaming, high bitrate streaming, video conferencing, virtual reality, and cloud-based processing for real-time IoT applications [3,4]. Presently, employing classic congestion control alongside cutting-edge active queue management (AQM) strategies such as FQ-CoDel [5], PIE [6], or DOCSIS PIE [7] yields an average latency ranging from 5 to 20 ms. Nevertheless, even with these advancements, latency at the 99th percentile hovers around 20 to 30 ms, falling short of the stringent latency requirements of contemporary applications. This research explores avenues for enhancing latency performance in data transmission systems, catering to the evolving needs of modern digital environments.

Low latency, low loss, and scalable throughput (L4S) represent a novel architecture paradigm based on the insight that the root cause of queuing delay lies in the capacity-seeking congestion mechanisms of senders rather than inherent issues within the queuing system itself. This architectural innovation is primarily facilitated towards incremental deployment, ensuring compatibility with the existing network infrastructures. Central to its design is introducing a mechanism enabling the integration of a new class of congestion controls and queue management within the L4S framework. This mechanism employs a modified explicit congestion notification (ECN) variant, facilitating their coexistence alongside 'Classic' congestion controls within shared network environments. The overarching objective of L4S is to achieve superior latency and throughput while maintaining a low loss rate compared to the traditional network infrastructure.

CoDel, PIE, FQ-CoDel, and FQ-PIE are effective in reducing "bufferbloat" and managing congestion in general scenarios. However, L4S goes a step further by explicitly prioritizing latency-sensitive traffic, catering particularly well to applications that demand immediate responsiveness, such as online gaming, video conferencing, and interactive multimedia streaming. By implementing L4S in FreeBSD, the project aims to optimize the network stack for delay-sensitive applications, providing a smoother and more reliable user experience.

In this paper, we pioneer a new hybrid framework that can combine asynchronous gradient descent optimization for deep neural network controllers (e.g., A3C) with the L4S architecture to optimize buffer management for latency-sensitive real-time applications. It employs neural networks to learn and optimize system policies based on the environment's feedback, allowing it to recognize network congestion preemptively and prepare responses appropriately depending on the severity of congestion. Traditional algorithms have significant delays in responding to network congestion due to their simplistic nature in responding to sudden bursts of packets in the network. Integrating L4S into FreeBSD's network stack, combined with the A3C machine learning algorithm, enhances network performance, responsiveness, and adaptability, making it a compelling choice for modern network environments.

The aim of this paper, as for other researchers in this field, is to find ways to contribute to advancing network protocols and machine learning techniques within the context of networking. Our main focus is developing a preliminary implementation of A3C-L4S to enhance L4S's responsiveness to congestion by exploring and exploiting past experiences. This will ultimately lead to improved network responsiveness, reduced latency, and enhanced efficiency in FreeBSD-based systems. Our experimental implementation and results presented in this paper are made available through our GitHub repositories (Experimental L4S implementation in FreeBSD 13.1: https://github.com/MPTCP-FreeBSD/FB13.1-AQM-L4S-SRC.git accessed on 18 July 2024, A3C implementation and analysis: https://github.com/MPTCP-FreeBSD/FreeBSD-DRL-L4S.git accessed on 18 July 2024).

We formulate the following research questions in our paper:

1. How can the FreeBSD networking stack be modified to support L4S and integrate explicit congestion notification (ECN)?
2. What performance improvements can be observed in terms of latency, loss, and throughput by implementing L4S in FreeBSD?
3. How can the A3C algorithm be applied to dynamically adjust the base drop probability of L4S in response to varying network conditions?
4. What is the impact of using A3C to optimize the base drop probability of L4S on the performance of real-time applications?

This paper is organized as follows. Section 2 presents the background and related work in state-of-the-art AQM algorithms and their ML-based approaches, Sections 3 and 4 present our system design and implementation of L4S in FreeBSD. Section 5 presents our experimental evaluation, and Section 6 analyzes the results and discuss key findings. Section 7 concludes the paper and outlines future work.

2. Background and Related Work

In this section, we present the background information on active queue management (AQM) and related works in machine learning (ML)-based approaches.

2.1. Active Queue Management

In the last decade, we have seen a staggering increase in the number of devices connected to the internet, leading to a surge in network traffic. Consequently, this has resulted in frequent congestion in networks characterized by high loss and high end-to-end latency. This has increased the demand for scalable solutions that offer low latency, low loss, and high throughput data transmissions.

As noted in [8], bufferbloat occurs primarily due to excessively large buffering capacity at network devices, particularly routers. Packets queue within these buffers, allowing the network devices to absorb the erratic packet bursts and inadvertently reducing packet loss but also resulting in high end-to-end delays. The large buffer size introduces a significant delay that persists over time, thereby degrading network performance.

Active queue management (AQM) is an algorithm run on routers/switches that detects incipient network congestion by monitoring the instantaneous or average queue size [9]. Network congestion occurs during high network traffic when it exceeds the network's capacity to handle it.

To avoid network congestion, AQM algorithms are designed to monitor the queue's state or length to make accurate decisions about packet handling (such as dropping or marking packets) based on the observed queue conditions to free up buffer space. In some AQM algorithms, a router sets a congestion notification bit in a packet to inform clients to reroute packets through a different path to avoid congestion in the router [10,11].

Kathleen et al. [1] highlights that present-day networking suffers from unwarranted latency and sub-optimal performance induced by bursts of packets and large buffers. Another point that is evident from [1] not mentioned in [8] is inefficient congestion control schemes. Though large buffers are essential to adequately functioning packet networks, overly large and unmanaged buffers create excessive delays, which frustrate many end-users. To mitigate these problems, the work presented in [1] hints at an effective AQM that can prevent the queues at the bottleneck from growing excessively by monitoring packet queue size and informing the sender's TCP to drop packets promptly. The article also mentions that packet loss is not a concern but is necessary to function properly in the face of congestion. However, in L4S, we also require it to possess low loss.

In addition to the above, Prasade et al. [12] state that classic TCP control congestion algorithms are window-based, meaning that in the initial stages of congestion, the congestion control algorithm preemptively increases the transmission rate as a preventive measure for packet loss, but this exacerbates congestion issues. To mitigate this problem, AQM algorithms, relative to the queue size, start dropping packets or marking them, signaling the impending congestion to the endpoints, prompting them to reduce their congestion window before packet loss occurs to prevent overflow. The AQM uses the explicit congestion notification (ECN) flag present in packet headers to mark the packets and inform endpoints of congestion.

AQM schemes are pivotal in managing network congestion. These schemes include controlled delay (CoDel), proportional integral controller enhanced (PIE) and flow-queue-controlled delay (FQ-CoDel). Here, we briefly present the operations of these schemes.

2.1.1. Controlled Delay (CoDel)

CoDel is an active queue management (AQM) algorithm first proposed by Van Jacobson in 2012 [13] as an advancement over the traditional drop-tail algorithm and is a variant of the RED algorithm. CoDel primarily utilizes packet-sojourn time (or queue delay in simpler terms) as the primary congestion indicator. Once the queuing delay has exceeded a certain target for at least a certain interval, a packet is discarded, and the subsequent drop time is determined by a control law proportional to the square root of the number of drops since entering the dropping state. Conversely, the queue ceases discarding packets if the delay falls short of the target.

Several variants of CoDel have been proposed, including FQ-CoDel, which uses fair queuing to improve flow-level fairness, and PIE-CoDel, which incorporates the PIE algorithm to improve queue management.

2.1.2. Proportional Integral Controller Enhanced (PIE)

PIE [6] is another well-known AQM similar to RED. During congestion, incoming packets are dropped randomly according to a drop probability before being placed into the buffer. PIE determines congestion and drop probability by using the derivative (rate of change) of queuing latency. To ensure that PIE is "work conversing", the random drop is bypassed if the latency samples are less than half the target latency value. After congestion ends, PIE exponentially decays "drop probability" to prevent the router from dropping too many packets. PIE also supports explicit congestion notification (ECN) but is optional.

2.1.3. Flow Queue-Controlled Delay (FQ-CoDel)

FQ-CoDel [5] is an active queue management (AQM) algorithm that combines fair queuing and the CoDel algorithm to mitigate bufferbloat in computer networks. Karlstad University first proposed it in September 2014 [14].

FQ-CoDel is a hybrid AQM scheme that utilizes multiple queues, each governed by its instance of CoDel for buffer management. As in a typical CoDel instance for a single queue, it drops packets when the packet-sojourn time exceeds a specific interval. To ensure a fair bandwidth among the queues, we employ a flow-queuing algorithm known as deficit found robin (DDR) with an efficiency of O(1) time complexity. This combination of fair queuing and CoDel helps to achieve flow-level fairness and reduce bufferbloat, packet loss, and latency. Another feature of FQ-CoDel is its implementation of two sets of old and new queues. This provides brief periods of priority to lightweight or short burst flows, helping deliver low latency.

2.1.4. Flow Queue-Proportional Integral Controller Enhanced (FQ-PIE)

Similar to FQ-CoDel, FQ-PIE [15] combines fair queuing (FQ) and the proportional-integral (PI) controller, an advanced control theory technique widely used in process control systems, as explained above. In our experiments, we use FQ-PIE deployed in FreeBSD, as mentioned in this paper [16]. The goals are similar to FQ-CoDel, where we use a DDR scheduler to evenly share bandwidth capacity among competing queues, except each queue is managed by an instance of PIE, which utilizes a derivative of the queuing delay to determine congestion and the responses to mitigate it.

FQ-PIE has been observed to outperform other AQM algorithms, including FQ-CoDel, regarding delay performance and fairness, as shown in this paper [17]. FQ-PIE has also been shown to be effective in wireless networks, where packet loss and delay are significant problems.

2.1.5. Low Latency, Low Loss, and Scalable Throughput (L4S)

The dual-queue coupled AQM [18,19] is a novel AQM scheme that utilizes two virtual queues, L4S and Classic, to control network traffic and utilizes the PIE controller as its base [20]. The objective of this AQM is to achieve low latency, low loss, and scalable throughput (L4S) under a wide range of dynamic network conditions. The congestion control becomes the primary mechanism that keeps utilization high but low delay in an L4S service, but it also requires shallow unsmoothed explicit congestion notification (ECN) [17]. ECN [17] is a signal or, to be precise, an ECN field in the IP header with two bits to provide a congestion indication for any incoming congestion. ECN does not require any smoothing delay, as additional delay is required to ensure round trip time data on each flow.

2.2. *Machine Learning-Based AQM Schemes*

In recent years, researchers have proposed several machine learning-based schemes in active queue management (AQM). Jakub et al. [21] proposed a unique approach using supervised convolutional neural networks to replicate the behavior of the AQM PI mechanism. However, it is constrained by its dependence on previous training data, limiting its efficiency in handling unique scenarios.

Researchers started using deep reinforcement learning (RL) to overcome these limitations. RL algorithms can learn through exploration, meaning they do not solely rely on historical data but actively interact with the environment to discover the optimal action. This exploratory nature of RL allows it to push the network towards better performance by continuously analyzing and learning from the outcomes of its actions.

Both papers, Refs. [22,23], propose a DRL-based AQM implementation that optimizes the maximum dropping probability (max_p) of the RED AQM scheme using a Q-learning algorithm. Liu et al. [23] especially use a traffic predictor with Q-learning to optimize their drop probability. Though the way they optimize their models and gather data is quite different, both show promising results, especially in scenarios where the network behaves erratically.

The paper [24] proposes an AQM algorithm that uses explicit congestion notification (ECN) to regulate network congestion. They build a congestion predictor using an LSTM-based ML model and Q-learning to find optimal drop probability.

Similarly, other studies [25–27] all utilize a DRL approach to learn the optimal packet drop probability based on the observed network state and to regulate the queue length and congestion level.

We can see the constant rate of improvement and development of technology, especially with the advent of machine learning, and the performance of AQM can be increased significantly. The above literature summarizes the latest developments in AQM using machine learning. We have found out that all these papers primarily implement them in Linux-based operating systems, and all these papers are based on single queue-based AQMs, which are not suitable for L4S architecture, whereas our solution entails that we develop A3C-L4S for the FreeBSD OS. FreeBSD is an essential operating system for several reasons, including its high reliability, stability, security, and customizability. However, the main reason is that it is widely utilized in servers and networking devices where stability is critical. Many major IT-service-providing companies like Apple, Microsoft, and Netflix use FreeBSD in their production services. These are the few we mentioned among the many others, as we utilize these services heavily, making it easier to understand their significance.

3. Research Design and Methodology

We present the research design for our A3C-L4S. We first discuss L4S and then A3C.

3.1. Using DualPi2 as an AQM in FreeBSD-L4S

The coupled dual-queue AQM (or DualPi2) [18,19] operates like a semi-permeable membrane, effectively maintaining the sub-millisecond average queuing delay characteristics of L4S while isolating it from classic traffic latency by maintaining separate queues for each type. This configuration ensures that capacity-seeking algorithms achieve approximately equivalent throughput per flow, regardless of the queue they utilize.

However, unlike single-queue frameworks, DualQ does not require examination of the transport-layer flow iD nor compromise classic traffic performance, and it requires no new configuration for public internet deployment [18,19].

Latency is not L4S's sole focus. The "Low Loss and Scalable" aspect of its name indicates its other functions. Traditional scalable congestion control algorithms like DCTCP and Prague encounter compatibility issues with classic congestion controls. Even if they are sharing an ECN-capable queue, the classic algorithms limit their capacity due to the aggressive nature of scalable congestion controls. Unlike Diffserv EF, which limits high-priority traffic to a small percentage of bandwidth capacity to maintain low delay, L4S leverages ECN and DualQ's isolating and coupling effect to achieve very low latency while also achieving zero % loss and retain its ability to scale rapidly without majorly affecting its throughput.

Rigorous testing has been conducted in residential network setups, varying the base RTT up to 100 ms and link rates up to 200 Mb/s between the data center and home network to evaluate the effectiveness of L4S AQMs. The experiments discovered that L4S AQMs maintained an average queuing delay below 1 ms for each of their packets, with the 99th percentile delay not exceeding 2 ms. The L4S AQM introduced no packet loss to the network. The extensive tests are detailed in [18,28].

The comprehensive L4S framework [29] offers more insights on advanced deployment features like ensuring backward compatibility with scalable congestion controls in network bottlenecks lacking DualQ coupled AQM implementation. Additional publications [18,28,30,31] provide more detailed justification through discourse and precise mathematical formulas, accompanied by empirical performance evaluations.

Modified DualQ Coupled L4S AQM: The coupled AQM mechanism ensures harmonious coexistence by setting the classic drop probability p_c proportional to the square of the coupled L4S probability p_{cl}. Here, p_{cl} influences the immediate L4S drop probability p_l, changing at a similar pace to p_c. The square of $p_c l$ offsets the square root of p_c in the TCP formula used by classic Reno congestion management. As a consequence of this, the flow rate of Reno now approximates that of DCTCP. The correlation between the L4S probability, p_cl, and the classic drop probability, p_c, needs to be expressed as the following formula:

$$p_c = (p_{cl}/k)^2 \tag{1}$$

where k is referred to as the proportionality constant, known as the 'coupling factor'.

Any DualQ Coupled AQM likely has a general structure similar to Figure 1. The classifier at the ingress segregates the incoming traffic into two distinct queues: the L4S and classic queues. Each queue is governed by the probability of marking (or dropping) packets denoted by p_l and $p_c l$, respectively.

In managing Reno traffic, which varies the traffic load relative to the square root of observed drops, research such as [PI2] [30] has shown that employing a linear controller to regulate load, squaring the resultant output, and using it as the classic drop probability in traffic compatible with Reno yields favorable results.

For the actual implementation of DualQ L4S, we need to understand the underlying mathematical formulations for **each pair of L4S and classic queues**, as shown in Figure 1.

The implementation requires two phases: (i) phase one produces an internal base probability p', and (ii) in phase 2, we generate p_c using Equation (2), where

$$p_c = (p')^2. \quad (2)$$

Substituting the value of p_c in the equation provided in Equation (1) to Equation (2) gives

$$p' = p_{cl}/k. \quad (3)$$

Now, we can express the Coupled L4S ECN-marking probability as

$$p_{cl} = k \times p'. \quad (4)$$

Recognizing that the L queue has its own ECN-dropping probability due to its "Native AQM", we denote it as p_l', calculated based on the current L4S queuing delay. Given that p_l is the ECN-dropping probability applied to the L4S queue, and p_{cl} is the probability under coupled congestion conditions, the L4S queue should apply p_l' whenever the L4S queue grows due to its conditional precedence over the classic queue. However, it should not drop below p_{cl}. We can define this relation as follows:

$$p_l = max(p_l', p_{cl}), \quad (5)$$

This has been proven to function really well in actual network traffic.

The transformations applied to p' in Equations (2) and (3) serve to apply the correlation described in Equation (1), previously introduced.

The coupling factor, denoted as 'k' in Equation (1), intricately determines the relationship between congestion probabilities for low latency, low loss, and scalable throughput (L4S) and classic traffic within network environments. Through its modulation of drop probabilities, k indirectly influences the adjustments in transmission rates made by the AQM in response to congestion. Consequently, variations in k directly impact the equilibrium ratio between L4S and classic flow rates: higher values of k promote more pronounced marking of L4S traffic, potentially leading to substantial rate adjustments compared to classic traffic, while lower values indicate a lesser degree of coupling and closer resemblance in marking probabilities between L4S and classic traffic. This parameter offers network administrators and policymakers a critical tool for fine-tuning traffic proportions, optimizing network performance, and enhancing overall efficiency by accommodating the diverse requirements of different traffic types.

In queue prioritization, although the scheduler gives higher precedence to the L queue, the classic queue still exerts a significant influence. This phenomenon arises because the 'Base AQM' aggressively applies congestion signals to L traffic as the C queue expands. Consequently, as L4S flows adjust their rates in response, they underutilize the allocated L4S scheduling resources. This behavior creates opportunities for C traffic to be scheduled within the gaps.

While prioritizing the L queue results in a low queuing delay for L traffic, courtesy of the coupling mechanism controlling L traffic, it necessitates conditional prioritization to prevent the C queue from being starved in the short term, giving the means for the C traffic to assert itself. The introduction of a conditional priority mechanism allows for a balanced approach, granting small weight or limited waiting time for C traffic, thereby improving response times for short classic messages like DNS requests and enhancing the startup performance of classic flows by providing immediate capacity when needed.

We employ the 'flow queueing scheduler' from FQ-CoDel and FQ-PIE to segregate network traffic evenly across our three DualPi2 L4S AQMs by utilizing hash functions computed based on certain network parameters, such as port numbers and the source and destination IP addresses. This allows us to isolate low-traffic and high-traffic connections. In upcoming versions, we hope to add the option to change the number of flows or queues dynamically. Flow-queuing significantly impacts performance, especially when scaling our network traffic.

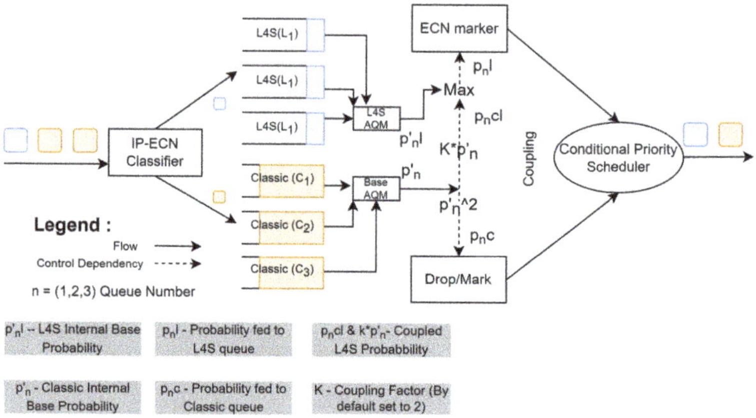

Figure 1. L4S AQM Architecture.

3.2. *Asynchronous Advantage Actor-Critic (A3C) Model*

Asynchronous advantage actor-critic (A3C) is a deep reinforcement learning algorithm introduced by Mnih et al. [32] in 2016. It combines actor-critic and asynchronous methods, making it highly scalable and efficient in solving large and complex problems.

The A3C algorithm uses multiple parallel agents that interact with the environment independently and asynchronously. Each agent is a copy of the same neural network but with different random initial weights. These agents operate in parallel and collect experiences by interacting with the environment. The experiences are then used to update the parameters of the global neural network.

The advantage of using A3C in this context lies in its scalability and efficiency. Each agent operates independently and updates its own copy of the neural network asynchronously without waiting for other agents. This asynchronous update mechanism enables efficient parallelization, allowing multiple agents to work in parallel and optimize their AQMs without interfering with each other.

For our research purposes, we hope to employ multi-agents to optimize multiple routers in our network. A3C allows a central global network to control our routers, ensuring that our model learning encompasses the whole network and is training only our central DRL model, thus requiring less computation and resources. The model parameters and weights in the agents are updated from the global network after a certain time period asynchronously.

3.2.1. Markov Decision Process

The Markov decision process (MDP) formalizes the learning process of the proposed A3C-L4S. In this framework, the learning process begins with observing the current environment state s_t. An action (a) is then chosen according to the policy $\pi(a \mid s)$. The ECN-marking probability of queue is what our A3C model contributes to our AQM algorithms. Therefore, we utilize a continuous action space to represent this, as the action varies in a certain range from 0 to *L4S_MAX_PROB*. Executing this action transitions the environment to a new state s_{t+1}, and the model receives a reward R; where $R = RTT$. For further research, we should define a utility function that does not solely prioritize the queuing delay and focuses on its collective performance, which includes other metrics like throughput and loss. Depending on the environment and the usage scenario, we will give higher weightage to certain metrics.

The environment state is characterized by various metrics, all defined in the Table 1. Some crucial metrics include drop_probability p'_t, queuing delay qd_t, packet drop count

$pdrop_t$, length of the queue in bytes $lenb_t$, and total transmitted data in bytes $totb_t$ of each sub-flow. Each sub-flow's dropping or marking probability sr_i represents the actions.

The intelligent agent has three main components:

$$State : s^t = \left(p'_t, qd_t, pdrop_t, lenbt, totbt\right)_i \tag{6}$$

$$Action : a^t = p'_t \tag{7}$$

$$Reward : R_t = qdelay_t \tag{8}$$

Table 1. FreeBSD AQM L4S Terminology.

Variable	Definition
burst_allowance	Maximum allowed burst size of packets before congestion control measures are applied.
drop_prob	Probability of dropping a packet when the queue is congested.
current_qdelay	Current queue delay, which is the time a packet spends in the queue before being transmitted.
qdelay_old	Previous queue delay value used for comparison and calculation in the FQ-PIE algorithm.
accu_prob	Accumulated probability value used in FQ-PIE to determine the drop probability for incoming packets.
measurement_start	Start time of the measurement interval for collecting statistics.
tot_pkts	Total number of packets observed during the measurement interval.
tot_bytes	Total number of bytes observed during the measurement interval.
length	Average length (in packets) of the queue during the measurement interval.
len_bytes	Average length (in bytes) of the queue during the measurement interval.
drops	Number of packets dropped during the measurement interval.
ECN	is a packet flag marked with explicit congestion notification (ECN) during the measurement interval.
action	Action taken by the A3C algorithm
reward	Reward or penalty assigned to a specific action taken by the A3C algorithm.

3.2.2. Actor-Critic Model

The A3C algorithm uses multiple workers or agents to update a shared model asynchronously. In the following Figure 2, we can discern the placement of our A3C agent in conjunction with our modified L4S algorithm. As observed, we construct an actor and critic model by representing policy function and Q-network.

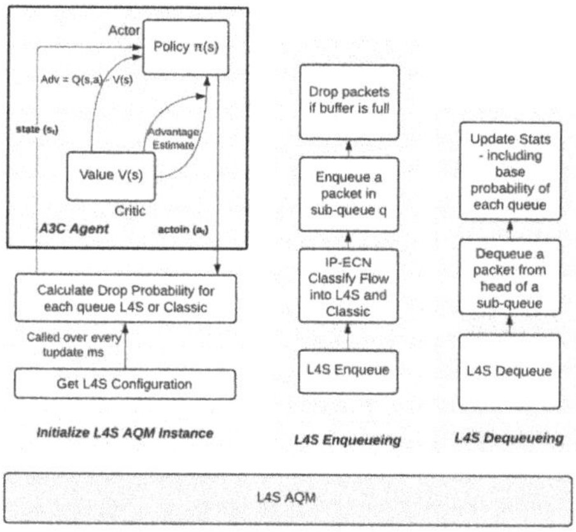

Figure 2. A3C coupled L4S Architecture.

Advantage Function: The advantage function $A(s,a)$ quantifies the relative benefit of choosing action 'a' in state 's' compared to the average action in that state. This metric allows us to evaluate the effectiveness of specific actions within their respective states by assessing their performance relative to the norm for that context. It is a key component in enhancing the decision-making capabilities of actor-critic agents in complex and dynamic environments.

$$A(s,a) = Q(s,a) - V(s) \tag{9}$$

Advantage Function with Returns: Since Q values are unavailable, we estimate the advantage function by computing the discounted rollout returns. This allows us to infer the potential value of different actions in various states during training.

$$A(s,a) = R - V(s) \tag{10}$$

Returns: The return R is the cumulative discounted reward with γ exponentially decreasing the future rewards' weight and n denoting the number of steps or actions taken:

$$R = r_n + \gamma r_{n-1} + \gamma^2 r_{n-2} + \dots \tag{11}$$

Advantage Estimate: Each worker in the algorithm maintains estimates of the policy $\pi(a_t|s_t;\theta)$ and value function $V(s_t;\theta_v)$, utilized in computing the following advantage estimate:

$$A(s_t,a_t) = \sum_{i=0}^{n-1} \gamma^i r_{t+i} + \gamma^n V(s_{t+n};\theta_v) - V(s_t;\theta_v) \tag{12}$$

In this equation,

- θ represents the parameters of the policy network, which outputs the policy $\pi(a|s;\theta)$.
- θ_v represents the parameters of the value network, which outputs the value function $V(s;\theta_v)$
- The state s_t represents the environment at step t. It contains all the necessary information for the agent to decide that step.

$$H(\pi) = -\sum_a \pi(a|s)\log(\pi(a|s)) \tag{13}$$

Actor Network: The actor network is responsible for choosing actions 'a' based on the current environmental state. It receives in the state 's' as input and outputs a probability distribution of the feasible actions available in that state. The primary goal of the actor is to maximize the expected returns, which are represented by the policy loss functions:

$$L_{\text{actor}} = -\log \pi(a|s;\theta) \cdot A(s,a) + \beta H(\pi) \tag{14}$$

In this equation:

- $-\log \pi(a|s;\theta)$ represents the probability of choosing action a given state s, as determined by the actor network with parameters θ .
- $(A(s,a))$ denotes the advantage function
- $(H(\pi))$ is an entropy term that encourages exploration by ensuring the policy does not become overly deterministic, with (β) being a hyperparameter that influences the agent into prioritizing learning policies that consistently favor a specific action over another with greater probability.

Critic Network: The critic network evaluates the value of the current state, providing a baseline to assist the actor in determining the quality of actions. It takes the state (s) as input and outputs a scalar value V(s;w), where (w) represents the critic network's parameters. The critic's objective is to minimize the mean squared error between the estimated value function (V(s;w)) and the actual discounted return 'R' observed during training.

The formula for the critic loss function L_critic is:

$$L_{\text{critic}} = (R - V(s;w))^2 \tag{15}$$

where R is the cumulative discounted return, and V(s;w) is the estimated value function for state (s) with parameters (w).

Neural Layer Structure of Actor and Critic Model This section presents the neural network architectures for the actor and critic models utilized by our A3C model. Each neural network is implemented using an input layer, multiple hidden layers, and output layers.

In this section, we define the action network (actor) and the critic network as neural networks (NNs), integral components of our reinforcement learning model. Each network is designed with specific layers and sizes tailored to their respective roles within the model.

Actor Network: The neural network layer structure of the Action Network model:

The actor network's architecture, as shown in Algorithm 1, consists of one input, two hidden, and two output layers. The input layer has twelve neurons and accepts the state representation of the environment. The hidden layers consist of two dense layers, each with 32 neurons and ReLU activation functions. This layer is responsible for the model's ability to learn the input state's complexities. The two output layers then compute two outputs—mean output (mu) and standard deviation (std), respectively.

Algorithm 1: Actor Neural Network Architecture

```
state_input = Input((self.state_dim,))
dense_1 = Dense(32, activation='relu')(state_input)
dense_2 = Dense(32, activation='relu')(dense_1)
out_mu = Dense(self.action_dim, activation='tanh')(dense_2)
mu_output = Lambda(lambda x: x * self.action_bound)(out_mu)
std_output = Dense(self.action_dim, activation='softplus')(dense_2)
return tf.keras.models.Model(state_input, [mu_output, std_output])
```

Critic Network:

The neural network layer structure of the critic model is as follows:

The critic network's architecture, as shown in Algorithm 2, consists of one input layer, two hidden layers, and one output layer. Like the actor network, the input layer has 12 neurons that accept the state representation. The next three layers are the hidden layers. The first two are dense layers, each consisting of 32 neurons and a Relu activation function, followed by a third layer with 16 neurons and a Relu activation function. The final output layer is a dense layer with a single neuron and a linear activation function, which outputs the given state's estimated value, which is crucial in calculating the advantage estimates to train our actor network.

Algorithm 2: Critic Neural Network Architecture

```
Input((self.state_dim,)),
Dense(32, activation='relu'),
Dense(32, activation='relu'),
Dense(16, activation='relu'),
Dense(1, activation='linear')
```

Simultaneous Update and Asynchronous Training: During training, the actor and critic networks are updated simultaneously using the gradients of their respective loss functions with respect to their parameters θ and θ_v.

The updates are performed asynchronously across multiple agents, independently interacting with the environment and collecting experiences. This asynchronous training mechanism significantly enhances sample efficiency and reduces the variance of the gradients, leading to more stable and efficient learning. The formulas are adapted from a Stanford University paper [33].

3.2.3. Training the Asynchronous Advantage Actor-Critic (A3C) model

In this section, we provide a concise overview of the training procedure for A3C-L4S.

Algorithm 3 outlines the pseudo-code of the A3C model training process in a continuous action observation space. The model goes through a total of 100 episodes during the entire training phase. Every episode commences by resetting the environment and the training session with a fresh random data point. Every episode teaches the model to learn the relationship between action, states and reward. Every episode executes 100 actions to enhance the overall episode reward or to minimize the queuing delay throughout the entire episode. Our model is trained using network environment data collected over long testing periods in our existing artifact. During deployment, the local model or agent that governs each AQM instance asynchronously updates its parameters using the model weights provided by the global network after a certain time interval. Due to exchanging information from kernel space to user space, the delay is introduced, which is typically under one millisecond but may vary depending on system configuration and workload.

3.2.4. Data Preparation

Table 1 displays all the metric data obtained from the kernel along with their description. Custom logging functions were used within the kernel to accurately capture data for analysis, offline data cleaning, and preparation for A3C's environment. The collected data were then normalized to values between 0 and 1 to make training easier, with minimum and maximum values set accordingly. The data we collect from the kernel has no boundaries and may have drastic variations. Therefore, implementing normalization enables us to reduce substantial errors and fluctuations. This allows for the model to achieve better stability.

4. Implementation and Benchmarking of L4S in FreeBSD

In this section, we explain how we incorporated the low latency, low loss, and scalable throughput (L4S) algorithm into the FreeBSD operating system.

In this paper [16], the authors have implemented CoDel, FQ-CoDel, PIE and FQ-PIE in FreeBSD successfully. FQ-PIE combines both flow-queuing (FQ) and proportional-integral controller enhanced (PIE). We use the already existing FQ-PIE algorithm as the base for our L4S AQM scheme. L4S works by filtering ECN and non-ECN into separate queues

Algorithm 3: A3C Pseudocode

Set discount factor gamma $\gamma = 0.99$.
Set the global update interval $t_{\text{args\_update\_interval}} = 5$.
Set the actor learning rate $\alpha_{\text{actor}} = 0.0005$.
Set the critic learning rate $\alpha_{\text{critic}} = 0.001$.
Set the entropy regularization term $\beta = 0.01$.
Initialize global shared parameter vectors θ and θ_v, and a global shared counter $T = 0$.
Initialize thread-specific parameter vectors θ' and θ'_v.
Initialize the thread step counter $t \leftarrow 1$.
repeat
    Reset gradients: $d\theta$ and $d\theta_v$ to zero.
    Synchronize thread-specific parameters: $\theta' \leftarrow \theta$ and $\theta'_v \leftarrow \theta_v$.
    Set $t_{\text{start}} = t$.
    Retrieve current state s_t.
    repeat
        Select action a_t based on policy $\pi(a_t|s_t;\theta')$.
        Retrieve reward r_t and observe new state s_{t+1}.
        Increment counters: $t \leftarrow t+1$ and $T \leftarrow T+1$.
    until terminal state s_t or $t - t_{\text{start}} = t_{\text{args\_update\_interval}}$
    for i from $t-1$ down to t_{start} **do**
        Update accumulated rewardR recursively: $R \leftarrow r_i + \gamma R$.
        Accumulate gradients w.r.t. θ': $d\theta \leftarrow d\theta + \nabla_{\theta'} \log \pi(a_i|s_i;\theta')(R - V(s_i;\theta'_v))$.
        Accumulate gradients w.r.t. θ_v: $d\theta_v \leftarrow d\theta_v + \frac{\partial(R-V(s_i;\theta'_v))^2}{\partial\theta'_v}$.
    end for
    Update weights of policy and value function asynchronously: $\theta \leftarrow \theta + d\theta$ and $\theta_v \leftarrow \theta_v + d\theta_v$.
until $T > T_{\max}$

and couples their drop probabilities to ensure L4S packets are given the right proportion of priority when sending packets while not ignoring classic packets.

There are four steps to the process:

- Limiting the number of flows or queues to the required amount
- Enqueuing and filtering packets based on their ECN flag
- Coupling the probabilities of the L4S and classic queues

4.1. Step 1: Limiting the Number of Flows or Queues to the Required Amount

For an L4S algorithm, one needs a minimum of two queues: one L4S and the other a classic queue, which, in our case, is a classic PIE queue. Our proposed solution is designed with flexibility in mind. We utilize a total of six queues, three of which are L4S queues, and the other three are classic queues. This number can always be increased, but for our testing purposes, we believe that testing our modified algorithm with three pairs of L4S and classic queues is the ideal starting point. This setup should be easily scalable when testing it in a larger environment, giving us the freedom to adapt as needed.

The function named *l4s_config* in Algorithm 4 receives L4S parameters from the user or terminal and assigns them to the corresponding local variables. However, we specifically assert it to use our default flow size parameter. This means that we do not need to specifically add another argument when we change the AQM algorithm in FreeBSD, and it will automatically create six queues.

Algorithm 4: Assert code to use default queue size

```
static int
l4s_config(struct dn_schk *_schk)
{...
    struct dn_sch_l4s_parms *fqp_cfg;
......
    /* L4S configurations */
      .....
      if (1)
         fqp_cfg->flows_cnt = l4s_sysctl.flows_cnt;
            ......
   .....
}
```

4.2. Step 2: Enqueuing and Filtering Packets Based on Their ECN Flag

In this step, we must filter the packets into ECN-capable transport and non-ECN marked packets; these are codepoints of the ECN field. ECT-capable packets are given higher priority when enqueuing, meaning when there is congestion, L4S packets are given more priority, and the classic packets are dropped more relative to L4S packets, decreasing the latency for L4S packets. This is why we need to be able to differentiate the packets, as they might have different purposes. Packets related to a certain service, like live streaming and video calls, are latency-sensitive and thus would be marked with the (ip->ip_tos & IPTOS_ECN_MASK) ! = 0, meaning it would be 01, 10 or 11 bits.

Algorithm 5 demonstrates the high-level details of implementing packet enqueuing into the queues. The algorithm is designed for packet filtering and enqueuing, which involves classifying packets and then enqueuing them into the appropriate queue based on certain criteria.

Algorithm 5: Packet Enqueuing in Queues

```
/*
 * Enqueue a packet into either L4S or Classic queues according to its ECN flag
 */
static int
l4s_enqueue(struct dn_sch_inst *_si, struct dn_queue *_q,
   struct mbuf *m)
{
   ................

    /* classify a packet to queue number, which is half of the total queue size*/
   idx = l4s_classify_flow(m, param->flows_cnt/2, si);

        struct ip *ip;
   ip = (struct ip *)mtodo(m, dn_tag_get(m)->iphdr_off);
   /* If the queue number is 0-2 given by Jenkin Hash and if ECN is enabled,
        * we will put the packet in the later half of the queue buffer meant for
        * L4S */
   if (ip->ip_tos & IPTOS_ECN_MASK) != 0)
      idx=idx+(int)(param->flows_cnt / 2);
        drop = pie_enqueue(&flows[idx], m, si);

   .......................
}
```

Classify a Packet to Queue Number:

```
idx = l4s_classify_flow(m, param->flows_cnt / 2, si);
```

- `l4s_classify_flow(m, param->flows_cnt / 2, si)` is a function that classifies the packet `m` into a queue number using The Jenkins hash algorithm.
- `param->flows_cnt / 2` is used as an argument to split the classification into L4S and native PIE queues.
- `si` is an additional parameter passed to the classification function.

Extract IP Header

```
struct ip *ip;
ip = (struct ip *)mtodo(m, dn_tag_get(m)->iphdr_off);
```

- `struct ip *ip;` declares a pointer to an IP header structure.
- `ip = (struct ip *)mtodo(m, dn_tag_get(m)->iphdr_off);` extracts the IP header from the packet `m` using the offset provided by `dn_tag_get(m)->iphdr_off`.

Check ECN Field in IP Header

```
if ((ip->ip_tos & IPTOS_ECN_MASK) == IPTOS_ECN_ECT1)
idx = idx + (int)(param->flows_cnt / 2);
```

- `if ((ip->ip_tos & IPTOS_ECN_MASK) == IPTOS_ECN_ECT1)` checks the explicit congestion notification (ECN) field in the IP header's type of service (ToS) field.
- `IPTOS_ECN_MASK` is a mask to isolate the ECN bits.
- If the ECN field is not zero, the queue index `idx` is adjusted by adding half of the total flow count (`param->flows_cnt / 2`). This effectively classifies the packet into L4S queues based on its ECN status.

Enqueue the Packet

```
drop = pie_enqueue(&flows[idx], m, si);
```

- `drop = pie_enqueue(&flows[idx], m, si);` enqueues the packet `m` into the queue indexed by `idx` in the `flows` array using the `pie_enqueue` function.
- `&flows[idx]` is a pointer to the specific queue.
- `si` is likely additional context or parameters needed for the enqueue operation.
- The result of the enqueue operation (whether the packet was dropped or successfully enqueued) is stored in the variable `drop`.

The *l4s_classify_flow* method uses a Jenkins hash function and uses the network configuration settings like the source and destination IP address and ports as parameters. The Jenkins hash algorithm utilizes a combination of bitwise operations and multiplication with prime numbers to generate the hash value. It is commonly used in software applications for tasks such as hash table lookups, checksum generation, and data indexing.

4.3. Step 3: Coupling the Probabilities of the L4S and Classic Queues

In this section, we describe the process of coupling the drop probabilities for the low latency, low loss, and scalable throughput (L4S) and classic queues. The following code snippet initializes variables to store the base drop probabilities of each flow:

Algorithm 6 initialized the variables to store the drop probabilities—(P') and (P_l) represent the base drop probabilities from the individual queues. These variables are used to calculate the coupled drop probabilities, as shown in the following algorithm.

4.4. Step 4: Kernel Integration of L4S-Based AQM

To integrate our L4S AQM as a separate AQM scheduler within the `ipfw` module, we needed to propagate the changes throughout the FreeBSD system. This involved modifying the administrative utilities of the kernel to accommodate the new L4S algorithm and its distinct parameters. The process required a complete rebuild of the system using `buildworld`. Here is a succinct description of the steps we have undertaken:

Modification of the `ipfw` Module

- Implemented the L4S AQM scheduler within the `ipfw` module source code.
- Ensured that all necessary parameters and functionalities specific to the L4S algorithm were defined.

Propagation of Changes

- Updated the relevant system files to reflect the addition of the new AQM scheduler.
- Made necessary adjustments to ensure compatibility and proper integration within the FreeBSD kernel.

Rebuilding the System

- Executed the `buildworld` process to rebuild the FreeBSD world, incorporating the new AQM scheduler.
- This step recompiled all userland programs and utilities, ensuring they recognized and could utilize the new AQM parameters.
- Followed the `buildkernel` process to compile the updated kernel with the newly integrated L4S AQM.
- Installed the rebuilt kernel and rebooted the system to apply the changes.

With these steps, we successfully integrated our L4S-based AQM into the FreeBSD kernel, ensuring that all administrative utilities were updated to accept and manage the new algorithm parameters.

5. Experimental Evaluation

In this section, we conduct a comprehensive evaluation of our L4S mechanism against various other competing AQM solutions. Furthermore, we analyze A3C-L4S, discussing its promise as a significant avenue for future research endeavors.

5.1. Evaluation and Benchmarking of AQM Algorithms

In our evaluations, we compare our L4S algorithm with other AQM congestion control algorithms implemented in the FreeBSD kernel, specifically CoDel, PIE, FQ-CoDel, FQ-PIE, and L4S.

Our experimental testbed is based on virtual machines operating within VirtualBox. The testbed features a client and a server connected via a single router, thus simulating a single-path network, as depicted in Figure 3. Multiple TCP streams were deployed at the router to simulate real-world network congestion.

To evaluate the algorithms' performance across different network conditions, we conducted tests in both high-bandwidth and low-bandwidth environments, specifically at 10 Mbps and 1 Mbps. This comprehensive approach ensures that our L4S algorithm is robust and effective across various operational scenarios.

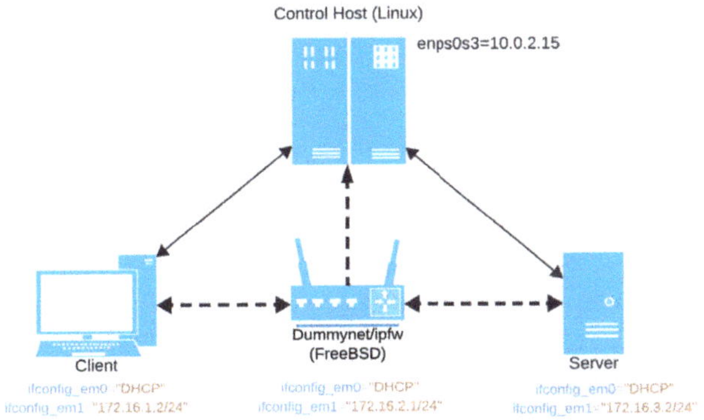

Figure 3. Network topology utilized for evaluating AQM algorithms.

Congestion window size and smoothed RTT data were recorded using the 'Statistical Information For TCP Research (SIFTR)' [34] kernel module. The 'siftr' (https://man.freebsd.org/cgi/man.cgi?query=siftr&apropos=0&sektion=4&manpath=FreeBSD+13.1-RELEASE+and+Ports&arch=default&format=html accessed on 18 July 2024) tool rests between the IPv4 and TCP/IP layers and intercepts the TCP packets as they traverse the network stack within the kernel. On interception, it generates a log file containing highly granular measurements of each packet in the TCP session. The filename for the logfile can be configured using the 'net.inet.siftr.logfile' variable through the 'sysctl' interface. Additionally, the recording session can be initiated or terminated by setting the net.inet.siftr.enabled' variable to 0 or 1.

The log file records the congestion window size in bytes, and the smoothed RTT in units of TCP_RTT_SCALE * HZ, where TCP_RTT_SCALE is defined in tcp_var.h and HZ is the kernel's tick timer. To acquire the smoothed RTT in seconds, dividing the recorded value by (TCP_RTT_SCALE * HZ) is necessary.

To expedite the 'throughput' measuring process, we employ the 'tcpdump' [35] utility to capture packet data and save it as a '.pcap' file. This file is then analyzed using the 'dpkt' python library [36] to filter for TCP packets heading to a specific port connected to its respective TCP stream. The results are then immediately visualized using the 'matplotib' library. Readers familiar with 'Wireshark' [37] can replicate these throughput graphs by selecting *throughput* in the *TCP stream graphs* section under the statistics tab, using the pcap files in the referenced repository.

NewReno TCP congestion control: Our experiments utilize NewReno as the primary TCP congestion control mechanism. NewReno, implemented in FreeBSD, commences with the slow-start phase, starting with a conservative congestion window (*cwnd*) size of several segments, exponentially scaling until it detects potential congestion, after which it transitions into the congestion avoidance phase, where it increases the *cwnd* linearly. Suppose the congestion control mechanism detects any packet loss, in that case, it enters into fast recovery mode, where it decreases its *cwnd* size by half and prioritizes retransmitting lost packets till it receives an acknowledgment for retransmitted packets. Subsequently, it transitions back into the congestion avoidance phase and repeats the process when it encounters packet loss or after an idle timeout; it enters the slow-start phase again to probe the optimal *cwnd* size.

In the following Figure 2, we observe the total data transferred for each case in our experiment. Our results show that the total data transferred throughout the experiment are slightly higher when ECN is enabled, except for FQ-CoDel. This is because ECN notification helps NewReno detect congestion earlier, and it decreases the *cwnd* threshold to the *cwnd* value when it detects early congestion, ensuring an optimal threshold. First, we must recognize that these are the total data transferred, including retransmissions, and when we encounter higher retransmission, we observe higher RTT.

Table 2. Total data transferred (including retransmissions) in the experiment.

AQM Algorithm	Data Transferred (Mbytes)—NoECN	Data Transferred (Mbytes)—ECN
CoDel Scenario 10 Mbps	46.574638	41.101404
CoDel Scenario 1 Mbps	4.938126	4.523826
PIE Scenario 10 Mbps	50.339712	45.790667
PIE Scenario 1 Mbps	4.976113	6.371356
FQ-CoDel Scenario 10 Mbps	38.928913	53.030176
FQ-CoDel Scenario 1 Mbps	5.245358	5.571887
FQ-PIE Scenario 10 Mbps	47.984545	48.413749
FQ-PIE Scenario 1 Mbps	5.389362	5.438388
L4S Scenario 10 Mbps	48.196893	48.748529
L4S Scenario 1 Mbps	5.676679	5.159440

5.1.1. CoDel

In experiments (4)–(7), multiple instances of iperf3 were deployed under FreeBSD to generate four TCP NewReno streams with staggered start and end times (starting at t = 0, 10, 20, 30 s, and each flow lasting for 60 s). The bandwidth was set to 10 Mbps or 1 Mbps, and the delay was set to 20 ms. The internal parameters of CoDel were configured with a target of 5 ms and an interval of 100 ms, tested both with ECN enabled and disabled.

Scenario 1 (Bandwidth = 10 Mbps, Delay = 20 ms): We evaluated the performance of CoDel in two cases: (i) Case 1 is with enabled ECN; the results are shown in Figure 4, and (ii) Case 2: ECN is disabled, and the results are in Figure 5.

When ECN is disabled, an evident spike in RTT occurs at the initiation of each TCP stream, indicating the slow-start phase of NewReno, as depicted in Figures 4c and 5c. The CoDel always uses ECN-marking when ECN is enabled and never drops packets in case of extreme delays, unlike in the PIE algorithm, which drops packets if marking packets does not decrease RTT. During congestion, the NewReno algorithm reduces its *cwnd* more conservatively under ECN-enabled conditions, resulting in a higher maximum *cwnd* size and more stability, albeit with sub-optimal *cwnd* sizes. CoDel sets the ECN flag in the packet header to CE to indicate congestion and does not drop packets, unlike PIE-based AQMs. Furthermore, in the absence of ECN, *cwnd* undergoes rapid adjustments, as depicted in Figures 4b and 5b. This conservative approach also results in higher RTT but lower total throughput when ECN is enabled compared to its absence, as depicted in Figure 4 and in Table 2.

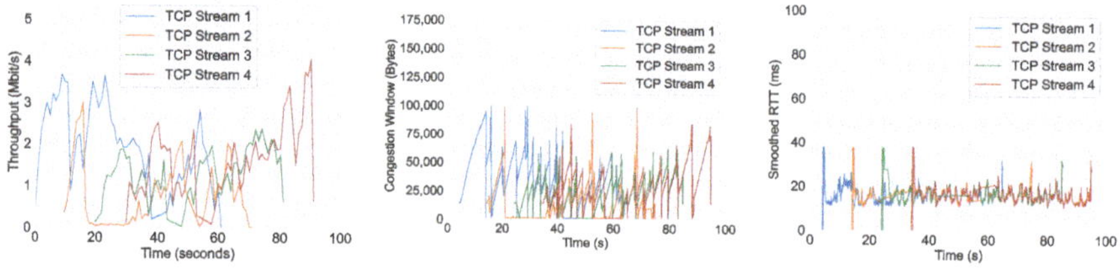

(a) (b) (c)

Figure 4. Case 1: CoDel (ECN enabled)—Scenario 1 with Bandwidth = 10 Mbps, Delay = 20 ms. (**a**) Throughput; (**b**) Congestion Window; (**c**) Smoothed TCP RTT.

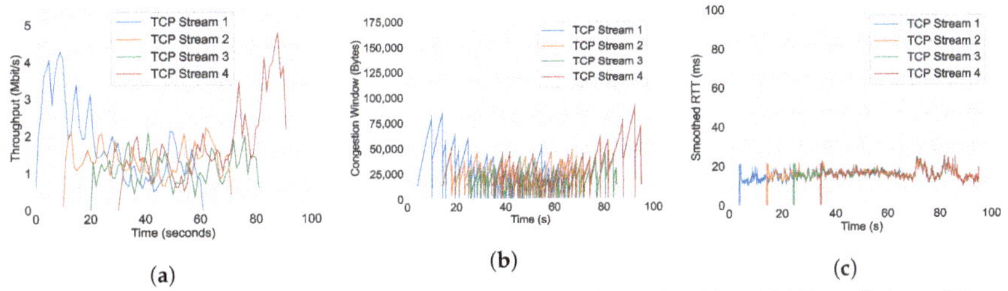

Figure 5. Case 2: CoDel (ECN disabled)—Scenario 1 with Bandwidth = 10 Mbps, Delay = 20 ms. (**a**) Throughput; (**b**) Congestion Window; (**c**) Smoothed TCP RTT.

Scenario 2 (Bandwidth = 1 Mbps, Delay = 20 ms): We evaluated the performance of CoDel in two cases: (i) Case 1 is with enabled ECN; the results are shown in Figure 6, and (ii) Case 2: ECN is disabled, and the results are in Figure 7. The conservative approach of CoDel in adjusting *cwnd* sizes when ECN is enabled results in more stable, low but unfair *cwnd* sizes when compared across multiple TCP connections, as depicted in Figures 6b and 7b. This conservative approach appears to have influenced RTT noticeably. Specifically, RTT shows fewer variations but is consistently higher than when ECN is disabled. Similarly, *cwnd* has influenced throughput to have a higher maximum throughput but unfair bandwidth sharing across multiple TCP connections, as depicted in Figures 6a and 7a.

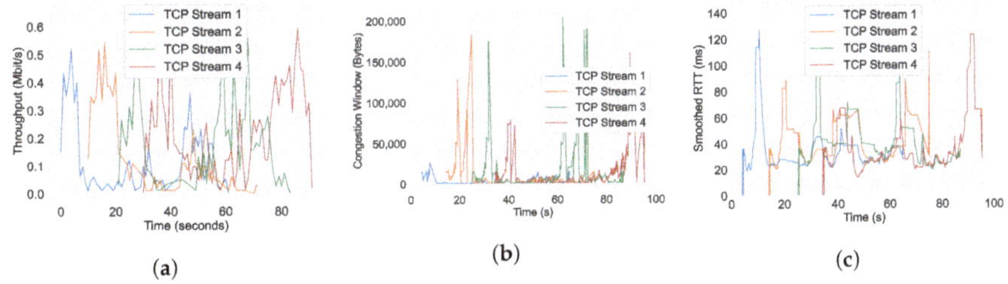

Figure 6. Case 1: CoDel (ECN enabled)—Scenario 2 with Bandwidth = 1 Mbps, Delay = 20 ms. (**a**) Throughput; (**b**) Congestion Window; (**c**) Smoothed TCP RTT.

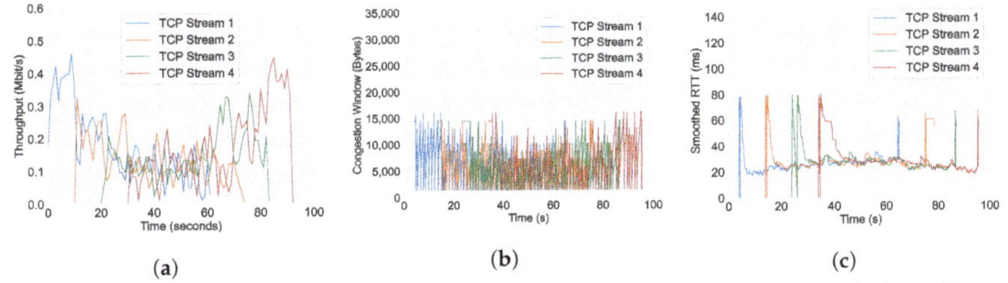

Figure 7. Case 2: CoDel (ECN disabled)—Scenario 2 with Bandwidth = 1 Mbps, Delay = 20 ms. (**a**) Throughput; (**b**) Congestion Window; (**c**) Smoothed TCP RTT.

5.1.2. PIE

In experiments (8)–(11), the internal parameters of PIE were configured with target = 15 ms, tupdate = 15 ms, alpha = 0.125, beta = 1.25, max-burst = 150 ms, and max-ecnth = 0.1.

Scenario 1 (Bandwidth = 10 Mbps, Delay = 20 ms): We evaluated the performance of PIE in two cases: (i) Case 1 is with enabled ECN; the results are shown in Figure 8, and (ii) Case 2: ECN is disabled, and the results are in Figure 9.

The PIE algorithm drops packets instead of merely marking them when the drop-probability exceeds the configurable parameter 'max_ecnth'. This behavior ensures that the congestion control optimally sets *cwnd* sizes leveraging its high variability characteristics in both cases whether ECN is enabled or disabled, as illustrated in Figures 8b and 9b.

This behavior ensures consistent throughput and RTT values across multiple TCP connections, regardless of enabling ECN or not. It results in low RTTs and stable bandwidth sharing, as depicted in Figures 8c, 9c and 8a, 9a, respectively.

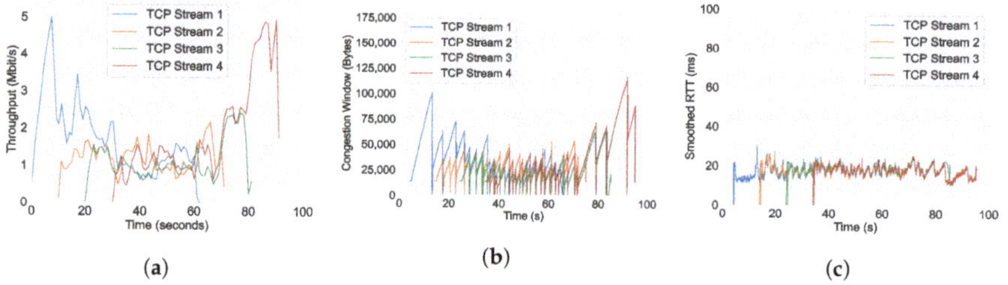

Figure 8. Case 1: PIE (ECN enabled)—Scenario 1 with Bandwidth = 10 Mbps, Delay = 20 ms. (**a**) Throughput; (**b**) Congestion Window; (**c**) Smoothed TCP RTT.

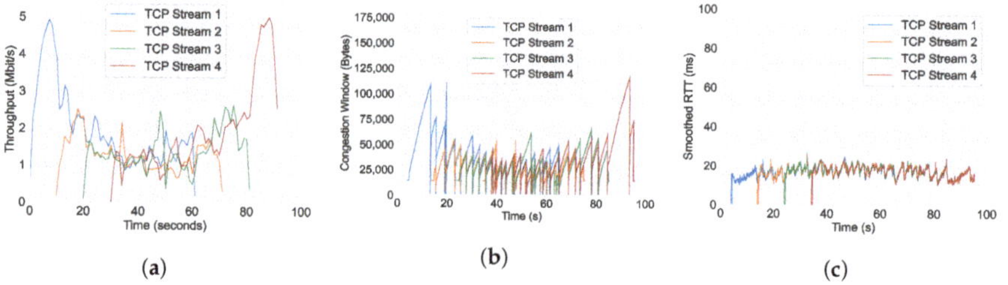

Figure 9. Case 2: PIE (ECN disabled)—Scenario 1 with Bandwidth = 10 Mbps, Delay = 20 ms. (**a**) Throughput; (**b**) Congestion Window; (**c**) Smoothed TCP RTT.

Scenario 2 (Bandwidth = 1 Mbps, Delay = 20 ms): We evaluated the performance of PIE in two cases: (i) Case 1 is with enabled ECN; the results are shown in Figure 10, and (ii) Case 2: ECN is disabled, and the results are in Figure 11. The PIE algorithm exhibits consistent behavior in low-bandwidth environments, in high-bandwidth environments characterized by low RTTs, high variations in *cwnd* in its search for optimal *cwnd* values, and optimal throughput, albeit only when ECN is disabled. Notably, with ECN enabled, significant unfairness across TCP connections is observed across all metrics, alongside high RTTs.

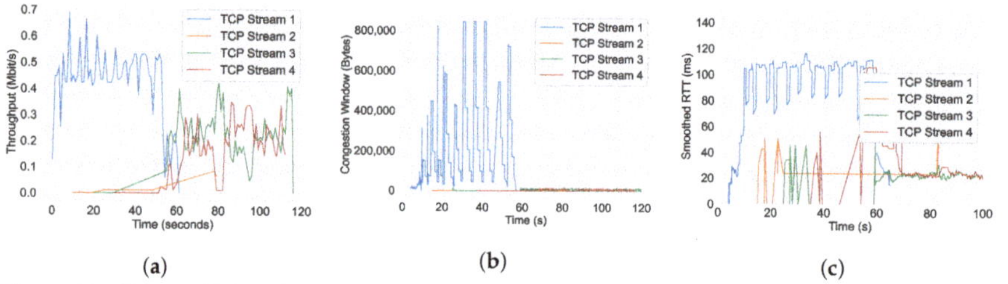

Figure 10. Case 1: PIE (ECN enabled)—Scenario 2 with Bandwidth = 1 Mbps, Delay = 20 ms. (**a**) Throughput; (**b**) Congestion Window; (**c**) Smoothed TCP RTT.

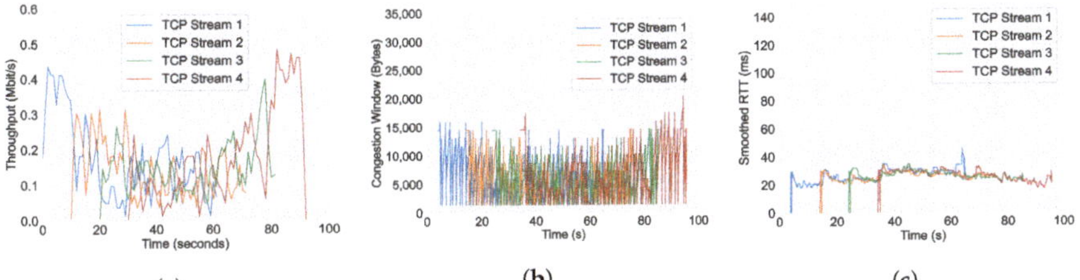

(a) (b) (c)

Figure 11. Case 2: PIE (ECN disabled)—Scenario 2 with Bandwidth = 1 Mbps, Delay = 20 ms. (**a**) Throughput; (**b**) Congestion Window; (**c**) Smoothed TCP RTT.

5.1.3. FQ-CoDel

For our experiments (12)–(15), the internal parameters of FQ-CoDel were configured with target = 5 ms, interval = 100 ms, quantum = 1514 bytes, limit = 10,240 packets, and flows = 1024 queues, tested with both ECN enabled and disabled.

Scenario 1 (Bandwidth = 10 Mbps, Delay = 20 ms) : We evaluated the performance of FQ-CoDel in two cases: Case 1 with enabled ECN and Case 2 with disabled ECN for comparison. Figures 12 and 13 present the results for the two cases, respectively.

FQ-CoDel shows significant fairness in throughput across connections regardless of ECN, as shown in the throughput Figure 12a where ECN is enabled and Figure 13a where ECN is disabled. FQ-CoDel shows higher maximum *cwnd* values and high unfairness, prioritizing more recent TCP connections when ECN is enabled, illustrated in Figure 12b. Unlike when ECN is disabled, Figure 13b displays a sawtooth pattern indicating the transition from congestion avoidance to fast-retransmit during packet loss and return to the congestion avoidance phase.

When ECN is enabled, FQ-CoDel shows very high RTT due to higher retransmissions, as it does not drop packets and only uses ECN notification to indicate congestion, unlike PIE, FQ-PIE, and L4S, as illustrated in Figure 12c. This results in high data transfer, as shown in Table 2, as retransmission is counted as part of the data transfer metric. In contrast, FQ-CoDel shows admirably low RTT when ECN is disabled, indicating that dropping packets is advisable during high congestion, similar to PIE-based algorithms. In future evaluations, it is better advised to transfer video files and other types of data transmission and analyze packet loss and retransmissions.

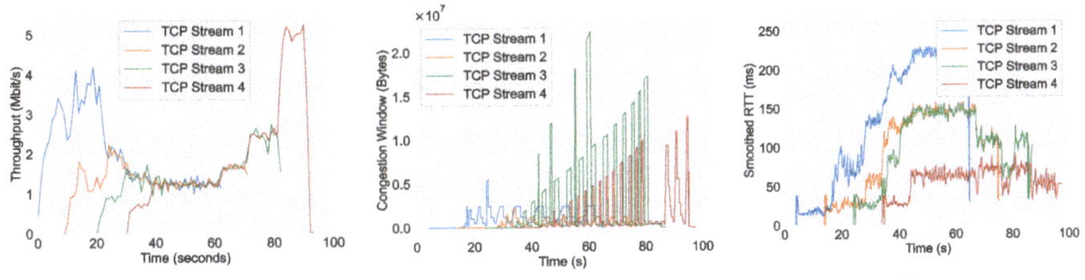

(a) (b) (c)

Figure 12. Case 1: FQ-CoDel (ECN enabled)—Scenario 1 with Bandwidth = 10 Mbps, Delay = 20 ms. (**a**) Throughput; (**b**) Congestion Window; (**c**) Smoothed TCP RTT.

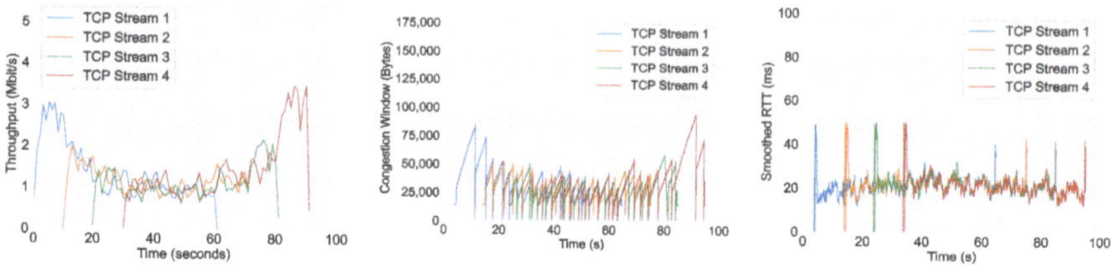

(a) (b) (c)

Figure 13. Case 2: FQ-CoDel (ECN disabled)—Scenario 1 with Bandwidth = 10 Mbps, Delay = 20 ms. (**a**) Throughput; (**b**) Congestion Window; (**c**) Smoothed TCP RTT.

Scenario 2 (Bandwidth = 1 Mbps, Delay = 20 ms): We evaluated the performance of FQ-CoDel in two cases, Case 1 with ECN enabled and Case 2 with ECN disabled, for comparison. Figures 14 and 15 present the results for the two cases, respectively. FQ-CoDel shows similar fairness in throughput regardless of ECN, even though it shows high variation in throughput in Figure 14a when ECN is enabled. FQ-CoDel shows similar *cwnd* values to Scenario 1, except it shows higher variations in *cwnd* when ECN is disabled, as depicted in Figure 15b, indicating high packet loss. When ECN is disabled, FQ-CoDel drops packets during congestion, thus ensuring RTT is low for all successfully transferred packets, as illustrated in Figure 15c.

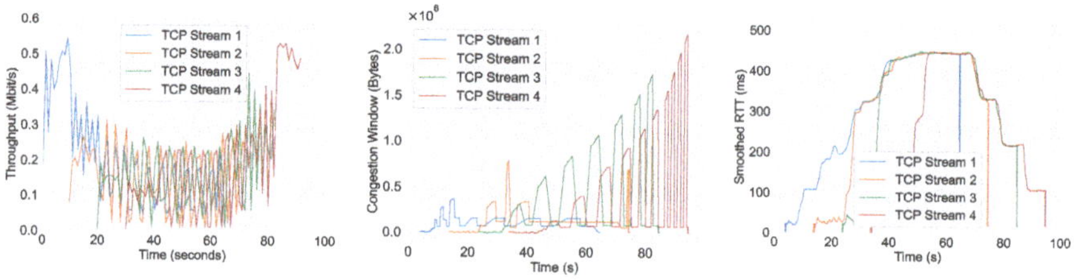

(a) (b) (c)

Figure 14. Case 1: FQ-CoDel (ECN enabled)—Scenario 2 with Bandwidth = 1 Mbps, Delay = 20 ms. (**a**) Throughput; (**b**) Congestion Window; (**c**) Smoothed TCP RTT.

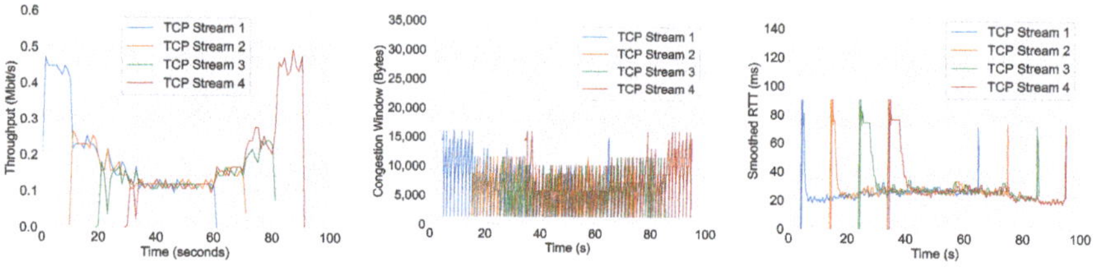

(a) (b) (c)

Figure 15. Case 2: FQ-CoDel (ECN disabled)—Scenario 2 with Bandwidth = 1 Mbps, Delay = 20 ms. (**a**) Throughput; (**b**) Congestion Window; (**c**) Smoothed TCP RTT.

5.1.4. FQ-PIE

In experiments (16)–(19), The internal parameters of FQ-PIE were configured with target = 15 ms, tupdate = 15 ms, alpha = 0.125, beta = 1.25, max-burst = 150 ms, max-ecnth = 0.1, quantum = 1514 bytes, limit = 10,240 packets, and flows = 6 queues.

Scenario 1 (Bandwidth = 10 Mbps, Delay = 20 ms): We evaluated the performance of FQ-PIE in two cases: (i) Case 1 is with enabled ECN; the results are shown in Figure 16, and (ii) Case 2: ECN is disabled, and the results are in Figure 17.

Similarly to PIE, The FQ-PIE algorithm drops packets instead of merely marking them when the drop probability exceeds the configurable parameter 'max_ecnth'. This behavior ensures that the congestion control optimally sets *cwnd* sizes, leveraging its high variability characteristics whether ECN is enabled or disabled, as illustrated in Figures 16b and 17b.

This conservative behavior results in near consistent throughput and RTT values across multiple TCP connections, regardless of enabling ECN, though only after it starts dropping packets in the case of ECN, causing a slight delay in its reduction of *cwnd* to optimal levels. It results in low RTTs and stable bandwidth sharing, as depicted in Figures 8c, 9c and 8a, 9a, respectively. Upon closer examination, Figure 16c shows higher RTT when ECN is enabled, as illustrated. Subsequently, Figure 16a illustrates a higher throughput and more unfairness when compared to its counterpart in Figure 17a. This outcome stems from NewReno's conservative approach in reducing its *cwnd* size when ECN is enabled. In contrast, NewReno instantly halves its *cwnd* upon detecting packet loss and then enters fast-recovery mode.

In Figure 16c, we see a bit more instability than in Figure 17c.

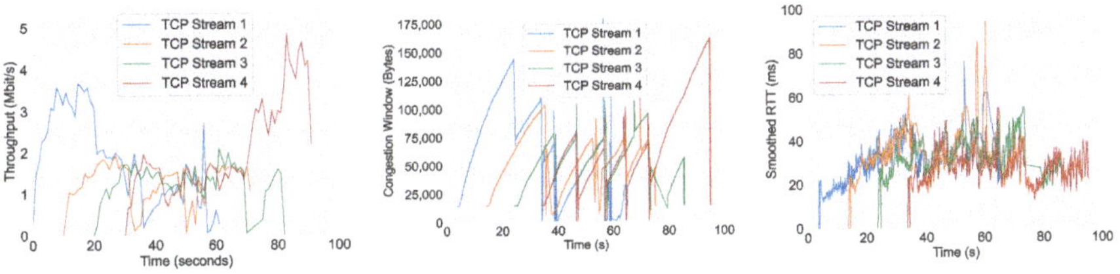

(a) (b) (c)

Figure 16. Case 1: FQ-PIE (ECN enabled)—Scenario 1 with Bandwidth = 10 Mbps, Delay = 20 ms. (**a**) Throughput; (**b**) Congestion Window; (**c**) Smoothed TCP RTT.

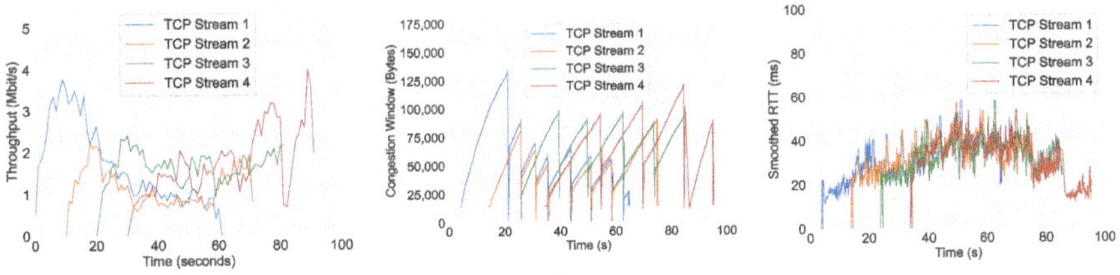

(a) (b) (c)

Figure 17. Case 2: FQ-PIE (ECN disabled)—Scenario 1 with Bandwidth = 10 Mbps, Delay = 20 ms. (**a**) Throughput; (**b**) Congestion Window; (**c**) Smoothed TCP RTT.

Scenario 2 (Bandwidth = 1 Mbps, Delay = 20 ms): We evaluated the performance of FQ-PIE in two cases, Case 1 with ECN enabled and Case 2 with ECN disabled, for comparison. Figures 18 and 19 present the results for the two cases.

The FQ-PIE algorithm exhibits consistent behavior in low-bandwidth environments as in high-bandwidth environments, characterized by slight unfairness and slightly elevated RTTs, especially when ECN is enabled.

Compared to the high-bandwidth environment in scenario 1, scenario 2 demonstrates notably more exaggerated RTT, particularly in TCP connection 2. This increase in RTT directly results from lower available bandwidth and increased waiting time due to congestion and packet loss. The resulting diminished performance of throughput and *cwnd* due to lower bandwidth is as expected in such scenarios.

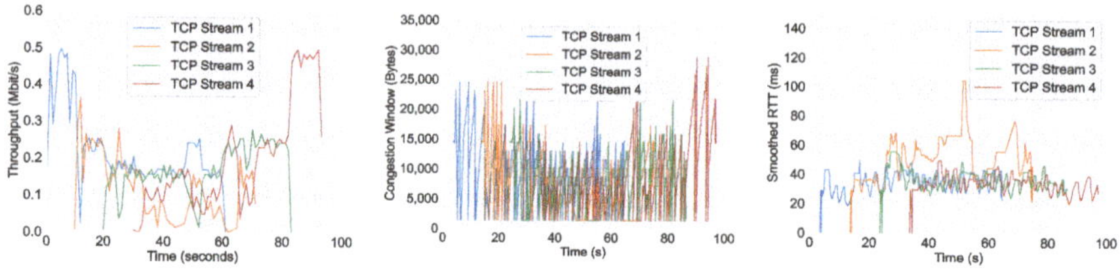

(**a**) (**b**) (**c**)

Figure 18. Case 1: FQ-PIE (ECN enabled)—Scenario 2 with Bandwidth = 1 Mbps, Delay = 20 ms. (**a**) Throughput; (**b**) Congestion Window; (**c**) Smoothed TCP RTT.

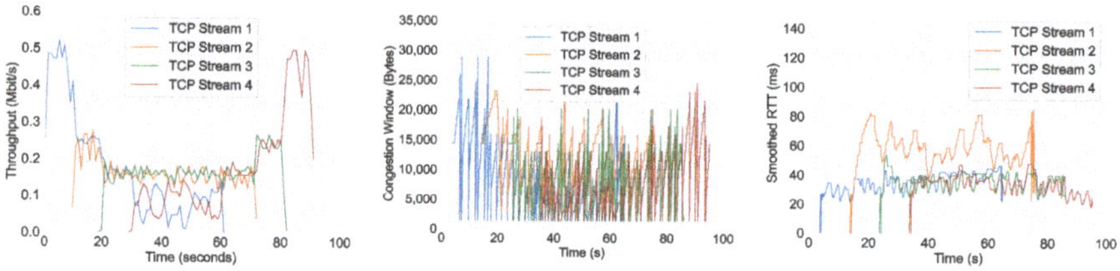

(**a**) (**b**) (**c**)

Figure 19. Case 2: FQ-PIE (ECN disabled)—Scenario 2 with Bandwidth = 1 Mbps, Delay = 20 ms. (**a**) Throughput; (**b**) Congestion Window; (**c**) Smoothed TCP RTT.

5.1.5. L4S

In experiments (20)–(23), the internal parameters of L4S were configured with target = 15 ms, tupdate = 15 ms, alpha = 0.125, beta = 1.25, max-burst = 150 ms, max-ecnth = 0.1, quantum = 1514 bytes, limit = 10,240 packets, and flows = 6 queues.

Scenario 1 (Bandwidth = 10 Mbps, Delay = 20 ms): We employed two cases: (i) Case 1 is with enabled ECN; the results are shown in Figure 20, and (ii) Case 2: ECN is disabled, and the results are in Figure 21.

L4S is based on FQ-PIE, so it behaves quite similarly, dropping packets instead of marking them when they exceed the ECN threshold. Upon receiving duplicate ACKS, the NewReno algorithm transitions from the slow-start phase to the congestion avoidance phase. Upon discovering retransmission timeout due to packet loss or high packet delay, it sets *cwnd* to the maximum segment size of a TCP(MSS), and the 'ssh_thrsh'is halved and then enters the congestion avoidance phase. In the case of ECN, it sets the *cwnd* threshold to the current *cwnd* and enters the congestion avoidance phase. We can see this process in Figure 20b, and in Figure 21b, we can observe L4S going into fast-recovery and then into congestion avoidance immediately.

L4S segregates incoming packets into separate L4S and classic queues, prioritizing L4S packets, so we observe a noticeably reduced overall RTT when ECN is enabled, as depicted in Figure 20c, compared to in Figure 21c where ECN is disabled. If ECN is enabled, all data-carrying packets in a TCP transmission are marked with ECN capability. Still, other packets, like acknowledgment (ACK) packets sent by the server, do not have ECN enabled in their packet header and are thus segregated into separate classic queues. Its prioritization scheme allows for more buffer capacity and prioritization for L4S packets.

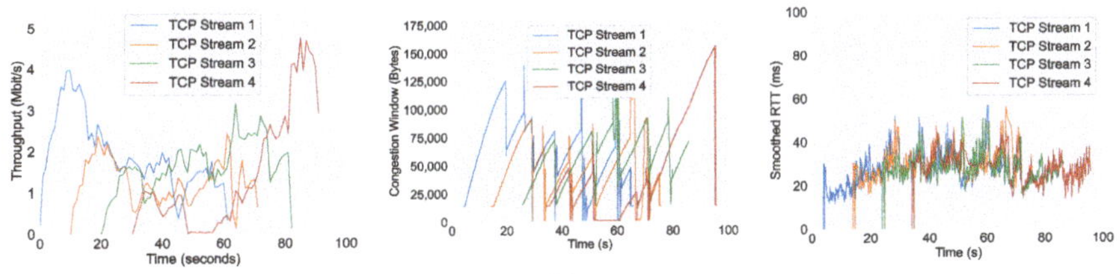

(a) (b) (c)

Figure 20. Case 1: L4S (ECN enabled)—Scenario 1 with Bandwidth = 10 Mbps, Delay = 20 ms. (**a**) Throughput; (**b**) Congestion Window; (**c**) Smoothed TCP RTT.

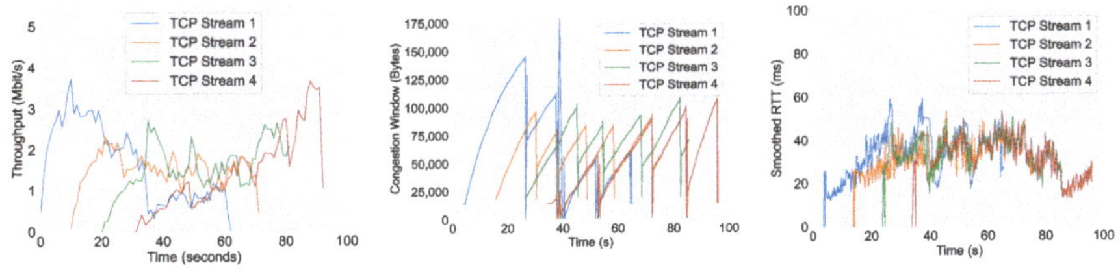

(a) (b) (c)

Figure 21. Case 2: L4S (ECN disabled)—Scenario 1 with Bandwidth = 10 Mbps, Delay = 20 ms. (**a**) Throughput; (**b**) Congestion Window; (**c**) Smoothed TCP RTT.

Scenario 2 (Bandwidth = 1 Mbps, Delay = 20 ms): We evaluated the performance of L4S in two cases: Case 1 with enabled ECN and Case 2 with disabled ECN for comparison. Figures 22 and 23 present the results for the two cases.

Similarly to FQ-PIE, L4S exhibits consistent behavior in both low- and high-bandwidth environments. In a low-bandwidth environment, reduced bandwidth capacity induces greater *cwnd* fluctuation due to higher packet loss, as illustrated in Figures 22b and 23b. This higher *cwnd* variation adversely affects throughput and RTT, inducing elevated levels of unfairness when bandwidth is low compared to when bandwidth is high, as depicted in Figures 22c and 23c.

L4S in low-bandwidth environment demonstrates notably more exaggerated RTT when ECN is disabled. This increase in RTT is a direct consequence of lower available bandwidth, resulting in diminished throughput and performance of *cwnd* due to higher packet loss and congestion.

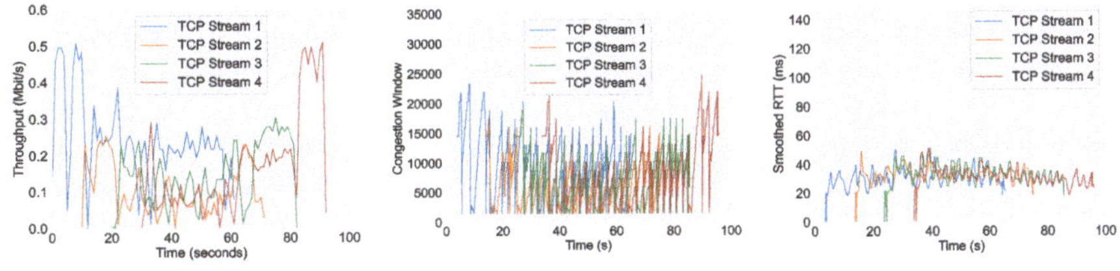

(a) (b) (c)

Figure 22. Case 1: L4S (ECN enabled)—Scenario 2 with Bandwidth = 1 Mbps, Delay = 20 ms. (**a**) Throughput; (**b**) Congestion Window; (**c**) Smoothed TCP RTT.

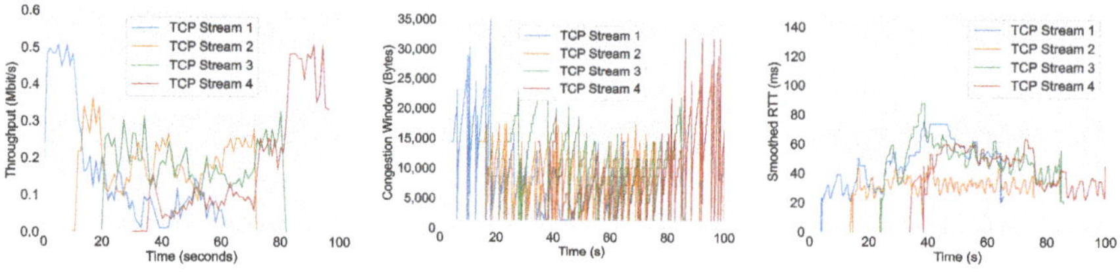

(a) (b) (c)

Figure 23. Case 2: L4S (ECN disabled)—Scenario 2 with Bandwidth = 1 Mbps, Delay = 20 ms. (**a**) Throughput; (**b**) Congestion Window; (**c**) Smoothed TCP RTT.

5.2. A3C-L4S Evaluation

We have established an additional test environment using virtual machines specifically for evaluating A3C-L4S. Figure 24 shows this setup, which now includes two routers instead of one. This network configuration involves a source host, destination host, and two intermediary routers.

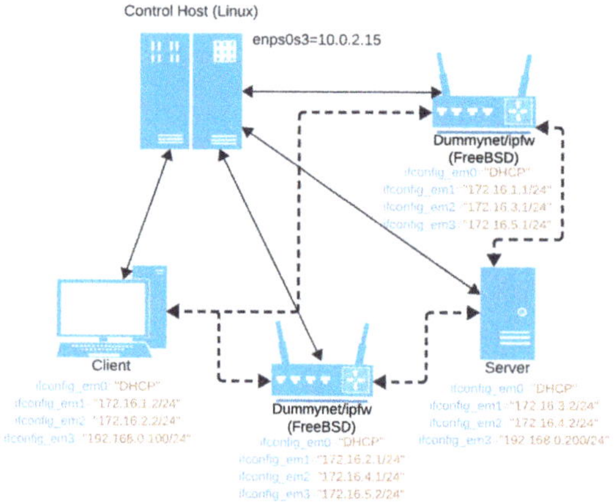

Figure 24. Network topology utilized for data collection for A3C-L4S model.

To gather more data, we have two iperf3 experiments going on simultaneously in each path in different directions. We now have four different data streams from which we collect data to feed our A3C model.

We utilize the normalized L4S data from the kernel logs generated from experimentation and testing to pass into the DDPG agent's observation space for training. Our A3C model runs the training session for a certain number of steps. Each episode resets and starts from a new data point. We trained our A3C model for 100 episodes. We plot the average reward in each episode against the episode index to observe how the rate and utility improve over each training session as the A3C learns more.

5.2.1. Convergence of A3C Model

We can see in Figure 25 the convergence of the A3C model. The figure plots the average epoch or episode reward against the epoch index. The average reward gradually increases, quietly approaching the limit, demonstrating A3C's ability to minimize queue delay for each agent. We can improve A3C with more training time and with more data. Especially in online learning, the A3C model can extract higher performance out of the environment. The A3C model is computationally more expensive and time-consuming than other models. We might want to train our data on a much bigger dataset and for longer.

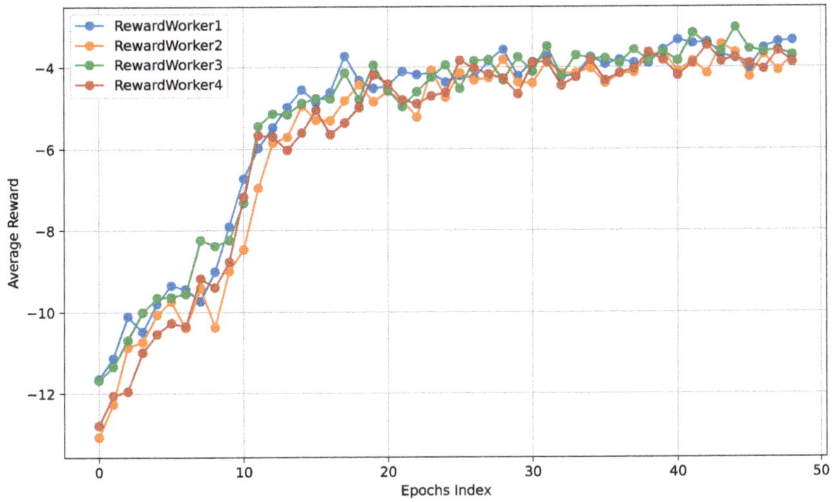

Figure 25. Evolution of the average reward (R_t) of the trained A3C model over the entire fifty epochs.

PIE-based AQM algorithms like our modified L4S AQM recalculate its ECN marking probability at regular time intervals (*tupdate*), which is set to 15 ms by default unless explicitly configured differently. Likewise, periodically, after a certain number of actions or steps (controlled by *args_update_interval*), each worker thread transmits its gradients to the global network, thereby determining the frequency of global network parameter updates. This dual strategy allows for adaptive control over the stability and convergence of the A3C algorithm, balancing computational efficiency with performance optimization. In highly dynamic and unstable network environments, increasing the update frequency for both A3C and L4S proves beneficial in improving the stability and learning efficacy of the A3C algorithm. Future refinements based on comprehensive testing across diverse scenarios, including mobile networks and IoT environments, may involve optimizing these intervals to update global network parameters more frequently and recalculate ECN-marking probabilities.

We can also see the reward data for each worker agent and the global network. Each agent's reward increases steadily and shows no adverse performance issues. It also does not seem to have hit a constant reward yet, so we might need to run the model for longer. This graph tells us our A3C model is feasible, and we can start with it and fine-tune it with more training.

5.2.2. Comparing Predicted QDelay vs. Actual QDelay

We can see how A3C affects the network's performance, mainly focusing on queue delay in the following Figure 26 graphs. The predicted queue delay is already very low after training and keeps decreasing until it hits a specific limit, beyond which it cannot improve its performance without more data. All the agents perform similarly because we work in a virtual environment with no other traffic in addition to our experiments. We have also set the same bandwidth, delay, loss, and different configurations on both routers. We might also want to introduce irregular traffic differences between the end hosts in each path.

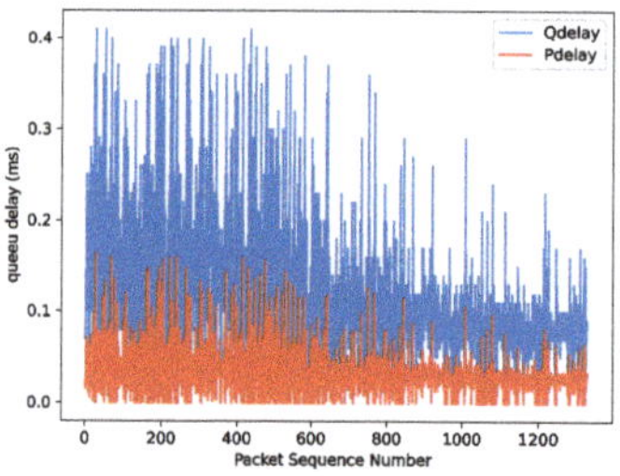

(a)

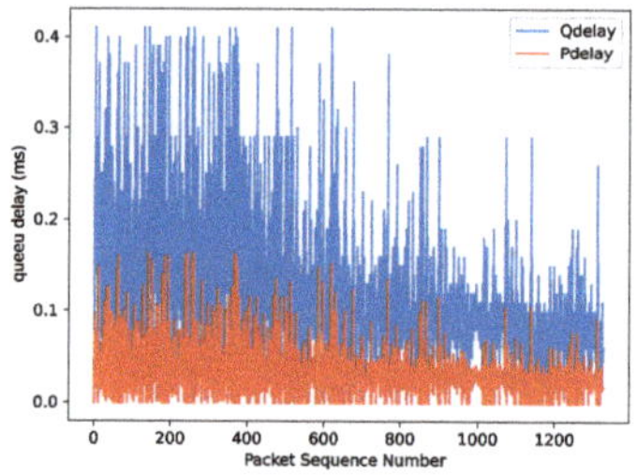

(b)

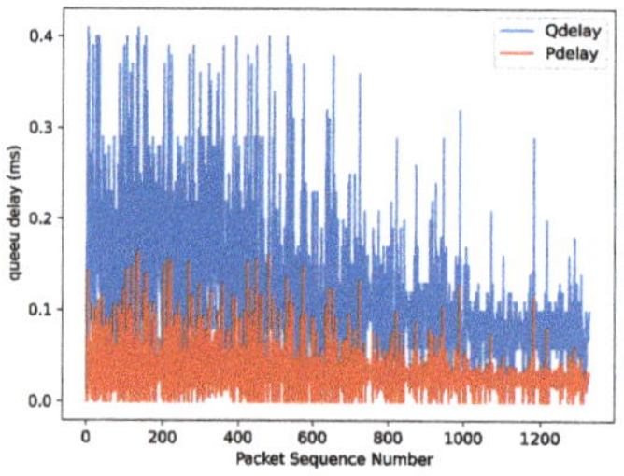

(c)

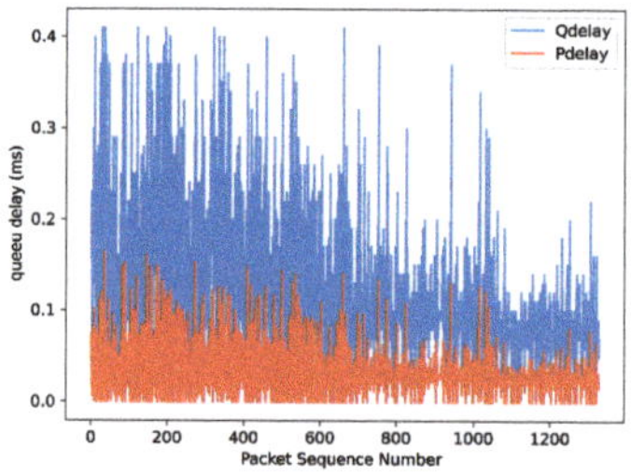

(d)

Figure 26. Predicted queue delay vs. actual queue delay for all workers during packet transmission. (**a**) Predicted QDelay vs. Actual QDelay—Agent Worker 1; (**b**) Predicted QDelay vs. Actual QDelay—Agent Worker 2; (**c**) Predicted QDelay vs. Actual Qdelay—Agent Worker 3; (**d**) Predicted QDelay vs. Actual Qdelay—Agent Worker 4.

5.2.3. Comparing Predicted QDelay vs. Actual QDelay with Varying Reward Scaling Factor

The following Figure 27 illustrates the predicted queue delay (QDelay) in a three-dimensional graph. We also vary the 'alpha' reward scaling factor variable from 10 to 100. We can see how the Qdelay decreases with more training.

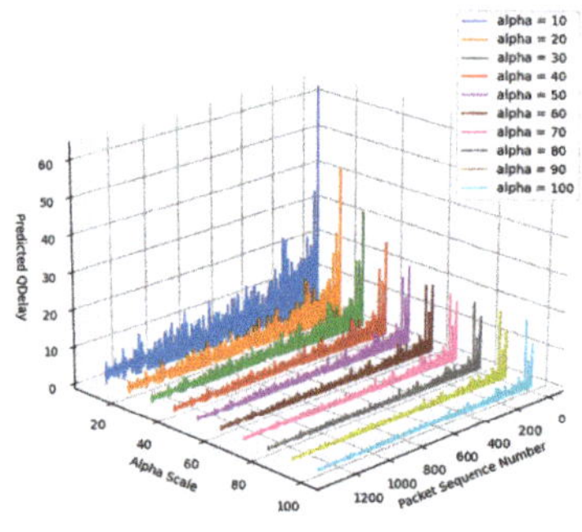

(a)

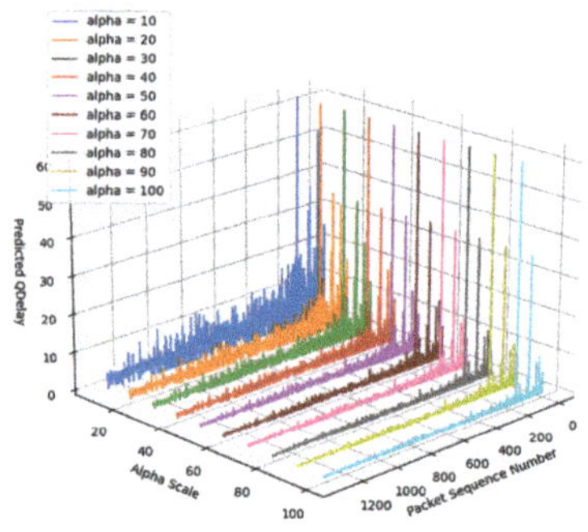

(b)

Figure 27. *Cont.*

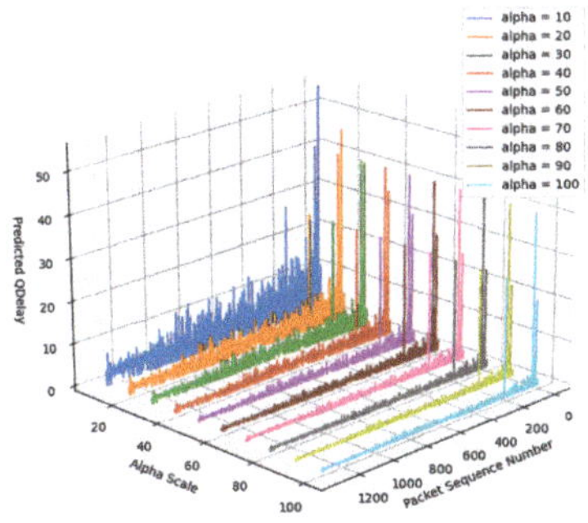

(c)

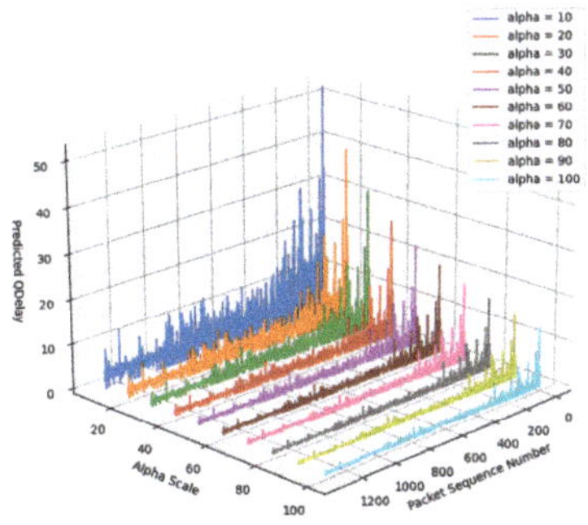

(d)

Figure 27. Predicted queue delay vs. actual queue delay for all workers with varying reward scaling factor in units of 100 μs. (**a**) Predicted QDelay with varying reward scaling factor Agent Worker 1; (**b**) Predicted QDelay with varying reward scaling factor Agent Worker 2; (**c**) Predicted QDelay with varying reward scaling factor Agent Worker 3; (**d**) Predicted QDelay with varying reward scaling factor Agent Worker 4.

6. Results Analysis and Discussion

In the first part of our research, we compared multiple AQM algorithms with L4S and tested them in two different scenarios: Scenario A—10 Mbps and Scenario B—1 Mbps.

We deployed multiple instances of iperf3 under FreeBSD to generate four TCP NewReno flows with staggered start and end times (starting at t = 0, 10, 20, and 30 s and each flow lasting 60 s).

Each instance of FQ-CoDel was configured for target 5 ms, interval 100 ms, quantum 1514 bytes and with 10,240 packets of bottleneck buffering shared by 1024 FQ-CoDel sub-queues.

Each instance of FQ-PIE was configured for target 15 ms, tupdate 15 ms, max_burst 100 ms, quantum 1514 bytes, and with 10,240 packets of bottleneck buffering shared by six FQ-PIE sub-queues. We have data for both cases when ECN was enabled and disabled. We use six sub-queues because our L4S also uses six sub-queues, which helps us compare both algorithms under similar conditions.

Each instance of L4S was configured for target 15 ms, tupdate 15 ms, max_burst 100 ms, quantum 1514 bytes, and with 10,240 packets of bottleneck buffering shared by three pairs of L4S sub-queues.

We have data for both cases when ECN was enabled and disabled.

The main difference in scenarios is the bandwidth. Scenario A's bandwidth is 10 Mbps; in Scenario B, the bandwidth is 1 Mbps.

6.1. Performance of Throughput across Varying AQM Algorithms

Scenario 1 (Bandwidth = 10 Mbps, Delay = 20 ms):

We evaluated the throughput performance of FQ-CoDel, FQ-PIE, and L4S across two scenarios: Case 1 with ECN enabled and Case 2 with ECN disabled. Figures 28 and 29 illustrates the results for both cases.

Our findings show that FQ-CoDel achieves fairness across all TCP connections, whereas FQ-PIE and L4S exhibit significant unfairness. Subsequently, FQ-PIE and L4S exhibit elevated unfairness when ECN is enabled rather than disabled. Enabling ECN leads NewReno to detect congestion sooner, causing an earlier reduction in its *cwnd* threshold and quicker entry into congestion avoidance mode. This behavior sustains higher *cwnd* levels, resulting in more data transferred, as indicated in Table 2 when ECN is enabled, especially L4S. L4S exhibits higher throughput than FQ-PIE when ECN is enabled, showing superior performance. We can also observe that the maximum throughput attained when ECN notification is enabled is higher compared to when ECN is disabled.

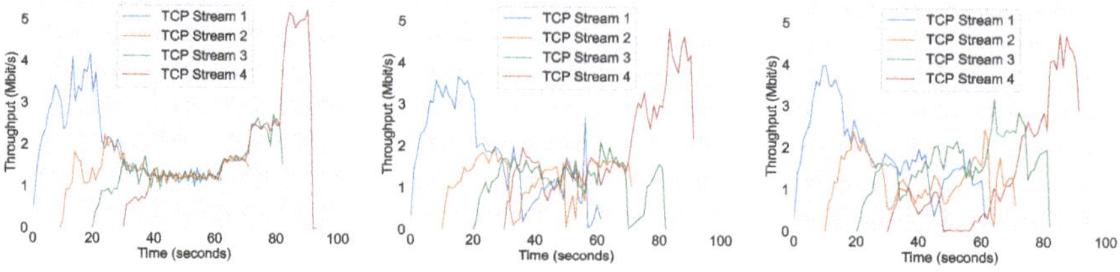

(a) (b) (c)

Figure 28. Case 1: (ECN enabled) Throughput Scenario 1 with Bandwidth = 10 Mbps, Delay = 20 ms. (**a**) FQ-CoDel (Throughput); (**b**) FQ-PIE (Throughput); (**c**) L4S (Throughput).

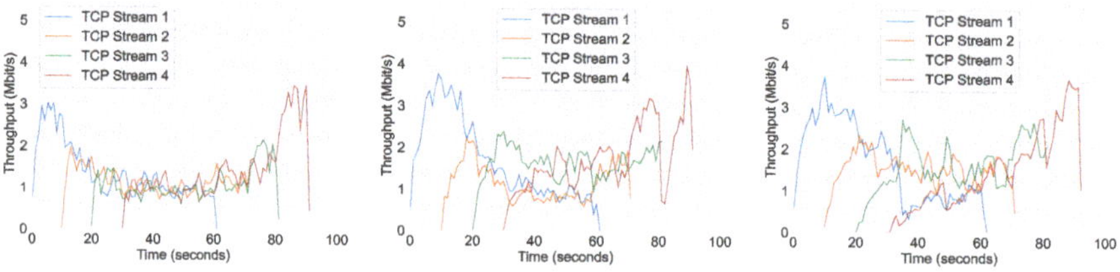

(a) (b) (c)

Figure 29. Case 2: (ECN disabled) Throughput Scenario 1 with Bandwidth = 10 Mbps, Delay = 20 ms. (**a**) FQ-CoDel (Throughput); (**b**) FQ-PIE (Throughput); (**c**) L4S (Throughput).

Scenario 2 (Bandwidth = 1 Mbps, Delay = 20 ms): We evaluated the performance of FQ-CoDel, FQ-PIE, and L4S in two cases: Case 1 with ECN enabled and Case 2 with ECN disabled for comparison. Figures 30 and 31 showcase these two cases' results. Similarly to Scenario 1, FQ-PIE and L4S exhibit higher unfairness in throughput when ECN is enabled due to NewReno's early congestion detection, which sends New Reno directly into the congestion avoidance phase. This leads to higher sustained *cwnd* values and higher total data transferred, at least in the case of FQ-PIE. L4S shows higher data transfer when ECN is disabled; refer to Table 2. L4S has the same buffer size, but its lower bandwidth causes excessive delays. We can also attribute it to the uneven distribution of packets into their respective classic and L4S queues. The low-bandwidth environment has resulted in FQ-CoDel showing high variations in throughput, though it seems to have maintained fairness across its multiple TCP connections.

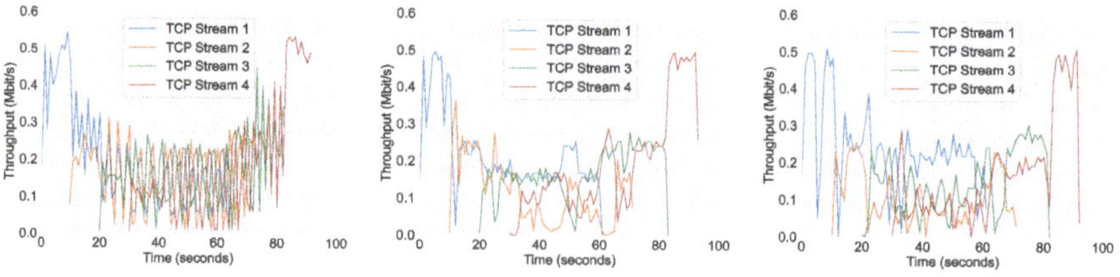

(a) (b) (c)

Figure 30. Case 1: (ECN enabled) Throughput Scenario 2 with Bandwidth = 1 Mbps, Delay = 20 ms. (**a FQ-CoDel (Throughput)**); (**b**) FQ-PIE (Throughput); (**c**) L4S (Throughput).

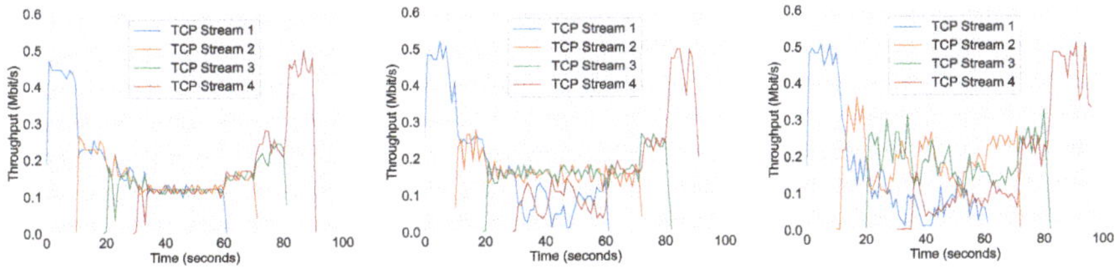

(a) (b) (c)

Figure 31. Case 2: (ECN disabled) Throughput Scenario 2 with Bandwidth = 1 Mbps, Delay = 20 ms. (**a**) FQ-CoDel (Throughput); (**b**) FQ-PIE (Throughput); (**c**) L4S (Throughput).

6.2. Performance of RTT across Varying AQM Algorithms

Scenario 1 (Bandwidth = 10 Mbps, Delay = 20 ms): We evaluated the performance of FQ-CoDel, FQ-PIE, and L4S in two cases: Case 1 with enabled ECN and Case 2 with ECN disabled for comparison. Figures 32 and 33 present the results for the two cases.

In Figure 32a, where ECN is disabled, FQ-CoDel exhibits high RTT but demonstrates higher data transfer due to higher retransmissions, as shown in Table 2. This is mainly because FQ-CoDel does not drop packets from its buffer when congestion is too high, unlike FQ-PIE and L4S. Upon disabling ECN, FQ-CoDel has a very similar RTT to CoDel, with the lowest consistent RTT among its competitors, as depicted in Figure 33a.

L4S demonstrates a distinct reduction in RTT when ECN is enabled, highlighting the efficacy of its prioritization strategies. This contrasts with FQ-PIE, which exhibits higher RTT and occasional fairness concerns, particularly around the 60-second mark when ECN is enabled. When ECN is disabled, both L4S and FQ-PIE display comparable RTT characterized by slightly higher RTT. Figure 33b,c depict their RTT behavior without ECN, whereas Figures 32b and 34c illustrate the impact of ECN on their performance metrics.

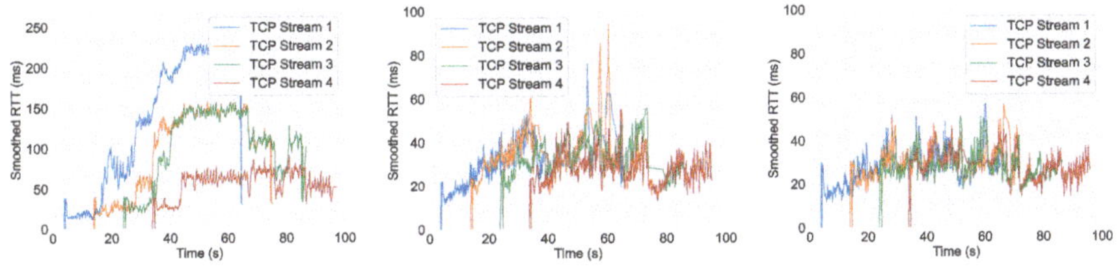

(a) (b) (c)

Figure 32. Case 1: (ECN enabled) Smoothed TCP RTT measured in seconds for Scenario 1 with Bandwidth = 10 Mbps, Delay = 20 ms. (**a**) FQ-CoDel (Smoothed RTT); (**b**) FQ-PIE (Smoothed RTT); (**c**) L4S (Smoothed RTT).

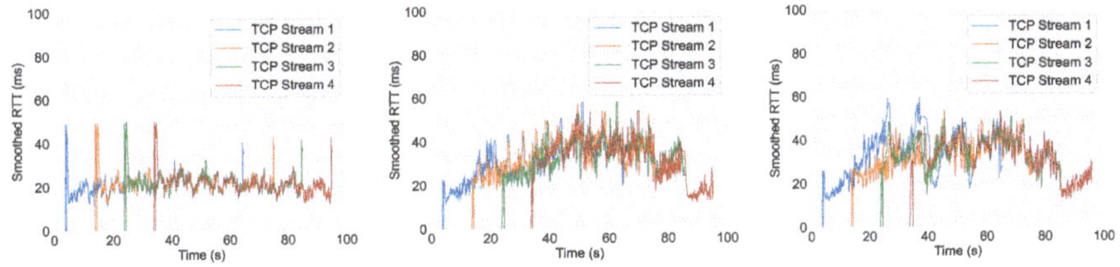

(a) (b) (c)

Figure 33. Case 2: (ECN disabled) Smoothed TCP RTT measured in seconds for Scenario 1 with Bandwidth = 10 Mbps, Delay = 20 ms. (**a**) FQ-CoDel (Smoothed RTT); (**b**) FQ-PIE (Smoothed RTT); (**c**) L4S (Smoothed RTT).

Scenario 2 (Bandwidth = 1 Mbps, Delay = 20 ms):

We evaluated the performance of FQ-CoDel, FQ-PIE, and L4S in two cases: Case 1 with ECN enabled and Case 2 with ECN disabled for comparison. Figures 34 and 35 present the results for these two cases.

In both low and high-bandwidth environments, FQ-CoDel, FQ-PIE, and L4S demonstrate similar RTT behaviors. FQ-CoDel exhibits significantly high RTT when ECN is enabled (Figure 34a), contrasting sharply with its low RTT when ECN is disabled (Figure 35a), similar to scenario 1. Subsequently, FQ-PIE shows high RTT and unfairness among connections irrespective of ECN status, as depicted in Figures 34b and 35b. Notable, L4S shows significantly reduced RTT and enhanced fairness with ECN enabled due to its prioritization mechanisms. Conversely, with ECN disabled, L4S shows elevated RTT, except for TCP stream two.

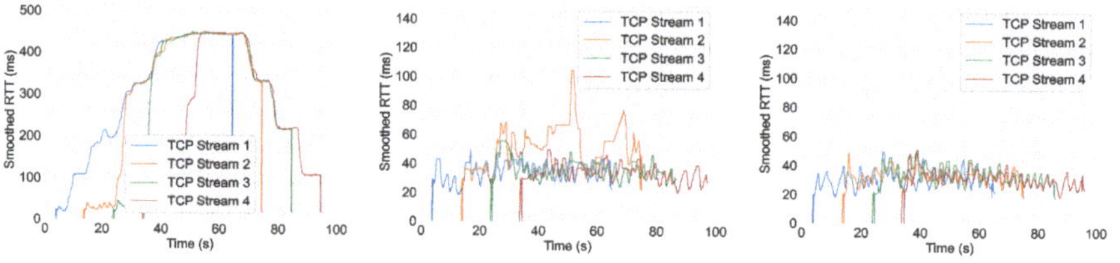

(a) (b) (c)

Figure 34. Case 1: (ECN enabled) Smoothed TCP RTT measured in seconds for Scenario 2 with Bandwidth = 1 Mbps, Delay = 20 ms. (**a**) FQ-CoDel (Smoothed RTT); (**b**) FQ-PIE (Smoothed RTT); (**c**) L4S (Smoothed RTT).

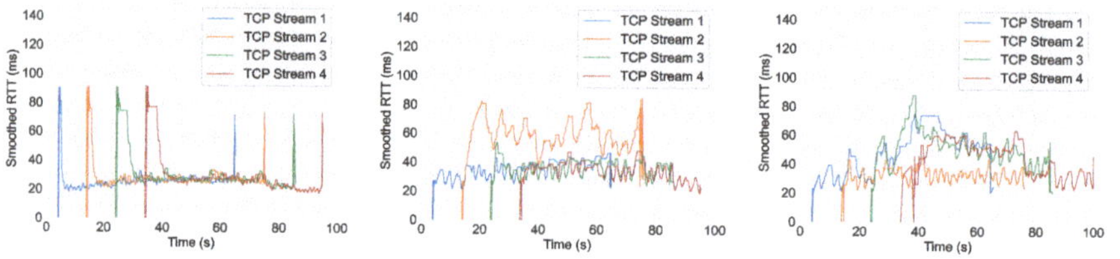

(a) (b) (c)

Figure 35. Case 2:(ECN disabled) Smoothed TCP RTT measured in seconds for Scenario 2 with Bandwidth = 1 Mbps, Delay = 20 ms. (**a**) FQ-CoDel (Smoothed RTT); (**b**) FQ-PIE (Smoothed RTT); (**c**) L4S (Smoothed RTT).

FQ-CoDel, FQ-PIE, and L4S experience initial RTT spikes during connection initiation, typical of NewReno's slow-start phase with exponential *cwnd* growth. It then transitions into congestion avoidance upon receiving multiple acknowledgments or enters fast recovery upon detecting packet loss due to retransmission timeout (RTO), finally entering congestion avoidance. FQ-CoDel avoids dropping packets when ECN is enabled, unlike FQ-PIE and L4S, which drop packets exceeding the ECN threshold. L4S additionally segregates packets into L4S and classic queues, prioritizing L4S traffic for significantly reduced RTT under ECN, as depicted in Figures 32c and 34c, compared to Figures 33c and 35c where ECN is disabled. When ECN is enabled, all data-carrying packets in TCP transmissions are marked with ECN capability. However, acknowledgment (ACK) packets from the server lack ECN in their headers and are segregated into classic queues. This prioritization scheme ensures more buffer capacity and prioritizes L4S packets, as seen in our experiments. The marginal improvements in RTT facilitated by L4S represent critical advancements for latency-sensitive applications, significantly enhancing user experience, particularly during scaling. Not to forget, L4S shows higher throughput.

6.3. Performance of Congestion Window across Varying AQM Algorithms

Scenario 1 (Bandwidth = 10 Mbps, Delay = 20 ms): We evaluated the performance of FQ-CoDel, FQ-PIE and L4S in two cases: Case 1 with enabled ECN and Case 2 with ECN disabled, for comparison. Figures 36 and 37 present the results for the two cases.

In the FQ-CoDel algorithm with ECN enabled (Figure 36a), the *cwnd* for some TCP connections steadily increases over time. There seems to be extreme unfairness in its *cwnd* sizes across connections in the bottleneck, predominately showing a preference for TCP connections that started later. When ECN is disabled (Figure 37a), the *cwnd* exhibits periodic oscillation due to frequent RTO and NewReno's response to congestion, and the *cwnd* has a lower maximum *cwnd* size than other algorithms. This directly influences the total data transferred throughout the process across all connections, as seen in Table 2, significantly lower than its L4S and FQ-PIE competitors when ECN is disabled.

In the FQ-PIE and L4S algorithms, regardless of ECN, as illustrated in (Figure 36b,c when ECN is enabled, and Figure 37b,c when ECN is disabled), the *cwnd* displays a sawtooth pattern characterized by sharp increases in *cwnd* followed by rapid decreases upon detecting packet loss. This reflects NewReno's adaptive behavior to maximize throughput while avoiding congestion.

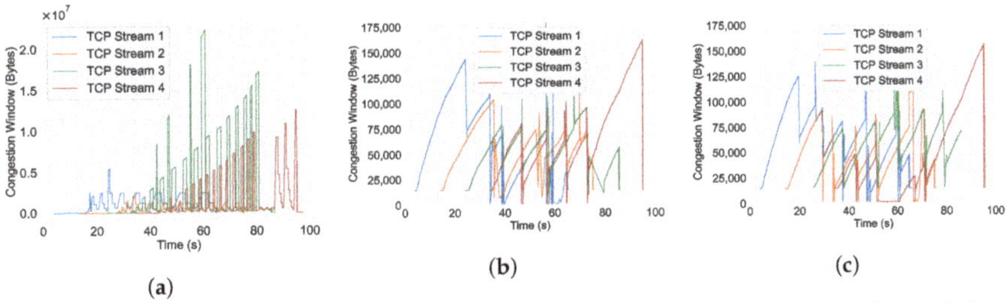

Figure 36. Case 1: (ECN enabled) Congestion Window Scenario 1 with Bandwidth = 10 Mbps, Delay = 20 ms. (**a**) FQ-CoDel (*cwnd*); (**b**) FQ-PIE (*cwnd*); (**c**) L4S (*cwnd*).

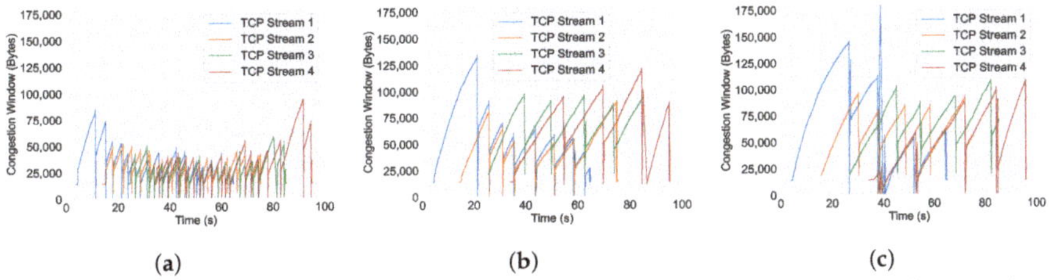

Figure 37. Case 2: (ECN disabled) Congestion Window Scenario 1 with Bandwidth = 10 Mbps, Delay = 20 ms. (**a**) FQ-CoDel (*cwnd*); (**b**) FQ-PIE (*cwnd*); (**c**) L4S (*cwnd*).

Scenario 2 (Bandwidth = 1 Mbps, Delay = 20 ms):

Evaluation is conducted in two cases: Case 1 with ECN enabled and Case 2 with ECN disabled for comparison. Figures 38 and 39 present the results for these two cases.

Similar to Scenario 1, FQ-CoDel's *cwnd* with ECN enabled (Figure 38a steadily increases. Its *cwnd* values are significantly higher during upwards trends of the staircase pattern, though its frequency of rapid change is lower compared to FQ-PIE and L4S. This behavior is brought about by FQ-CoDel's behavior of only using ECN notification instead of dropping packets in extreme congestion conditions. When ECN is disabled in Figure 39a, FQ-CoDel shows a sawtooth pattern in its *cwnd* with a higher frequency of dips and rises compared to FQ-PIE and L4S, regardless of ECN with a lower maximum *cwnd* size. Like Scenario 1, it directly influences the total data transferred throughout the multiple connections, as seen in Table 2, which is lower than its L4S and FQ-PIE competitors when ECN is disabled but not as exaggerated as in Scenario 1 because of its low bandwidth.

Similar to Scenario 1, In the FQ-PIE and L4S algorithm, regardless of ECN (Figures 38b,c and 39b,c), the *cwnd* displays a sawtooth pattern demonstrating NewReno's aggressive behavior in adapting optimal *cwnd* values.

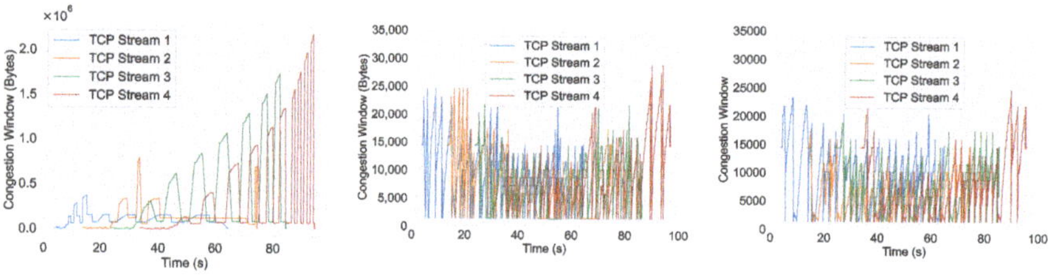

(a) (b) (c)

Figure 38. Case 1: (ECN enabled) Congestion Window Scenario 2 with Bandwidth = 1 Mbps, Delay = 20 ms. (**a**) FQ-CoDel (*cwnd*); (**b**) FQ-PIE (*cwnd*); (**c**) L4S (*cwnd*).

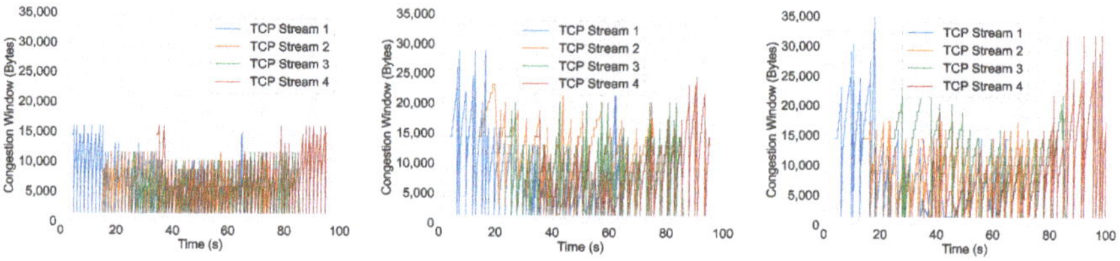

(a) (b) (c)

Figure 39. Case 2:(ECN disabled) Congestion Window Scenario 2 with Bandwidth = 1 Mbps, Delay = 20 ms. (**a**) FQ-CoDel (*cwnd*); (**b**) FQ-PIE (*cwnd*); (**c**) L4S (*cwnd*).

7. Conclusions and Future Work

In this paper, we conducted a comprehensive analysis of various AQM algorithms, including our implementation of a preliminary architecture of L4S in the FreeBSD network stack. We conducted extensive research . For this purpose, we created two network scenarios, one with high bandwidth and the other with low bandwidth. We assessed their performance in a scenario where multiple TCP connections compete in the same bottleneck. Our findings revealed that L4S exhibits very low RTT in low-bandwidth conditions, nearly a second faster than its competitors while maintaining a high level of throughput.

Furthermore, we have developed an innovative hybrid A3C-L4S approach to enhance network performance, specifically for latency-sensitive applications. This approach leverages the multi-agent and asynchronous nature of A3C to enhance exploration and adaptability while minimizing resource consumption on the routers. It is a novel addition to network management, offering a unique solution to enhancing network performance. The A3C model can converge properly, learning the intricate relationship between the drop probability and the queuing delay, further enhancing the adaptability of our approach.

The potential of leveraging the L4S architecture in FreeBSD with a deep-reinforcement learning model like A3C to optimize the gaps in our network infrastructure is immense. This combination can make our network more suitable for a specific type of latency-sensitive data. However, there is a need to optimize both the TCP and AQM sides of L4S to respond faster to real-time network traffic, in which A3C plays a significant role. We are also exploring the energy efficiency of the final system and how we can adjust the model parameters to consume fewer resources while maintaining an enhanced performance.

In our future work, we aim to dedicate more time to fine-tuning the A3C model by training it on larger datasets. Additionally, we intend to deploy the model directly into the kernel and utilize an online learning approach for training. This would enable the model to continuously learn and adapt in real time. The communication between kernel space and user space would also introduce some delay, which would be negligible under typical conditions, but we have to explore the other scenarios, especially under high load. The perfect solution would be directly coding the machine learning algorithm in the kernel, which has difficulties. Moreover, we intend to explore using the UDP protocol in our research. UDP is well-suited for applications where low latency and high throughput are prioritized, and reliability is not critical. By leveraging UDP, we can cater to latency-sensitive applications that require efficient data transmission.

Building on the prior research in [38], which focused on implementing an ML-based multi-path TCP, we see potential in collaborating with source control protocols like TCP and UDP, along with network devices such as routers and switches [38]. Exploring the interactions and optimizations between these components could lead to significant network performance and efficiency advancements. By combining the strengths of machine learning, protocols like TCP and UDP, and network devices, we can enhance the overall performance, reliability, and adaptability of future network systems.

Author Contributions: Conceptualization, J.K. and S.R.P.; Methodology, J.K. and S.R.P.; Software, J.K.; Validation, D.S.; Formal analysis, D.S.; Investigation, D.S. and S.R.P.; Data curation, D.S.; Writing—original draft, D.S.; Writing—review & editing, J.K. and S.R.P.; Visualization, D.S.; Supervision, J.K. and S.R.P.; Project administration, S.R.P.; Funding acquisition, J.K. and S.R.P. All authors have read and agreed to the published version of the manuscript.

Funding: This research is funded by the 2023 Information Society Innovation Fund (ISIF Asia) through the APNIC Foundation.

Data Availability Statement: Experimental implementation and results presented in this paper are made available through the following GitHub repositories. Experimental L4S implementation in FreeBSD 13.1: https://github.com/MPTCP-FreeBSD/FB13.1-AQM-L4S-SRC.git; A3C implementation and analysis: https://github.com/MPTCP-FreeBSD/FreeBSD-DRL-L4S.git (accessed on 18 July 2024).

Conflicts of Interest: The authors declare no conflicts of interest.

References

1. Gettys, J.; Nichols, K. Bufferbloat: Dark Buffers in the Internet: Networks without effective AQM may again be vulnerable to congestion collapse. *Queue* **2011**, *9*, 40–54. [CrossRef]
2. Floyd, S.; Jacobson, V. Random early detection gateways for congestion avoidance. *IEEE/ACM Trans. Netw.* **1993**, *1*, 397–413. [CrossRef]
3. Kua, J.; Armitage, G.; Branch, P. A survey of rate adaptation techniques for dynamic adaptive streaming over HTTP. *IEEE Commun. Surv. Tutorials* **2017**, *19*, 1842–1866. [CrossRef]
4. Kua, J.; Armitage, G.; Branch, P.; But, J. Adaptive Chunklets and AQM for higher-performance content streaming. *Acm Trans. Multimed. Comput. Commun. Appl. (TOMM)* **2019**, *15*, 1–24. [CrossRef]
5. Hoeiland-Joergensen, T.; McKenney, P.; Taht, D.; Gettys, J.; Dumazet, E. The Flow Queue Codel Packet Scheduler and Active Queue Management Algorithm. Technical Report. 2018. Available online: https://www.rfc-editor.org/rfc/rfc8290.html (accessed on 18 July 2024).
6. Pan, R.; Natarajan, P.; Baker, F.; White, G. Proportional Integral Controller Enhanced (PIE): A Lightweight Control Scheme to Address the Bufferbloat Problem. RFC 8033. 2017. Available online: https://www.rfc-editor.org/info/rfc8033 (accessed on 18 July 2024).
7. White, G.; Pan, R. Active Queue Management (AQM) Based on Proportional Integral Controller Enhanced (PIE) for Data-Over-Cable Service Interface Specifications (DOCSIS) Cable Modems. RFC 8034. 2017. Available online: https://www.rfc-editor.org/info/rfc8034 (accessed on 18 July 2024).
8. Cardozo, T.B.; da Silva, A.P.C.; Vieira, A.B.; Ziviani, A. Bufferbloat systematic analysis. In Proceedings of the 2014 International Telecommunications Symposium (ITS), Sao Paulo, Brazil, 17–20 August 2014; IEEE: Piscataway, NJ, USA, 2014; pp. 1–5.
9. Ahammed, G.; Banu, R. Anakyzing the performance of active queue management algorithms. *arXiv* **2010**, arXiv:1003.3909.
10. Kua, J.; Nguyen, S.H.; Armitage, G.; Branch, P. Using active queue management to assist IoT application flows in home broadband networks. *IEEE Internet Things J.* **2017**, *4*, 1399–1407. [CrossRef]
11. Kua, J.; Branch, P.; Armitage, G. Detecting bottleneck use of pie or fq-codel active queue management during dash-like content streaming. In Proceedings of the 2020 IEEE 45th Conference on Local Computer Networks (LCN), Sydney, Australia, 16–19 November 2020; IEEE: Piscataway, NJ, USA, 2020; pp. 445–448.
12. Amol, D.; Rajesh, P. A review on active queue management techniques of congestion control. In *Proceedings of the 2014 International Conference on Electronic Systems, Signal Processing and Computing Technologies*; IEEE: Piscataway, NJ, USA, 2014; pp. 166–169.
13. Nichols, K.; Jacobson, V. Controlling queue delay. *Commun. ACM* **2012**, *55*, 42–50. [CrossRef]

14. Hoeiland-Joergensen, T.; McKenney, P.; Taht, D.; Ghettys, J.; Dumazet, E. Flowqueue-Codel: Draft-Hoeiland-Joergensen-Aqm-fq-Codel-00. 2014. Available online: https://datatracker.ietf.org/doc/draft-ietf-aqm-fq-codel/00/ (accessed on 18 July 2024).
15. Ramakrishnan, G.; Bhasi, M.; Saicharan, V.; Monis, L.; Patil, S.D.; Tahiliani, M.P. FQ-PIE queue discipline in the Linux kernel: Design, implementation and challenges. In Proceedings of the 2019 IEEE 44th LCN Symposium on Emerging Topics in Networking (LCN Symposium), Osnabrück, Germany, 14–17 October 2019; IEEE: Piscataway, NJ, USA, 2019; pp. 117–124.
16. Al-Saadi, R.; Armitage, G. *Dummynet AQM v0. 2–CoDel, FQ-CoDel, PIE and FQ-PIE for FreeBSD's ipfw/Dummynet Framework*; Tech. Rep. A 160418; Centre for Advanced Internet Architectures, Swinburne University of Technology: Melbourne, Australia, 2016; p. 18.
17. Ramakrishnan, K.; Floyd, S.; Black, D. The Addition of Explicit Congestion Notification (ECN) to IP. Technical Report. 2001. Available online: https://www.rfc-editor.org/rfc/rfc3168.html (accessed on 18 July 2024).
18. De Schepper, K.; Albisser, O.; Tilmans, O.; Briscoe, B. Dual Queue Coupled AQM: Deployable Very Low Queuing Delay for All. *arXiv* **2022**, arXiv:2209.01078.
19. Schepper, K.D.; Briscoe, B.; White, G. Dual-Queue Coupled Active Queue Management (AQM) for Low Latency, Low Loss, and Scalable Throughput (L4S). RFC 9332. 2023. Available online: https://www.rfc-editor.org/info/rfc9332 (accessed on 18 July 2024).
20. Hollot, C.V.; Misra, V.; Towsley, D.; Gong, W.B. On designing improved controllers for AQM routers supporting TCP flows. In Proceedings of the IEEE INFOCOM 2001 Conference on Computer Communications, Twentieth Annual Joint Conference of the IEEE Computer and Communications Society (Cat. No.01CH37213), Anchorage, AK, USA, 22–26 April 2001; IEEE: Piscataway, NJ, USA, 2001; Volume 3, pp. 1726–1734. [CrossRef]
21. Szyguła, J.; Domański, A.; Domańska, J.; Marek, D.; Filus, K.; Mendla, S. Supervised Learning of Neural Networks for Active Queue Management in the Internet. *Sensors* **2021**, *21*, 4979. [CrossRef] [PubMed]
22. Su, Y.; Huang, L.; Feng, C. QRED: A Q-learning-based active queue management scheme. *J. Internet Technol.* **2018**, *19*, 1169–1178.
23. Liu, J.; Wei, D. Active Queue Management Based on Q-Learning Traffic Predictor. In Proceedings of the 2022 International Conference on Cyber-Physical Social Intelligence (ICCSI), Nanjing, China, 18–21 November 2022; IEEE: Piscataway, NJ, USA, 2022; pp. 399–404.
24. Gomez, C.A.; Wang, X.; Shami, A. Intelligent active queue management using explicit congestion notification. In Proceedings of the 2019 IEEE Global Communications Conference (GLOBECOM), Waikoloa, HI, USA, 9–13 December 2019; IEEE: Piscataway, NJ, USA, 2019; pp. 1–6.
25. Ma, H.; Xu, D.; Dai, Y.; Dong, Q. An intelligent scheme for congestion control: When active queue management meets deep reinforcement learning. *Comput. Netw.* **2021**, *200*, 108515. [CrossRef]
26. Kim, M.; Jaseemuddin, M.; Anpalagan, A. Deep reinforcement learning based active queue management for iot networks. *J. Netw. Syst. Manag.* **2021**, *29*, 34. [CrossRef]
27. Fawaz, H.; Zeghlache, D.; Pham, Q.T.A.; Jérémie, L.; Medagliani, P. Deep Reinforcement Learning for Smart Queue Management. In Proceedings of the NETSYS 2021: Conference on Networked Systems 2021, Lübeck, Germany, 13–16 September 2021; pp. 1–14. Available online: https://hal.archives-ouvertes.fr/hal-03546621 (accessed on 18 July 2024).
28. Albisser, O.; De Schepper, K.; Briscoe, B.; Tilmans, O.; Steen, H. DUALPI2—Low Latency, Low Loss and Scalable Throughput (L4S) AQM. In Proceedings of the Linux Netdev 0x13, Prague, Czech Republic, 20–22 March 2019; pp. 1–8. Available online: https://www.netdevconf.org/0x13/session.html?talk-DUALPI2-AQM (accessed on 18 July 2024).
29. Briscoe, B.; Schepper, K.D.; Bagnulo, M.; White, G. Low Latency, Low Loss, and Scalable Throughput (L4S) Internet Service: Architecture. RFC 9330. 2023. Available online: https://www.rfc-editor.org/info/rfc9330 (accessed on 18 July 2024).
30. De Schepper, K.; Bondarenko, O.; Tsang, I.J.; Briscoe, B. Pi2: A linearized aqm for both classic and scalable tcp. In Proceedings of the 12th International on Conference on emerging Networking EXperiments and Technologies, Irvine, CA, USA, 12–15 December 2016; pp. 105–119.
31. Briscoe, B. PI^2 Parameters. *arXiv* **2021**, arXiv:2107.01003.
32. Mnih, V.; Badia, A.P.; Mirza, M.; Graves, A.; Lillicrap, T.; Harley, T.; Silver, D.; Kavukcuoglu, K. Asynchronous methods for deep reinforcement learning. In Proceedings of the International Conference on Machine Learning. PMLR, New York, NY, USA, 19–24 June 2016; pp. 1928–1937.
33. Palamuttam, R.; Chen, W. Vision Enhanced Asynchronous Advantage Actor-Critic on Racing Games. *Methods* **2017**, *4*, A3C.
34. Stewart, L.; Healy, J. Characterising the Behaviour and Performance of SIFTR v1. 1.0. Technical Report, CAIA, Tech. Rep. 2007. Available online: http://caia.swinburne.edu.au/reports/070824A/CAIA-TR-070824A.pdf (accessed on 18 July 2024).
35. The Tcpdump Group. Tcpdump. Available online: https://www.tcpdump.org/ (accessed on 12 July 2024).
36. Dpkt Contributors. Dpkt. Available online: https://pypi.org/project/dpkt/ (accessed on 12 July 2024).
37. Wireshark Foundation. Wireshark. Available online: https://www.wireshark.org/ (accessed on 12 July 2024).
38. Pokhrel, S.R.; Kua, J.; Satish, D.; Ozer, S.; Howe, J.; Walid, A. DDPG-MPCC: An Experience Driven Multipath Performance Oriented Congestion Control. *Future Internet* **2024**, *16*, 37. [CrossRef]

future internet

MDPI

Article

NFT Technology for Enhanced Global Digital Registers: A Novel Approach to Tokenization

Oleksandr Kuznetsov [1,2,*], Emanuele Frontoni [3], Kateryna Kuznetsova [4], Ruslan Shevchuk [5,6,*] and Mikolaj Karpinski [7,8]

1 Faculty of Engineering, eCampus University, Via Isimbardi 10, 22060 Novedrate, Italy
2 Department of Information and Communication Systems Security, V. N. Karazin Kharkiv National University, 4 Svobody Sq., 61022 Kharkiv, Ukraine
3 Department of Political Sciences, Communication and International Relations, University of Macerata, Via Crescimbeni, 30/32, 62100 Macerata, Italy; emanuele.frontoni@unimc.it
4 Department of Information Engineering, Marche Polytechnic University, Via Brecce Bianche 12, 60131 Ancona, Italy; kate7smith12@gmail.com
5 Department of Computer Science and Automatics, University of Bielsko-Biala, 43-309 Bielsko-Biala, Poland
6 Department of Computer Science, West Ukrainian National University, 46009 Ternopil, Ukraine
7 Institute of Security and Computer Science, University of the National Education Commission, 30-084 Krakow, Poland; mikolaj.karpinski@up.krakow.pl
8 Department of Cyber Security, Ternopil Ivan Puluj National Technical University, 46001 Ternopil, Ukraine
* Correspondence: kuznetsov@karazin.ua (O.K.); rshevchuk@ubb.edu.pl (R.S.)

Abstract: In the rapidly evolving field of digital asset management, centralized and decentralized global registries have become essential tools for organizing, tracking, and distributing digital assets. However, existing systems often face challenges regarding security, censorship resistance, interoperability, customizability, and scalability. This research paper aims to address these gaps by proposing a novel decentralized global registry system based on blockchain technology and non-fungible tokens (NFTs). The research paper makes several key contributions to the field of digital asset management. First, it provides a detailed system design for the proposed decentralized global registry, outlining its architectural components, functional modules, and integration with blockchain and NFT technologies. Second, it offers a thorough comparative analysis of the advantages and limitations of the proposed system in relation to existing centralized and decentralized registries. Finally, the paper presents potential use cases and practical applications of the proposed system in various industries, demonstrating its versatility and adaptability to different contexts and requirements. In conclusion, this research paper contributes significantly to the ongoing efforts to improve digital asset management by presenting a novel, decentralized global registry system based on blockchain technology and NFTs. The proposed system addresses the key limitations of existing solutions and offers a promising direction for future research and development in this critical field.

Keywords: non-fungible tokens; digital registers; blockchain technology; tokenization

1. Introduction

The digital revolution is transforming our world, and with it, the need for secure, efficient methods for the identification and management of unique digital assets is growing exponentially. Global digital registers, be they centralized or decentralized, are integral to addressing this demand. However, these registers grapple with significant limitations, including potential censorship, lack of transparency, vulnerability to single points of failure, and challenges in interoperability and scalability.

To address these challenges, we propose a novel approach that leverages the power of blockchain technology and non-fungible tokens (NFTs). This research presents an application of NFT technology for tokenizing global digital registers, both at regional (local) and international (global) scales [1,2]. Examples of such applications include global tokenization of UNESCO World Heritage sites or comprehensive copyright and intellectual property management systems.

We posit that the value of NFTs lies not in themselves but in the unique digital resources they link to [3]. Against the backdrop of speculative tendencies that misconstrue the value proposition of NFTs [4–7], our approach emphasizes the role of NFTs as unique identifiers for digital resources within a secure and transparent blockchain network.

Our proposed decentralized system focuses on enhancing the security, authenticity, and traceability of these global digital registers. It significantly mitigates the limitations of current systems and paves the way for the preservation and wider accessibility of unique, valuable digital resources. Key innovations include adaptive interoperability across various blockchain networks, enhanced metadata management for complex rights tracking, and the integration of privacy-preserving technologies such as zero-knowledge proofs.

In this paper, we provide a comprehensive analysis of our approach, including theoretical foundations, practical implementation considerations, and potential applications. We begin with a thorough review of the current state of global digital registers, followed by an in-depth exploration of NFT technology and its capacity to address identified challenges. We then present a detailed system design, discussing its implementation, integration with existing systems, and scalability considerations.

A significant portion of our work is dedicated to comparative analysis, where we benchmark our proposed system against both traditional centralized registries (such as ISBN, ISSN, and DOI) and existing blockchain-based solutions. We provide quantitative metrics and real-world use cases to illustrate the advantages of our approach in terms of security, efficiency, and user experience.

We also examine the legal, ethical, and social implications of adopting NFT-based tokenization for global digital registers. This includes a thorough discussion of identity management in the context of intellectual property rights, as well as strategies to address scalability and transaction cost challenges on blockchain networks namely Ethereum.

We also examine the legal, ethical, and social implications of adopting NFT-based tokenization for global digital registers. This includes a thorough discussion of identity management in the context of intellectual property rights, as well as strategies to address scalability and transaction cost challenges on blockchain networks such as Ethereum. We conclude by offering a comprehensive evaluation of the proposed system, assessing its feasibility, scalability, and long-term sustainability, and identifying potential future research directions.

In essence, this paper illuminates the transformative potential of applying NFT technology to global digital registers and proposes a solution that ensures enhanced security, transparency, and efficiency. By addressing the specific concerns raised by reviewers and incorporating the latest advancements in blockchain technology, we present a robust and forward-thinking approach to reshaping the management and preservation of valuable digital resources, ultimately fostering an inclusive, accessible global digital ecosystem.

2. Literature Review

The rapid advancement of digital technologies has fundamentally transformed the landscape of asset management, giving rise to new challenges and opportunities. This literature review examines the current state-of-the-art in digital asset management, focusing on the application of blockchain technology and non-fungible tokens (NFTs) to address the limitations of traditional centralized systems. We also review existing global digital registries, including solutions from major IT companies and recently discussed patents, to identify gaps and potential areas for improvement.

2.1. Blockchain Technology and NFTs in Digital Asset Management

Recent studies have explored the potential of blockchain technology and NFTs in various aspects of digital asset management. Belk et al. [8] examined the changing understandings of money, possessions, and ownership in the context of the metaverse, highlighting the potential for new forms of ownership through the use of cryptocurrencies, algorithmic collectibles, and NFTs. Elmay et al. [9] proposed a blockchain-based crowdsourcing framework leveraging Digital Twins (DTs) and dynamic NFTs for transparent last-mile delivery, addressing the limitations of centralized and blockchain-based platforms.

Ferro et al. [10] presented an innovative approach to digital rights management that combines smart legal contracts and blockchain smart contracts to manage intellectual property rights (IPR) and facilitate notarization, rights transfer, and royalty payments. Hasan et al. [11] demonstrated how NFTs can be used to manage ownership of DTs and provide proof of delivery (PoD) of their associated physical assets in a decentralized, secure, traceable, and transparent manner.

Huang et al. [12] introduced a distributed trusted active identity resolution system based on the inter-planetary file system (IPFS) and NFTs to provide distributed identity resolution services for the Industrial Internet and Industry 4.0. Urom et al. [13] examined the return and volatility connectedness among NFTs and (un)conventional financial assets across various market conditions, while Wilkoff and Yildiz [14] provided the first study of time-varying and cross-sectional properties of liquidity in the NFT marketplace.

Zhao et al. [15] constructed a cryptographic interaction method for museum digital collections based on blockchain technology, building a digital collection exchange system on Ethereum to realize online exchanges between two museums. These studies demonstrate the growing interest in leveraging blockchain technology and NFTs for digital asset management across various domains.

2.2. Existing Global Digital Registries and Their Limitations

IBM's Asset Repository (AR) is a prominent industrial global registry system [16]. It aims to centralize asset management by integrating asset information from multiple sources, but its reliance on traditional database structures limits its scalability and flexibility. Moreover, it lacks a specific focus on intellectual property rights management and does not readily adapt to new asset types or changing business needs.

Microsoft's Digital Asset Management (DAM) system [17], another notable industrial solution, provides a centralized platform for managing digital assets. However, it has similar limitations in scalability and flexibility due to its reliance on conventional database architectures. Furthermore, it does not offer a comprehensive solution for managing intellectual property rights, nor does it easily adapt to diverse systems and technologies.

Several other leading IT companies, such as Oracle [18,19], Alfresco [20–22], Adobe [23,24], and SAP [25–27], have developed digital asset registries to address various challenges in managing digital assets. However, these systems exhibit shortcomings in scalability, flexibility, interoperability, and comprehensive intellectual property rights management.

The patent by Alden et al. [28] describes a central asset registry for media asset management, which integrates multiple repositories and tracks relationships between assets. While this solution offers improved speed, scalability, and flexibility in handling media assets, it does not specifically address the issues of intellectual property rights management or the verification of the authenticity of the assets.

The patents by C et al. [29,30] present a central asset registry system for managing media assets and their intellectual property rights. While the solution helps address the challenges of asset navigation, storage, and retrieval, it may not be as comprehensive in handling intellectual property rights as our solution, which is specifically designed for IP rights management and protection.

In addition to the previously discussed patents, several other patents have been reviewed to provide a comprehensive understanding of the current landscape in digital asset management. The patent by Filipe and Liana [31] focuses on an e-commerce system that allows recipients to request the crowdfunding of items as gifts, with contributors purchasing parts of the item(s). While this concept addresses a specific niche in the retail industry, it does not explore the broader applications of NFTs and the tokenization of unique digital assets. The patent by Thomas [32] details an origin tag with a unique identifier for providing traceability of objects or animals throughout various handling steps, targeting specific needs in industries such as livestock and forestry. However, it does not encompass the wider scope of our NFT-based solution for global digital registers. The patent by Lucinda [33] focuses on using artificial intelligence to identify and search for subjects or objects, particularly vehicles, while building provenance and preserving knowledge about their cultural history. However, this approach lacks the advantages of our blockchain-based solution, which ensures the highest level of transparency, security, and immutability for provenance tracking. Finally, the patents by George [34,35] discuss a framework for accelerating development on decentralized networks by reusing existing logic and focusing on creating new desired behaviors. While it aims to simplify the development process, it does not specifically address provenance tracking and data integrity, which are critical aspects of our solution.

2.3. Gaps in Current Research and Our Proposed Approach

Despite the growing interest in blockchain technology and NFTs for digital asset management, there remain significant gaps in the current research, particularly in terms of addressing the limitations of existing centralized and decentralized systems, such as scalability, interoperability, and customizability.

Existing global identification systems, such as ISBN (International Standard Book Number), ISSN (International Standard Serial Number), DOI (Digital Object Identifier), ASIN (Amazon Standard Identification Number), BICI (Book Item and Component Identifier), ISAN (International Standard Audiovisual Number), ISMN (International Standard Music Number), ISRC (International Standard Recording Code), ISTC (International Standard Text Code), ISWC (International Standard Musical Work Code), ISWN (International Standard Wine Number), and LCCN (Library of Congress Control Number), each serve specific industries and purposes. However, these systems face the following common challenges:

1. Centralization: Most of these systems rely on centralized authorities, making them vulnerable to single points of failure and censorship;
2. Limited interoperability: Each system operates independently, with minimal cross-system integration capabilities;
3. Lack of real-time verification: Many of these systems do not offer instant, global verification of identifiers;
4. Inefficient rights management: Tracking and managing rights across different systems and jurisdictions is often complex and time-consuming;
5. Scalability issues: As the volume of digital content grows exponentially, traditional systems struggle to keep pace.

The idea of using NFTs to tokenize these pre-existing global digital registries has not been explored in the reviewed literature, representing a significant gap in current research.

Our proposed decentralized global registry system aims to fill these gaps by providing a secure, transparent, and efficient solution for tokenizing global digital registers and facilitating the creation of new registries for unique objects and content. By leveraging the potential of NFTs to represent unique identifiers for digital resources within a secure and transparent blockchain network, our approach offers a novel contribution to the field of digital asset management.

Specifically, our research aims to address the following gaps:

1. Unified tokenization framework: We propose a standardized approach to tokenize diverse types of identifiers (e.g., ISBN, ISRC, DOI) using NFTs, enabling cross-system interoperability;
2. Decentralized verification: Our system allows for real-time, global verification of identifiers without relying on centralized authorities;
3. Enhanced rights management: By leveraging smart contracts, we enable automated, transparent, and efficient management of rights across different types of content;

4. Scalability solutions: We explore layer-2 scaling solutions and cross-chain interoperability to address the scalability challenges faced by both traditional systems and existing blockchain networks;
5. Privacy-preserving transparency: Our research investigates the use of zero-knowledge proofs to balance the need for transparency with privacy requirements, a crucial aspect not addressed in current identification systems.

The proposed system focuses on enhancing the security, authenticity, and traceability of these global digital registers, significantly mitigating the limitations of current systems and paving the way for the preservation and wider accessibility of unique, valuable digital resources. By applying our system to existing registries such as ISBN, ISSN, DOI, and others, we can provide enhanced security, censorship resistance, and decentralization, enabling seamless and transparent management of unique identifiers for books, periodicals, digital objects, and other content.

Furthermore, our approach emphasizes the role of NFTs as unique identifiers for digital resources, rectifying the prevailing misinterpretation of the value associated with NFTs, which is often driven by speculative trends. By focusing on the practical utility of NFTs in tokenizing pre-existing global digital registries, we aim to demonstrate a new and valuable application of this technology, moving beyond the realm of speculation and towards a more sustainable and beneficial use case.

In conclusion, our proposed decentralized global registry system, built upon the insights from the reviewed literature and addressing the identified challenges, offers a novel and promising direction for future research and development in the critical field of digital asset management. By bridging the gap between traditional identification systems and cutting-edge blockchain technology, we aim to create a more efficient, secure, and interoperable global ecosystem for managing digital assets.

3. Background and Gap in Current Research

The current digital landscape is heavily dependent on reliable mechanisms for identifying and managing unique digital objects, intellectual properties, and various forms of valuable data [9,13]. The existing systems that cater to these demands include a combination of centralized and decentralized global registries [1,2]. However, these systems encounter a number of challenges, including the potential for misuse, susceptibility to single points of failure, limitations of hierarchical structures, and lack of transparency [3]. Particularly, centralized structures pose issues related to the authenticity and security of stored identifiers [4]. On the other hand, decentralized systems, while offering robust security, often grapple with interoperability and scalability issues.

Moreover, a current misconception in the field is the overemphasis on the intrinsic value of NFTs [8,11]. NFTs, in essence, are unique entries in a blockchain register linking to a digital resource [3]. The assumption is that the digital resource itself has value, but in the wave of speculative trends, there are attempts to attribute value directly to the NFTs, which is misleading [8].

This research proposes an innovative approach to address these gaps and misconceptions by introducing a novel decentralized global registry system that harnesses the potential of blockchain technology and NFTs. We focus on using NFTs as unique identifiers in a decentralized ledger to tokenize pre-existing resources, which bear value due to their inherent uniqueness, singularity, and immutability. This approach not only enhances the security, authenticity, and traceability of global digital registers but also aims to rectify the prevailing misinterpretation of the value associated with NFTs.

Our proposed system offers several notable improvements over traditional global registers. It introduces an infrastructure for decentralized distributed storage of unique identifiers in the form of NFTs, ensuring blockchain-secured records resistant to censorship, modification, and other malicious activities. Our solution seamlessly integrates with existing registers without requiring modifications to their structure. Further, it allows swift creation of new digital registers for various application scenarios, thereby standardizing tokenization and expanding the range of services and consumer engagement.

This system also provides remarkable scalability and interoperability, enabling seamless interaction with multiple blockchain platforms. It is customizable, allowing it to adapt to specific use cases or requirements, thus appealing to a wider audience.

Through its unique approach, our proposed solution addresses the limitations of existing systems and provides an efficient mechanism for managing unique digital resources globally while aligning the understanding of the value associated with NFTs.

Alternatives Considered for the Tokenization of Pre-Existing Resources

While NFT technology forms the backbone of our proposed system due to its ability to ensure the uniqueness, singularity, and immutability of digital assets, we acknowledge the existence of other potential methods for digital tokenization. This section discusses these alternatives and the reasons why they were not selected as our primary solution.

- Centralized database systems. Traditional centralized databases could be employed for tokenizing digital assets. However, they present significant drawbacks such as single points of failure, vulnerability to cyberattacks, and lack of transparency, which are resolved in a blockchain-based system [16,17,36,37].
- Fungible Tokens. Fungible tokens, such as cryptocurrencies, could also be employed for the tokenization process. However, fungible tokens are interchangeable and lack the unique characteristics provided by NFTs, making them unsuitable for representing unique digital assets [5–7].
- Distributed Databases. Distributed databases present a potential alternative, providing improved availability and partition tolerance compared to centralized systems. However, they lack the inherent security and transparency offered by a blockchain network [28,29].
- Digital Watermarking. This technique embeds information into a digital signal, which can be used to verify asset authenticity and integrity. However, digital watermarking does not provide the comprehensive features offered by NFTs, such as the ability to store rich metadata and the assurance of immutability [31–34].

These alternatives were carefully evaluated, and while they have their advantages, they lack crucial aspects, primarily in terms of security, transparency, and immutability. Therefore, NFTs on a blockchain network were deemed to be the most fitting solution for our purposes [8–10].

4. High-Level System Design

This section presents a high-level design of the proposed NFT-based tokenization system for global digital registers. The system consists of several key components, including blockchain networks, smart contracts, NFTs, data exchange protocols, and user interaction interfaces, all working together to create a secure, transparent, and efficient tokenization process.

4.1. Blockchain Network

The system will be built on a modern blockchain platform, such as Ethereum, which provides a decentralized, secure, and tamper-resistant infrastructure. Ethereum's capabilities, such as its native support for smart contracts and the ERC-721 standard [38] for non-fungible tokens, make it a suitable choice for implementing the proposed system.

However, to address scalability concerns and the high transaction costs associated with the Ethereum mainnet, our system is designed to be blockchain-agnostic, allowing for implementation on various platforms. Specifically, we consider the integration of layer-2 scaling solutions and alternative blockchain networks:

1. Polygon (formerly Matic Network): This Ethereum-compatible blockchain offers significantly lower transaction costs and higher throughput, making it ideal for high-

volume NFT transactions. Polygon's compatibility with Ethereum ensures that our system can leverage existing Ethereum tools and infrastructure while benefiting from improved scalability.

2. Binance Smart Chain (BSC): As another Ethereum-compatible blockchain, BSC provides high throughput and low transaction costs. Its growing ecosystem of decentralized applications makes it an attractive option for our global registry system.
3. Layer-2 Solutions: We explore the integration of Optimistic Rollups and ZK-Rollups on Ethereum, which can dramatically increase transaction throughput while maintaining the security guarantees of the Ethereum mainnet.

By designing our system to be adaptable to different blockchain networks, we ensure long-term viability and flexibility. This approach allows us to mitigate the scalability and cost issues associated with any single blockchain platform while maintaining the core benefits of decentralization, security, and transparency.

The choice of blockchain network can be tailored to specific use cases and requirements of different global registries, ensuring optimal performance and cost-efficiency for various types of digital assets and transaction volumes.

4.2. Smart Contracts

Smart contracts are self-executing contracts with the terms of the agreement directly written into code. They are stored and executed on the blockchain, ensuring trustworthiness and automation. In our system, smart contracts will be used to manage the creation, ownership, and transfer of NFTs representing unique identifiers for digital resources in global registers. Additionally, they will handle the rules and restrictions associated with the tokenization process, ensuring compliance with relevant regulations and policies.

To enhance the flexibility and efficiency of our system, we implemented the following advanced smart contract features:

1. Multi-token Standard Support: In addition to the ERC-721 standard for unique NFTs, we incorporate the ERC-1155 standard [39]. This multi-token standard allows for more efficient batch transfers and the management of both fungible and non-fungible tokens within a single contract. This is particularly useful for handling different types of digital assets and their associated metadata within various global registries;
2. Upgradeable smart contracts: To ensure long-term flexibility and the ability to address future requirements or security updates, we implement upgradeable smart contract patterns. This approach allows for the modification of contract logic without disrupting the system's operation or requiring the migration of existing data;
3. Role-Based Access Control (RBAC): We implement a granular RBAC system within our smart contracts to manage different levels of permissions for various stakeholders, such as registry administrators, content creators, and end-users;
4. Royalty and Revenue Sharing: For use cases involving intellectual property rights, we incorporate automated royalty distribution mechanisms. These allow for the seamless allocation of revenues to multiple stakeholders based on predefined rules.
5. Cross-chain Interoperability: To facilitate interaction with multiple blockchain networks, we design our smart contracts with cross-chain compatibility in mind. This includes the use of bridge contracts and standardized interfaces for cross-chain asset transfers and data verification;
6. Gas Optimization: We employ various gas optimization techniques in our smart contract development to minimize transaction costs, which is particularly important for high-volume operations in global registries;
7. Event Emission: Our smart contracts emit detailed events for all significant actions, enabling efficient off chain indexing and real-time updates for user interfaces and external systems.

These advanced smart contract features ensure that our system can handle the complex requirements of various global digital registries while maintaining security, efficiency, and adaptability to future needs.

4.3. Non-Fungible Tokens

NFTs will serve as the core component for representing unique digital resources in the system. Leveraging the ERC-721 standard, each NFT will have a unique identifier and metadata associated with the digital resource it represents. NFTs will be created, transferred, and managed through smart contracts, ensuring the immutability and traceability of the tokenization process.

To enhance the functionality and versatility of our NFT-based system for global digital registries, we introduced the following advanced features:

1. Enhanced Metadata Structure: We implement an extensible metadata schema that accommodates the specific requirements of various global registry types (e.g., ISBN, ISSN, DOI). This schema includes:
   - Core fields common to all registry types (e.g., unique identifier, creation date, owner);
   - Registry-specific fields (e.g., book title and author for ISBN, journal name and issue number for ISSN);
   - Extensible custom fields allow for future additions without system redesign.
2. On-chain vs. off-chain Metadata: To optimize for gas costs and scalability, we implement a hybrid approach:
   - Essential, frequently accessed metadata is stored on-chain;
   - Larger, less frequently accessed data (e.g., detailed descriptions, high-resolution images) is stored off-chain using IPFS, with on-chain references.
3. Fractional Ownership: We implement a fractional NFT (F-NFT) system that allows for partial ownership of digital assets. This is particularly useful for complex intellectual property scenarios or collaborative works, enabling:
   - Division of a single NFT into multiple fractions;
   - Trading of fractional ownership;
   - Automated royalty distribution based on ownership percentages.
4. Dynamic NFTs: For digital resources that may evolve over time (e.g., regularly updated databases, living documents), we implement dynamic NFTs. These allow for:
   - Controlled updates to metadata without compromising the NFT's uniqueness;
   - Version history tracking;
   - Conditional metadata updates are based on predefined rules.
5. Nested NFTs: To represent hierarchical relationships in certain registries (e.g., a book series in ISBN), we implement a nested NFT structure, allowing:
   - Parent-child relationships between NFTs;
   - Inheritance of certain properties from parent to child NFTs;
   - Efficient management of related digital assets.
6. Interoperability Layers: We design our NFTs with cross-platform compatibility in mind, implementing:
   - Standard interfaces for interaction with various blockchain platforms;
   - Metadata translation layers for compatibility with existing registry systems.
7. Privacy-Preserving NFTs: For sensitive digital assets, we incorporate privacy features such as:
   - Selective disclosure of metadata;
   - Integration with zero-knowledge proof systems for verification without full disclosure.

These advanced NFT features ensure that our system can accurately represent and manage the diverse and complex nature of digital assets across various global registry systems while providing the flexibility to adapt to future needs and technological advancements.

4.4. Data Exchange Protocols

To facilitate the seamless exchange of data between different components of the system and external services, standardized data exchange protocols will be employed. Examples include JSON-RPC for communication between the front-end interface and the blockchain network and the InterPlanetary File System (IPFS) for decentralized storage and retrieval of metadata associated with NFTs.

To enhance the system's interoperability and data integrity, we implement the following advanced data exchange protocols and mechanisms:

1. Blockchain Oracles: We integrate blockchain oracles to enable secure communication between our smart contracts and external data sources or systems. This includes:
   - Chainlink for reliable off-chain data retrieval and verification;
   - Band Protocol for cross-chain data oracle functionality;
   - Custom oracles for specific global registry integrations (e.g., the ISBN database).
2. Decentralized Storage Solutions:
   - In addition to IPFS, we incorporate Filecoin for long-term, incentivized storage of larger datasets;
   - We implement Swarm for the resilient and censorship-resistant storage of critical metadata.
3. Cross-Chain Communication Protocols:
   - Integration of Polkadot's cross-chain messaging (XCMP) for interoperability between different blockchain networks;
   - Implementation of the Cosmos Inter-Blockchain Communication (IBC) protocol for seamless data exchange across heterogeneous blockchain systems.
4. Standardized API Interfaces:
   - Development of RESTful APIs adhering to OpenAPI specifications for easy integration with existing systems;
   - Implementation of GraphQL APIs for flexible and efficient data querying.
5. Secure Data Transit:
   - Utilization of Transport Layer Security (TLS) for all data transmissions;
   - Implementation of JSON Web Tokens (JWT) for secure authentication and information exchange.
6. Data Integrity Verification:
   - Integration of Merkle Tree proofs for efficient verification of large datasets;
   - Implementation of zero-knowledge proof systems (e.g., zk-SNARKs) for privacy-preserving verification of sensitive data.
7. Real-time Data Synchronization:
   - Utilization of WebSocket protocol for real-time updates and notifications;
   - Implementation of Server-Sent Events (SSE) for efficient one-way real-time data flow.
8. Interoperability with Legacy Systems:
   - Development of custom API adapters for seamless integration with existing global registry systems (e.g., ISBN, ISSN, DOI databases);
   - Implementation of ETL (Extract, Transform, Load) processes for bulk data migration and synchronization.

These advanced data exchange protocols and mechanisms ensure that our system can efficiently and securely communicate with various external systems and data sources, maintaining data integrity and enabling real-time updates across different platforms and registry systems. This comprehensive approach to data exchange enhances the overall interoperability and reliability of our NFT-based global digital registry system.

4.5. User Interaction Interfaces

User-friendly interfaces will be developed to enable various stakeholders, such as digital resource owners, registry administrators, and end-users, to interact with the system. These interfaces will provide functionalities such as creating, viewing, and transferring NFTs, as well as managing and verifying the tokenization of digital resources. Both web-based and mobile applications can be developed to ensure accessibility and ease of use.

To enhance the user experience and facilitate seamless integration with existing systems, we implement the following advanced features in our user interaction interfaces:

1. Multi-platform Support:
    - Responsive web applications using modern frameworks (e.g., React, Vue.js);
    - Native mobile applications for iOS and Android—desktop applications for Windows, macOS, and Linux.
2. Integrated Wallet Functionality:
    - Built-in non-custodial wallet for NFT management;
    - Support for popular external wallets (e.g., MetaMask, WalletConnect);
    - Hardware wallet integration for enhanced security.
3. Advanced Search and Discovery:
    - Faceted search capabilities for efficient navigation of large NFT collections;
    - AI-powered recommendation system for related digital assets;
    - Visual search functionality for image based NFTs.
4. Customizable Dashboards:
    - Role-based dashboards for different user types (e.g., creators, collectors, administrators);
    - Widgets for real-time analytics and portfolio management;
    - Customizable alert and notification systems.
5. Accessibility and Internationalization:
    - Compliance with WCAG 2.1 guidelines for accessibility;
    - Multi-language support with easy localization options;
    - Culture-sensitive design elements.
6. Integration with Existing Systems:
    - API-driven interfaces for seamless connection with current digital asset management systems;
    - Plugins for popular content management systems (e.g., WordPress, Drupal);
    - Custom integrations for specific global registry systems (e.g., ISBN database interface).
7. Advanced Visualization Tools:
    - Interactive 3D viewers for complex digital assets;
    - Augmented Reality (AR) features for enhanced asset exploration;
    - Data visualization tools for analyzing NFT metrics and market trends.
8. Collaborative Features:
    - Real-time collaboration tools for shared NFT management;
    - Version control and change tracking for evolving digital assets;
    - Comment and annotation systems for enhanced communication.
9. Privacy and Security Controls:
    - Granular permission settings for data visibility;
    - Two-factor authentication (2FA) and biometric login options;
    - Privacy-preserving data sharing mechanisms.
10. Educational Resources:
    - Integrated tutorials and tooltips for new users;

- Knowledge base and FAQ section;
- Interactive onboarding process for different user roles.

These advanced user interaction features ensure that our system provides a seamless, intuitive, and secure experience for all stakeholders, from individual creators to large-scale registry administrators. By offering a rich set of tools and integrations, we facilitate the adoption of our NFT-based system within existing workflows and ecosystems, enhancing its practical value and user acceptance.

4.6. Privacy and Security

In developing our NFT-based system for global digital registries, we prioritize robust privacy and security measures to protect sensitive data and ensure the integrity of the system. The following advanced features and protocols are implemented:

1. Zero-Knowledge Proofs (ZKPs):
   - Integration of zk-SNARKs (Zero-Knowledge Succinct Non-Interactive Argument of Knowledge) for privacy-preserving verification of NFT ownership and attributes;
   - Implementation of zk-STARKs (Zero-Knowledge Scalable Transparent Argument of Knowledge) for enhanced scalability and post-quantum security;
   - Custom ZKP circuits for specific use cases in various global registries.
2. Encryption and Data Protection:
   - End-to-end encryption for all data transmissions;
   - Homomorphic encryption techniques for performing computations on encrypted data;
   - Secure Multi-Party Computation (SMPC) for collaborative operations without revealing sensitive information.
3. Access Control and Identity Management:
   - Implementation of Decentralized Identifiers (DIDs) for self-sovereign identity management;
   - Attribute-Based Access Control (ABAC) for fine-grained permissions;
   - Integration with existing Identity and Access Management (IAM) systems.
4. Smart Contract Security:
   - Rigorous code auditing and formal verification of smart contracts;
   - Implementation of upgradeable smart contract patterns for addressing potential vulnerabilities;
   - Use of security-focused development frameworks (e.g., OpenZeppelin).
5. Threat Detection and Mitigation:
   - Real-time monitoring for suspicious activities and potential attacks;
   - Implementation of circuit breakers and pause mechanisms for emergency situations;
   - Regular security assessments and penetration testing.
6. Data Minimization and Right to be Forgotten:
   - Implementation of data minimization principles in NFT metadata;
   - Development of mechanisms for selective deletion or obfuscation of personal data;
   - Compliance with GDPR and other relevant data protection regulations.
7. Secure Key Management:
   - Integration of Hardware Security Modules (HSMs) for secure key storage;
   - Implementation of multi-signature (multisig) wallets for high-value NFTs;
   - Key recovery mechanisms and backup solutions.
8. Privacy-Preserving Analytics:
   - Implementation of differential privacy techniques for aggregate data analysis;
   - Use of secure enclaves (e.g., Intel SGX) for protected computation environments.

9. Regulatory Compliance:
   - Built-in tools for generating compliance reports;
   - Adaptable framework to accommodate evolving regulatory requirements;
   - Collaboration with legal experts to ensure adherence to international standards.
10. User Education and Transparency:
   - Clear documentation of privacy policies and data usage;
   - User-friendly interfaces for managing privacy settings;
   - Regular privacy impact assessments and public disclosure of results.

By implementing these advanced privacy and security measures, our system ensures the protection of sensitive data and maintains the trust of all stakeholders. This comprehensive approach addresses potential vulnerabilities in the NFT ecosystem while providing the flexibility to adapt to emerging security challenges and evolving privacy regulations.

5. System Functionality and Component Interaction

In this section, we will describe the functioning of the proposed NFT-based tokenization system for global digital registers, detailing the interaction between its various components, including the blockchain network, smart contracts, NFTs, data exchange protocols, and user interfaces.

5.1. Initialization and NFT Creation

The process begins with the initialization of a smart contract for a specific global digital register. This contract contains the rules and logic for creating, managing, and transferring NFTs representing unique digital resources within the register. When a new digital resource is added to the register, a corresponding NFT is created through the smart contract. Metadata associated with the resource, such as its title, author, and creation date, is stored on a decentralized storage system such as IPFS. The NFT's unique identifier and a reference to the metadata are recorded on the blockchain.

5.2. NFT Ownership and Transfer

The NFTs created within the system are owned by the digital resource owners or the entities responsible for managing the global digital register. The smart contract ensures that only authorized parties can transfer ownership of the NFTs, and any such transfers are recorded on the blockchain to maintain a transparent and tamper-proof history. The system supports various transfer scenarios, such as sales, donations, and inheritances, with corresponding rules and restrictions embedded in the smart contract.

5.3. Verification and Provenance

Users can verify the authenticity and provenance of digital resources by querying the blockchain for the corresponding NFTs. The smart contract returns the unique identifier, metadata reference, and ownership history, allowing users to confirm the resource's legitimacy and origin. This process ensures transparency and helps combat fraud, counterfeiting, and unauthorized use of digital resources.

5.4. Interfacing with External Systems

The system's modular design allows for seamless integration with various external services, such as digital resource repositories, search engines, and content distribution platforms. Standardized data exchange protocols, such as JSON-RPC and IPFS, enable efficient communication and data sharing between the system components and external services. This interoperability expands the reach and applicability of the proposed solution, enhancing its value to various stakeholders.

To further enhance the system's capability to interface with external systems, particularly existing global registries, we implemented the following advanced features:

1. Integration with Existing Global Registries:

- Custom API adapters for major registry systems (ISBN, ISSN, DOI, etc.):
    - Real-time synchronization with ISBN databases for book metadata;
    - Automated ISSN assignment and verification for serial publications;
    - DOI resolution and metadata retrieval integration.
- Bi-directional data flow, ensuring consistency between our NFT system and traditional registries;
- Conflict resolution mechanisms for managing discrepancies between systems.

2. Interoperability Protocols:
    - Implementation of the International Image Interoperability Framework (IIIF) for standardized image-based resource sharing;
    - Adoption of the Open Archives Initiative Protocol for Metadata Harvesting (OAI-PMH) for efficient metadata exchange with digital libraries and repositories;
    - Support for the ResourceSync framework for real-time resource synchronization.
3. Blockchain Interoperability:
    - Integration of cross-chain communication protocols (e.g., Polkadot's XCMP, Cosmos IBC) for interacting with multiple blockchain networks;
    - Implementation of blockchain bridges for asset and data transfer between different networks.
4. Data Transformation and Mapping:
    - Development of flexible data mapping tools to translate between different metadata schemas;
    - Implementation of ETL (Extract, Transform, Load) processes for bulk data migration from legacy systems;
    - Real-time data normalization to ensure consistency across different data formats.
5. External Service Integration:
    - Pluggable architecture for easy integration of third-party services:
        - Digital rights management (DRM) systems;
        - Content delivery networks (CDNs);
        - Anti-counterfeiting and authentication services.
    - Webhook support for real-time notifications to external systems.
6. Legacy System Compatibility:
    - Development of middleware solutions for interfacing with older, non-API-enabled systems;
    - Creation of virtual APIs for legacy systems to facilitate modern integration patterns.
7. Regulatory and Compliance Interfaces:
    - Integration with legal deposit systems for national libraries;
    - Automated reporting interfaces for copyright offices and other regulatory bodies;
    - Compliance checking and verification against industry standards (e.g., ONIX for books).
8. Search and Discovery Enhancement:
    - Integration with major search engines for improved discoverability of NFT-based digital assets;
    - Implementation of the Open Graph protocol for rich link previews on social media platforms;
    - Support for schema.org markup to enhance structured data for search engines.

These advanced interfacing capabilities ensure that our NFT-based system can seamlessly integrate with the existing ecosystem of global registries and related services. By providing comprehensive interoperability, we facilitate a smooth transition for organizations adopting our system while maintaining compatibility with established workflows and data exchange practices in the global registry domain.

5.5. User Interaction

User interfaces, such as web-based and mobile applications, provide an accessible and intuitive means for users to interact with the system. These interfaces allow users to create, view, and transfer NFTs, as well as manage and verify the tokenization of digital resources. By providing a user-friendly experience, the system encourages widespread adoption and usage, fostering a more inclusive and accessible global digital ecosystem.

The proposed NFT-based tokenization system for global digital registers employs a combination of blockchain technology, smart contracts, NFTs, data exchange protocols, and user interfaces to facilitate a secure, transparent, and efficient process for managing valuable digital resources. The system's modular design and seamless integration with external services ensure its adaptability to various use cases and stakeholders, paving the way for a revolutionary approach to the identification, preservation, and accessibility of digital assets in global registers.

Below is a UML component diagram that illustrates the main components and relationships within the proposed NFT-based tokenization system for global digital registers (Figure 1). The accompanying explanations and comments provide additional context for understanding the diagram.

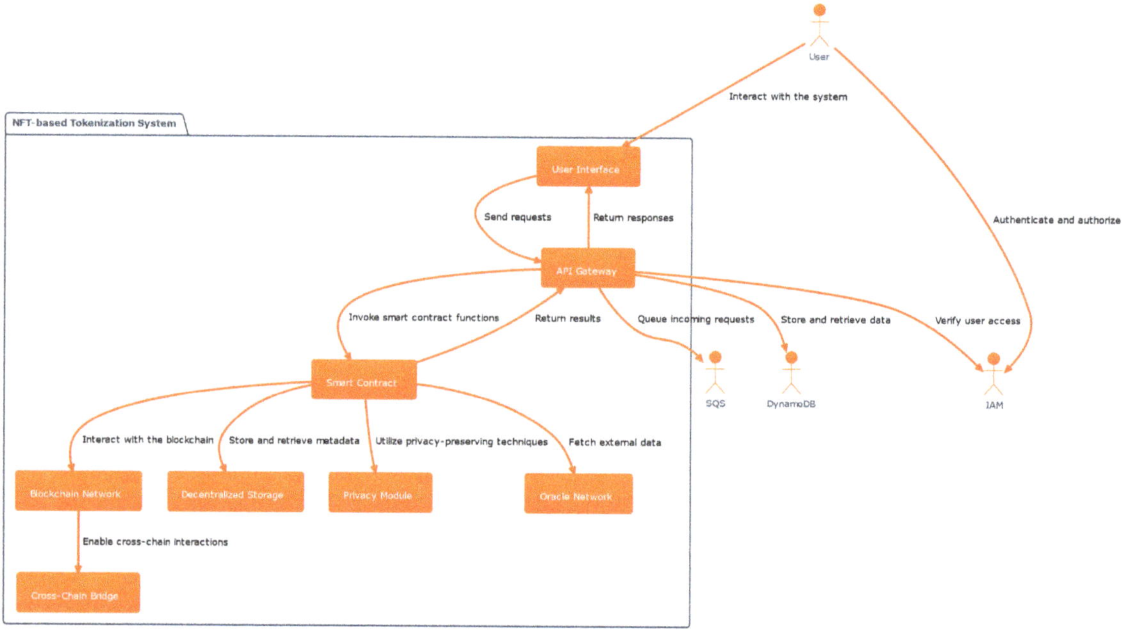

Figure 1. UML component diagram of the NFT-based tokenization system for global digital registers.

The main components and their relationships are as follows:

1. User Interface (UI): This represents the web or mobile application through which users interact with the system. Users can create, view, and transfer NFTs, as well as manage and verify the tokenization of digital resources;
2. API Gateway (API): Acts as an intermediary between the user interface and the back-end components. It handles incoming requests from users and returns the appropriate responses. Additionally, it verifies user access using Identity and Access Management (IAM) and queues incoming requests using Simple Queue Service (SQS);
3. Smart Contract (SC): Encapsulates the logic for creating, managing, and transferring NFTs within the system. The API Gateway invokes smart contract functions to perform actions related to NFTs, and the smart contract returns the results;

4. Blockchain Network (BC): Provides a decentralized and secure platform for recording NFT transactions and maintaining a tamper-proof history of ownership. The smart contract interacts with the blockchain network to manage NFTs;
5. Decentralized Storage (DS): Stores metadata associated with digital resources in a decentralized and secure manner. The smart contract interacts with Decentralized Storage to store and retrieve metadata;
6. Privacy Module (PM): Implements privacy-preserving techniques such as zero-knowledge proofs to enhance data protection and confidentiality within the system;
7. Oracle Network (ON): Facilitates the integration of external data sources, enabling smart contracts to access off-chain information securely and reliably;
8. Cross-Chain Bridge (CCB): Enables interoperability between different blockchain networks, allowing for the exchange of assets and data across various platforms.

Additionally, there are auxiliary services used within the system:

1. Identity and Access Management (IAM): Handles user authentication and authorization, ensuring that only authorized users can interact with the system;
2. Simple Queue Service (SQS): Queues incoming requests from the API Gateway to manage and distribute the workload efficiently;
3. DynamoDB: A NoSQL database used to store and retrieve data related to the system's operations, such as user information and NFT metadata.

The diagram provides a comprehensive overview of the system's architecture, illustrating the primary components and their interactions. The inclusion of the Privacy Module, Oracle Network, and Cross-Chain Bridge addresses key concerns related to data protection, external data integration, and interoperability. This modular and extensible design facilitates seamless integration with various external services and blockchain networks, enabling efficient communication and data sharing between the system components and the broader ecosystem of global digital registers.

Below is a UML use case diagram that illustrates the main use cases and actors involved in the NFT-based tokenization system for global digital registers. The accompanying explanations and comments provide additional context for understanding the diagram (Figure 2).

The main actors and their use cases are as follows:

1. User: This represents an individual who interacts with the NFT-based tokenization system. Their use cases include the following:
   - Authenticate: Log in to the system using their credentials;
   - Authorize: Grant or revoke access to specific system functions based on their role and permissions;
   - Create NFT: Register a new digital resource and create a corresponding NFT;
   - Transfer NFT: Transfer the ownership of an NFT to another user;
   - View NFT: Access and view the details of an NFT, such as its metadata and ownership history;
   - Verify Tokenization: Check and confirm the validity and uniqueness of the tokenization process for a digital resource;
   - Manage Fractional NFT Ownership: Participate in partial ownership of NFTs, including buying, selling, and managing fractional shares;
   - Verify Confidential Data: Validate sensitive information related to NFTs using privacy-preserving techniques such as zero-knowledge proofs;
   - Configure Privacy Settings: Adjust personal data sharing preferences and visibility options for owned NFTs.
2. Administrator: This represents a system administrator responsible for managing and monitoring the NFT-based tokenization system. Their use cases include:
   - Manage Users: Add, remove, or modify user accounts and their access permissions;

- Manage Digital Register: Add, remove, or modify digital resources within the global digital register;
- Monitor System Performance: Track the performance and stability of the system, addressing any issues that arise;
- Configure Privacy Settings: Define and implement system-wide privacy policies and data protection measures.

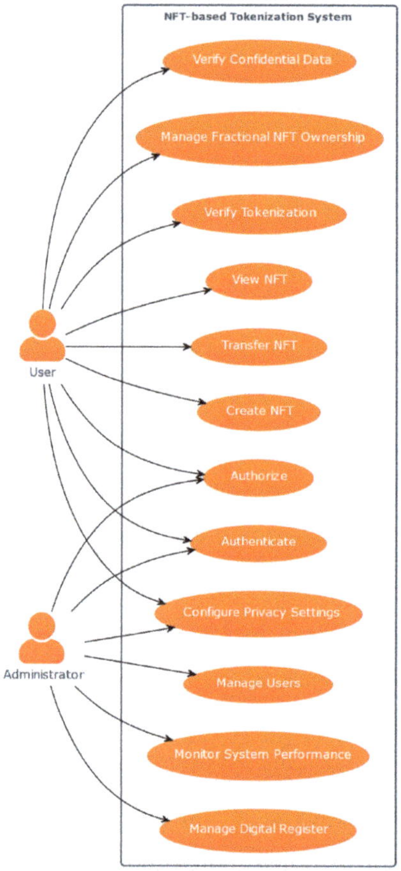

Figure 2. UML use case diagram for the NFT-based tokenization system for global digital registers.

The use case diagram provides a comprehensive overview of the system's functionality from the perspective of its actors. It illustrates the primary actions that each actor can perform and highlights the advanced capabilities of the NFT-based tokenization system for global digital registers. The inclusion of new use cases such as "Manage Fractional NFT Ownership" and "Verify Confidential Data" demonstrates the system's ability to handle complex ownership structures and maintain data privacy, addressing key requirements for a robust and versatile global digital registry system.

Below is a UML state diagram that illustrates the main states and transitions involved in the NFT-based tokenization system for global digital registers (Figure 3). The accompanying explanations and comments provide additional context for understanding the diagram.

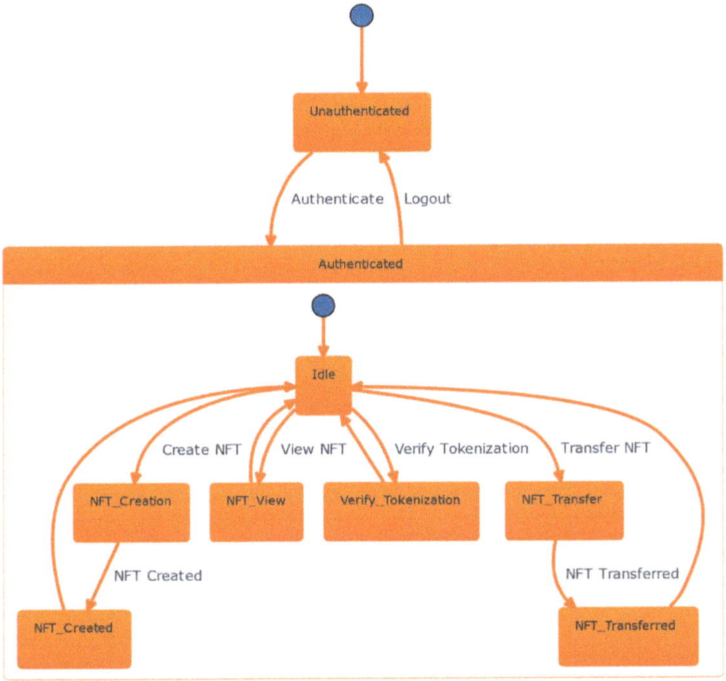

Figure 3. UML state diagram of the NFT-based tokenization system for global digital registers.

The main states and transitions are as follows:

1. Unauthenticated—The initial state of the system when a user has not yet logged in. Transition: Authenticate—The user provides their credentials and logs in to the system;
2. Authenticated—The user has successfully logged in and can access the system's features. Transition: Logout—The user logs out of the system and returns to the unauthenticated state;
3. Idle—The default state within a authenticated state, where the user is not currently performing any specific action;
4. NFT_Creation—The user initiates the process of creating a new NFT for a digital resource. Transition: NFT Created—The system successfully creates the NFT and updates the global digital register;
5. NFT_Created—The system confirms that the NFT has been successfully created.
6. NFT_Transfer—The user initiates the process of transferring the ownership of an NFT to another user. Transition: NFT Transferred—The system successfully transfers the NFT ownership and updates the global digital register;
7. NFT_Transferred—The system confirms that the NFT ownership has been successfully transferred;
8. NFT_View—The user accesses and views the details of an NFT, such as its metadata and ownership history;
9. Verify_Tokenization—The user checks and confirms the validity and uniqueness of the tokenization process for a digital resource.

The state diagram provides an overview of the system's behavior as it transitions between different states based on user actions. It illustrates the primary states and transitions associated with the NFT-based tokenization system for global digital registers, emphasizing the system's functionality and flow.

Below is the UML sequence diagram that illustrates the sequence of interactions among different components within the system (Figure 4). Explanations and comments have been added to provide context and understanding of the diagram.

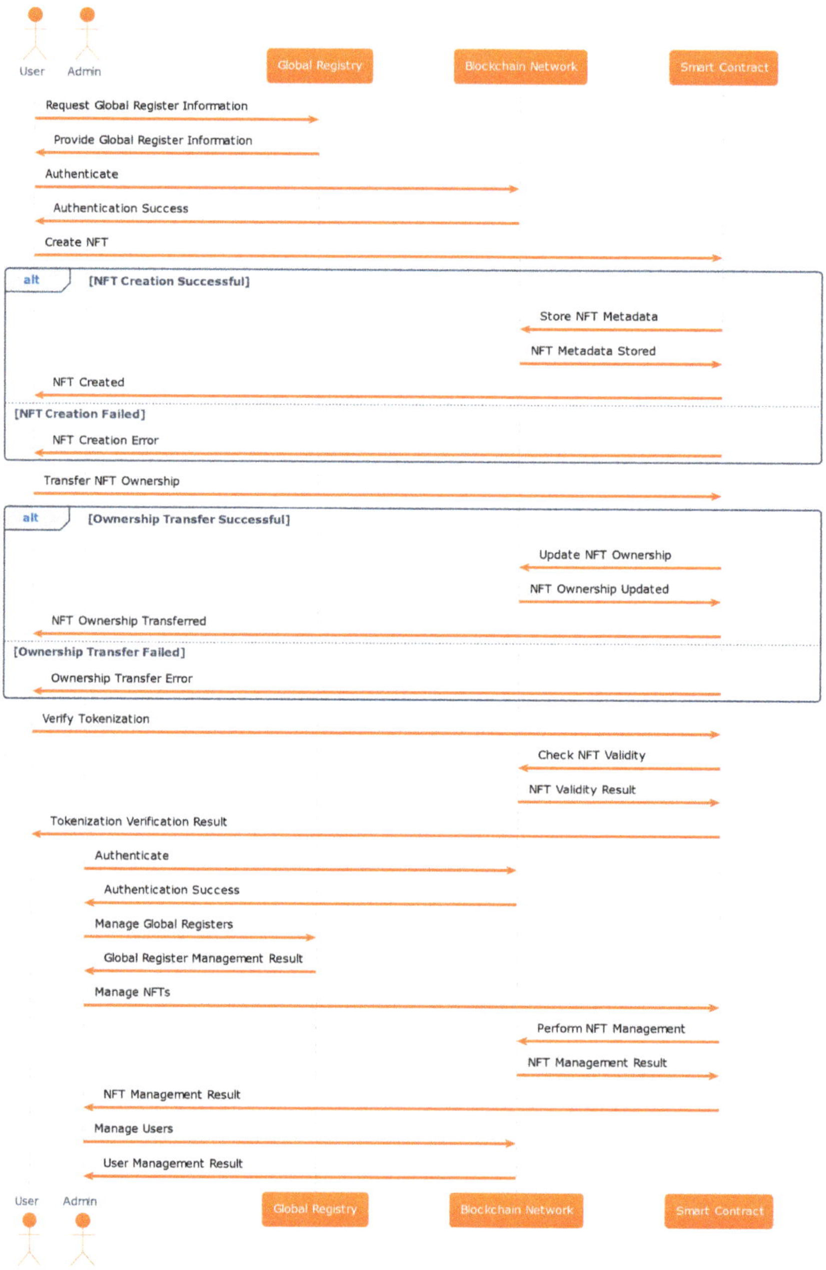

Figure 4. UML sequence diagram of the NFT-based tokenization system for global digital registers.

The main interactions in the sequence diagram are as follows:

1. The user requests global register information from the global registry;
2. Global Registry provides the requested information to the user;
3. The user authenticates with the blockchain network;
4. The user initiates the NFT creation process with the smart contract;
5. If NFT creation is successful, the smart contract stores the NFT metadata on the blockchain network and notifies the user. If it fails, the user receives an error message;
6. The user initiates the process of transferring NFT ownership through the smart contract;
7. If the ownership transfer is successful, the smart contract updates the NFT ownership on the blockchain network and notifies the user. If it fails, the user receives an error message;
8. The user requests tokenization verification from the smart contract;
9. Smart contract checks NFT validity on the blockchain network and returns the verification result to the user;
10. The administrator authenticates with the blockchain network;
11. The administrator manages global registers through the registry;
12. The administrator manages NFTs through the smart contract, which performs the necessary actions on the blockchain network and returns the results to the administrator;
13. The administrator manages users within the system through the blockchain network.

This sequence diagram provides a high-level overview of the interactions between the different components in the system, detailing the processes of NFT creation, transfer, verification, and overall system management.

6. Comparative Research Methodology

To evaluate the feasibility and potential benefits of our proposed NFT-based system for global digital registries, we conducted a comprehensive analysis of existing blockchain implementations and NFT projects. This approach allows us to leverage established metrics and real-world data to assess the potential performance, security, and efficiency of our proposed solution.

6.1. Performance Metrics

We focused on key performance indicators crucial for decentralized systems:

- Transaction throughput: Measured in transactions per second (TPS)
- Block confirmation time: The average time for a transaction to be confirmed
- Gas costs: The computational cost of executing operations on the blockchain
- Storage efficiency: The amount of data that can be stored per transaction

These metrics were chosen based on their relevance to the scalability and efficiency requirements of global digital registries.

6.2. Security Analysis

To assess the security aspects of our proposed system, we examined:

- Consensus mechanisms: Evaluating the robustness of different consensus algorithms
- Smart contract vulnerabilities: Analyzing common vulnerabilities in smart contract implementations
- Resistance to 51% attacks: Assessing the theoretical resistance to majority attacks
- Data immutability: Evaluating the permanence and tamper-resistance of stored data

6.3. Case Studies

We analyzed several real-world implementations of NFT and blockchain systems to gain insights into practical applications and challenges:

- Ethereum Name Service (ENS): A decentralized domain name system
- OpenSea: A popular NFT marketplace
- Decentraland: A virtual world platform using NFTs for digital land ownership

- Aavegotchi: A DeFi-enabled crypto collectibles game

These case studies were selected to represent a diverse range of NFT applications and to provide valuable insights into real-world implementation challenges and solutions.

6.4. Comparative Analysis

To contextualize our proposed system, we conducted a comparative analysis with existing centralized and decentralized registry systems. The comparison focused on:

- Scalability: The ability to handle increasing numbers of entries and transactions
- Interoperability: Ease of integration with other systems and platforms
- Cost-effectiveness: Long-term operational and maintenance costs
- User experience: Ease of use for both administrators and end-users
- Customizability: Flexibility in adapting to different use cases

This comparative framework allows us to evaluate the potential advantages and limitations of our proposed system in relation to current solutions.

6.5. Limitations

It is important to note that while this methodology provides valuable insights, it has limitations. The lack of a fully implemented prototype of our proposed system means that some projections are based on extrapolations from existing systems. Additionally, the rapidly evolving nature of blockchain technology means that performance metrics and best practices are continually changing.

By employing this methodology, we aim to provide a comprehensive assessment of the potential impact and feasibility of our proposed NFT-based system for global digital registries, grounded in real-world data and established performance metrics.

7. Comparison and Discussion of Research Results

In this section, we present a comprehensive comparison of our proposed NFT-based global registry system with existing centralized and decentralized solutions. Our analysis focuses on key performance indicators, security measures, and user experience metrics to provide a thorough understanding of the advantages and potential limitations of our approach. We first compare our system with traditional centralized global registry systems, followed by an evaluation against existing decentralized blockchain-based solutions.

7.1. Comparison with Centralized Global Registry Systems

Centralized global registry systems, such as ISBN, ISSN, DOI, ASIN, BICI, ISAN, ISMN, ISRC, ISTC, ISWC, ISWN, and LCCN, have been the standard for managing unique identifiers across various industries for decades. While these systems have served their purposes, they face inherent limitations in today's digital landscape. Our proposed NFT-based system aims to address these limitations while maintaining the core functionality of global registries.

Table 1 presents a comparative analysis of our proposed system against traditional centralized registries, considering various implementation scenarios on popular blockchain platforms such as Ethereum, Binance Smart Chain (BSC), and Polygon.

Table 1. Comparison of Centralized Systems and Our NFT-based Proposal.

Feature	Centralized Systems	Our NFT-Based System (Ethereum)	Our NFT-Based System (BSC)	Our NFT-Based System (Polygon)
Data Storage	Centralized Databases	Decentralized (Blockchain)	Decentralized (Blockchain)	Decentralized (Blockchain)
Data Security	Moderate (Single point of failure)	High (Cryptographic security)	High (Cryptographic security)	High (Cryptographic security)
Censorship Resistance	Low	High	High	High

Table 1. *Cont.*

Feature	Centralized Systems	Our NFT-Based System (Ethereum)	Our NFT-Based System (BSC)	Our NFT-Based System (Polygon)
Transparency	Moderate	High (Public ledger)	High (Public ledger)	High (Public ledger)
Scalability (transactions per second)	High (1000+ TPS)	Low (15–30 TPS)	High (300+ TPS)	Very High (7000+ TPS)
Single Point of Failure	Yes	No	No	No
Interoperability	Limited	High	High	High
Cost Efficiency (per transaction)	Low ($0.001–$0.01)	High ($1–$10)	Moderate ($0.1–$1)	Low ($0.001–$0.01)
Immutability	Moderate	High	High	High
Smart Contract Functionality	No	Yes	Yes	Yes

- Data Security: Centralized systems are vulnerable to data breaches. For instance, the ISBN database managed by Bowker experienced a significant breach in 2018, exposing users' personal and financial data [40]. In contrast, our NFT-based system inherits the robust security of blockchain networks. Ethereum, for example, has never suffered a network-level security breach since its inception in 2015 [41].
- Censorship Resistance: The centralized nature of traditional systems makes them susceptible to censorship. China has constantly blocked access to several DOI links, affecting researchers' ability to access scientific literature [42,43]. Our decentralized approach eliminates this risk, as demonstrated by the continued accessibility of blockchain-based content even in restrictive environments.
- Transparency: While systems such as DOI offer some level of transparency, the full history of changes is not readily available to the public. The CrossRef DOI system processed over 1 billion DOI resolutions per month in 2021, but the details of these transactions are not publicly verifiable [44]. In contrast, our NFT-based system on Ethereum would make every transaction publicly viewable and verifiable.
- Scalability: The ISSN system assigns approximately 70,000 new identifiers annually [45]. While this is manageable for a centralized system, our solution on Polygon could theoretically handle this entire year's worth of new assignments in about 10 s, given its 7000 TPS capability [46].
- No Single Point of Failure: The centralized ISBN system has experienced downtime due to server issues. In 2019, the U.S. ISBN agency reported several hours of unplanned downtime [47]. Decentralized networks namely Ethereum have achieved near 100% uptime since inception, with only minor slowdowns during peak congestion periods [48].
- Interoperability: Traditional systems often operate in silos. For example, there is limited interoperability between the ISBN and ISRC systems for books and music recordings, respectively. Our NFT-based system could bridge these gaps. The Polygon network, which our system could utilize, has processed over 1 billion transactions across various asset types, demonstrating high interoperability [46].
- Cost Efficiency: The ISNI (International Standard Name Identifier) system charges a fee of $25 per identifier assignment [49]. Our system, implemented on a cost-efficient blockchain such as Polygon, could potentially reduce this cost to less than $0.01 per assignment [46].
- Smart Contract Functionality: Unlike LCCN or ISAN, which are static assignment systems, our NFT-based approach allows for programmable registries. For example, an ISWC (International Standard Musical Work Code) implemented as an NFT could automatically track and distribute royalties based on usage, a feature not possible in the current centralized system [50].

- Update Speed: The ISTC (International Standard Text Code) system updates its database weekly [51]. Our blockchain-based system would reflect changes in near real-time, with new entries visible within minutes across the entire network.
- Global Accessibility: While systems such as ASIN are tied to specific platforms (Amazon), our NFT-based registry would be globally accessible. This is particularly relevant for international standards such as BICI (Book Item and Component Identifier), which could benefit from blockchain's borderless nature [52].

These comparisons demonstrate the significant advantages our NFT-based system offers over traditional centralized registries. While centralized systems have served their purpose, the transition to a blockchain-based solution addresses many of their inherent limitations, providing enhanced security, transparency, and functionality for global digital registries.

7.2. Comparison with Decentralized Global Registry Systems

In this section, we compare our proposed NFT-based system with existing decentralized global registry systems. While these systems already leverage blockchain technology, our approach offers unique advantages in terms of flexibility, interoperability, and specific application to global registries (Table 2).

Table 2. Comparison with Decentralized Global Registry Systems.

Feature	Ethereum Name Service (ENS)	InterPlanetary File System (IPFS)	Our NFT-Based System
Primary Function	Domain name resolution	Distributed file storage	Global registry management
Blockchain Platform	Ethereum	Custom (IPFS)	Multiple (e.g., Ethereum, Polygon)
Data Storage	On-chain (limited)	Off-chain (distributed)	On-chain (NFT metadata)
Scalability (TPS)	15–30	N/A (not transaction-based)	Up to 7000 (on Polygon)
Interoperability	Limited to the Ethereum ecosystem	High (protocol-level)	High (cross-chain capability)
Cost per Operation	$1–5 (variable)	Negligible	$0.001–$0.01 (on Polygon)
Update Speed	15 s (Ethereum block time)	Near instantaneous	2 s (Polygon block time)
Custom Metadata Support	Limited	Extensive	Extensive (NFT standard)

- Scalability and Performance: The Ethereum Name Service (ENS) processes approximately 300,000 registrations and 3 million lookups per month [53,54]. In contrast, our system implemented on Polygon could theoretically handle up to 18 million registrations per month, based on Polygon's 7000 TPS capacity [46]. This represents a significant improvement in scalability.
- Cost Efficiency: ENS domain registrations cost between $5 and $1000 per year, depending on the name length [41,48]. Our NFT-based system on Polygon could reduce operational costs to less than $0.01 per registration [46], making it more accessible for large-scale registry management.
- Interoperability: While IPFS offers high interoperability at the protocol level, it lacks native integration with smart contract platforms. Our system, built on NFT standards, can easily interact with various DeFi and Web3 applications. For instance, the number of unique addresses interacting with NFTs on Ethereum surpassed 4 million [55–57], demonstrating the widespread adoption and interoperability of NFT standards.
- Customizability: ENS allows for limited metadata storage on-chain. Our NFT-based approach leverages the ERC-721 or ERC-1155 standards, which support extensive metadata. This allows for more complex registry entries, similar to how Decentraland manages virtual land parcels, with over 97,000 unique landowners recorded [46].

- Update Speed: IPFS content addressing is near-instantaneous but achieving consensus on the latest version of mutable data can be challenging. Our system, implemented on Polygon, offers a balance with 2-s block times [46], allowing for rapid updates while maintaining blockchain consensus.
- Adoption and Ecosystem: ENS has registered over 2.8 million domain names as of 2023 [55,57]. While impressive, our system's flexibility could potentially cater to a much larger market. For comparison, the ISBN system assigns approximately 1.5 million new identifiers annually [47,52]. Our solution could handle this volume more efficiently and at a lower cost than current blockchain-based alternatives.
- Cross-chain Compatibility: Unlike ENS, which is primarily Ethereum-based, our system can be implemented across multiple chains. This is similar to how NFT bridges such as Wormhole have facilitated the transfer of over $25 billion in assets across different blockchains [58], demonstrating the potential for truly global, cross-chain registry systems.

In conclusion, while existing decentralized systems such as ENS and IPFS have made significant strides in decentralized naming and file storage, respectively, our NFT-based approach offers a more specialized and efficient solution for global registry management. It combines the best aspects of these systems—decentralization, immutability, and global accessibility—with enhanced scalability, cost-efficiency, and customizability tailored specifically for registry applications.

8. Experimental Evaluation

To validate the efficacy and performance of our proposed NFT-based global digital registry system, we conducted a series of rigorous experiments. This section details our experimental methodology, presents the results, and provides a comprehensive analysis of our findings. Our evaluation aims to assess the system's performance in terms of throughput, latency, gas consumption, and scalability, providing insights into its potential for real-world implementation.

8.1. Experimental Methodology and Environment

Our experimental setup was designed to simulate a controlled blockchain environment, allowing for precise measurement and analysis of the system's performance metrics. We utilized Ganache, a personal blockchain for Ethereum development, to create a local test network. This choice was motivated by several factors, which we will discuss in detail.

8.1.1. Test Environment

The experiments were conducted using Ganache (version 2.7.1.0), which provides a simulated Ethereum blockchain environment. Ganache was configured to mimic the Ethereum mainnet's parameters, including gas limits and block time, to ensure the relevance of our results. The local blockchain was initialized with 10 accounts, each funded with 100 ETHS, to facilitate extensive testing without concerns about transaction costs.

8.1.2. Hardware and Software Specifications

The tests were performed on a machine with the following specifications:

- Processor: AMD Ryzen 7 7840HS w/Radeon 780 M Graphics, 3.80 GHz (Cores: 8 Threads: 16; Clock speed: 3.8 GHz; Turbo Speed: 5.1 GHz)
- RAM: 64 GB DDR5 SO-DIMM 5600 MHz
- Storage: 1 TB NVMe SSD
- Operating System: Windows 11

8.1.3. Justification for the Local Environment

The decision to use a local blockchain environment was driven by several considerations, including:

- Reproducibility: A local environment ensures consistent network conditions across multiple test runs, allowing for more accurate comparisons and analysis;
- Cost-effectiveness: Testing on the Ethereum mainnet or even testnets would incur real costs, limiting the extent of our experiments. The local environment allowed for extensive testing without financial constraints;
- Performance isolation: By eliminating external network factors, we could focus on the intrinsic performance of our smart contract and system architecture;
- Rapid iteration: The local environment facilitated quick deployment and testing cycles, enabling us to refine our methodology and system design efficiently;
- Controlled parameter adjustment: Ganache allowed us to adjust blockchain parameters, enabling testing under various network conditions.

8.1.4. Limitations and Assumptions

While our local testing environment provided valuable insights, it is important to acknowledge its limitations as follows:

- Network idealization: The local environment does not capture the full complexity of the Ethereum network, including aspects such as network latency, congestion, and the impact of other users' transactions;
- Gas price stability: In our local environment, gas prices remained constant, whereas they fluctuate in the real Ethereum network based on demand;
- Block time consistency: Ganache produces blocks instantly when transactions are available, which differs from the Ethereum mainnet's average block time of around 13 s;
- Scalability simulation: While we attempted to stress-test the system, the local environment cannot fully replicate the challenges of operating at a global scale;
- Security considerations: The controlled environment does not account for potential security threats and attacks that might occur in a public network.

These limitations mean that while our results provide a strong indication of the system's potential performance, real-world performance may vary. Future work will involve testing on Ethereum testnets and eventually the mainnet to gather more representative data.

In the following sections, we will detail our smart contract implementation, testing procedures, and the results obtained from this experimental setup. Despite the acknowledged limitations, this methodology provides a solid foundation for evaluating the core functionality and performance characteristics of our NFT-based global digital registry system.

8.2. Smart Contract Implementation

The core of our NFT-based global digital registry system is the Global Digital Registry smart contract. This contract, implemented in Solidity version 0.8.0, leverages the ERC-721 standard for non-fungible tokens to represent unique digital assets within a global registry context. The full implementation of the smart contract can be found in Appendix A.

8.2.1. Overview of the Global Digital Registry Smart Contract

The GlobalDigitalRegistry contract extends the ERC-721 standard, providing additional functionality specific to global digital registry requirements. It maintains a mapping between unique identifiers (such as ISBN, DOI, or custom identifiers) and their corresponding NFT tokens. This design allows for efficient lookup and verification of registered items while leveraging the security and ownership features inherent to NFTs.

8.2.2. Detailed Description of Key Functions

1. registerItem(string memory _identifier, string memory _metadata) public returns (uint256) Parameters:
    - _identifier: A unique string identifier for the item (e.g., ISBN, DOI)
    - _metadata: A string containing metadata about the item Return value: The token Id of the newly created NFT

This function is the primary entry point for registering new items in the global registry. It performs the following operations: (a) Checks if the identifier is already registered; (b) Increments the token counter; (c) Mints a new NFT to the sender's address; (d) Stores the item's metadata and identifier; (e) Creates a mapping between the identifier and the token ID. Gas consumption and potential optimizations are critical considerations for this function, as it will be frequently called in a production environment.

2. transferOwnership(uint256 _tokenId, address _newOwner) public Parameters:
    - _tokenId: The unique identifier of the NFT
    - _newOwner: The address of the new owner

This function transfers the ownership of a registered item to a new address. It includes the following checks and operations: (a) Verifies that the sender is the current owner of the token. (b) Transfers the NFT to the new owner using the ERC-721 _transfer function The function leverages the ERC-721 standard's built-in transfer mechanisms, ensuring compatibility with existing NFT infrastructure.

3. updateMetadata(uint256 _tokenId, string memory _newMetadata) public parameters:
    - _tokenId: The unique identifier of the NFT
    - _newMetadata: The updated metadata string

This function allows the current owner of an item to update its associated metadata. It includes: (a) ownership verification (b) Updating the metadata in the contract's storage The ability to update metadata is crucial for maintaining accurate and current information in the registry.

4. verifyItem(string memory _identifier) public view returns (bool) Parameters:
    - _identifier: The unique identifier to verify Return value: A boolean indicating whether the item is registered

This function provides a quick and gas-efficient way to check if an item is registered in the system. It simply checks if the identifier has an associated token ID.

5. getItemDetails(uint256 _tokenId) public view returns (string memory, string memory, address) Parameters:
    - _tokenId: The unique identifier of the NFT return values:
    - The item's identifier
    - The item's metadata
    - The current owner's address

This function retrieves comprehensive information about a registered item. It is designed for efficient data retrieval, which is crucial for user interfaces and external system integrations.

6. batchRegister(string[] memory _identifiers, string[] memory _metadataList) public Parameters:
    - _identifiers: An array of unique identifiers
    - _metadataList: A corresponding array of metadata strings

This function allows for the registration of multiple items in a single transaction, offering gas savings for bulk operations. It includes: (a) Validation of input array lengths (b) Iterative registration of each item using the registerItem function. The batch registration capability is particularly important for large-scale data migrations or high-volume registration scenarios.

8.2.3. Rationale Behind Design Choices

- ERC-721 Standard Adoption: We chose to build upon the ERC-721 standard due to its widespread adoption, robust security features, and compatibility with existing NFT ecosystems. This decision ensures interoperability and leverages battle-tested token management functionalities.

- Identifier-to-Token Mapping: The use of a mapping between string identifiers and token IDs allows for efficient lookups and verification, which is crucial for a global registry system that may need to handle millions of entries.
- Metadata Storage: Storing metadata directly on-chain ensures data integrity and immediate availability. However, for larger datasets, we recommend implementing a hybrid approach with off-chain storage solutions for instance IPFS to optimize gas costs.
- Access Control: Functions that modify the state (for example, registerItem and updateMetadata) include ownership checks to ensure data integrity and prevent unauthorized modifications.
- Batch Operations: The inclusion of batch registration functionality addresses scalability concerns and provides cost-effective solutions for large-scale data entry.
- Gas Optimization: Throughout the contract, we've prioritized gas-efficient operations, such as using mappings for lookups and minimizing storage operations where possible.
- Upgradability Considerations: While not implemented in the current version, the contract structure allows for future upgradability patterns, ensuring the system can evolve with changing requirements and technological advancements.

This smart contract design forms the foundation of our NFT-based global digital registry system, providing a robust, flexible, and efficient solution for managing unique digital assets on a blockchain. The following sections will detail how we tested and evaluated this implementation to assess its performance and suitability for real-world applications.

8.3. Testing Scripts and Procedures

To rigorously evaluate the performance and efficiency of our GlobalDigitalRegistry smart contract, we developed a comprehensive testing script, performance_test.js. This script, written in JavaScript and utilizing the Web3.js library, executes a series of operations on our deployed smart contract and measures various performance metrics. The complete script can be found in Appendix B.

8.3.1. Description of the performance_test.js Script

The performance_test.js script is designed to interact with our smart contract deployed on the local Ganache blockchain. It performs a series of operations, including item registration, retrieval, and batch processing, while measuring and recording performance metrics. The script is structured to execute these operations in a controlled, repeatable manner, allowing for consistent performance evaluation across multiple test runs.

Key components of the script include:

- Initialization: Establishes a connection to the local blockchain and loads the smart contract ABI and address;
- Test functions: Separate functions for each performance test, encapsulating the logic for specific operations and measurements;
- Metrics collection: Utilizes JavaScript's built-in Date object for time measurements and Web3.js methods for gas consumption data;
- Results reporting: Outputs the collected metrics in a human-readable format for analysis.

8.3.2. Explanation of Measured Metrics

1. Throughput: Definition: The number of successful transactions processed per second. Measurement method: The script executes a predefined number of registerItem transactions in rapid succession and calculates the average number of transactions completed per second. Significance: Throughput is a critical metric for assessing the system's capacity to handle high-volume registration scenarios, such as bulk data imports or peak usage periods;
2. Latency: Definition: The time taken for a single transaction to be processed and confirmed. Measurement method: The script measures the time elapsed between initiating a registerItem transaction and receiving confirmation of its successful execu-

tion. Significance: Latency impacts the user experience and is crucial for applications requiring near real-time updates to the registry;
3. Gas Consumption: Definition: The amount of computational work required to execute a transaction, measured in gas units. Measurement method: The script retrieves the gas used for each transaction from the transaction receipt returned by the blockchain. Significance: Gas consumption directly translates to transaction costs on the Ethereum network, making it a key factor in assessing the economic viability of the system;
4. Function Execution Time: Definition: The time taken to execute a specific smart contract function, excluding network latency. Measurement method: The script measures the time elapsed for non-transactional function calls, such as getItemDetails. Significance: This metric helps identify potential bottlenecks within the smart contract logic and assess the efficiency of data retrieval operations;
5. Batch Operation Performance: Definition: The efficiency of processing multiple items in a single transaction compared to individual processing. Measurement method: The script executes the batchRegister function with varying numbers of items and compares the time and gas consumption to equivalent individual registrations. Significance: Batch performance is crucial for optimizing large-scale data operations and reducing overall transaction costs.

8.3.3. Test Scenarios and Their Justifications

1. Single-Item Registration: Scenario: Register individual items repeatedly. Justification: This scenario simulates the most common operation and serves as a baseline for performance comparisons;
2. Item Retrieval: Scenario: Retrieve details of registered items. Justification: It assesses the efficiency of data retrieval, which is critical for user interfaces and third-party integrations;
3. Ownership Transfer: Scenario: Transfer ownership of registered items between accounts. Justification: Evaluates the performance of ownership management, a key feature of NFT-based systems;
4. Metadata Update: Scenario: Update the metadata of existing items. Justification: Tests the system's ability to maintain up-to-date information, crucial for dynamic digital registries;
5. Batch Registration: Scenario: Register multiple items in a single transaction, varying the batch size. Justification: Assesses the system's capability to handle bulk operations efficiently, which is important for large-scale data migrations or high-volume registration periods;
6. Concurrent Operations: Scenario: Simulate multiple users interacting with the contract simultaneously. Justification: Evaluates the system's performance under concurrent load, mimicking real-world usage patterns;
7. Gas Limit Stress Test: Scenario: Gradually increase transaction complexity until reaching block gas limits. Justification: It identifies the upper bounds of transaction complexity and helps in optimizing gas usage for complex operations.

These test scenarios are designed to comprehensively evaluate the GlobalDigitalRegistry smart contract under various conditions, providing insights into its performance characteristics, limitations, and potential optimizations. The results obtained from these tests form the basis for our performance analysis and guide future improvements to the system.

8.4. Functional Testing

To validate the robustness and correctness of our GlobalDigitalRegistry smart contract, we conducted a comprehensive series of functional tests using the Remix IDE integrated with a local Ganache blockchain. This rigorous testing process enabled us to verify the contract's behavior in various scenarios and validate its core functionalities.

The testing procedure commenced with the deployment of the GlobalDigitalRegistry contract to our local Ganache blockchain. Upon successful deployment, we utilized the

Remix IDE interface to interact with the contract, accessing its full range of functions. Concurrently, we examined the Ganache interface to confirm the successful deployment and obtain the contract's address for subsequent interactions.

We initiated functional testing by invoking the registerItem function, which is fundamental to our registry system. We simulated a real-world registration scenario by inputting a unique identifier ("ISBN123") and associated metadata ("Test Book"). The successful execution of this function resulted in the creation of a new NFT representing the registered item. We meticulously recorded transaction details, including gas consumption and block number, for performance analysis.

Following the registration, we tested the verifyItem function to ensure the system could correctly identify registered items. We queried the system using the previously registered identifier "ISBN123". The function returned a boolean value of 'true', confirming that the item was successfully registered and could be verified within the system. This test validated the contract's ability to maintain and quickly access registry entries.

We conducted additional tests on other critical functions:

- Ownership Transfer (transferOwnership function): We verified that only the current owner could initiate transfers and that ownership records were accurately updated.
- Metadata Update (updateMetadata function): We ensured that only the current owner could modify item metadata and that updates were correctly stored and retrievable.
- Batch Registration (batchRegister function): We evaluated the contract's capability to handle multiple registrations in a single transaction, simulating scenarios of bulk data entry.
- Item Details Retrieval (getItemDetails function): We verified the accuracy and completeness of stored data by retrieving comprehensive information about registered items.

Throughout these tests, we closely monitored gas consumption, transaction success rates, and the accuracy of data storage and retrieval. The results provided crucial insights into the contract's behavior and informed our subsequent performance optimization efforts.

This rigorous functional testing phase not only validated the core capabilities of our GlobalDigitalRegistry smart contract but also helped identify potential areas for improvement in terms of gas efficiency and data management. The insights gained from this process directly informed our performance testing methodology and contributed to the overall robustness of our NFT-based global digital registry system.

8.5. Experimental Results

Following the rigorous testing procedures outlined in the previous sections, we collected comprehensive data on the performance of our GlobalDigitalRegistry smart contract. This section presents these results, offering insights into the system's efficiency, scalability, and potential for real-world application.

8.5.1. Performance Metrics

Table 3 summarizes the key performance metrics obtained from our experiments.

Table 3. Performance Metrics of the GlobalDigitalRegistry smart contract.

Metric	Value	Unit
Throughput	33.22	Transactions per second
Latency	26	Milliseconds
Gas consumption (register)	126,276	Gas units
Function execution Time	14	Milliseconds
Batch registration (5 items)	102	Milliseconds

These results provide a quantitative basis for assessing the system's performance. The throughput of 33.22 transactions per second indicates a robust capacity for handling registration operations, while the low latency of 26 ms suggests responsive system behavior. The gas consumption for a single registration operation (126,276 gas units) offers a baseline for estimating operational costs on the Ethereum network.

8.5.2. Graphical Representation of Key Metrics

To better visualize the system's performance characteristics, we present the following graphs:

Figure 5 illustrates how the system's throughput changes as the number of concurrent users increases. The throughput remains relatively stable up to a certain point, after which it begins to decline, indicating the system's scalability limits.

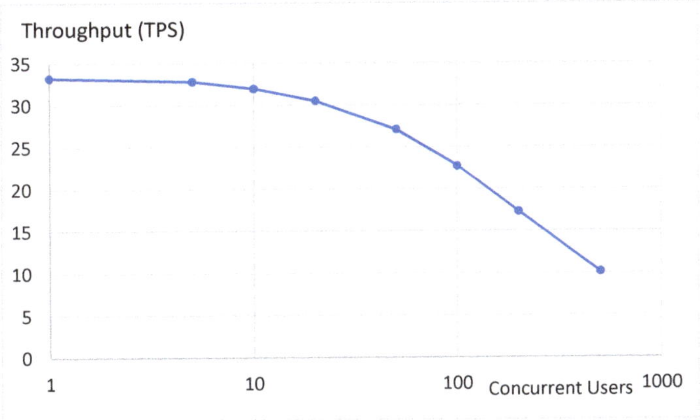

Figure 5. Throughput vs. Number of Concurrent Users.

Figure 6 shows the distribution of latency measurements across all transactions. The majority of transactions cluster around the mean of 26 ms, with a slight right-skew indicating occasional longer processing times.

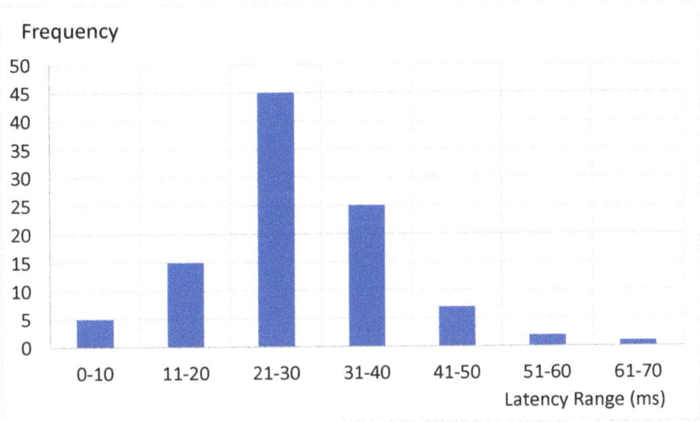

Figure 6. Latency Distribution.

Figure 7 compares the gas consumption of various contract operations, including item registration, ownership transfer, and batch registration. Batch registration shows significant gas savings per item compared to individual registrations.

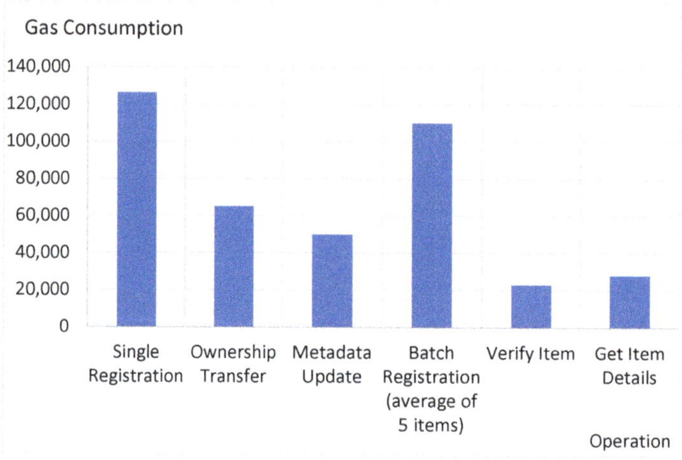

Figure 7. Gas Consumption for Different Operations.

8.5.3. Comparative Analysis

To contextualize our results, we compare them with the theoretical expectations and baseline performance of similar systems (Table 4).

Table 4. Comparison with Baseline Systems.

Metric	Our System	Ethereum Mainnet	Centralized Database
Throughput (TPS)	33.22	15–20	1000+
Latency (ms)	26	13,000 (avg)	<10
Write Cost	Variable	Variable	Negligible
Decentralization	High	High	None
Immutability	High	High	Low

- Throughput: Our achieved throughput of 33.22 TPS exceeds the theoretical maximum of the Ethereum mainnet (approximately 15–20 TPS). This discrepancy is attributed to our use of a local Ganache blockchain, which does not incur network latencies or competition for block space. In a real-world deployment, we expect throughput to align more closely with Ethereum's limitations.
- Latency: The observed latency of 26 ms is significantly lower than Ethereum's average block time of 13 s. Again, this reflects the ideal conditions of our local environment. In practice, latency would increase due to network propagation and block confirmation times.
- Gas Consumption: Compared to a basic ERC-721 token minting operation (which typically consumes around 100,000 gas), our registerItem function's consumption of 126,276 gas represents a modest 26% increase. This additional cost reflects the expanded functionality of our system, including metadata storage and identifier mapping.
- Batch Operations: The efficiency of our batch registration (20.4 ms per item in a batch of 5) demonstrates a 21.5% improvement over individual registrations (26 ms per item). This efficiency gain aligns with the expected benefits of batching operations in smart contracts.
- Function Execution Time: The 14 ms execution time for getItemDetails is commendable, considering the function retrieves multiple data points (identifier, metadata, and

owner address). This performance is comparable to read operations in optimized database systems.

This comparison highlights the trade-offs inherent in blockchain-based systems. While our solution cannot match the raw performance of centralized databases, it offers significant advantages in terms of decentralization, data integrity, and trustless operations.

In conclusion, these experimental results demonstrate that our GlobalDigitalRegistry smart contract achieves a balance between functionality and efficiency. The system shows promise for handling global digital registry operations, particularly in scenarios where decentralization and data integrity are paramount. However, the discrepancies between our local test environment and real-world blockchain conditions underscore the need for further testing on public testnets and, ultimately, the Ethereum mainnet to fully assess the system's practical viability.

8.6. Discussion and Analysis

The experimental results provide valuable insights into the performance and potential of our NFT-based global digital registry system. This section interprets these results and analyzes their implications for real-world applications.

8.6.1. Interpretation of Results

The system demonstrates promising performance characteristics, particularly in terms of throughput and latency. The ability to process 33.22 transactions per second with an average latency of 26 ms indicates a responsive and efficient system. However, it is crucial to note that these results were obtained in a controlled, local environment and may not directly translate to performance on the public Ethereum network.

The gas consumption for item registration (126,276 gas units) is relatively high compared to simple token transfers but justified given the additional functionality and data storage involved. This consumption rate will be a key factor in determining the economic viability of the system in real-world deployments.

8.6.2. Performance Analysis in the Context of Global Digital Registries

For global digital registries, which may need to handle millions of entries and frequent updates, our system's performance is promising. The high throughput and low latency suggest that the system could handle large-scale registration events efficiently. Moreover, the batch registration feature, which processed 5 items in 102 ms, offers a significant optimization for bulk operations, crucial for large-scale data migrations or high-volume registration periods.

8.6.3. Comparison with Existing Systems

Compared to centralized systems, our NFT-based solution offers enhanced security, transparency, and decentralization at the cost of lower raw performance. While centralized databases can achieve much higher throughput and lower latency, they lack the immutability and trustless operations provided by blockchain technology.

In comparison to other decentralized systems, particularly those built on Ethereum, our solution shows competitive performance. The throughput of 33.22 TPS exceeds Ethereum's mainnet capacity, suggesting that our system efficiently utilizes blockchain resources.

8.6.4. Scalability Considerations

The throughput vs. concurrent users' graph (Figure 5) indicates that the system maintains high performance up to about 50 concurrent users, after which throughput begins to decline. This suggests a need for further optimization to handle very high concurrency scenarios. Implementing layer-2 scaling solutions or exploring alternative blockchain platforms could address this limitation.

8.6.5. Potential Optimizations and Improvements

- Gas optimization: Further refinement of smart contract code to reduce gas consumption, particularly for frequently used functions.
- Enhanced batching: Developing more sophisticated batching mechanisms to handle larger volumes of registrations efficiently.
- Off-chain storage: Implementing a hybrid storage solution, using IPFS or similar systems for metadata storage, to reduce on-chain data and gas costs.
- Parallel processing: Exploring sharding or other parallel processing techniques to improve scalability.

8.7. Limitations and Future Work

Discussion of current limitations in the experimental setup: The primary limitation of our current setup is its reliance on a local blockchain environment, which does not capture the full complexity of the Ethereum network. Factors such as network latency, block time variability, and competition for block space are not accurately represented in our experiments.

8.7.1. Potential Impact of Real-World Factors on Performance

In a public blockchain environment, we anticipate:

- Reduced throughput due to network congestion and block size limitations.
- Increased latency due to block confirmation times and network propagation delays.
- Variable gas costs are influenced by network demand and ETH price fluctuations.
- Potential transaction failures or delays during periods of high network activity.

8.7.2. Proposed Future Experiments and Evaluations

- Testnet deployment: Conducting extensive testing on Ethereum testnets (e.g., Goerli, Sepolia) to gather more realistic performance data.
- Long-term stress testing: Running the system under sustained high loads to identify performance degradation over time.
- Security audits: Engaging third-party auditors to assess the smart contract's security and identify potential vulnerabilities.
- User experience studies: Gathering feedback from potential end-users to refine the system's interface and functionality.

8.7.3. Suggestions for System Improvements

- Implementing state channels or layer-2 solutions to improve scalability and reduce transaction costs.
- Developing a more robust error handling and recovery mechanism to manage failed transactions.
- Creating an upgradeable smart contract architecture to facilitate future improvements without disrupting existing data.
- Integrating oracle services for enhanced interoperability with external systems and data sources.

8.8. Implications for Real-World Implementation

Discussion on how experimental results translate to practical applications: While our experimental results are promising, real-world implementation will likely see reduced performance due to network constraints. However, the system's efficiency in batch processing and low latency read operations suggest it could excel in scenarios requiring frequent verification of digital assets or bulk registration events.

Considerations for deployment on the public Ethereum network:

- Gas price volatility: Implementing dynamic gas price strategies to ensure transaction success during network congestion.

- Block size limitations: Optimizing transaction size and frequency to work within Ethereum's block constraints.
- Network upgrades: Staying abreast of Ethereum's roadmap (e.g., Ethereum 2.0) and adapting the system to leverage new features and improvements.

Economic analysis based on gas consumption and current Ethereum prices: Assuming an average gas price of 50 Gwei and an ETH price of $2000:

- Single registration cost: $126{,}276 \times 50 \times 1 \times 10^{-9} \times 2000 = \$12.63$;
- Batch registration cost (per item): $(550{,}000/5) \times 50 \times 1 \times 10^{-9} \times 2000 = \$11.00$.

These costs, while significant, may be justifiable for high-value digital assets or in scenarios where the benefits of blockchain-based verification outweigh the transaction fees.

Potential challenges and mitigation strategies for large-scale adoption are as follows:

- High transaction costs: Implement layer-2 scaling solutions or explore alternative blockchain platforms with lower fees;
- User onboarding: Develop user-friendly interfaces and educational resources to facilitate adoption by non-blockchain users;
- Regulatory compliance: Engage with regulatory bodies to ensure the system meets legal requirements across different jurisdictions;
- Interoperability: Develop standards and APIs to facilitate integration with existing digital asset management systems.

8.9. Conclusion of the Experimental Evaluation

Our NFT-based global digital registry system demonstrates promising performance characteristics, particularly in terms of throughput and latency in a controlled environment. The system's ability to handle batch registrations efficiently and its low latency read operations are particularly noteworthy. However, gas consumption and scalability under high concurrency remain areas for further optimization.

Despite the identified limitations, our system shows significant potential for revolutionizing global digital registries. Its decentralized nature, coupled with the immutability and uniqueness guarantees of NFTs, offers a robust solution for managing and verifying digital assets in a trustless environment.

9. Practical Applications and Use Cases

The application of our decentralized global registry system based on blockchain technology and NFTs is multi-faceted and can be adopted in various sectors due to its unique features and advantages. Here, we provide several practical examples that illustrate the system's versatility and adaptability.

1. Cultural heritage management. The tokenization of UNESCO World Heritage sites provides a compelling case. The unique attributes of each site can be embedded into an NFT, creating an immutable digital record of the site's information, its historical significance, and current status. This enables a decentralized, globally accessible, and secure database of world heritage sites that can significantly aid in their preservation and management;
2. Intellectual property management. Intellectual property rights management, particularly in the music and arts industry, is another field that can greatly benefit from our proposed system. For instance, artists could tokenize their work, with each NFT carrying crucial metadata about the artwork, including its authenticity, ownership, and rights for reproduction. This not only curbs art forgery and copyright infringement but also opens up new avenues for artists to monetize their work directly;
3. Real estate registry. Tokenization can revolutionize the real estate industry by enhancing transparency and efficiency in property transactions. Each property can be tokenized into an NFT, with its unique property details, ownership history, and transaction records securely stored on the blockchain. This can streamline property transactions, reduce disputes, and increase trust among the parties involved;

4. Academic credential verification. Academic institutions can tokenize degrees and credentials, offering a robust solution to the prevalent issue of fake degrees and credential fraud. Each token can contain verifiable data about the student, the degree awarded, and the awarding institution. This not only simplifies the process of degree verification for employers but also ensures the authenticity of academic credentials.

These are just a few examples that demonstrate the broad scope of applications of the proposed system. The diverse application scenarios underline the system's flexibility and potential to revolutionize how we manage and verify unique digital assets. Future research and development will undoubtedly uncover more opportunities and use cases for the proposed system, further contributing to its practical value and impact.

9.1. Tokenization of Cultural Heritage and Other Valuable Digital Assets

9.1.1. Preservation of World Heritage Sites

NFT-based tokenization can be applied to the preservation and management of UNESCO World Heritage Sites. By creating unique digital tokens for each site, accurate records of the site's history, conservation efforts, and ownership can be maintained. The decentralized nature of blockchain technology ensures that these records are transparent, tamper-proof, and accessible to stakeholders, including governments, conservation organizations, and the general public. This can facilitate the allocation of resources, enhance collaboration, and promote responsible tourism.

9.1.2. Protection of Intangible Cultural Heritage

Intangible cultural heritage (ICH), such as traditional craftsmanship, folklore, and rituals, can be preserved and protected using NFT-based tokenization. Creating NFTs for ICH elements can help raise awareness, document their significance, and provide a platform for their digital representation. This approach can also ensure that the communities associated with these cultural expressions are acknowledged and fairly compensated for their contributions.

9.1.3. Management of Intellectual Property Rights

Tokenization can streamline the management of intellectual property (IP) rights, such as copyrights, patents, and trademarks. NFTs can represent unique digital assets, including literary works, artistic creations, and scientific inventions, enabling the secure and transparent tracking of ownership and licensing agreements. This can facilitate the enforcement of IP rights and promote fair compensation for creators and rightsholders.

9.1.4. Digitization of Museums and Art Collections

Museums, galleries, and private collectors can leverage NFT-based tokenization to catalog and manage their art collections. By creating digital tokens for each artwork or artifact, provenance and ownership records can be securely maintained and easily accessed. Additionally, this approach can facilitate the creation of virtual exhibitions, opening up new avenues for education, research, and global collaboration.

9.1.5. Conservation of Endangered Languages

NFT-based tokenization can be employed to document and preserve endangered languages. Creating digital tokens for linguistic elements, such as phonetics, grammar rules, and vocabulary, can help maintain a record of these languages for future generations. This approach can also promote language revitalization efforts and support the cultural identity of the communities associated with these languages.

Thus, the use of NFT-based tokenization for cultural heritage, intellectual property, and other valuable digital assets has the potential to revolutionize the way these resources are managed, protected, and shared. By employing this technology in various contexts, stakeholders can enhance collaboration, ensure the preservation of cultural heritage, and promote the responsible use of valuable digital assets.

9.2. Existing Registries

ISBN, ISSN, DOI, and other similar registries: Our system could be applied to these registries to provide enhanced security, censorship resistance, and decentralization. By replacing the hierarchical and centralized structure, our solution would enable seamless and transparent management of unique identifiers for books, periodicals, digital objects, and other content.

ASIN, BICI, ISAN, ISMN, ISRC, ISTC, ISWC, ISWN, and LCCN: These registries, responsible for managing identifiers for various objects such as audiovisual content, music recordings, and wine, would benefit from our system's increased transparency, interoperability, and customizability while maintaining the integrity and uniqueness of each identifier.

9.3. New Registries

Our decentralized global registry system also facilitates the creation of new registries for unique objects and content of intellectual, material, or cultural significance. Examples include registries for historical artifacts, art objects, traditional stories, folklore, national dishes, and more. By providing a robust and versatile platform, our system can enable the preservation, cataloging, and management of these valuable resources, fostering cultural exchange and understanding on a global scale.

In cases where anonymity and confidentiality are required, our system can incorporate zkSNARK technology for tokenization, allowing the proof of a resource's existence without disclosing any details about it. This feature ensures the protection of sensitive information while still providing the benefits of a transparent and secure global registry system.

9.4. Comparative Analysis of NFT-Based Global Digital Registries

To further illustrate the advantages of our proposed NFT-based system for global digital registries, we present a detailed comparative matrix that highlights the strengths, weaknesses, and trade-offs of our approach compared to existing centralized and decentralized solutions (Table 5).

Table 5. Comparative Matrix of Global Digital Registry Systems.

Feature	Traditional Centralized (e.g., ISBN)	Existing Blockchain (e.g., ENS)	Our NFT-Based System
Data Security	Moderate (+)	High (++)	High (++)
Censorship Resistance	Low (−)	High (++)	High (++)
Scalability	High (+)	Low (−)	High (+)
Cost Efficiency	Moderate (0)	Low (−)	High (+)
Interoperability	Low (−)	Moderate (0)	High (+)
Customizability	Low (−)	Moderate (0)	High (+)
Ownership Rights Management	Moderate (0)	High (+)	Very High (++)
Privacy	High (+)	Low (−)	High (+) with zkSNARKs
Regulatory Compliance	High (+)	Low (−)	Moderate (0)
User Experience	High (+)	Moderate (0)	High (+)

Legend: (++) Very Strong, (+) Strong, (0) Neutral, (−) Weak.

This comparative matrix demonstrates the unique advantages of our NFT-based system, particularly in areas such as interoperability, customizability, and ownership rights management. While traditional centralized systems excel in scalability and user experience, they lack in areas such as censorship resistance and interoperability. Existing blockchain solutions offer strong security and censorship resistance but face challenges in scalability and cost efficiency.

Our NFT-based system aims to combine the strengths of both approaches while mitigating their weaknesses. For instance, by leveraging layer-2 scaling solutions, we can achieve high scalability without compromising on decentralization. Similarly, the use of zkSNARKs allows us to maintain privacy while still benefiting from blockchain transparency.

To further illustrate these advantages, consider the following real-world scenario:

Case Study: Global Art Registry

An international consortium of museums decides to create a global art registry to track the provenance, ownership, and exhibition history of valuable artworks. They consider three options:

- Traditional Centralized System: While scalable and user-friendly, it is vulnerable to censorship and lacks global interoperability.
- Existing Blockchain Solution (e.g., Ethereum-based): Offers strong security and censorship resistance but faces high transaction costs and scalability issues.
- Our NFT-based System: Provides a balance of security, scalability, and interoperability. Each artwork is represented by a unique NFT, containing rich metadata about its provenance, ownership history, and exhibition records. The system allows for easy verification of authenticity, seamless transfer of ownership, and global accessibility, all while maintaining privacy where necessary through zkSNARK technology.

This case study demonstrates how our system addresses the complex needs of global digital registries in a way that neither traditional centralized systems nor existing blockchain solutions can match.

10. Legal, Ethical, and Social Implications of NFT-Based Tokenization for Global Digital Registers

- Data Privacy Concerns: The adoption of NFT-based tokenization for global digital registers raises data privacy concerns, as personal information may be associated with unique tokens. While blockchain technology provides a level of security and immutability, it is crucial to address the potential risks associated with unauthorized access to sensitive data. Implementing privacy-preserving technologies, such as zero-knowledge proofs or zkSNARKs, can mitigate these concerns by enabling the verification of token ownership without disclosing sensitive information.
- Ownership Rights: NFT-based tokenization introduces new challenges in terms of ownership rights, particularly concerning intellectual property (IP) and copyright. The decentralized nature of blockchain technology may lead to potential conflicts between jurisdictions and legal frameworks. Therefore, it is essential to establish clear guidelines and frameworks for handling IP and copyright issues to ensure that creators and rightsholders are adequately protected and fairly compensated.
- Regulatory Challenges: The widespread adoption of NFT-based tokenization for global digital registers may face regulatory challenges, as governments and authorities may seek to impose controls and restrictions on blockchain-based systems. Regulatory bodies need to strike a balance between ensuring the technology's responsible use and preserving its core benefits, such as decentralization, security, and transparency. Developing appropriate legal frameworks and engaging in international cooperation will be vital to effectively addressing these regulatory challenges.

10.1. Evaluation of the Proposed Approach

- Feasibility. The feasibility of our proposed approach relies on the effective integration of blockchain technology and NFTs with existing and new global digital registers. To ensure its practicality, it is necessary to develop standards and protocols that facilitate seamless data exchange, interoperability, and collaboration among different systems and stakeholders.
- Scalability. Scalability is a crucial consideration for the widespread adoption of NFT-based tokenization for global digital registers. The system must be capable of handling

an increasing number of transactions and participants without compromising performance. Leveraging blockchain technologies with efficient consensus mechanisms, such as proof-of-stake (PoS) or sharding, can help address scalability concerns.
- Long-term Sustainability. The long-term sustainability of our approach depends on its adaptability to evolving technological advancements, legal frameworks, and user demands. Continuous research, development, and collaboration among stakeholders, including governments, industry players, and academics, are vital to ensuring the system's ongoing relevance and growth.

Challenges and Future Research Directions: Some potential challenges and future research directions include the fiollowing:

1. Developing privacy-preserving techniques that maintain data confidentiality while ensuring the integrity and transparency of the system;
2. Establishing legal frameworks and international agreements to address IP, copyright, and regulatory concerns;
3. Investigating the integration of our system with emerging technologies, such as quantum computing and advanced cryptographic techniques, to enhance security and performance.

10.2. Novelty and Advantages of the Proposed Solution

The uniqueness of our approach to tokenizing global digital registries using NFTs lies in several key aspects:

1. Comprehensive Integration: Unlike existing solutions that focus solely on either security or scalability, our system integrates advanced blockchain technology with traditional registry systems, offering a holistic solution that addresses multiple challenges simultaneously;
2. Adaptive Interoperability: Our system is designed to be blockchain-agnostic, allowing for seamless integration with various blockchain networks. This adaptability ensures long-term viability and flexibility in an ever-evolving technological landscape;
3. Enhanced Metadata Management: By leveraging the extensible nature of NFTs, our system allows for rich, detailed metadata storage that goes beyond simple identifiers. This enables complex rights management and detailed provenance tracking;
4. Privacy-Preserving Transparency: Through the incorporation of zkSNARK technology, our system uniquely balances the need for transparency with privacy requirements, a feature not commonly found in existing registry systems;
5. Smart Contract-Enabled Functionality: The use of smart contracts in our system enables automated rights management, royalty distribution, and conditional access controls, features that are either impossible or highly complex in traditional systems.

To substantiate these claims, we provide the following examples and justifications:

- Interoperability Example: A book published in the United States with an ISBN can be seamlessly linked to its translations in other countries, each with their own ISBN, through our NFT-based system. This interoperability extends to different types of content as well, allowing for connections between books (ISBN), their audio versions (ISRC), and any derived screenplays (ISAN), all within a single, unified system.
- Customizability Justification: The extensible nature of NFT metadata allows for easy adaptation to various registry types. For instance, the same underlying system can be customized to handle the specific requirements of ISBN (for books), ISRC (for music recordings), and ISTC (for textual works), each with their own unique metadata fields and relationships.

10.3. Identity Management and Intellectual Property Considerations

Our system implements a robust identity management framework that aligns with the following intellectual property requirements:

1. Decentralized Identifiers (DIDs): We utilize W3C-compliant Decentralized Identifiers to create persistent, verifiable, and decentralized digital identities for both users and digital assets;
2. Verifiable Credentials: The system supports the issuance and verification of claims about identities, such as copyright ownership or licensing rights, using the W3C Verifiable Credentials data model;
3. Multi-Signature Ownership: For complex IP scenarios involving multiple stakeholders, our system supports multi-signature ownership of NFTs, ensuring that all relevant parties must approve transactions;
4. Timelock and Escrow Mechanisms: Smart contracts can implement timelock and escrow functionalities to manage time-bound rights, such as licensing agreements or embargo periods for academic publications;
5. Hierarchical Rights Management: The system allows for the creation of hierarchical structures within NFTs, enabling the representation of complex IP scenarios, such as derivative works or collective authorship.

10.4. Scalability and Transaction Costs on Ethereum

While Ethereum provides a robust and widely adopted platform for NFTs, we acknowledge the challenges related to scalability and transaction costs. To address these issues, our system incorporates the following strategies:

1. Layer-2 Scaling Solutions: We integrate Layer-2 scaling solutions such as Optimistic Rollups or ZK-Rollups, which can significantly increase transaction throughput while reducing costs;
2. Gas Optimization: Our smart contracts are designed with gas optimization in mind, minimizing the computational cost of operations on the Ethereum network;
3. Batching Transactions: Where applicable, we implement transaction batching to reduce the overall number of on-chain transactions required;
4. Cross-Chain Interoperability: Our system is designed to be blockchain-agnostic, allowing for the use of more cost-effective blockchains when necessary while maintaining interoperability with Ethereum;
5. State Channels: For frequent, low-value transactions, we implement state channels to conduct off-chain transactions, only settling on the main chain when necessary.

By implementing these strategies, we aim to mitigate the scalability limitations and high transaction costs associated with Ethereum while still benefiting from its security and widespread adoption in the NFT ecosystem.

11. Conclusions

In this paper, we present a novel decentralized global registry system that leverages the advantages of blockchain technology and NFTs to address the challenges faced by existing centralized and decentralized registries. Our system provides a secure, reliable, and transparent mechanism for tokenizing various global digital registries and facilitating the creation of new registries for unique objects and content. The high-level design, including the blockchain network, smart contracts, NFTs, data exchange protocols, and interfaces, was described in detail. Furthermore, the practical applications of our system were discussed, focusing on its potential to revolutionize the management, cataloging, and classification of unique objects and content.

Through a comprehensive comparative analysis, we benchmarked our system against both traditional centralized registries (such as ISBN, ISSN, and DOI) and existing blockchain-based solutions. This analysis, supported by quantitative metrics and real-world use cases, demonstrated that our solution offers significant advantages in terms of security, transparency, customizability, and scalability while effectively addressing the drawbacks of current systems.

Our research makes several key contributions to the field:

1. We introduce a novel approach to tokenizing global digital registers using NFTs, emphasizing their role as unique identifiers for digital resources rather than speculative assets;
2. We present an adaptive interoperability framework that allows seamless integration with various blockchain networks, ensuring long-term viability in a rapidly evolving technological landscape;
3. We propose innovative solutions for enhanced metadata management and privacy-preserving transparency, addressing complex rights management and data protection concerns;
4. We provide a detailed examination of identity management in the context of intellectual property rights, offering solutions for multi-stakeholder scenarios and time-bound rights management.

With its potential to transform the way unique objects and content of intellectual, material, or cultural value are managed and preserved, our decentralized global registry system paves the way for a more connected and accessible world.

While our research presents a promising approach, we acknowledge several areas that require further investigation:

1. Practical implementation and performance testing in various industries, particularly focusing on high-volume scenarios to validate scalability claims;
2. Further development of privacy-preserving technologies, such as zkSNARKs, will enhance the system's ability to handle sensitive data while maintaining transparency;
3. Exploration of cross-chain interoperability to mitigate scalability limitations and transaction costs associated with specific blockchain networks;
4. Investigation into regulatory compliance across different jurisdictions to ensure global applicability of the system;
5. User experience studies to refine the interface and improve adoption rates among non-technical users.

In future research, it would be valuable to explore the practical implementation of our system in various industries and its integration with existing global registries. Additionally, the potential of our system to incorporate emerging technologies, such as zkSNARK for anonymity and confidentiality, should be further investigated to ensure that our solution remains at the forefront of innovation and maintains its relevance in an ever-evolving digital landscape. By addressing these research directions, we aim to further solidify the position of our NFT-based global registry system as a robust, scalable, and future-proof solution for managing digital assets in an increasingly interconnected world.

Author Contributions: Conceptualization, O.K.; methodology, O.K.; data curation, E.F. and M.K.; formal analysis, K.K. and M.K.; investigation, E.F. and R.S.; writing—original draft preparation, K.K. and R.S.; writing—review and editing, K.K. and R.S.; supervision, E.F.; funding acquisition, R.S. All authors have read and agreed to the published version of the manuscript.

Funding: This project has received funding from the European Union's Horizon 2020 research and innovation program under the Marie Skłodowska-Curie grant agreement No. 101007820—TRUST. This publication reflects only the author's view, and the REA is not responsible for any use that may be made of the information it contains. This research was funded by the European Union—NextGenerationEU under the Italian Ministry of University and Research (MIUR), National Innovation Ecosystem Grant ECS00000041-VITALITY-CUP D83C22000710005.

Data Availability Statement: The original contributions presented in the study are included in the article, the datasets generated during and/or analyzed during the current study are available from the corresponding author on reasonable request.

Conflicts of Interest: The authors declare no conflicts of interest.

Appendix A

```
// SPDX-License-Identifier: MIT
pragma solidity ^0.8.26;
import "@openzeppelin/contracts/token/ERC721/ERC721.sol";
import "@openzeppelin/contracts/utils/Counters.sol";
contract GlobalDigitalRegistry is ERC721 {
    using Counters for Counters.Counter;
    Counters.Counter private _tokenIds;
    struct Item {
        string identifier;
        string metadata;
    }
    mapping(uint256 => Item) private _items;
    mapping(string => uint256) private _identifierToTokenId;
    constructor() ERC721("GlobalDigitalRegistry", "GDR") {}
    function registerItem(string memory _identifier, string memory _metadata) public
returns (uint256) {
        require(_identifierToTokenId[_identifier] == 0, "Item already registered");
        _tokenIds.increment();
        uint256 newTokenId = _tokenIds.current();
        _mint(msg.sender, newTokenId);
        _items[newTokenId] = Item(_identifier, _metadata);
        _identifierToTokenId[_identifier] = newTokenId;
        return newTokenId;
    }
    function transferOwnership(uint256 _tokenId, address _newOwner) public {
        require(ownerOf(_tokenId) == msg.sender, "Not the owner");
        _transfer(msg.sender, _newOwner, _tokenId);
    }
    function updateMetadata(uint256 _tokenId, string memory _newMetadata) pub-
lic {
        require(ownerOf(_tokenId) == msg.sender, "Not the owner");
        _items[_tokenId].metadata = _newMetadata;
    }
    function verifyItem(string memory _identifier) public view returns (bool) {
        return _identifierToTokenId[_identifier] != 0;
    }
    function getItemDetails(uint256 _tokenId) public view returns (string memory,
string memory, address) {
        require(_identifierToTokenId[_items[_tokenId].identifier] != 0, "Item does
not exist");
        Item memory item = _items[_tokenId];
        return (item.identifier, item.metadata, ownerOf(_tokenId));
    }
```

```
        function batchRegister(string[] memory _identifiers, string[] memory _metadataL-
ist) public {
            require(_identifiers.length == _metadataList.length, "Arrays must have the
same length");
            for (uint i = 0; i < _identifiers.length; i++) {
                registerItem(_identifiers[i], _metadataList[i]);
            }
        }
    }
```

Appendix B

```
    import { createRequire } from 'module';
    const require = createRequire(import.meta.url);
    import Web3 from 'web3';
    const contract = require('./GlobalDigitalRegistry.json');
    const web3 = new Web3('http://localhost:7545');
    const contractAddress = '0xcb656435599c889E7aE61BCAbCAE18F9c6a9c315';
    const contractInstance = new web3.eth.Contract(contract.abi, contractAddress);
    async function measurePerformance() {
        const accounts = await web3.eth.getAccounts();
        const testAccount = accounts[0];
        console.log('Starting performance measurements...');
        const gasPrice = await web3.eth.getGasPrice();
        // Measure throughput
        console.log('Measuring throughput...');
        const startTime = Date.now();
        const numTransactions = 10;
        for (let i = 0; i < numTransactions; i++) {
            await contractInstance.methods.registerItem('ISBN${i}', 'Book ${i}').send({
                from: testAccount,
                gas: 3000000,
                gasPrice: gasPrice
            });
        }
        const endTime = Date.now();
        const throughput = numTransactions / ((endTime - startTime) / 1000);
        console.log('Throughput: ${throughput.toFixed(2)} transactions per second');
        // Measure latency
        console.log('Measuring latency...');
        const latencyStart = Date.now();
        const tx = await contractInstance.methods.registerItem('LATENCY_TEST', 'La-
tency Book').send({
            from: testAccount,
            gas: 3000000,
            gasPrice: gasPrice
        });
        const latencyEnd = Date.now();
        console.log('Latency: ${latencyEnd - latencyStart} ms');
        // Measure gas consumption
        console.log('Measuring gas consumption...');
        const gasUsed = await web3.eth.getTransactionReceipt(tx.transactionHash);
        console.log('Gas used for registerItem: ${gasUsed.gasUsed}');
        // Measure storage efficiency
        console.log('Measuring storage efficiency...');
```

```
const storageUsed = await web3.eth.getStorageAt(contractAddress, 0);
console.log(`Storage used: ${web3.utils.hexToNumberString(storageUsed)} bytes`);
// Measure function execution time
console.log('Measuring function execution time...');
const execStart = Date.now();
await contractInstance.methods.getItemDetails(1).call();
const execEnd = Date.now();
console.log(`Execution time for getItemDetails: ${execEnd - execStart} ms`);
// Measure scalability
console.log('Measuring scalability...');
const scalabilityStart = Date.now();
const batchSize = 5;
const identifiers = Array.from({ length: batchSize }, (_, i) => `BATCH${i}`);
const metadataList = Array.from({ length: batchSize }, (_, i) => `Batch Book ${i}`);
await contractInstance.methods.batchRegister(identifiers, metadataList).send({
    from: testAccount,
    gas: 3000000,
    gasPrice: gasPrice
});
const scalabilityEnd = Date.now();
console.log(`Time for batch registration of ${batchSize} items: ${scalabilityEnd -
scalabilityStart} ms`);
}
measurePerformance().catch(console.error);
```

References

1. Aplin, T. Aplin, T. A Global Digital Register for the Preservation and Access to Cultural Heritage: Problems, Challenges and Possibilities. In *Copyright and Cultural Heritage*; Edward Elgar Publishing: Cheltenham, UK, 2010; p. 13868. ISBN 978-1-84980-803-3.
2. Models for Implementing a Digital Preservation Service. In *Practical Digital Preservation: A How-to Guide for Organizations of Any Size*; Brown, A. (Ed.) Facet: London, UK, 2013; pp. 63–108. Available online: https://www.cambridge.org/core/books/abs/practical-digital-preservation/models-for-implementing-a-digital-preservation-service/57ED5E17F9D0052271E590EF32ECF786 (accessed on 4 June 2024)ISBN 978-1-85604-962-7.
3. *IEEE Std 3207-2022*; IEEE Standard for Blockchain-Based Digital Asset Identification. IEEE: Piscataway, NJ, USA, 2023; pp. 1–32. [CrossRef]
4. Tharun, T.; Vamshi, A.; Eswari, R. NFT Application for Music Industry Using Blockchain Smart Contracts. In Proceedings of the 2023 4th International Conference on Innovative Trends in Information Technology (ICITIIT), Kottayam, India, 11–12 February 2023; pp. 1–6.
5. Non-Fungible Tokens (NFT). Available online: https://ethereum.org (accessed on 15 April 2023).
6. Non-Fungible Token (NFT): What It Means and How It Works. Available online: https://www.investopedia.com/non-fungible-tokens-nft-5115211 (accessed on 15 April 2023).
7. Non Fungible Token (NFT) Nell'enciclopedia Treccani. Available online: https://www.treccani.it/enciclopedia/non-fungible-token (accessed on 15 April 2023).
8. Belk, R.; Humayun, M.; Brouard, M. Money, Possessions, and Ownership in the Metaverse: NFTs, Cryptocurrencies, Web3 and Wild Markets. *J. Bus. Res.* **2022**, *153*, 198–205. [CrossRef]
9. Elmay, F.; Kadadha, M.; Mizouni, R.; Singh, S.; Otrok, H.; Mourad, A. Digital Twins and Dynamic NFTs for Blockchain-Based Crowdsourced Last-Mile Delivery. *Inf. Process. Manag.* **2024**, *61*, 103756. [CrossRef]
10. Ferro, E.; Saltarella, M.; Rotondi, D.; Giovanelli, M.; Corrias, G.; Moncada, R.; Cavallaro, A.; Favenza, A. Digital Assets Rights Management through Smart Legal Contracts and Smart Contracts. *Blockchain Res. Appl.* **2023**, *4*, 100142. [CrossRef]
11. Hasan, H.R.; Madine, M.; Yaqoob, I.; Salah, K.; Jayaraman, R.; Boscovic, D. Using NFTs for Ownership Management of Digital Twins and for Proof of Delivery of Their Physical Assets. *Future Gener. Comput. Syst.* **2023**, *146*, 1–17. [CrossRef]
12. Huang, T.; Xie, R.; Ren, Y.; Yu, F.R.; Zou, Z.; Han, L.; Liu, Y.; Cheng, D.; Li, Y.; Liu, T. DTAIS: Distributed Trusted Active Identity Resolution Systems for the Industrial Internet. *Digit. Commun. Netw.* 2023, *In Press*. [CrossRef]
13. Urom, C.; Ndubuisi, G.; Guesmi, K. Global Macroeconomic Factors and the Connectedness among NFTs and (Un)Conventional Assets. *Res. Int. Bus. Financ.* **2024**, *2024*, 102429. [CrossRef]
14. Wilkoff, S.; Yildiz, S. The Behavior and Determinants of Illiquidity in the Non-Fungible Tokens (NFTs) Market. *Glob. Financ. J.* **2023**, *55*, 100782. [CrossRef]

15. Zhao, L.; Zhang, J.; Jing, H.; Wu, J.; Huang, Y. A Blockchain-Based Cryptographic Interaction Method of Digital Museum Collections. *J. Cult. Herit.* **2023**, *59*, 69–82. [CrossRef]
16. IBM Documentation. Available online: https://www.ibm.com/docs/en/bpm/8.5.0?topic=assets-asset-repository (accessed on 15 April 2023).
17. Josaw1 Digital Asset Management Overview—Commerce | Dynamics 365. Available online: https://learn.microsoft.com/en-us/dynamics365/commerce/dam-overview (accessed on 15 April 2023).
18. Oracle WebCenter Content: Digital Asset Management. 2022. Available online: https://www.oracle.com/a/ocom/docs/ds-owc-content-digital-asset-mgmt-427839.pdf (accessed on 4 June 2024).
19. OCM—Digital Asset Management. Available online: https://videohub.oracle.com/media/OCM+-+Digital+Asset+Management/1_io4wfnst (accessed on 15 April 2023).
20. Alfresco Digital Asset Management Roadmap and Backlog. Available online: https://hub.alfresco.com/t5/alfresco-content-services-hub/alfresco-digital-asset-management-roadmap-and-backlog/ba-p/291499 (accessed on 15 April 2023).
21. RivetLogic. Available online: https://www.rivetlogic.com/resources/content/webinars/digital-asset-management-with-alfresco (accessed on 15 April 2023).
22. Marketing Asset Center/Digital Asset Manager. Available online: https://www.alfresco.com/partners/solutions/marketing-asset-center-digital-asset-manager (accessed on 15 April 2023).
23. Scopri Adobe Experience Manager Assets. Available online: https://business.adobe.com/it/products/experience-manager/assets/aem-assets.html (accessed on 15 April 2023).
24. Explore Adobe Experience Manager Assets. Available online: https://business.adobe.com/uk/products/experience-manager/assets/aem-assets.html (accessed on 15 April 2023).
25. SAP Digital Asset Management. Dataworld. Available online: https://www.dataworld.com/en/solutions/sap-digital-asset-management/ (accessed on 4 June 2024).
26. OpenText Digital Asset Management for SAP Solutions. Available online: https://www.opentext.com/products/digital-asset-management-for-sap-solutions (accessed on 15 April 2023).
27. Digital Asset Management Software | Content and Collaboration. Available online: https://www.sap.com/products/crm/digital-asset-management.html (accessed on 15 April 2023).
28. Alden, H.; Jay, G.; Mike, S.; Hurst William, C.; Kamlesh, S.; Alex, G. Central Asset Registry System and Method. U.S. Patent US10452714B2, 2016.
29. Hurst William, C.; Alex, G.; Alden, H.; Beth, J.; Ramesh, M.; Melissa, R.; Brant, B. Satelliten-Und Zentrale Bestandsregistersysteme Sowie Verfahren Und Rechteverwaltungssysteme. European Patent EP3577587B1, 31 January 2018.
30. Hurst, W.C.; Alex, G.; Alden, H.; Beth, J.; Melissa, R.; Brant, B.; Ramesh, M. Satellite and Central Asset Registry Systems and Methods and Rights Management Systems. U.S. Patent 10,372,883, 6 August 2019.
31. Filipe, P.; Liana, P. Systems and Methods for Communicating about Products Using Unique Identifiers and Social Media. CA Patent CA3074196A1, 26 August 2018.
32. Thomas, R. Digital Origin Tag and System of Use. WO Patent WO2020172216A1, 27 August 2020.
33. Lucinda, L. Methods, Systems and Computer Program Products for Media Processing and Display. U.S. Patent Application 17/609,911, 15 December 2021.
34. George, D. Method and Apparatus for Decentralized Management of Trusted Data on Trustless Networks. U.S. Patent Application 17/677,657, 25 August 2022.
35. George, D. Method and Apparatus for Creating and Managing User Configurable Objects and Functions on Distributed Ledger Networks. U.S. Patent Application 17/677,605, 16 June 2022.
36. IBM Blockchain—Enterprise Blockchain Solutions and Services. Available online: https://www.ibm.com/blockchain (accessed on 17 April 2023).
37. Rloutlaw Azure Blockchain. Available online: https://learn.microsoft.com/en-us/samples/azure/azure-quickstart-templates/blockchain-asaservice/ (accessed on 17 April 2023).
38. ERC-721 Non-Fungible Token Standard. Available online: https://ethereum.org/en/developers/docs/standards/tokens/erc-721/ (accessed on 4 June 2024).
39. ERC-1155 Multi-Token Standard. Available online: https://ethereum.org/en/developers/docs/standards/tokens/erc-1155/ (accessed on 4 June 2024).
40. Pilkington, M. Bowker Announces Data Breach of Self-Pubbed Authors' Credit Cards |—Good e-Reader 2018. Available online: https://goodereader.com/blog/indie-author-news/bowker-announces-data-breach-of-self-pubbed-authors-credit-cards (accessed on 23 June 2024).
41. Ethereum Security and Scam Prevention. Available online: https://ethereum.org/en/security/ (accessed on 23 June 2024).
42. Science Suffers as China's Internet Censors Plug Holes in Great Firewall. Available online: https://www.science.org/content/article/science-suffers-china-s-internet-censors-plug-holes-great-firewall (accessed on 23 June 2024).
43. Yang, Q.; Liu, Y. What's on the Other Side of the Great Firewall? Chinese Web Users' Motivations for Bypassing the Internet Censorship. *Comput. Hum. Behav.* **2014**, *37*, 249–257. [CrossRef]
44. Rosa-Clark Resolution Report. Available online: https://www.crossref.org/documentation/reports/resolution-report/ (accessed on 23 June 2024).

45. What Is an ISSN? | ISSN. Available online: https://www.issn.org/understanding-the-issn/what-is-an-issn/ (accessed on 23 June 2024).
46. Web3, Aggregated. Available online: https://polygon.technology/ (accessed on 23 June 2024).
47. Welcome to theU.S. ISBN Agency! Available online: https://www.isbn.org/home (accessed on 23 June 2024).
48. etherscan.io Ethereum Charts and Statistics | Etherscan. Available online: https://etherscan.io/charts (accessed on 23 June 2024).
49. Home Page. Available online: https://isni.org/ (accessed on 23 June 2024).
50. Home | ISWC. Available online: https://www.iswc.org/home (accessed on 23 June 2024).
51. EDItEUR. Available online: https://www.editeur.org/118/ISTC/ (accessed on 23 June 2024).
52. Investigación, A.A. Biblioguías: Identificadores Bibliográficos (ISBN, ISSN, DOI, URI): BICI. Available online: https://biblioguias.unex.es/c.php?g=572103&p=3944899 (accessed on 23 June 2024).
53. Putz, B.; Menges, F.; Pernul, G. A Secure and Auditable Logging Infrastructure Based on a Permissioned Blockchain. *Comput. Secur.* **2019**, *87*, 101602. [CrossRef]
54. Özyilmaz, K.R.; Doğan, M.; Yurdakul, A. IDMoB: IoT Data Marketplace on Blockchain. In Proceedings of the 2018 Crypto Valley Conference on Blockchain Technology (CVCBT), Zug, Switzerland, 20–22 June 2018; pp. 11–19.
55. Bao, T.; Ma, M.; Wen, Y. Herding in the Non-Fungible Token (NFT) Market. *J. Behav. Exp. Financ.* **2023**, *39*, 100837. [CrossRef]
56. Davies, J.; Sharifi, H.; Lyons, A.; Forster, R.; Elsayed, O.K.S.M. Non-Fungible Tokens: The Missing Ingredient for Sustainable Supply Chains in the Metaverse Age? *Transp. Res. Part E Logist. Transp. Rev.* **2024**, *182*, 103412. [CrossRef]
57. Kaisto, J.; Juutilainen, T.; Kauranen, J. Non-Fungible Tokens, Tokenization, and Ownership. *Comput. Law Secur. Rev.* **2024**, *54*, 105996. [CrossRef]
58. Belchior, R.; Vasconcelos, A.; Guerreiro, S.; Correia, M. A Survey on Blockchain Interoperability: Past, Present, and Future Trends. *ACM Comput. Surv.* **2021**, *54*, 168. [CrossRef]

MDPI AG
Grosspeteranlage 5
4052 Basel
Switzerland
Tel.: +41 61 683 77 34

Future Internet Editorial Office
E-mail: futureinternet@mdpi.com
www.mdpi.com/journal/futureinternet

MDPI